TOWARD
ACCEPTANCE

Sexual Orientation
Issues on Campus

EDITED BY
VERNON A. WALL
AND
NANCY J. EVANS

American College Personnel Association

Copyright © 2000 by
University Press of America,® Inc.
4501 Forbes Boulevard, Suite 200
Lanham, Maryland 20706

12 Hid's Copse Rd.
Cumnor Hill, Oxford OX2 9JJ

Library of Congress Cataloging-in-Publication Data

Toward acceptance : sexual orientation issues on campus /
Edited by Vernon A. Wall and Nancy J. Evans.
p.   cm.
Includes bibliographical references.
I.   Homosexuality and education—United States. 2. Homophobia in higher
education —United States. 3. Gay college students—United States—
Social conditions. 4. Bisexual college students—United States—Social
conditions. I. Wall, Vernon A. II. Evans, Nancy J.
LC192.6.T69   1999   378.1'982664—dc21   99-055912 CIP

ISBN 1-883485-17-7 (cloth: alk. ppr.)
ISBN 1-883485-18-5 (pbk: alk. ppr.)

Content

Introduction

What Have We Accomplished?

Nancy J. Evans and Vernon A. Wall

In 1991, the book *Beyond Tolerance: Gays, Lesbians, and Bisexuals on Campus* was published by the American College Personnel Association. For years, student affairs professionals had requested a comprehensive publication that addressed the issues of lesbian, gay, and bisexual (LGB) students, faculty, and staff. *Beyond Tolerance* was the first attempt at filling that void. As such, it was a beginning.

The 1990s saw a significant increase in awareness of the concerns of gay, lesbian, and bisexual people. For instance, in 1991, the year in which *Beyond Tolerance* was published, sexual orientation issues were quite present in the mainstream press. The focus of this attention was mainly the rights of gay, lesbian, and bisexual people to equal treatment under the law (Newton, 1994; Thompson, 1994). In some cases, such as the passage of a gay rights bill in Connecticut, advances were made. Other cases, such as the establishment of a policy by the Cracker Barrel restaurant chain that forbade employing people "whose sexual preferences fail to demonstrate normal heterosexual values," underscored that additional work was needed.

As the world reacted to a barrage of human rights related issues, the college campus was no different. *The Chronicle of Higher Education* (Dodge, 1991) reported that gay and lesbian students were waging civil-rights campaigns on college campuses demanding that universities allow homosexual couples to live in on-campus housing for married students, create special offices staffed by gay people to deal with gay campus issues, and establish gay and lesbian studies departments.

Dodge (1991) stated that the tactics ranged from "arranging high profile demonstrations and lobbying efforts to meeting quietly with administrators and serving on campus committees" (p. A31). As students became more active, they often stirred resentment among faculty members and students who think homosexuality is wrong.

Today, our world is still a confusing mix of encouraging gains and heartbreaking set-backs in the sexual orientation arena. The *Advocate* (The year in review, 1999) listed the following key events for the year 1998:

- Voters in Maine passed a measure that repealed the state's ban on anti-gay discrimination.
- Green Bay Packers football star Reggie White stated that homosexuality was a "sin" and that the plight of gay men and lesbians should not be compared to that of blacks.
- President Clinton issued an executive order that added sexual orientation to the list of categories for which discrimination is prohibited in federal civilian employment.
- Senate majority leader Trent Lott (R – Miss.) stated that homosexuality was a sin and compared it to alcoholism and kleptomania.
- A coalition of 15 different religious-right groups launched a newspaper ad campaign claiming that homosexuality could be cured.
- In a keynote address at a fundraising dinner in Washington, D.C. for the Human Rights Campaign, Vice-president Al Gore declared that "all people, regardless of sexual orientation, should be able to be a part of a loving relationship and raise a family without fear of recrimination or discrimination."
- Tammy Baldwin, a Wisconsin legislator, became the first openly lesbian candidate to win election to the House of Representatives.
- Matthew Shepard, a 21 year-old gay college student is savagely beaten to death generating enormous press coverage and spontaneous demonstrations against hate crimes in dozens of cities around the country.

Since *Beyond Tolerance* was released, much has happened in the higher education community also. Campus administrators are beginning to discuss openly the needs and concerns of LGB students, faculty, and staff. Gay, lesbian, and bisexual student organizations are growing in numbers. Programming around sexual orientation topics is more commonplace. A number of universities are offering coursework addressing LGBT topics. Bisexual and transgender identities are being discussed and debated. Sexual orientation is addressed in many non-discrimination policies and some institutions of higher education are providing domestic partner benefits.

Unfortunately, these gains are offset by alarming incidents of hate crimes against gay, lesbian, bisexual, and transgender persons and a resurgence of propaganda designed to incite discrimination against and oppression of this group. Some schools have seen the establishment of "straight" organizations whose only purpose is promotion of a heterosexist perspective. Television programs, such as "Sixty Minutes" have aired sensationalist attacks on gay studies programs and state funding of LGBT-related initiatives has been prohibited in some locales. These issues, along with the brutal murder of Matthew Shepard are indicators that our work is certainly not complete.

Toward Acceptance: Sexual Orientation Issues on Campus, is designed to provide an updated examination of the complex issues facing gay, lesbian, bisexual, and transgendered persons on college campuses. To insure that the book would take sexual orientation awareness to the next level, we solicited chapter proposals from a broad base of potential authors who were doing cutting edge work in this arena. We believe that the contributions we have included have achieved the goals we set for the book.

Content

Toward Acceptance is organized into five distinct sections: (I) Research, (II) Institutional issues and interventions, (III) Interventions in student services, (IV) Diversity within the lesbian, gay, bisexual and transgender community, and (V) Addressing campus issues.

The book begins with an overview of what the research tells us about gay, lesbian, and bisexual issues on campus. In Chapter 1, James M.

Croteau and Donna M. Talbot review studies and integrate their findings to paint an empirically-based picture of the current state of the student affairs profession in relation to gay, lesbian, and bisexual awareness. Implications for the profession's continuing journey toward affirmation and acceptance are also drawn from this empirical landscape

In Chapter 2, Kathleen J. Bieschke, Amy B. Eberz, and D'Andre Wilson share what is known about gay, lesbian, and bisexual college students based on existing empirical research. They then make recommendations for conducting research with this population and unveil a research agenda for the field.

In Part II, the authors discuss institutional issues and interventions. Chapter 3 includes a discussion of the complex issues of recognizing gay and lesbian domestic partnerships as families in the university setting. Using data collected by the Domestic Partners Project for the ACPA Standing Committee for Lesbian, Gay, Bisexual, and Transgender Awareness, authors John Leppo, Scott R. Boden, and Donald A. Stenta present reasons why colleges and universities should offer domestic partner employment benefits and critique the most common objections. Strategies for seeking domestic partner benefits and considerations in implementation are also discussed.

Lesbian, gay, and bisexual people attend, teach, and work at religiously affiliated institutions, despite assumptions otherwise. While some issues related to creating more accepting campus communities for gay, lesbian, and bisexual students, faculty, and staff are universal, special considerations exist at these institutions. In Chapter 4, Heidi Levine and Patrick G. Love explore the barriers that exist at many religiously affiliated colleges and universities and some steps student affairs professionals, faculty, and students can take on those campuses.

Drawing on a key study of classroom concerns of gay, lesbian, and bisexual college students as well as literature about creating inclusive classroom environments, in Chapter 5 Mark Connolly identifies important issues for gay, lesbian, and bisexual students. Mark also offers recommendations for students, faculty, and student affairs professionals who may work with students either in or out of the college classroom.

Chapter 6, written by Wallace Eddy and Deanna S. Forney, presents an assessment measure developed to aid in creating and enhancing higher education environments facilitative of lesbian, gay, and bisexual identity

x

development. Their instrument, which is grounded in developmental and environmental theory, can provide convincing data when advocating for change on campus.

In Part III, the authors discuss interventions in student services. Training and awareness programs on sexual orientation issues have become increasingly popular. In Chapter 7, noted trainers Vernon A. Wall, Jamie Washington, Nancy J. Evans, and Ross A. Papish share effective strategies for facilitating awareness programs on sexual orientation issues for college students. The chapter contains an extensive appendix with exercises to assist individuals in program development.

In Chapter 8, Ruperto M. Perez, Kurt DeBord, and Kathleen J. Brock explore the issues and practical considerations involved in developing and offering group counseling to college students struggling with issues related to sexual orientation. Different types of groups are introduced and questions that group facilitators must address are considered.

Little has been written or documented on relationship violence within the lesbian, gay, bisexual and transgender community. In Chapter 9, Claire N. Kaplan and Sandy L. Colbs focus on strategies for prevention of violence and intervention with gay, lesbian, bisexual, and transgender assault survivors.

Part IV, Diversity within the Lesbian, Gay, Bisexual, and Transgender Community, begins with a chapter that examines current understandings of bisexual identities and communities. This chapter, written by Leah Robin and Karl Hamner, also discusses implications for college students and professionals.

In Chapter 11, Kelly A. Carter defines terms, discusses stereotypes and addresses typical issues faced by transgender students on campus. Ways that student affairs professionals can be more inclusive will also be addressed.

Women of color who embrace a lesbian or bisexual identity are often hidden on college campuses. In Chapter 12, Angela D. Ferguson and Mary F. Howard-Hamilton discuss the complexities of multiple oppressions, their implications for personal identity development and recommendations for student affairs professionals who wish to provide inclusive environments.

In Chapter 13, Rosa Cintrón discusses the challenge involved in appreciating and understanding the diversity among Latino men and explores the cultural imperative of the concept "macho." This concept is core to understanding sexual orientation issues in the Latin culture.

It seems that religion and spirituality are playing larger roles in the lives of students today. In Chapter 14, Valsin L. DuMontier addresses the role of spirituality and religion in the lives of lesbians, gay men, and bisexual people. He also examines the intersection of spiritual development and gay and lesbian identity development.

In Part V, the authors address campus issues. While *Beyond Tolerance* offered a chapter on being an ally to members of the lesbian, gay, and bisexual communities, in Chapter 15, Ellen M. Broido goes beyond this work by examining the developmental process of becoming an ally as well as concrete strategies for being an ally—as an individual and as a campus change agent.

In Chapter 16, Mark von Destinon, Nancy J. Evans, and Vernon A. Wall discuss strategies for maneuvering around and working with perceived obstacles when attempting to effect change related to sexual orientation issues on campus. Drawing on models of change and environmental intervention, the authors provide suggestions for moving toward a true commitment to equity on campus.

The editors of this book, Nancy J. Evans and Vernon A. Wall, offer some parting thoughts in Chapter 17 on how student affairs professionals can continue to be proactive in the area of sexual orientation awareness and support. They point out that although progress has been made, there is always more work to be done.

Finally, John Leppo has updated the list of resources from *Beyond Tolerance* to provide one of the most complete listings of helpful books, pamphlets, articles, videotapes, and other media ever produced. National organizations promoting gay, lesbian, bisexual, and transgender rights and those assisting gay, lesbian, bisexual, and transgender individuals and their supporters are also listed.

As with *Beyond Tolerance*, this project has been a collaborative effort involving gay, lesbian, and bisexual individuals and heterosexual allies. We sincerely hope that *Toward Acceptance* will be yet another step toward equity, inclusion, and appreciation for all people involved in the higher education community. We have that vision. Join us in making that vision a reality.

References

The year in review. (January 19, 1999). *The Advocate, 776/777*, pp. 10-16.

Dodge, S. (April 3, 1991). Vigorous civil rights drives by homosexual students bring both changes and resentment on campuses. *The Chronicle of Higher Education*, pp. A31-32.

Evans, N., & Wall, V. (Eds). (1991). *Beyond Tolerance: Gays, lesbians and bisexuals on campus*. Alexandria, VA: ACPA Media.

Newton, D. (1994). *Gay & lesbian rights: A reference handbook*. Santa Barbara, CA: Instructional Horizons.

Thompson, M. (Ed.). (1994). *The Advocate history of the gay & lesbian movement*. New York: St. Martin's Press.

PART I

RESEARCH

Chapter 1

ಐღ

Understanding the Landscape: An Empirical View of Lesbian, Gay, and Bisexual Issues in the Student Affairs Profession

JAMES M. CROTEAU AND DONNA M. TALBOT

In a comprehensive review of the student affairs literature on lesbian, gay, or bisexual (LGB) issues, Lark (1998) found a small, but growing body of literature that directly addresses how student affairs professionals can be affirmative in their work. Most notable among that literature is the predecessor to this book, *Beyond tolerance: Gays, lesbians and bisexuals campus* (Evans & Wall, 1991). This emerging literature, however, is almost never based on empirical research about the profession. It is our contention that without an empirical knowledge base about the student affairs profession regarding sexual minority concerns, the advancement of literature that can guide professionals in this area is severely hampered.

Lark (1998) noted that it was only in the late 1980s and early 1990s that the first empirical research on lesbian, gay, and bisexual (LGB) issues appeared in the student affairs literature. She found only 17 published research articles, of which the vast majority focused on students (e.g., documenting or improving students' attitudes toward sexual minorities; examining the experiences and/or perceptions of lesbian, gay, and bisexual students). Chapter 2 of this book (Bieschke, Eberz, & Wilson) addresses the research on LGB college students.

Minimal research has been conducted examining the student affairs profession itself in relation to LGB issues. Several recent studies and publications (Croteau & Lark, 1995a, b; Croteau & von Destinon, 1994; Hogan & Rentz, 1996; Hoover, 1994; Talbot, 1992, 1996; Talbot & Harvey, 1993; Talbot & Kocarek, 1997), however, do provide initial empirical information about the status of the student affairs profession in regard to LGB concerns. This chapter is an integration of findings from these studies and an examination of their implications for student affairs practice and future research.

Table 1 overviews the samples, authors, content areas, and general design of these studies. In the remainder of the chapter, the particular studies are referred to by the designation given each study in the first column of Table 1. In the first section of the chapter, we summarize the findings into conclusions and draw implications for the profession's continued efforts to become increasingly inclusive and affirmative. In the second section, we make recommendations for future research that will help paint a fuller and more useful picture of the profession regarding this important topic.

Painting the Landscape through Empirical Findings

In this section, we draw eight conclusions based only on findings found most compelling due to one or both of the following reasons. Findings were seen as compelling due to the relative methodological rigor from which the finding was established (i.e., replicated across studies, derived from relatively sound quantitative measurement, or derived from systematic qualitative data collection and analysis processes). Findings were also considered compelling if the information involved had clear and direct implications for moving the profession towards more affirmation and inclusion. Each conclusion is numbered and serves as a

Table 1:
Overview of the Studies on the Student Affairs Profession in Relation to Lesbian, Gay, and Bisexual Concerns

Study	Authors	Sample	Content Area of Study	General Design
Original graduate program study	Talbot (1992; 1996); Talbot & Kocarek (1997)	321 master's degree students; 56 graduate faculty from 8 different programs	Knowledge, skills, comfort, and behavior with diversity including LGB issues; student attitudes toward gay men and lesbians	Written survey; quantitative self-report items; semi-structured interviews
Follow-up graduate program study	Talbot & Harvey (1993)	88 graduate faculty from 18 student affairs programs	Knowledge, skills, comfort and behavior with diversity including LGB issues	Written survey; quantitative self-report items
Professional preparedness study	Hoover (1993)	394 practitioner members of ACPA and/or NASPA	Knowledge, skills, comfort and behavior with diversity including LGB issues	Written survey; quantitative self-report items; semi-structured interviews
Biased and exemplary practices study	Croteau & Lark (1995a)	270 members of ACPA's Standing Committee on LGB Awareness	Descriptions of biased and exemplary practices in regards to LGB issues	Written survey, qualitative descriptions of practices
Homophobic attitudes study	Hogan & Rentz (1996)	310 university faculty and student affairs practitioners at two Midwestern universities	Homophobia by position, gender, and the interaction of these two variables	Written survey; quantitative self-report items
Job search study	Croteau & von Destinon (1994)	249 LGB student affairs professionals from LGBT events at national conferences	Information on job search experiences related to LGB issues (e.g., openness about sexual orientation, discrimination)	Written survey; quantitative self-report items; qualitative descriptions of discrimination
Job experiences study	Croteau & Lark (1995b)	174 LGB members of ACPA's Standing Committee on LGB Awareness	Information about job experiences related to LGB issues (e.g., openness about sexual orientation; frequency & description of discrimination)	Written survey; quantitative self-report items; qualitative descriptions of discrimination

subheading. The data supporting that conclusion and the implications for professional practice and training are described under each subheading.

1. *Discrimination appears to be a frequent occurrence in the work lives of LGB student affairs professionals. Qualitative descriptions of discrimination from the research form a basis for identifying and eliminating such discrimination in student affairs work environments.*

Twenty-six percent of all sexual minority student affairs professionals in the "job search study" reported being discriminated against in the job search process. Among those who were most open about their sexual orientation, an even greater percentage reported discrimination (42%). Sixty percent of sexual minority student affairs professionals in the "job experiences study" reported at least one incident of discrimination on the job, while 38% indicated they had experienced two or more incidents of discrimination. Forty-four percent of that same sample said they expected discrimination at work in the future. Despite some methodological concerns (see Croteau, 1996), these data clearly support the notion that discrimination against sexual minority professionals is a significant issue for the profession.

The *quantitative* results in the "job search" and "job experiences" studies document the problem of discrimination in the profession. On the other hand, the *qualitative* results in these same studies describe the range of discrimination against sexual minority professionals that occurs. Results of the qualitative analysis in the "job search study" indicated that discrimination occurred either during the process of the job search or in the actual employment decisions that were made as a result of the job search. Discrimination that occurred during the job search most often involved biased actions of interviewers (e.g., requiring sexual minorities to go through a more rigorous process or failing to be inclusive of sexual minority people or issues during the interview). Discrimination in employment decisions involved "candidates being evaluated negatively, screened out of job searches, or even having offers rescinded because of the candidate's sexual orientation" (Croteau & von Destinon, 1994, p. 43). Detailed descriptions and illustrations of these categories of job search discrimination are described by the authors (see Croteau & von Destinon, 1994, pp. 42-43).

Results of the qualitative analysis in the "job experiences study" indicated that discrimination experienced by sexual minority professionals on the job can be grouped into two broad categories. The first broad category involved inequitable employer decisions and policies targeted at sexual minorities. These included negative job evaluations, failures to promote, lack of salary increases, actual or threatened job losses, and personnel policies denying same sex partners of professionals the benefits that heterosexual married partners receive.

The second broad category involved discriminatory actions that occur during everyday work activities. This category included: (a) "overt expressions of homophobic sentiment as well as harassment or violence," (b) "actions perceived to arise out of homophobia but not involving direct expression of homophobic sentiment," (c) "attempts to interfere with respondents' choices about how open or secretive to be about their sexual orientation," and (d) "actions which exclude LGB professionals or their concerns" (Croteau & Lark, 1995b, p. 194). Detailed descriptions and illustrations of these categories of "on the job" discrimination are described by the authors (see Croteau & Lark, 1995b, pp. 193-195).

The descriptive categories of job search and on the job discrimination map the broad range of potential discriminatory practices. In other words, the use of these descriptive maps can prevent professionals from being overly narrow in their efforts to eliminate discrimination. For instance, if professionals examine only employment decisions for possible discrimination, they will overlook discrimination during job interviews, what happens concerning inclusion and exclusion in everyday work activities, etc.

In the discussion of the job search survey, Croteau and von Destinon (1994) illustrate a constructive use of the mapping of discriminatory actions provided by these studies. They took the map of discriminatory interview practices and used it to infer guidelines or suggestions for affirmative interviewing in student affairs job searches. Table 2 lists these guidelines.

2. *LGB student affairs professionals are making a variety of decisions about how open to be about their sexual orientation while at work and in searching for work. There are indications that student affairs professionals who are completely open about their minority sexual orientation at work may find their jobs satisfying despite experiencing more discrimination than their less open counterparts.*

Results from both the "job experiences study" and "job search study" indicate that student affairs professionals made a variety of choices about how open to be in their professional lives. In the "job experiences study," 47% of sexual minority professionals reported that all or most people in their work setting knew about their sexual orientation, 32% reported that

Table 2
Suggestions for Affirmative Interviewing in the Student Affairs Profession

---

1. The interviewer will be at ease and comfortable discussing issues of sexual orientation.
2. The interviewer will be open to discussing issues of sexual orientation appropriate to the position, neither avoiding, nor over emphasizing these issues.
3. The applicant's decision regarding whether to disclose sexual orientation will be respected and the interviewer will not attempt to manipulate the applicant into disclosing his/her sexual orientation.
4. The interviewer will not attempt to discern the candidate's sexual orientation indirectly through speculation about appearance or directly through inquiring from other professionals.
5. If the interviewer knows a candidate is lesbian, gay, or bisexual, the interviewer will not share that information without the candidate's permission, and will not attempt to restrict the candidate's choices concerning how "out" to be in the prospective job.
6. The interviewer will not engage in activities that directly discriminate such as derogatory comments about sexual minorities or more rigorous interview procedures for these applicants.
7. The interviewer will not assume that the applicant of unknown sexual orientation is heterosexual, but will instead use inclusive references and non-heterosexist language.

Note. These recommendations are taken directly from the discussion of a qualitative study of the job search experiences of sexual minority student affairs professionals (Croteau & von Destinon, 1994, pp. 44-45).

some people knew, 15% reported that only close friends in the work setting knew, and 6% reported that no one at work knew. In the "job search study," 38% of the sexual minority professionals disclosed their sexual orientation during the job search (i.e., prior to knowing they had a job offer, most often during interviews). The majority (62%) waited until after accepting the job to disclose, if at all.

Another common finding in both the "job experiences study" and the "job search study" is that sexual minority students affairs professionals who were more open about their sexual orientation reported experiencing more discrimination than those who were less open. One possible explanation for this finding could be that those who were more open had broader definitions of discrimination. On the other hand, it makes sense intuitively that sexual minority people who are open about their sexual orientation are visible targets for prejudice and discrimination. In isolation, this finding may be discouraging for those student affairs professionals hoping to be more open about their sexual orientation. However, when those professionals who were completely open about their sexual orientation were compared on other factors with those who were more closeted, a different picture emerged. Despite higher rates of reported discrimination on the job, those professionals who were completely open were at least as satisfied with their jobs as those who were less open. Further, those professionals who were completely open about their sexual orientation were more satisfied with their "level of openness" than were professionals who were more closeted. Croteau and Lark (1995b) speculated that the satisfaction openly LGB professionals feel about their choice to be out "may relate to such factors as freedom from the burden of keeping a secret" or "the rewards of serving as role models" for sexual minority students (p. 197). In fact, the authors concluded that the data should give hope to student affairs professionals who want to be open about their sexual orientation at work. Despite apparently experiencing more discrimination, openly LGB professionals appear to "feel content with their jobs and satisfied with their choice to be 'out' in student affairs" (p. 197).

3. *Ten themes emerged from a national survey on biased and exemplary student affairs practices concerning sexual minority issues. The themes allow student affairs professionals to assess the breadth of their efforts to end bias and increase affirmation in their student affairs work.*

Table 3 lists the 10 themes that were developed through qualitative analysis of the 1605 incidents of biased and exemplary practice described by members of what was then called ACPA's Standing Committee on Lesbian, Gay, and Bisexual Awareness. Each theme has a biased and an exemplary component for which the authors provided description and illustration in their research article (see Croteau & Lark, 1995a, pp. 474-479).

Sensitivity to multicultural and diversity issues in student affairs needs to be examined and improved at multiple levels (e.g., individual, institutional, etc.) (Stage & Hamrick, 1994). The authors of the "biased and exemplary practice study" suggested that the 10 themes can be used as an assessment device at three levels. At the individual level, the themes are a means for critical self-examination. In what areas am I doing an exemplary job? What am I neglecting? In what ways do I act in a biased manner?

At a broader level, the themes can provide a map for what needs to be incorporated into in-service training or graduate education on LGB issues. The 10 themes remind trainers and educators of the range of practices that need to be discussed in such training. If the graduate curriculum in a preparation program focuses only on understanding the unique developmental and situational needs of sexual minority students (theme 5) and on how to provide anti-homophobia education to the campus community (theme 7), eight other areas or themes central to non-biased and affirmative practice are neglected. Organizers of in-service training in student affairs divisions can also use the themes in planning their efforts. What has been the content of in-service training on LGB concerns in recent years? What content has yet to be covered and should be incorporated into future training sessions?

Finally, the 10 themes can be used at even a broader level—in the development of a consensus on principles of practice for the profession. While the themes themselves do not represent such a consensus, the themes do "map a universe of possible biased and exemplary practices" that should be considered, if and when much needed principles of practice are developed for the profession (Croteau & Lark, 1995a, p. 481).

4. *The qualitative research provides student affairs professionals with specific stories and descriptions about the homophobic sentiment and actions that occur within student affairs. The "storytelling" nature of the data is compelling and "may motivate professionals at an emotional level" by illustrating the "reality" of such bias (Croteau & Lark, 1995a, p. 481).*

Table 3
Themes of Biased and Exemplary Practice

1. **EXEMPLARY**: Student Affairs professionals openly express affirmation of lesbian, gay and bisexual people and confront homophobic remarks made by others. **BIASED**: Student Affairs professionals fail to express affirmation, do not confront homophobic remarks, or make homophobic remarks themselves.

2. **EXEMPLARY**: Student Affairs professionals respond to homophobic harassment and violence with support for victims, sanctions for perpetrators and anti-homophobia education for all. **BIASED**: Student Affairs professionals ignore or minimize homophobic violence and harassment.

3. **EXEMPLARY**: Student Affairs professionals are inclusive of lesbian, gay and bisexual people in language, programming, written materials, social events, and diversity activities/policies. **BIASED**: Student Affairs professionals are exclusive of lesbian, gay and bisexual people in these areas.

4. **EXEMPLARY**: Student Affairs professionals treat lesbian, gay and bisexual people with the same level of regard they would any student or colleague. **BIASED**: Student Affairs professionals fail to treat this population with such equity.

5. **EXEMPLARY**: Student Affairs professionals are sensitive to the unique developmental and situational needs of lesbian, gay and bisexual people. **BIASED**: Student Affairs professionals ignore or misunderstand the unique needs of this population.

6. **EXEMPLARY**: Student Affairs professionals value students and staff being "out," work to promote a climate that supports openness, and respect the confidentiality of those who choose not to be "out." **BIASED**: Student Affairs professionals discourage openness and/or fail to respect the confidentiality of those not "out."

7. **EXEMPLARY**: Student Affairs professionals provide staff training and campus programs designed to reduce homophobia and increase awareness. **BIASED**: Student Affairs professionals do not provide such training and programs.

8. **EXEMPLARY**: Student Affairs professionals provide or support programs specifically for lesbian, gay or bisexual persons on campus. **BIASED**: Student Affairs professionals fail to support or provide such programs.

(continued)

Table 3 *(continued)*
Themes of Biased and Exemplary Practice

---

9. **EXEMPLARY**: Student Affairs professionals advocate for lesbian, gay and bisexual organizations and individuals. **BIASED**: Student Affairs staff fail to advocate.
10. **EXEMPLARY**: Student Affairs professionals are equitable and affirmative in employment procedures, decisions, and benefits. **BIASED**: Student Affairs professionals are not equitable, or are discriminatory, in these employment practices.

Note. These themes are taken directly from the results of a qualitative study of student affairs professionals with experience on lesbian, gay, and bisexual issues (Croteau & Lark, 1995a, pp. 474-479).

Three examples of the compelling nature of these stories follow. First, in the "job experiences study," one gay student affairs professional described being harassed on the job. He reported that his office was vandalized in a number of ways. The words "fag," "homo" and "bugger" were written on his door and a "condom covered with chocolate sauce" was placed on his door (Croteau & Lark, 1995b, p. 194).

The second example is from the "original graduate program" study. Graduate students stated that rarely did their classroom learning or practicum experiences include exposure to issues of sexual minorities. Several students said that sexual minority issues were "taboo" in their programs. Many reported that when these issues did come up in the classroom it was usually students who initiated the discussion and not faculty.

The final example is from the "biased and exemplary practices study" and is about how student affairs professionals minimize the significance of homophobic violence and harassment. One student affairs professional told a story about how the residence hall door of two "out" lesbian students was set afire. The participant said that "the professional staff of the institution disregarded the incident as a college prank" even though the women were in their room at the time and "the guilty party was outside the door yelling such things as 'burn, dyke, burn.'" Further, a dean of students was quoted by another participant in the study as saying "all 18 to 21 year old men are homophobic; don't overreact to gay bashing." Yet another professional was quoted as having told gay students who were receiving threatening notes, "when you're gay you should expect this and no real harm should come" (Croteau & Lark, 1995a, p. 475).

The qualitative portions of the studies contain many more examples of this "storytelling" type of data about the spectrum of homophobic sentiment and actions that are still occurring in the profession. There are stories and descriptions of: (a) job search discrimination (Croteau & von Destinon, 1994), (b) "on the job" discrimination (Croteau & Lark, 1995a), (c) biased practices (Croteau & Lark, 1995a), and (d) negative experiences in professional preparation (Hoover, 1994; Talbot, 1992, 1996). Direct exposure to LGB people's stories of struggle with oppression can be a powerful component in positive attitude change (Geasler, Croteau, Heineman, & Edlund, 1995). Many student affairs professionals may be ignorant of the reality of oppression in the profession. It may be these powerful stories, rather than quantitative documentation of homophobia, that motivate involvement in anti-homophobia efforts in the profession.

5. *Faculty and graduate students in student affairs have a variety of levels of knowledge, skills, behaviors, and comfort with sexual minority issues. Inconsistencies in faculty and graduate students' self reports of this information indicate that they may at times overestimate their own overall competencies on LGB issues.*

Only data from the "original graduate program" study are available on graduate students. Some data on faculty are available, however, from both the original and follow-up graduate program studies. Thus, we will present data from both studies when available, delineating which is from the original and which is from the follow-up.

Only 8.7% of the graduate students from the original study reported having taken courses that focused on the experiences of LGB people. When asked about having read books on the history and experiences of sexual minorities, 29.9% of the graduate student sample indicated they had. Approximately 75% of the same sample felt capable of identifying individual heterosexism while 66% felt they could identify institutional heterosexism. Fifty-five percent of this same sample reported being capable of teaching others about issues related to sexual orientation. Less than half the sample (42.7%) were moderately to very comfortable with their skill level in providing professional programs and services for LGB students.

Approximately 80% of the faculty sample from the original study strongly agreed or agreed that they were capable of designing courses and advising in a way that reflects sensitivity to LGB students. When asked to evaluate their ability to teach about the needs and developmental issues of sexual minorities, 35% and 43% of the faculty (from the original and follow-up studies respectively) reported being moderately to very comfortable. When asked about attending professional workshops or conferences which focused specifically on the issues of sexual minorities, 51% and 61% of each faculty sample indicated they had. Fewer faculty (49% and 59%) had taken the initiative to read books written about the history or experiences of LGB people. These findings seem consistent with faculty's written comments about the lack of resources (books, articles, and training) available regarding sexual minorities.

Approximately half the faculty samples in both the original and follow-up graduate program studies indicated that they didn't know the name/topic or content of Cass' Sexual Identity Formation Model (Cass, 1979). A majority of the faculty had heard of the Kinsey Scales (Kinsey, Pomeroy, & Martin, 1948; Kinsey, Pomeroy, Martin, & Gebhard, 1953) before, but only 37% (original study) and 48% (follow-up study) indicated they had either general or specific knowledge about the Kinsey Scales. When asked about LGB developmental issues, 41% and 50% of the faculty samples indicated they were knowledgeable or very knowledgeable. When asked about the unique contributions and history of sexual minorities, 18% and 25% of the faculty indicated they were knowledgeable or very knowledgeable.

Some of this self-reported data seem inconsistent for both graduate students and faculty. Low percentages of graduate students had engaged in activities to learn about sexual minorities (classes, reading books). More than half the sample also felt less than moderately comfortable with their skill level in providing professional programs and services for LGB students. Despite the fact that few graduate students engaged in activities to learn about sexual minorities and few were comfortable with their skill level, over half of the sample believed they could teach others about issues related to sexual orientation.

Even more striking inconsistencies appeared in the faculty data. When asked about their knowledge of certain concepts or topics related to sexual minority issues (e.g., Cass' Model, Kinsey scale), few faculty reported having specific knowledge. Further, half or more of faculty in both samples reported being less than knowledgeable about the developmental issues and unique contributions of sexual minorities. Despite this lack of knowledge, 80% of the faculty in the original study indicated they were capable of teaching and advising in a way that reflects sensitivity to sexual minority students!

6. *Graduate faculty and students have lower levels of knowledge, skills, and comfort with sexual minority issues as compared to other areas of diversity (gender, race/ethnicity). Student affairs practitioners have lower levels of skill but equal or higher levels of knowledge and comfort with sexual minority issues compared to other areas of diversity (gender, age and race/ethnicity).*

Overall, student affairs practitioners in the "professionals' preparedness study," as well as graduate students and faculty in the "original and follow-up graduate program studies," reported moderately high to high levels of comfort and skill with issues of diversity, though there were differences by the diverse population being addressed. For all the studies, *Comfort* subscale mean scores for each diverse population are presented in Table 4. Both faculty samples and the graduate student sample had similar patterns in reporting on the *Comfort Scale*; their mean scores for comfort in situations with sexual minorities were lower than mean scores in situations with racial/ethnic minorities. Unlike the faculty and graduate students, practitioners had nearly equal mean scores for the sexual orientation and race/ethnicity subscales, with comfort in situations involving sexual minorities slightly higher than that for ethnic minorities.

The subscale mean scores regarding skill level (for the faculty, graduate student, and practitioner samples) are also reported in Table 4. Mean scores indicated that faculty felt more capable of working with and teaching about women than people of color; they felt least skilled in working with or teaching about sexual minorities. Once again, the graduate students followed the same patterns with slightly lower mean scores than the faculty. In the "practitioners' preparedness study," practitioners had similar patterns to the graduate students and faculty except their comfort level subscale scores for ethnicity and sexual orientation were nearly the same.

Relatively speaking, the populations surveyed (faculty and practitioners) scored lower on the *Knowledge Scale* than on other scales. For example, the faculty in the "follow-up graduate program study" had

Table 4

Average of the Comfort and Skill Item Means Separately for Items on LGB, Race, Gender and Age.

	Graduate Students n=321	Faculty (Original) n=49	Faculty (Follow-up) n=88	Practitioners n=389
Comfort Subscales (1=Low Comfort, 5=High Comfort)				
LGB	3.79	4.10	4.34	4.43
Race	4.23	4.35	4.50	4.42
Gender	—	—	—	4.71
Age	—	—	—	4.52
Skill Subscales (1=Low Skill, 4=High Skill)				
LGB	2.58	2.85	2.86	3.03
Race	2.91	3.24	3.24	3.13
Gender	3.13	3.37	3.42	3.40
Age	—	—	—	3.21

Note. Data are taken from two unpublished dissertations, one research study, and two publications (Hoover, 1994; Talbot, 1992, 1996; Talbot & Harvey, 1993; Talbot & Kocarek, 1997). Since figures are averages of item means, standard deviations are not appropriate. "N's" in the table represents the maximum number of participants who responded to any item that went into that item mean average. Each item mean that was averaged may have a smaller "n" by one or two.

a mean score of 2.8 for knowledge of women's issues, needs, unique history, and contributions (1 = no knowledge or familiarity with the topic/content area, 4 = thorough, specific knowledge). They had a knowledge score mean of 2.4 for topics related to ethnic minorities and 2.2 for topics related to sexual minorities. The practitioners had a higher mean score for knowledge of sexual minority topics (2.0) than for ethnic minorities (1.6); they scored higher for knowledge about issues related to age (2.5) and women (2.2).

According to the self-reported levels of comfort, skill, and knowledge regarding diversity, all the participants (graduate students, faculty and practitioners) indicated that they were comfortable and skilled in working with or teaching about diverse populations, even though they reported low levels of knowledge about these populations. The scores also suggest that a hierarchy exists in participants' comfort, skill, and knowledge across the diverse populations being addressed. Nearly every time, sexual minorities are at the bottom of this hierarchy.

7. *There is a positive relationship between faculty's level of knowledge, skills, and comfort with sexual orientation and their students' level of knowledge, skills, and comfort.*

In the "original graduate program study," a correlation matrix was produced to test the relationship between faculty's and graduate students' total mean scores on the *Knowledge Scale* and *Comfort Scale* (see Table 5). Not surprisingly, knowledge and comfort with issues of diversity were highly correlated in both faculty and students. In addition, there was a strong positive relationship between students' level of knowledge and faculty's level of knowledge, as well as a positive relationship between students' level of comfort and faculty's level of comfort. There were also strong positive correlations between faculty's level of comfort and students' level of knowledge. These correlations included all items, not just those specific to sexual orientation.

The implications of the correlations between faculty's comfort and knowledge and graduate students' comfort and knowledge are extremely important. One interpretation of this finding is that faculty do indeed have a great influence on the student body; faculty's ability to model comfort and knowledge with diverse populations, including sexual minorities, impacts graduate students' level of comfort and knowledge. In semi-structured interviews, graduate students indicated that they watched their faculty closely, looking for consistency between what they taught and what they did in their lives. Some graduate students shared stories

Table 5

Correlation Matrix for Knowledge and Comfort Scale Scores Among Graduate Students and Faculty in Student Affairs

	Student Knowledge	Student Comfort	Faculty Knowledge	Faculty Comfort
Student Knowledge	1.00			
Student Comfort	0.92	1.00		
Faculty Knowledge	0.80	0.54	1.00	
Faculty Comfort	0.73	0.56	0.74	1.00

Note. Data are taken from an unpublished dissertation (Talbot, 1992)—the "original graduate program study." "N" for faculty is 49 and "n" for graduate students is 321.

about how the faculty seemed uncomfortable as they tried to teach about or discuss issues related to sexual orientation or ethnicity. In their minds, the awkward delivery of the message outweighed the content.

The high correlation between faculty and graduate student scores points toward an important overall notion about how to increase affirmation in the profession. Student affairs faculty may need to increase their levels of knowledge and comfort with sexual minority concerns in order to "produce" future graduates for the profession who are more knowledgeable and comfortable with these issues.

8. *The student affairs profession (and future profession as indicated by graduate student demographics) is diverse in relation to sexual orientation. Other areas of diversity are not as representative of the*

general population. Data support the notion that such diversity of persons within the profession is important in creating more knowledgeable, skilled, and sensitive professionals.

The graduate student sample in the "original graduate program study" was 78% female, 82% White, and 90% heterosexual. The faculty samples from the original and follow-up graduate program studies were 41% and 43% female respectively, 92% and 84% White respectively, and 91% heterosexual (follow-up study only; sexual orientation was not included as a demographic variable in the original faculty survey). The student affairs practitioners were predominantly female (58%), predominantly White (90%), and predominantly heterosexual (87%). Even though these samples are predominantly "majority," except related to gender, they are diverse compared to most populations in higher education. Given the percentages of sexual minorities frequently found in research samples measuring sexual orientation by self-identification (see Gonsiorek & Weinrich, 1991), the student affairs samples were well represented with LGB people.

High levels of knowledge, comfort, skill, and affirmative behavior toward minorities are not inherent in, nor exclusive to, environments with significant minority populations. However, exposure to, and interaction with, diverse populations can reduce biased and prejudiced behaviors. In fact, a pattern that affirms this notion existed in the "original graduate program study." Graduate programs that had the most diverse student body tended to have the highest scores for knowledge, skills, and comfort with diversity (for both students and faculty). Similarly, the programs with the least diversity tended to have the lowest scores. This finding was reinforced by the interviews with the graduate students. When asked how they best learned about diversity, most of the students indicated that it was through personal contact and knowledge. They viewed the "book learning" as important but needed the experience to fully integrate their learning.

Encouraging and Improving Future Research

The first section of this chapter summarized major findings from the studies on LGB issues in the student affairs profession that are listed in Table 1. These studies have addressed the experiences of LGB student affairs professionals, biased and exemplary student affairs practices in regard to LGB issues, and the LGB-related knowledge, skill, and attitudes of student affairs graduate students, faculty, and practitioners. The research-based information described in the previous section is limited in both scope and methodological rigor. In this section, we focus on improving and expanding future research efforts related to LGB issues in student affairs.

This section is divided into three parts. In the first part, we focus on ways to improve the methods, and increase the variety, of *quantitative designs* employed in future research. In the second part, we focus on ways to improve the methods, and increase the variety, in *qualitative* designs for future research. Finally, in the third part, we recommend several approaches for increasing research in relation to sexual minority concerns in the profession.

Improving and Expanding Quantitative Designs in Future Research

First, we discuss the strength of the existing research in the area of sampling and encourage future researchers to emulate this success. Second, we discuss how the quality of measurement has varied in existing research and make suggestions for improved measurement in future research. Lastly, we point out the limited variety of quantitative approaches that have been employed thus far. We suggest, through specific illustrations, the use of a wider variety of approaches to quantitative research.

The studies of the student affairs profession reviewed in this chapter used written surveys and had very good return rates. With one exception (Hogan & Rentz, 1996), the studies utilized large, national samples, mirroring the diversity of the profession in regard to demographics and student affairs positions. Future research should examine the sampling procedures used in these studies so that future efforts can be as successful.

Existing research on LGB issues in the student affairs profession is quite varied in terms of the rigor of quantitative measurement. For instance, the "job search" and "job experiences" studies utilized two key variables: discrimination and degree of openness about sexual orientation. These variables, like many in this area of research, were not well defined and were measured by a single item that had no established validity or reliability. The "original and follow-up graduate program studies" and "practitioners preparedness study" did a better job of measurement. Conceptual definitions were assigned to variables and multiple items were generated to measure those concepts. Once the initial measures were so generated, the measures were submitted to student affairs faculty and practitioners so that their feedback on content and face validity could be used for further refinement. Test-retest studies were also conducted to establish reliability of measures designed for their research. Future research should improve measurement by using suggestions from a review of work experiences research (Croteau, 1996) and by emulating or extending the methods employed in the "graduate program studies" (see Talbot, 1992; Talbot, 1996; Talbot & Kocarek, 1997) and the "professional preparedness study" (see Hoover, 1994).

An extremely limited scope of quantitative research designs have been employed in existing research on the student affairs profession in regard to sexual minority issues. All of the quantitative approaches have been correlational in nature (i.e., involving written surveys on existing data with no manipulation of variables). Future research should expand the scope of designs considered, which in turn would allow different types of research questions to be addressed. For instance, different designs would allow researchers to address how divisions, offices, or preparation programs can become more LGB affirmative. More specifically, a longitudinal design would allow tracking of information across time as positive or negative changes occur regarding sexual minority concerns. Another important design, the intervention outcome study, would allow researchers to test the effectiveness of intentional strategies aimed at increasing affirmation in student affairs environments.

Even within the general category of correlational survey designs employed by all existing research in this area, the variety of approaches have been limited. The existing studies have focused on descriptive information; little attention has been directed toward hypothesis testing and theory building research. For instance, in the "job search" and "job experiences" studies, the level of student affairs professionals' openness about their own sexual orientation was measured and correlated with the level of discrimination and job satisfaction. Openness was defined simply as the number of colleagues who knew the participant's sexual orientation. In contrast, a model that describes the dynamics of managing one's sexual identity (e.g., Griffin, 1992) could be employed as the theoretical context for defining and measuring openness, as well as generating hypotheses about its relationship to other variables. This process of confirming or disconfirming theory-based hypotheses can then lead student affairs professionals toward useful theoretical concepts that can be used in a variety of ways in day to day student affairs work (e.g., knowing how a discriminatory incident may influence sexual minority professionals' identity management; understanding the factors in student affairs environments that impact sexual minority professionals' decisions about identity management strategies).

Improving and Expanding
Qualitative Designs in Future Research

In this discussion, we first argue that qualitative methods are especially appropriate for research on LGB issues in the student affairs profession and should continue to be used. Then we encourage the use of a wider variety of qualitative data collection methods and basic designs than have been employed in existing research.

Almost all of the existing research on the profession in relation to sexual minority concerns have employed qualitative methods. A number of scholars (Croteau, 1996; Hoshmand, 1989; Sang, 1989) have advocated for the use of qualitative methods in research focusing on issues and populations that have historically been ignored and/or devalued. The "discovery" orientation of qualitative methods (i.e., its freedom from *a priori* defining of all data to be collected) allows "the native experiences, meanings and perspectives of unfamiliar" or devalued groups to emerge (Hoshmand, 1989, p. 20). In contrast, quantitative approaches require a body of established knowledge to adequately define, measure, and hypothesize about variables. In fact, the lack of such a body of knowledge makes measurement in quantitative research difficult as suggested in the previous discussion. Though the studies reviewed here provide some greater basis for developing research questions suited to quantitative inquiry, the lack of information regarding sexual minorities in student affairs remains enormous.

The variety of questions and designs being employed in qualitative research, however, needs to be expanded. In developing research questions and designing qualitative studies, Patton (1990) identifies a key decision qualitative researchers must make between breadth or depth of information. The qualitative parts of the existing research have focused on breadth; that is, relatively large samples employing written surveys requiring relatively brief responses. This method of data collection has been appropriate to the research questions and purposes of the studies: mapping the universe of possible exemplary and biased practices in regard to sexual minority concerns or mapping the universe of possible discriminatory actions toward LGB student affairs professionals. Research questions and designs focused on depth of information are also needed. Any one of the 10 themes developed in the biased and exemplary practices study (Table 3) could be the focus of a study. For example, the second theme calls student affairs professionals to respond to incidents of homophobic harassment and violence with support for victims, sanctions for perpetrators, and education for the whole community in which the incident occurred. In the study focused on all 10 themes, information about this one theme is limited. A depth-focused study could target directors in residential life who have handled numerous such incidents with varying levels of success. These individuals could then participate in semi-structured interviews with researchers. The use of in-depth interviews concentrating on a more narrowly focused topic would allow a different kind of information to emerge. Instead of generating information about the range of exemplary and biased practices, information would emerge that specifically describes effective responses to harassment and violence. In the tradition of "grounded theory" qualitative research (Strauss & Corbin, 1990), this would allow the development of models of antiharassment intervention that are "grounded" in the experiences of student affairs professionals who handle harassment on college campuses. Another in-depth qualitative approach, the case study using observational and archival methods of data collection, could also be used in a study of an incident of harassment. This method would produce detailed information on the institutional response and community dynamics that occurred during and after the incident. Thus, both breadth and depth approaches to future qualitative research need to be considered and choices made dependent on the research question and type of information sought.

Increasing Future Research Efforts

The previous parts of this section focused on improving the quality of research on the profession regarding LGB issues. In this part, we recommend several approaches for increasing the quantity of research in this area. The conclusions drawn earlier in this chapter are tentative and limited in both scope and usefulness. More research is necessary if we are to draw conclusions with any more certainty, breadth, or meaningfulness.

Findings from the "original and follow-up graduate program studies" and the "professional preparedness" study suggest one explanation for the lack of research in this area. Student affairs practitioners seem to be more affirmative about, and active in, addressing sexual minority concerns than are student affairs faculty and graduate students. In other words, the primary setting from which research is generated, graduate preparation programs, may be the least affirmative environment in the student affairs profession. Therefore, the first approach we recommend for increasing research in this area is to work toward making graduate preparation programs more affirmative. Within a more affirmative environment, faculty and graduate students may feel more supported and motivated towards conducting research on LGB issues.

A second approach capitalizes on the relatively affirmative practices in student affairs divisions. Student affairs professionals could expand their LGB affirmative work to include research activities. This approach fits well with the recent push in student affairs for scholarly practitioners to play an increasing role in the generation of empirical knowledge directly useful to student affairs practice. Further, student affairs practitioners who are conducting research need to publish their work. In preparing this chapter, the authors reviewed only those empirical studies that had received a relatively high degree of critical review; that is, only those studies that had been published or undergone the scrutiny of a doctoral dissertation process. We know of some studies, and suspect many more, that have been conducted for institutional planning/evaluation purposes but have never been widely circulated through publication. These studies represent campus environment and case study approaches that can contribute to an overall research base for LGB affirmative work in student affairs. An empirically based body of knowledge will be built "only as each small piece of scholarly work is compared, contrasted, and integrated with other such work" (Croteau & Bieschke, 1996, p. 122). Only through publication can each piece of research be disseminated broadly enough to allow access for researchers to begin this cumulative building process.

A final approach to increasing research is to encourage heterosexual researchers to consider involvement in research on LGB issues. There are legitimate concerns about heterosexuals investigating sexual minority issues. These concerns may be similar to those expressed about Whites conducting research about ethnic minority issues (e.g., Mio & Iwamasa, 1993). Should and can a heterosexual researcher play a leading role in studying LGB concerns? Can a heterosexual researcher adequately understand the issues to represent sexual minority voices? According to Gerschick (1993), the answer to these questions is yes, with qualifiers.

One qualifier relates to the heterosexual researcher's level of self-awareness and development regarding sexual minority issues. A second qualifier relates to the type of methodology and focus of the research being conducted. A number of scholars address these two qualifiers in greater detail in reference to "majority" researchers focusing on "minority" issues (Gerschick, 1993; Helms, 1993; Mio & Iwamasa, 1993; Ponterotto, 1993; Sue, 1993).

Conclusion

The "original and follow-up graduate program studies" (Talbot, 1992, 1996; Talbot & Harvey, 1993; Talbot & Kocarek, 1997), "profession preparedness study" (Hoover, 1994), "homophobic attitudes study" (Hogan & Rentz, 1996), "job search study" (Croteau & von Destinon, 1994), "job experiences study" (Croteau & Lark, 1995b), and the "biased and exemplary practice study" (Croteau & Lark, 1995a) are the beginnings of empirical research on LGB issues in the student affairs profession. This chapter's integration of findings from these studies provide only a tentative and limited picture of the profession in regard to LGB issues. Most research questions in this area have not even been asked and the few that have been asked need much more exploration.

Drawing on our own knowledge and experience with research on LGB issues, we believe that there is an overarching, additional reason that only minimal research is being conducted and published in this area. It is our contention that the lack of research on sexual minority issues is due, in large part, to heterosexism and homophobia among scholars in student affairs and higher education (Chan, 1996; Tierney, 1997). Simply put, researchers fear overt and covert stigmatization if they do research on LGB issues. The individual and professional growth and rewards of doing scholarly research in this area are often overlooked in the face of this fear. Progress, however, cannot occur without risk.

References

Cass, V. C. (1979). Homosexual identity formation: A theoretical model. *Journal of Homosexuality, 4,* 214-219-235.

Chan, C. S. (1996). Combating heterosexism in educational institutions: Structural changes and strategies. In E. D. Rothblum & L. A. Bond (Eds.), *Preventing heterosexism and homophobia* (pp. 20-35). Thousand Oaks, CA: Sage.

Croteau, J.M. (1996). Research on the work experiences of lesbian, gay and bisexual people: An integrative review of methodology and findings. *Journal of Vocational Behavior, 48,* 195-209.

Croteau, J. M., & Bieschke, K. J. (1996). Beyond pioneering: An introduction to the special issue on the vocational issues of lesbian women and gay men. *Journal of Vocational Behavior, 48,* 119-124.

Croteau, J. M., & Lark, J. S. (1995a). A qualitative investigation of biased and exemplary student affairs practice concerning lesbian, gay and bisexual issues. *Journal of College Student Development, 36,* 472-482.

Croteau, J. M., & Lark, J. S. (1995b). On being lesbian, gay or bisexual in student affairs: A national survey of experiences on the job. *NASPA Journal, 32,* 189-197.

Croteau, J. M., & von Destinon, M. (1994). A national survey of job search experiences of lesbian, gay and bisexual student affairs professionals. *Journal of College Student Development, 35,* 40-45.

Evans, N. J., & Wall, V. A. (Eds.). (1991). *Beyond tolerance: Gays, lesbians and bisexuals on campus.* Alexandria, VA: American College Personnel Association.

Garnets, L., Hancock, K. A., Cochran, S. D., Goodchilds, J., & Peplau, L. A. (1991). Issues in psychotherapy with lesbians and gay men: A survey of psychologists. *American Psychologist, 46,* 964-972.

Geasler, M. J., Croteau, J. M., Heineman, C. J., & Edlund, C. J. (1995). A qualitative study of students' expression of change after attending panel presentations by lesbian, gay and bisexual speakers. *Journal of College Student Development, 36,* 483-492.

Gerschick, T. J. (1993). Should and can a White, heterosexual, middle-class man teach students about social inequality and oppression? One person's experience and reflections. In D. Shoem, L. Frankel, X. Zuinga, & E. A. Lewis (Eds.), *Multicultural teaching in the university* (pp. 200-311). Westport, CT: Praeger.

Gonsiorek, J. C., & Weinrich, J. D. (1991). The definition and scope of sexual orientation. In J. C. Gonsiorek & J. D. Weinrich (Eds.), *Homosexuality: Research implications for public policy* (pp. 1-12). Newbury Park, CA: Sage.

Helms, J. E. (1993). I also said, "White racial identity influences White researchers." *Counseling Psychologist, 21,* 240-243.

Hogan, T. L., & Rentz, A. L. (1996). Homophobia in the academy. *Journal of College Student Development, 37,* 309-314.

Hoover, C. K. (1994). *An investigation of the preparedness of student affairs professionals to work effectively with diverse populations on campus.* Unpublished doctoral dissertation, University of Maryland, College Park.

Hoshmand, L. (1989). Alternate research paradigms: A review and teaching proposal. *The Counseling Psychologist, 17,* 3-80.

Kinsey, A. C., Pomeroy, W. B., & Martin, C. E. (1948). *Sexual behavior in the human male.* Philadelphia: Saunders

Kinsey, A. C., Pomeroy, W. B., Martin, C. E., & Gebhard, P. H. (1953). *Sexual behavior in the human female.* Philadelphia: Saunders.

Lark, J. S. (1998). Lesbian, gay, and bisexual concerns in student affairs: Themes and transitions in the development of the professional literature. *NASPA Journal, 35,* 157-168.

Mio, J. S., & Iwamasa, G. (1993). To do, or not to do: That is the question for White cross-cultural researchers. *Counseling Psychologist, 21,* 197-212.

Patton,M.Q. (1990).*Qualitative evaluation and research methods.* Newbury Park, CA:Sage.

Ponterotto, J. G. (1993). White racial identity and the counseling professional. *Counseling Psychologist, 21,* 213-217.

Sang, B. E. (1989). New directions in lesbian research, theory, and education. *Journal of Counseling and Development, 68,* 92-96.

Stage, F. K., & Hamrick, F. (1994). Diversity issues: Fostering campus wide development of multiculturalism. *Journal of College Student Development, 35,* 331-335.

Strauss, A., & Corbin, J. (1990). *Basics of qualitative research: Grounded theory procedures and techniques.* Newbury Park, CA: Sage.

Sue, D. W. (1993). Confronting ourselves: The White and racial/ethnic-minority researcher. *Counseling Psychologist, 21,* 244-249.

Talbot, D. M. (1992). *A multimethod study of the diversity emphasis in master's degree programs in college student affairs.* Doctoral dissertation, University of Maryland, College Park.

Talbot, D. M. (1996). Master's students' perspectives on their graduate education regarding issues of diversity. *NASPA Journal, 33,* 163-178.

Talbot, D. M., & Harvey, K. A. (1993). [A follow-up multimethod study of the diversity emphasis in a broad range of master's degree programs in student affairs]. Unpublished raw data. (Information available from the authors.)

Talbot, D. M., & Kocarek, C. (1997). Student affairs graduate faculty's level of knowledge, comfort and skill with issues of diversity. *Journal of College Student Development, 38,* 278-287.

Tierney, W. G. (1997). *Academic outlaws: Queer theory and cultural studies in the academy.* Thousand Oaks, CA: Sage.

Chapter 2

ℰℐℭℛ

Empirical Investigations of the Gay, Lesbian, and Bisexual College Student

KATHLEEN J. BIESCHKE, AMY B. EBERZ,
AND D'ANDRE WILSON

The gay, lesbian, and bisexual college student has received increasing attention in the published literature (for example, Baker, 1991; D'Emilio; 1990; Evans & Wall, 1991) and in an increasing number of reports for the university community (see Rankin, 1998), but the published empirical research pertaining to this population remains sparse. The difficulties researchers encounter when attempting to study the behaviors of gays, lesbians, and bisexuals are well-documented (see Buhrke, Ben-Ezra, Hurley, & Ruprecht, 1992; Catania, McDermott, & Pollack, 1986; Croteau, 1996; Lonborg & Phillips, 1996) and much of the research is methodologically flawed. Yet relying on the speculative and theoretical literature regarding these students is risky, especially if one is making policy decisions, designing training programs for student affairs professionals, or making personal decisions about one's interactions regarding this population. Certainly, conducting investigations pertaining to the gay, lesbian, and bisexual college student not only provides student affairs professionals with valuable information, but also legitimizes, empowers, and demonstrates acceptance of this population (see D'Augelli, 1989a for a compelling discussion of this argument).

This chapter has two primary goals. First, we will synthesize and critically review the current empirical literature focused on gay, lesbian, and bisexual college students. As part of that review, it is our intention to provide an integrative summary of research findings, critique the studies methodologically, and develop a research agenda. Our second goal is to provide recommendations for researchers who are contemplating further study of gay, lesbian, and bisexual college students.

Because there were a number of articles and chapters that focused on this population, we developed a set of criteria specifically designed to concentrate our review on the empirical research pertaining exclusively to gay, lesbian, and bisexual college students. First, we included all empirical (that is, data-based) research studies published in refereed journals during the 1980s or 1990s. Our definition of empirical research encompassed both quantitative and qualitative research studies. Articles that were exclusively speculative or theoretical were not included (for example, Cass, 1979; D'Augelli, 1989a; Henderson, 1984).

Second, we included only research studies that clearly focused on the college student. If other comparison groups were included, we included the study only if it was possible to draw separate conclusions about gay, lesbian, or bisexual college students. A number of studies we considered were eliminated on this basis (for example, Cass, 1984; Etringer, Hillerbrand, & Hetherington, 1990; Hershberger & D'Augelli, 1995; Levine, 1997; Savin-Williams, 1995; Schneider, Farberow, & Kruks, 1989; Troiden, 1979; Walters & Simoni, 1993).

Third, we eliminated those studies that focused on the attitudes of heterosexuals towards those who identify as gay, lesbian, or bisexual. Such studies only addressed the gay, lesbian, and bisexual student indirectly (for example, D'Augelli & Rose, 1990; Dillon, 1986; McCord & Herzog, 1991; Stevenson & Gajarsky, 1991).

Finally, we included only research studies published in refereed journals. Dissertations, presentations, and unpublished manuscripts that we located (for example, Banzhaf, 1990; Bieschke, Grubbs, Peterson, Agee, & Surbeck, 1995; DeSurra & Church, 1994; Evans, 1996, Levine & Bahr, 1989) were excluded. Our rationale for not including such research is that it is not known whether presentations and unpublished manuscripts have undergone any type of peer review process and thus the results presented remain suspect. Furthermore, none of these types of studies are readily accessible to researchers.

Literature Review

An attempt was made to locate every published study focused on gay, lesbian, or bisexual college students that met our criteria. We attempted to "cast our net broadly." In other words, we did not just focus on those journals most closely associated with student affairs (such as the *Journal of College Student Development* (JCSD); the *NASPA Journal)*. Had we done so, we would have found only one-third of the articles we finally gathered as no empirical articles have been published in the *NASPA Journal*, and only four were found in *JCSD*. In all, we located twelve articles, representing nine separate studies (the results of some studies have been published more than once: Rhoads, 1994; 1995a; 1995b; and D'Augelli, 1989a; 1989b).

A summary of all the published research articles reviewed for this chapter is provided in Table 1. The table (and our subsequent literature review) is organized around the three themes that emerged from the literature: the identity development process, experiences on campus, and health issues. Included in Table 1 are the names of the authors, a brief description of the stated purpose, the sample, and the general design for each study.

Given the small number of published studies regarding this population and the methodological limitations discussed later in this chapter, one might wonder whether it is possible to draw any firm conclusions regarding gay, lesbian, and bisexual college students. After scrutinizing the methodology and data analyses for each study, we present only those conclusions in which we have some confidence. In addition, we indicate when a particular conclusion has been supported in multiple studies.

It is important to bear in mind that none of the reviewed studies separately analyzed data regarding bisexual men and women. Many of the studies, however, included bisexuals in their sample of lesbian or gay students. Any conclusions regarding bisexual college students, then, must be seen as tentative and requiring further investigation.

Table 1
Summary of Studies Addressing the Gay, Lesbian, and Bisexual College Student

College Experiences

Authors	Sample.	Stated Purpose	General Design
D'Augelli (1989)	125 lesbian, gay, or bisexual individuals attending a GLB student organization meeting.	To examine patterns of victimization of lesbian, gay, or bisexual individuals in a university community.	Responses were obtained using a questionnaire used in a study of discrimination at Yale University (Herek, 1986).
D'Augelli (1992)	Responses from a 1989 study were combined with replies to the same survey instrument in 1990. The final sample consisted of 65 gay men, 32 lesbians, 16 bisexual men, and 8 bisexual women.	To focus on harassment and discrimination specifically directed at self-identified lesbian, gay, or bisexual undergraduate students, and to describe the nature of that harassment and discrimination.	Responses were obtained using a survey developed by Herek (1986) that was distributed by members of a gay, lesbian, bisexual student organization at meetings, social events, lectures, films, and dances.
Herek (1993)	166 lesbian, gay, and bisexual respondents from within a university community.	To provide date from an empirical study of anti-gay prejudice, and to provide a model for researchers to follow in conducting similar studies.	A questionnaire was distributed in three ways within the university community: (1) at a campus dance sponsored by lesbian and gay student groups; (2) at meetings of various lesbian and gay student groups; and (3) through friendship networks.

Table 1 (*continued*)
Summary of Studies Addressing the Gay, Lesbian, and Bisexual College Student

Authors	Sample	Stated Purpose	General Design
Baier, et al. (1991)	Random sample of 1650 students; 36 students reported being either gay or bisexual.	To examine the pattern of sexual behavior among college students; to determine if victimization is a function of gender, sexual orientation, or class level; to determine when students are victimized, before or after entering the university.	Modified version of Koss' Sexual Experiences Survey was mailed to a random sample of 1650 students. Responses of "gay/bisexual" students were compared to heterosexual students.
Reynolds (1989)	32 gay/bisexual male students and 32 heterosexual students.	To explore differences in perception of university climate between gay and heterosexual male students.	Heterosexual and 32 matched pairs of gay male students were identified. Pairs were matched on six background variables. Each student was given a questionnaire packet containing the outcome (University Climate Scale) and predictor (Alienation Scale, Bem Sex-Role Inventory, Rosenberg Self-Esteem Scale, and University Homophobia Scale) variables.
Lopez & Chism (1993)	16 lesbian and gay students known to a GLB office on campus.	To examine "their identity as lesbian, or gay, their campus and classroom experiences, their relationships with instructors, and general learning issues." (p. 97)	Students chose one of three methods to respond to a similar set of questions, including a focus group, individual interviews, and open-ended questionnaires.

Table 1 (*continued*)
Summary of Studies Addressing the Gay, Lesbian, and Bisexual College Student

		Identity Development	
Authors	**Sample**	**Stated Purpose**	**General Design**
D'Augelli (1991)	61 undergraduate gay men.	"To shed light on identity processes of self-identified gay men in college." (pp. 140-141)	Anonymous questionnaires (38% return rate).
Lopez & Chism (1993)	16 lesbian and gay students known to a GLB office on campus.	To examine "their identity as lesbian, or gay, their campus and classroom experiences, their relationships with instructors, and general learning issues," (p. 97)	Students chose one of three methods to respond to a similar set of questions, including a focus group, individual interviews, and open-ended questionnaires.
Rhoads (1994, 1995a, 1995b)	40 gay and bisexual college men, a majority were active in a GLB student organization.	To examine the coming out experiences of gay and bisexual men as they attempt to develop an identity within a context of heterosexist societal norms.	2-year ethnographic study; 40 formal interviews, informal interviews, participant observation of GLB culture, examination of documents (such as articles from the student newspaper).
Baier, et al. (1991)	Random sample of 1650 students; 36 students reported being either gay or bisexual.	To examine the pattern of sexual behavior among college students; to determine if victimization is a function of gender, sexual orientation, or class level; to determine when students are victimized, before or after entering the university.	Modified version of Koss' Sexual Experiences Survey was mailed to a random sample of 1650 students. Responses of "gay/bisexual" students were compared to heterosexual students.

Table 1 (*continued*)
Summary of Studies Addressing the Gay, Lesbian, and Bisexual College Student

Health-Related

Authors	Sample	Stated Purpose	General Design
Kline, et al. (1987)	58 gay/bisexual students attending a gay/lesbian student organization or conference.	Explored whether changes in the sexual behavior of gay men occurred in response to the AIDS epidemic.	Self-report questionnaires, prediction of proportional decrease in AIDS risk behaviors among gay and bisexual male students compared to a sample of gay physicians.
Yager, et al. (1988)	48 gay and bisexual male students attending meetings of a student organization.	"To investigate whether homosexuality predisposes males to eating disorders." (p. 145)	Self-report questionnaires, including demographics and the Eating Disorders Inventory. Gay/bisexual men compared to a sample of heterosexual men.

Studies of Gay, Lesbian, and Bisexual College Student Experiences on Campus

We located only six published articles representing five separate studies that addressed the gay, lesbian, and bisexual college student experience on campus. Half the studies focused on gay, lesbian, and bisexual college students' experiences of discrimination and harassment.

Two such studies (D'Augelli, 1989b, 1992; Herek, 1993) described the experiences of gay, lesbian, and bisexual college students on campus. They found that the vast majority of these students reported that they had been victims of some form of harassment, discrimination, or intimidation due to their sexual orientation. Ways in which students had been harassed or intimidated included the following: receiving verbal insults and threats of physical violence; having personal property vandalized or objects thrown at them; and being chased, followed, spat on, punched, kicked, beaten, or assaulted with a weapon. Findings also indicated that most of these incidents were not reported to the authorities. Further, it was found that many of the gay, lesbian, and bisexual students expected future harassment and were fearful of it. The majority of the gay, lesbian, and bisexual students made conscious changes in their daily routines in an attempt to avoid harassment.

Unlike the previous two studies, which focused exclusively on describing a gay, lesbian, or bisexual sample, Baier, Rosenzweig, and Whipple (1991) conducted a study that compared these students to a sample of heterosexual students. They reported that the gay, lesbian, and bisexual students were more likely than heterosexual students to experience sexual victimization.

These three studies all support the conclusion that gay, lesbian, and bisexual students experience high rates of harassment, victimization, and intimidation. This finding implies that the majority of gay, lesbian, and bisexual students lack the level of security and comfort afforded most heterosexual students on college campuses. Indeed, Reynolds (1989) found that gay male students had a very different perception of the campus climate than their heterosexual male counterparts. The gay students in this study felt less safe, comfortable, and supported within the university community.

Only one study (Lopez & Chism, 1993) focused more narrowly on the classroom experiences of gay and lesbian students (their attempts to locate bisexual volunteers were unsuccessful). It was also the only study of campus experiences that was based exclusively on qualitative data. The results of their study indicated that gay and lesbian students are discriminated against more on campus than in the classroom. They found that in the classroom the professor was the most important determinant of classroom environment. Students reported experiencing a wide range of attitudes towards gays and lesbians from instructors, the most common one being avoidance. Students reported being much affected by the indirect and subtle messages conveyed by instructors. One student in their study simply stated "Doing nothing is doing something. To a gay, lesbian, or bisexual student, failure to act could make a student feel that the instructor is not supportive and possibly hostile" (p. 101).

Studies of Gay, Lesbian, and Bisexual Identity Development

Although a variety of theoretical models (for example, Cass, 1979; Coleman, 1982; Faderman, 1985; Minton & McDonald, 1984; Troiden, 1988) and empirical studies (for example, Cass, 1984; Loiacano, 1989; McDonald, 1982; Miranda & Storms, 1989; Sophie, 1986; Walters & Simoni, 1993) have attempted to explain the complex process of gay, lesbian, and bisexual identity development, only five empirically-based publications, based on three studies, have examined this process in college students. Two of the three studies examined general identity development experiences. Two studies focused exclusively on gay and/or bisexual men, one of which addressed particular aspects of the coming-out process.

With respect to general identity development issues, D'Augelli's (1991) and Lopez and Chism's (1993) studies investigated several broad aspects of identity. First, D'Augelli examined the following experiences among gay college men: development and management of a gay identity; issues influencing disclosure or nondisclosure to family members; social relationships with other lesbian, gay, and bisexual people; and involvement in gay social and political activities. The results suggested that respondents varied widely in the way they became aware of and acknowledged their gay feelings, disclosed to others, and managed relationships with partners. Many men reported having made attempts to disguise their gay identity (for example, using opposite-sex pronouns when referring to partners or introducing a partner as a friend) in uncomfortable situations. Moreover, many participants reported having experienced a considerable amount of tension about whether to disclose their orientation to family members.

Less than half of the men had come out to their families. Often this disclosure was selective, including only family members who were perceived as tolerant and accepting. Mothers were perceived as significantly more tolerant than were fathers. In addition to the challenge of disclosing to family members, respondents expressed concern about ending close relationships, worrying about HIV infection, and disclosing to coworkers and supervisors.

Supportive relationships outside the family were especially significant to these men. They indicated that their most important interpersonal connections involved friendships with other gay men and with straight friends who were aware of their gay identity. With respect to involvement in the gay community, many men reported socializing with other gay people in a variety of settings, such as gay bars and social activities sponsored by the university's gay, lesbian, and bisexual student organization.

Lopez and Chism (1993) examined factors in the classroom environment that impacted identity development for gay and lesbian students. Qualitative analyses of the data indicated that these students encountered a variety of identity issues on a continual basis. With respect to coming out, many participants initially reported experiencing "inescapable" (p. 98) feelings of confusion, anxiety, and self-loathing. This initial period often involved a decrease in academic performance, followed by an improvement as students experienced increased self-awareness and further identity development.

The classroom environment significantly impacted students' coming-out experiences in several ways. First, instructors' supportive or unsupportive behaviors (such as addressing homophobic and heterosexist remarks, making demeaning comments) particularly affected students who were just beginning to come out. Perceptions of both classroom environment and instructor receptivity towards gay and lesbian issues influenced students' daily decisions to disclose their identity to others. Students reported feeling more comfortable coming out to peers in upper-division courses and being less likely to come out in situations where the professor might reduce their grades or treat them differently from other students who had not disclosed a gay, lesbian, or bisexual identity. Participants also reported feeling considerable discomfort and resentment about being considered spokespersons for all gay and lesbian people in order to help educate classmates and professors.

In contrast to D'Augelli's (1991) and Lopez and Chism's (1993) descriptive studies of general developmental issues, the other study considered more specific aspects of the process of coming out for gay and bisexual men. Rhoads (1994, 1995a, 1995b) conducted a two-year ethnographic study that focused on gay and bisexual college men who were in their later years of college and were politically active. His findings identified several aspects of the coming-out experiences of gay and bisexual college men. These results suggest that coming out is a continual process that results in personal changes, negative experiences, and incidents of harassment and discrimination.

Coming out was described as a process that begins with self-acknowledgment and is necessarily ongoing because of pervasive heterosexist societal expectations. As a result of coming out, students reported experiencing significant positive personal changes, including an improved sense of self-worth, increased openness with others, and greater self-confidence and self-understanding. However, students also described a variety of negative results of coming out, such as periods of intense questioning of their sexual identity. Moreover, students reported ongoing experiences of harassment and discrimination in a variety of settings. In social settings and on campus, students were physically and verbally assaulted. In the classroom, students were frequently excluded and marginalized by class discussions about issues such as dating, committed relationships, and sexuality.

Rhoads (1994, 1995a) also addressed the role of cultural politics in the process of coming out. As noted earlier, 27 of the 40 men in this study indicated that political involvement comprised part of their gay or bisexual identity and was an essential progression in the coming-out process. Rhoads noted that students' self-identification as "queer" represented an effort to unify gay, lesbian, and bisexual people and to claim a proud and positive gay, lesbian, or bisexual identity. Thus, many students described coming out as a political act that educates others about heterosexist norms and gay, lesbian, and bisexual issues. Queer students in this sample expressed pride in their gay and bisexual identities and a desire to challenge heterosexist norms of sexuality. The process of coming out for some students, then, may include developing a queer identity and becoming politically active in support of gay, lesbian, and bisexual issues.

Studies of the Health Issues of Gay, Lesbian, and Bisexual College Students

Three published studies have addressed aspects of gay, lesbian, and bisexual student life that can be broadly categorized as "health issues." Except for falling under this umbrella term, the three studies are not particularly related to one another. Each study had significant methodological flaws that make it impossible to draw any firm conclusions from the data presented. Below are the results in which we have some confidence; however, the results of these studies are perhaps most useful if viewed as suggestive of future research.

The Baier et al. (1991) study described earlier provides some limited data about the patterns of sexual behavior of gay, lesbian, and bisexual college students in comparison to a sample of heterosexuals. Their results indicate that gay, lesbian, and bisexual students are more likely to be sexually active and to have more partners than their heterosexual counterparts.

Another study explored whether gay college students perceived changes in their AIDS-risk behaviors in response to the AIDS epidemic (Klein, Sullivan, Wolcott, Landsverk, Namir, & Fawzy, 1987). Results indicated that students reported markedly decreasing their AIDS-risk behaviors and moderately increasing their behaviors not considered to increase AIDS risk.

Yager, Kurtzman, Landsverk, and Wiesmeier (1988) examined whether identifying as gay or bisexual predisposes males to eating disorders in comparison to a group of college-age heterosexual men. After we corrected for Type I error (far too many analyses were conducted given the sample size), the results suggested that gay men (in comparison to a sample of heterosexual males) are more likely to report feeling terrified of being and feeling fat despite others' perceptions.

Methodological Critique and Research Guidelines

Before we begin our methodological critique, we commend these authors for their empirical investigations of an under-researched and often invisible segment of the college population. Research in this area is difficult to conduct and, as we will demonstrate, it is impossible to construct the "perfect study." Researchers in this area can take some solace in Gelso's (1979) thoughts about investigating the counseling process. He states that though all research is flawed in some way, knowledge about a domain is furthered through repeated empirical investigations, hopefully each with a different set of methodological shortcomings. Below we discuss the methodological strengths and weaknesses of the literature reviewed. Each methodological concern is followed by recommendations for future research. A summary of our recommendations can be found in Table 2.

Research Design

Emerging theory can provide a useful framework for guiding research. Most of the studies reviewed were atheoretical in both their conceptualization and discussion of results. Furthermore, most of the studies reviewed are unrelated to each other. This may be due to the small number of research articles in this area. Nonetheless, researchers should be sure to consult previous studies in order to build upon knowledge in a domain. The results from the Herek (1993) and D'Augelli (1989b; 1992) studies illustrate the usefulness of such a method. Our confidence in their findings is strengthened by use of the same instrument and similar populations at different universities. Two of the areas we reviewed (the identity development of gay males and the experiences on campus of gays, lesbians, and bisexuals) are addressed by multiple studies that should be consulted prior to the design of future studies.

It is also important to consider research designs that best answer the research questions being posed. In particular, we would like to encourage researchers to consider utilizing qualitative research designs. Only two of the studies reviewed utilized a qualitative research design exclusively. Rhoads's (1994, 1995a, 1995b) design was particularly enhanced by a triangulated method of data collection. Similarly, the Lopez and Chism (1993) article provided much richer information about the complex experiences of gays and lesbians on campus because of their utilization of a variety of qualitative methods. Certainly, one of the drawbacks of a qualitative research design is that the results are not generalizable to all gay, lesbian, and bisexual college students. Given the complexities one encounters when sampling from this population, however, the results of most quantitative studies we reviewed are not generalizable either. Again, we would like reemphasize Gelso's (1979) assertion that multiple studies, each with different methodological drawbacks, contribute to our growing understanding of a domain of knowledge.

Table 2
Guidelines for Researching the Gay, Lesbian, and Bisexual College Student

Research Design
- When possible, use existing theory about gay, lesbian, and bisexual college students to design research and explain results.
- Be sure to consult previous research studies.
- Consider a variety of research designs, including qualitative one, and choose the one that best answers the research questions.
- Carefully consider whether to include a comparison group of heterosexuals.

Sampling
- When doing quantitative research, attempt to use creative methods of sampling.
- Fully describe the sample, including demographic information and stage of identity development.
- Carefully consider whether to merge those who identify as bisexual with gay and lesbian individuals.
- Guarantee anonymity if possible.
- Conduct multi-university studies.

Data Collection
- Avoid single-item, self-report measure of constructs.
- Attempt to use established measures with accompanying psychometric information. If unavailable, attempt to construct measures that allow for the assessment of psychometric properties.
- Use multiple methods of data collection.

Data Analysis
- Clearly outline data analysis procedures.
- Conduct data analyses appropriate to the sample size and question.

Discussion of Results
- Use existing theory to interpret results.
- Discuss limitations to research findings (for example, sampling concerns).

Another design consideration is whether to compare gay, lesbian, and bisexual students to a sample of heterosexual students. Three of the studies reviewed (Baier, et al. 1991; Reynolds, 1989; Yager, et al., 1988) utilized such a methodology. Indeed, comparing gay, lesbian, and bisexual students with heterosexual students, with the heterosexual students serving as the "normative" group, seems heterosexist by its very nature.

However, there are times when the research question justifies such comparisons. For example, Reynolds (1989) examined differences in perceptions of the university climate between male heterosexual and gay students. This study attempted to demonstrate empirically that gay students perceive the climate more negatively on a variety of dimensions. If one believes that no one group should experience more adversity than another, such a comparison seems particularly warranted. Similarly, Yager et al. (1988) attempted to identify prevalence rates for eating disorders among gay and bisexual males. Given that the incidence of eating disorders is very small among heterosexual men, a significant change in incidence among gay or bisexual males is relevant, as it may inform health care workers about special issues relevant to the population. However, not all of the studies reviewed presented a compelling justification for comparing gay, lesbian, and bisexual students to heterosexual students. The Baier et al. (1991) study examined differences in patterns of sexual behavior, coercion, and victimization for these two groups. Methodological problems notwithstanding, a compelling rationale for this comparison was not provided. Given the potential for misuse of the results from this study, such a rationale should have been thoughtfully conceived and presented. If a heterosexual comparison group is utilized, it seems essential to have this group indicate their sexual identity rather than to assume that all in the sample are heterosexual. One of the studies (Yager, et al., 1988) compared a sample of men who identified as gay to a sample of "heterosexual" men, yet neglected to ask males in the heterosexual group to indicate their sexual orientation or identity. Further, when comparing heterosexual groups to gay, lesbian, and bisexual groups, researchers should try to ensure comparability by matching relevant demographic characteristics (Reynolds, 1989).

To summarize, we believe that to design a strong research study, researchers must first consult the previous literature and existing theory, consider a variety of research designs, including qualitative ones, and choose one that is particularly suited to the research question being asked. When making the choice of research design, researchers should carefully consider whether incorporating a heterosexual comparative group is warranted.

Sampling

The problems inherent in sampling from the gay, lesbian, and bisexual population are well-documented (see Croteau, 1996; Harry, 1986; Herek, Kimmel, Amaro, & Melton, 1991; Lonborg & Phillips, 1996). The quantitative studies reviewed in this chapter illustrate some of these sampling problems. (While sampling is less of an issue for qualitative studies because results are not intended to be generalized to a larger population, it is still important to consider participant selection to enhance transferability of findings.)

It is particularly noteworthy that of the studies reviewed, all except Baier, et al. (1991) used at least in part some type of convenience sample. That is, participants were typically drawn from those gay, lesbian, or bisexual students who attended some type of organization, meeting, or function that would attract members of the gay, lesbian, and bisexual population. It is interesting to note that both the qualitative studies utilized participants from this population as well.

Other methods of sampling were used as an adjunct to convenience sampling. Two studies utilized a friendship network; that is, asking members of the convenience sample to distribute the research packet to their friends, and two other studies used newspaper advertisements. In addition, some authors made surveys available at larger events such as dances.

Many of the research studies we reviewed guaranteed participants anonymity and reported response rates, when possible, ranging from 38-98%. Guaranteeing anonymity when sampling from this population seems particularly important if striving for the highest possible response rate. And while a high response rate is important and seen as one guard against sampling bias, researchers may find it difficult to calculate response rates when utilizing a friendship network or blanketing large events with questionnaires. We are not suggesting that methods such as friendship networks are inappropriate. On the contrary, for some research questions one is left with very few alternatives to such a method. Researchers must decide which methodological flaw they are most willing to tolerate: a small sample size or a biased sample. Again, we urge future researchers to let their research questions guide their decision-making.

Baier et al. (1991) avoided the problems associated with convenience sampling by randomly sampling 1,650 college students who were asked to indicate their sexual orientation, but were not guaranteed anonymity. They achieved a return rate of 43% after two follow-up contacts. While this method has its merits, it may compromise the sample size of the non-heterosexual group, especially if, as in this study, the researchers do not guarantee anonymity. Baier et al. also suggested using a "captive" audience such as students in a class for whom anonymity can be guaranteed rather than a mail survey format without the guarantee of anonymity. They had only 36 students identify themselves as gay, lesbian, or bisexual of the 702 who participated.

These types of sampling methods clearly compromise the researcher's ability to generalize as they typically lead to a greater representation of older and politically active or "out" individuals. Such sampling concerns can affect the interpretation of significant results. For example, results of the D'Augelli (1989b; 1992) and Herek (1993) studies indicate that gay, lesbian, and bisexual students experience more discrimination and harassment on campus. This result, however, may not be true for all gay, lesbian, and bisexual college students. One might well argue that such a result is only true for those individuals who feel comfortable enough to attend functions particularly focused on the gay, lesbian, and bisexual community. Those who are politically active or more "out" might be at greater risk for harassment due to their more visible status as members of the gay, lesbian, and bisexual community.

If these studies cannot be seen as representative of all gay, lesbian, and bisexual college students, who are they describing? Most participants in these studies were older male college students. With one exception, all of the studies categorized in either the health or identity development areas focused exclusively on bisexual or gay men. The exception was the Lopez and Chism (1993) study that included seven lesbians and only secondarily addressed the issue of identity. In contrast, most of the studies in the college experiences area included not only gay and bisexual men, but lesbians and bisexual females as well. None of the studies reviewed focused exclusively on either lesbians or bisexuals. Interestingly, of the nine studies reviewed, three were conducted at the same northeastern university.

Though demographic information about the samples would have been extremely useful, it was often not provided. Three studies collected data about race, but only one reported the breakdown for the sample (D'Augelli, 1991). D'Augelli (1991) was also the only researcher to report any other demographic information, including family income and parents' level of education. It would have been easier to determine the applicability of findings if the researchers provided detailed demographic information about participants (for example, year in college, ethnicity, socioeconomic status) as well as length of time a participant has been out and stage of identity development.

Researchers also need to describe participants with unambiguous terminology. For example, in the Baier et al. (1991) study, the non-heterosexual group was labeled gay/bisexual; it is unclear if lesbians were included in the sample. It is only by inference that a reader is able to conclude that lesbians *were* included in the sample.

Another sampling issue relates to bisexual students. As noted earlier, none of the studies treated bisexuality separately, but instead grouped these participants with those who identified as gay or lesbian. As a result, no empirical comparisons can be made between these groups, nor can any conclusions be drawn about bisexual students. Further, such a method assumes that bisexual participants in the sample will respond in a manner similar to those who identify as gay or lesbian. One way to address this issue is to employ the method implemented by Yager et al. (1988), who tested for significant differences between bisexual and gay men. Finding none, they were able to have some confidence that the data for the two groups could be combined. This method may also be used when researchers combine a gay and lesbian sample.

Clearly, sampling from the gay, lesbian, and bisexual population is complicated. It is difficult to identify a sample when members of the larger population are in the throes of identifying themselves. How can researchers ask people to identify as gay, lesbian, or bisexual on a questionnaire if they haven't yet come to that conclusion themselves?

Researchers must apply creativity to standard sampling procedures in order to increase sample size as well as the diversity of participants. For example, if using a convenience sample in combination with a friendship network, one might explain to participants why such networks are commonly utilized as a method of data collection, emphasize how important their cooperation is, and thank participants for their willingness to participate. In addition, one might ask participants in the convenience sample to contact one other person who is less "out" about his or her sexual identity. Further, in order to increase sample size as well as confidence in the generalizability of results, multi-university studies should be seriously considered.

It may be necessary to collect data outside the usual research settings and consider such events as marches, rallies, and special lectures, or solicit participants from list-serves and ally networks. One might also consider advertising in newspapers targeted to liberal, gay, lesbian, or bisexual readers. Another possibility is to routinely collect information about sexual identity at agencies where such data would be kept confidential (Eldridge & Barnett, 1991). The regular collection of data would facilitate programmatic research and perhaps give agencies more detailed information about their clientele.

Data Collection

In the nine studies reviewed, six were exclusively quantitative and used self-report paper-and-pencil measures. Of the remaining three, two were exclusively qualitative and one represented a mixture of quantitative and qualitative. We believe that neither method of data collection is inherently better than the other. Each, however, has important issues that must be considered when designing a study.

The questionnaires that explicitly examined behaviors specific to the gay, lesbian, and bisexual population did not have accompanying psychometric information. Because of the newness of the research area, it may not be possible to use measures of constructs that have psychometric information specific to the gay, lesbian, bisexual student population. Some of the researchers used single items as the measurement of a variable (for example, an item like "ability to count on lover for emotional support" was used as the sole measurement of social support). Such a solution is unwise, as it is difficult to know whether the one item researchers chose is either reliable or valid.

Researchers have a choice when deciding how to measure a construct: they can create their own measure or use a measure that exists for another population. When researchers create a measure, they should make sure the measure can be assessed for reliability and validity. Reliability can be assessed if multiple items are used to measure constructs; this procedure allows one to calculate a measure's internal consistency. While internal consistency coefficients can contribute to knowledge about the content validity of a measure, content validity can be further assessed by convening a panel of experts to create and judge items to be included in a scale.

Another solution to this complex measurement issue may be using or adapting instruments that have been used with other populations. Researchers should be somewhat wary, however, as existing validity and reliability data may not be relevant. Researchers should reassess the measure's psychometric properties for the sample under investigation.

Only three studies used multiple methods of data collection. Rhoads's (1994, 1995a, 1995b) study provides a model for others to follow. In his two-year ethnographic study, Rhoads formally interviewed participants for one to three hours, informally interviewed them in social settings, observed and participated in the gay and bisexual culture, and analyzed relevant documents such as articles in the student newspaper. The incorporation of triangulated methods to collect data is a notable strength of the study. Another strength is Rhoads' stated commitment to critical postmodernist theory that is woven throughout his study and informs readers' interpretation of his results. An advisory panel of students assisted with qualitative analysis; however, Rhoads did not clearly state the exact composition of his advisory panel. For example, the sexual identity or ethnicity of panelists is unclear.

The Lopez and Chism (1993) study also used multiple methods of data collection, but not in the manner one might expect. Participants were asked to provide information in their choice of one of three ways: in a focus group, in an individual interview, or through an open-ended questionnaire. All three methods included similar questions for students to address. Eight students chose to participate in a focus group, four completed individual interviews, and four responded to open-ended questionnaires. While allowing students to choose their level of involvement is a creative way to increase participation, the results of the study would have been strengthened had the students all participated in some standard, minimal way (for example, responding to open-ended questionnaires) in addition to the other methods of data collection.

Herek (1993) also used multiple methods of data collection, though to a lesser extent. In addition to a survey instrument, he also gave participants the opportunity to respond to some open-ended questions at the end of his survey. Though certainly such a methodology does not allow for extensive exploration of complex processes, it at least allows for some elaboration of results as well as possible directions for future researchers.

We would like to encourage future researchers to consider qualitative designs because they allow one to collect data about complex processes, such as the coming out process. One way to investigate these processes is to utilize qualitative studies that ask post-graduate participants to consider retrospectively what that process was like for them. Boatwright, Gilbert, Forrest, and Ketzenberger (1996) successfully utilized such a methodology when investigating the impact of identity development on the career behavior of lesbians. Memory, however, often alters the actual experience, particularly those events that were unclear or were denied earlier. Another possible way to investigate identity development might be to utilize longitudinal designs. But whatever method is chosen, researchers need to thoroughly document their data collection procedures so that others can more easily replicate the studies.

Data Analysis

Several articles lacked a detailed data analysis section. The purpose of the data analysis section is so that readers can better evaluate findings and future researchers can replicate findings. Given the somewhat "sketchy" descriptions of the data analyses, we at times found it difficult to be sure whether the data analysis procedures employed were done correctly. It was clear, however, that many of our questions centered around the suitability of the analyses for the sample size obtained.

Given the small sample size that is typical when sampling from this population, it is particularly important to pay attention to issues of power and Type I error. According to Tabachnik and Fiddell (1996), power is the probability of rejecting the null hypothesis when the alternative is true. Researchers should strive to increase power whenever possible. A researcher's desire to increase power, however, must be balanced by a commitment to guard against Type I error. A Type I error is considered very serious and occurs when the null hypothesis is rejected when it is actually true.

In a number of studies reviewed, the sample size obtained was far too small for the number of statistical tests conducted. Multiple univariate or pairwise comparisons increase the chance of a Type I error (that is, rejecting a true null hypothesis). Researchers should consider using omnibus tests to assess for differences prior to conducting multiple univariate or t-tests. Another way to control Type I error rate is to divide the level of significance among the number of pairwise tests to be conducted. We employed this method ourselves when evaluating the research findings of several studies.

Inequality in sample size of comparison groups must also be addressed to provide some statistical control of Type I error as tests are often sensitive to extreme differences (Tabachnik & Fiddell, 1996). This issue (in addition to the problems associated with multiple pairwise comparisons) is of particular concern in the Baier et al. (1991) study. They compared a sample of 666 heterosexual students to 36 gay/bisexual students on 37 different variables. They chose to employ a chi square statistic to control the Type I error rate. We believe that choosing fewer comparisons and creating a matched comparison group of 36 heterosexual students would have been a more efficient strategy for controlling Type I error rate.

Discussion of Results

While valuable research results can be obtained when the research questions are not based on theory, it seems important to at least consider using existing theory to explain results. For example, in the study by Klein et al. (1987) regarding safe sex behavior, the authors noted that gay and bisexual male college students (as compared to a group of gay and bisexual male physicians) were more likely to agree with a statement that it is pointless to change sexual behavior. In the discussion, theory about adolescent development was not discussed as a possible explanation for this behavior, limiting the ability of the reader to understand how this finding might influence the development of psychoeducational strategies. Furthermore, some studies did not clearly address limitations to the research findings as a result of methodological flaws.

A Research Agenda for Studying the Gay, Lesbian, and Bisexual College Student

Previous empirical research has uncovered valuable information about gay, lesbian, and bisexual college students' issues. Indeed, such empirical research has helped legitimize the recognition and validity of issues salient to this population (D'Augelli, 1989a). Additional research is essential to further our understanding of this often invisible and frequently unacknowledged population.

With respect to the experiences of gay, lesbian, and bisexual college students on campus, the existing empirical literature focuses primarily on harassment and victimization of these students. Results from this body of research as a whole suggest that gay, lesbian, and bisexual students are often victims of verbal harassment and abuse, physical assault, intimidation, discrimination, and marginalization in the college environment. These incidents occur at higher rates among gay, lesbian, and bisexual students than among heterosexual students. Gay, lesbian, and bisexual students often do not experience a sense of support and security on campus, and incidents of harassment and discrimination are likely under-reported. These students are typically fearful of future harassment and discrimination and may make conscious changes in their behaviors and activities to reduce the possibility of such incidents occurring. Finally, the research also suggests that gay, lesbian, and bisexual students are often aware of which segments of the college community—such as residence halls, departments, faculty, and staff—are affirmative and openly supportive.

In light of these initial findings, a variety of issues pertaining to campus experiences seem ripe for future research. We wondered what sorts of affirmative factors (for example, staff and faculty training, or negative consequences for those who harass or discriminate against gay, lesbian, and bisexual students) may help to create a positive and supportive environment for these students on campus. How might such an environment influence students' choices to attend an institution or to become involved on campus? How might such an environment be associated with students' coming-out experiences and coping mechanisms? How might these factors impact students' future career decisions?

We also had further questions about students' negative experiences. We wondered whether some students may be more or less targeted for discrimination or harassment. For instance, are more politically active students as likely to be victimized as those who are not as politically active? Are lesbian or bisexual women victimized differently than gay or bisexual men? Do bisexual students experience different types of harassment or discrimination than do gay men or lesbian women? How does the fear of victimization influence students' decisions to attend an institution or become involved on campus? In what ways do gay, lesbian, and bisexual students cope with the stress of such a hostile environment? How does this environment affect students' academic performance, relationships, and general psychological functioning?

Further empirical studies are also needed to advance our understanding of identity development issues for these students. To date, this literature suggests findings that are most generalizable to a select group: gay and bisexual men who have disclosed their identities to at least some others.

These preliminary findings suggest considerable variance in the process of developing a gay, lesbian, or bisexual identity. This process seems to begin with a period of self-acknowledgment followed by selective disclosure to others. Often students may initially experience feelings of self-loathing, followed by increased self-confidence, self-understanding, and self-acceptance. Yet some may also engage in efforts to disguise their identities when they feel threatened. For certain students, becoming politically active in the gay, lesbian, and bisexual community represents an aspect of identity development as well. Coming out seems to be an ongoing process, perhaps because of the vast prevalence of heterosexist societal norms.

Supportive relationships with other gay, lesbian, and bisexual students and with heterosexual students who are aware of the students' identity appear to be critical for students to develop a positive and proud identity. Gay, lesbian, and bisexual students likely experience strained or extinguished relationships with family members, friends, acquaintances, supervisors, or faculty members as a result of coming out.

Given these somewhat tentative findings about identity development, we offer a variety of possible research questions. First, we wonder whether identity development issues differ between men and women as well as among gay men, lesbian women, and bisexual men and women. Further, how might identity development occur for students who are not politically active, unlike many of the politically active students examined in the current literature? How might this process interact with other developmental issues, such as racial identity development, psychosocial development, cognitive development, or career development? What factors influence the development of a positive identity or a negative identity? How does this identity development process affect students' psychological well-being?

Finally, the literature offers no conclusive findings about the health behaviors of gay, lesbian, and bisexual college students. Although the three studies we reviewed addressed issues such as sexual behavior, AIDS-risk behaviors, and prevalence of eating disorders, this very limited body of research provides no definite implications for our understanding of this population. Some issues for future research in this area might include investigating how a student's stage of identity development or stage of the coming out process influences health behavior, or investigating whether confusion over sexual identity affects a willingness to seek either medical or mental health treatment.

Conclusions

So, are studies of gay, lesbian, and bisexual college students worth our time and effort? Undeniably, this population is a difficult one to study. Researchers must be especially cognizant of the many methodological hazards that may befall them. But the body of research that currently exists provides researchers and practitioners in the field with important information. In particular, we have a good foundation of knowledge about the discrimination and harassment college students may experience on campus as well as the identity development of gay and bisexual men. Careful attention to theory and previous research studies in this area in combination with the development of thoughtful research questions will help guide researchers to make sound methodological choices. And while each methodological choice made represents a trade-off, ultimately we will accumulate a body of knowledge which will both inform students affairs professionals as well as contribute to the growing status of these students on the college campus.

References

Baier, J. L., Rosenzweig, M. G., & Whipple, E. G. (1991). Patterns of sexual behavior, coercion, and victimization of university students. *Journal of College Student Development, 32,* 310-322.

Baker, J. (1991). Gay nineties: Addressing the needs of homosexual community and junior college students and faculty. *Community and Junior College, 15,* 25-32.

Banzhaf, J. (1990). *Role model choice of gay college students: A study of gay white males attending college during the 1960's, 70s and 80s.* Unpublished dissertation, University of Rochester.

Bieschke, K. J., Grubbs, V., Peterson, K., Agee, L., & Surbeck, B. (1995). *The utilization of counseling services by gay, lesbian, and bisexual students.* Paper presented at the national convention of the American College Personnel Association, Boston, MA.

Boatwright, K. J., Gilbert, M. S., Forrest, L., & Ketzenberger, K. (1996). Impact of identity development upon career trajectory: Listening to the voices of lesbian women. *Journal of Vocational Behavior, 48,* 210-228.

Buhrke, R. A., Ben-Ezra, L. A., Hurley, M. E., & Ruprecht, L. J. (1992). Content analysis and methodological critique of articles concerning lesbian and gay male issues in counseling journals. *Journal of Counseling Psychology, 39,* 91-99.

Cass, V. C. (1979). Homosexual identity formation: A theoretical model. *Journal of Homosexuality, 4,* 219-235.

Cass, V. (1984). Homosexual identity formation: Testing a theoretical model. *Journal of Sex Research, 20,* 143-167.

Catania, J. A., McDermott, L. J., & Pollack, L. M. (1986). Questionnaire response bias and face-to-face interview sample bias in sexuality research. *Journal of Sex Research, 22,* 52-72.

Coleman, E. (1981-1982). Developmental stages of the coming out process. *Journal of Homosexuality, 7,* 31-43.

Croteau, J. M. (1996). Research on the work experiences of lesbian, gay, and bisexual people: An integrative review of methodology and findings. *Journal of Vocational Behavior, 48,* 195-208.

D'Augelli, A. R. (1989a). Lesbians and gay men on campus: Visibility, empowerment, and educational leadership. *Peabody Journal of Education, 66* (3), 124-142.

D'Augelli, A. R. (1989b). Lesbians' and gay men's experiences of discrimination and harassment in a university community. *American Journal of Community Psychology, 17,* 317-321.

D'Augelli, A. R. (1991). Gay men in college: Identity processes and adaptations. *Journal of College Student Development, 32,* 140-146.

D'Augelli, A. R. (1992). Lesbian and gay male undergraduates' experiences of harassment and fear on campus. *Journal of Interpersonal Violence, 7,* 383-395.

D'Augelli, A. R., & Rose, M. L. (1990). Homophobia in a university community: Attitudes and experiences of heterosexual freshmen. *Journal of College Student Development, 31,* 484-491.

D'Emilio, J. (1990). The campus environment for gay and lesbian life. *Academe, 76,* 16-19.

DeSurra, C. J., & Church, K. A. (1994). *Unlocking the classroom closet: Privileging the marginalized voices of gay/lesbian college students.* Paper presented at the Annual Meeting of the Speech Communication Association, New Orleans, LA.

Dillon, C. (1986). Preparing college health professionals to deliver gay-affirmative services. *Journal of American College Health, 35,* 36-40.

Eldridge, N. S., & Barnett, D. C. (1991). Counseling gay students. In N. J. Evans & V. A. Wall (Eds.), *Beyond tolerance: Gays, lesbians and bisexuals on campus* (pp. 147-178). Alexandria, VA: American College Personnel Association.

Etringer, B. D., Hillerbrand, E., & Hetherington, C. (1990). The influence of sexual orientation on career decision-making: A research note. *Journal of Homosexuality, 19,* 103-111.

Evans, N. J. (1996, June). *Experiences of gay, lesbian, and bisexual youths in university communities.* Paper presented at the Penn State Conference on Research with Gays, Lesbians, and Bisexuals, University Park, PA.

Evans, N. J., & Wall, V. A. (Eds.). (1991). *Beyond tolerance: Gays, lesbians and bisexuals on campus.* Alexandria, VA: American College Personnel Association.

Faderman, L. (1984). The "new gay" lesbians. *Journal of Homosexuality, 10,* 85-95.

Gelso, C. J. (1979). Research in counseling: Methodological and professional issues. *Counseling Psychologist, 8,* 7-35.

Harry, J. (1986). Sampling gay men. *Journal of Sex Research, 22,* 21-34.

Henderson, A. F. (1984). Homosexuality in the college years: Developmental differences between men and women. *Journal of American College Health, 32,* 216-219.

Herek, G. M. (1993). Documenting prejudice against lesbians and gay men on campus: The Yale sexual orientation survey. *Journal of Homosexuality, 25,* 15-30.

Herek, G. M., Kimmel, D. C., Amaro, H., & Melton, G. B. (1991). Avoiding heterosexist bias in psychological research. *American Psychologist, 46,* 957-963.

Hershberger, S. L., & D'Augelli, A. R. (1995). The impact of victimization on the mental health and suicidality of lesbian, gay, and bisexual youths. *Developmental Psychology, 31,* 65-74.

Klein, D. E., Sullivan, G., Wolcott, D. L., Landsverk, J., Namir, S., & Fawzy, F. I. (1987). Changes in AIDS risk behaviors among homosexual male physicians and university students. *American Journal of Psychiatry, 144,* 742-747.

Levine, H. (1997). A further exploration of the lesbian identity development process and its measurement. *Journal of Homosexuality, 32,* 67-78.

Levine, H., & Bahr, J. (1989). *Relationship between sexual identity formation and student development among gay and lesbian students.* Unpublished manuscript.

Loiacano, D. K. (1989). Gay identity issues among Black Americans: Racism, homophobia, and the need for validation. *Journal of Counseling and Development, 68,* 21-25.

Lonborg, S.D., & Phillips, J.M. (1996). Investigating the career development of gay, lesbian, and bisexual people: Methodological considerations and recommendations. *Journal of Vocational Behavior, 48,* 176-194.

Lopez, G., & Chism, N. (1993). Classroom concerns of gay and lesbian students: The invisible minority. *College Teaching, 41,* 97-103.

McCord, D. M., & Herzog, H.A. (1991). What undergraduates want to know about homosexuality. *Teaching of Psychology, 18,* 243-244.

McDonald, G. J. (1982). Individual differences in the coming out process for gay men: Implications for theoretical models. *Journal of Homosexuality, 8,* 47-90.

Minton, H. L., & McDonald, G. J. (1984). Homosexual identity formation as a developmental process. *Journal of Homosexuality, 9,* 91-104.

Miranda, J., & Storms, M. (1989). Psychological adjustment of lesbians and gay men. *Journal of Counseling and Development, 68,* 4 1-45.

Rankin, S. (1998). Campus climate for lesbian, gay, bisexual, and transgendered students, faculty, and staff: Assessment and strategies for change. In R. Sanlo (Ed.), *Working with lesbian, gay, and bisexual college students: A guide for administrators and faculty* (pp. 203-212). Westport, CT: Greenwood.

Reynolds, A. J. (1989). Social environmental conceptions of male homosexual behavior: A university climate analysis. *Journal of College Student Development, 30,* 62-69.

Rhoads, R. A. (1994). *Coming out in college: The struggle for a queer identity.* Westport, CT: Bergin & Garvey.

Rhoads, R. A. (1995a). The cultural politics of coming out in college: Experiences of male students. *The Review of Higher Education, 19,* 1-22.

Rhoads, R. A. (1995b). Learning from the coming-out experiences of college males. *Journal of College Student Development, 36,* 67-74.

Savin-Williams, R. C. (1995). An exploratory study of pubertal maturation timing and self-esteem among gay and bisexual male youths. *Developmental Psychology, 31,* 56-64.

Schneider, S. G., Farberow, N. L., & Kruks, G. N. (1989). Suicidal behavior in adolescent and young adult gay men. *Suicide and Life-Threatening Behavior, 19,* 381-394.

Sophie, J. (1985-1986). A critical examination of stage theories of lesbian identity development. *Journal of Homosexuality, 12,* 39-51.

Stevenson, M. R., & Gajarsky, W. M. (1991). Issues of gender in promoting tolerance for homosexuality. *Journal of Psychology & Human Sexuality, 3,* 155-163.

Tabachnik, B. G., & Fiddell, L. 5. (1996). *Using multivariate statistics* (3rd ed.). New York: HarperCollins.

Troiden, R. R. (1979). Becoming homosexual: A model of gay identity acquisition. *Psychiatry, 42,* 362-373.

Troiden, R. R. (1988). Homosexuality identity development. *Journal of Adolescent Health Care, 9,* 105-113.

Walters, K. L., & Simoni, J. M. (1993). Lesbian and gay male group identity attitudes and self-esteem: Implications for counseling. *Journal of Counseling Psychology, 40,* 94-99.

Yager, J., Kurtzman, F., Landsverk, J., & Wiesmeier, E. (1988). Behaviors and attitudes related to eating disorders in homosexual male college students. *American Journal of Psychiatry, 145* (4), 495-497.

PART II

INSTITUTIONAL ISSUES AND INTERVENTIONS

Chapter 3

ೞಎೞ

Recognition of Gay and Lesbian Relationships

JOHN LEPPO, SCOTT R. BODEN, AND DONALD A. STENTA

In the past decade, student affairs educators have been at the forefront of diversity education on college campuses. Arising out of the institutional mission to prepare students to be future citizens and leaders, diversity programs conducted by student affairs educators have recognized the importance of developing the capability in students to live, work and function in an increasingly diverse society. Through education and social programming for students, faculty, and staff, student affairs professionals have been effective change agents in fashioning a campus environment that is more accepting and inclusive of diversity on campus. They are attuned to the power and importance of role modeling, of setting an example both as an institution and as individuals, in communicating commitment to embracing the diversity that exists on campus and in society (Fried, 1995; McEwen & Roper, 1994; Pope & Reynolds, 1997).

Laudably, many of these efforts have included programs that recognize the diversity in sexual orientation that exists among students, faculty and staff. Because of this leadership role in developing a more inclusive campus environment, student affairs educators frequently have the awareness and sensitivity to the issues facing gays and lesbians on campus, as well as the experience in institutional change that uniquely prepares them to assume a leadership role in recognition of the diverse types of family structures that exist in our society, including those families in which gays and lesbians are participants. Working with human resources professionals on campus, student affairs educators have both the opportunity and the challenge of using their awareness of gay and lesbian families and relationships to change the institutional environment to be more equitable and non-discriminatory in the arena of employment benefits and institutional recognition of these relationships and families in the workplace.

Beyond these philosophical and educational foundations for involvement by student affairs officers in recognition of domestic partnerships for gay and lesbian employees, however, is a much more practical concern. Each year student affairs recruits and hires many new professionals to be student affairs educators and to administer its programs. Increasingly, these new professionals are emerging from campus environments in which they have learned to be sensitive to and supportive of diversity on campus. As employees in relatively lower-paid positions, new professionals are very much aware of the importance of employment benefits in overall compensation. Fired with idealism and enthusiasm, they want their new employers to be consistent with the values presented in diversity education efforts on the campus. This consistency, evidenced by the availability of domestic partner benefits for gays and lesbians, is a matter of importance both to gay, lesbian and non-gay new professionals alike.

Perhaps of equal importance to student affairs officers and faculty in student affairs preparation programs, however, is the increasing competition for new talent posed by the corporate sector (Dalton, 1996). Undergraduates who are the beneficiaries of our leadership and diversity education may have a choice between a career in student affairs or work in a corporate human relations environment that is already well on its way towards domestic partner benefits as a standard element of benefits packages. The most promising students for the future of student affairs, whom we have taught to be sensitive to these matters, may well choose to work where practice and the work environment reflect the inclusive approach indicated in institutional publications.

This chapter will examine domestic partner employment benefits, a benchmark in the recognition of gay and lesbian relationships and families. Societal trends in recognition of gay and lesbian families and the importance of domestic partner benefits to both the individual employee and the employer will be examined, along with potential institutional objections to equalization of benefits. Results of the Domestic Partners Survey that profiles current practice at colleges and universities will be reviewed, and considerations for change will be discussed.

The Need for Domestic Partner Benefits

Gay marriage has burst upon the consciousness of the American public as a topic of controversy and discussion as the result of a 1993 court decision in Hawaii. In *Baehr v. Lewin* (1993), the Hawaii Supreme Court held that the state of Hawaii could not prohibit same-sex marriages. Under the "full faith and credit" clause of the U.S. Constitution, other states would be potentially required to recognize a same-sex marriage from Hawaii. In reaction to the pending Hawaii decision, many state legislatures rushed to approved new laws defining for state purposes marriage as only between a man and a woman, prohibiting same-sex marriages, and denying recognition of same-sex marriages performed in other states. Partners Task Force for Gay and Lesbian Couples (1995) reported that 16 states had passed such legislation as of December, 1996. In addition, Congress passed the Defense of Marriage Act (DOMA) in September 1996, which allows states to refuse to recognize same-sex marriages performed in other states, and which defines marriage for federal purposes as only between a man and a woman. Although it is generally believed that both DOMA and the state statutes will eventually be found unconstitutional, extensive litigation will be required (Ladner, 1994). To date, Massachusetts has emerged as the only state where a same-sex marriage from Hawaii will be recognized as having legal legitimacy.

For the first time, the controversy generated by news reports and public discussion surrounding *Baehr v. Lewin* and DOMA exposed the public to the concept that gay and lesbian people form loving relationships that parallel opposite sex partners in heterosexual marriage but suffer invidious injustice and discrimination because their relationships do not have legal recognition. Civil marriage for opposite-sex couples brings with it many legalities and economic benefits to the couple. Depending upon state laws; they may include inheritance rights, funeral decisions, participation in a partner's medical decisions, tax breaks, hospital visitation, pensions, joint custody of children, immigration rights, housing on military bases, US Citizenship, employment benefits, automatic access to facilities and services, and more.

Until same-sex marriage is legally recognized throughout the United States, however, same-sex couples can obtain some measure of support and economic relief through employment benefits for domestic partners. Partnership benefits first emerged as one of a group of "family" and "workplace" issues in the mid-80s, along with domestic partnership registration, non-discrimination policies, gay and lesbian employee groups, adoption and custody rights, and similar concerns. The *New York Times* reported in 1996 that 313 companies, 36 cities, 12 counties, and 4 states (Delaware, Massachusetts, New York, and Vermont) have adopted domestic partnership employment benefits. The extension of health insurance and other employment benefits to domestic partners is expected to be increasingly "mainstream." At the 1996 National Gay and Lesbian Task Force conference on gay and lesbian issues in the workplace, it was reported that more than 400 U.S. corporations have either adopted policies that ban discrimination against gays and lesbians or that allow company benefits for domestic partners (San Francisco Examiner On-Line edition, 1996). While national polls indicate that only 45% of Americans support recognition of same-sex marriage (Gover, 1997), polls suggest that 84% of Americans surveyed favored equal treatment in the workplace for gays and lesbians (Poll shows, 1997).

What is a Family?

The American nuclear family is traditionally thought to consist of a man, woman, and their 2.2 children but the nature of the American family has been changing since 1970. The number of cohabiting couples (unmarried, both same-sex and opposite-sex) increased 300% between 1970 and 1980, according to the Family Diversity Project (1989). The U.S. Bureau of the Census, which does not define "family," recorded 4,497,000 households with two unrelated adults, about one-third of which (1,458,000) were same-sex partner households (U.S. Bureau of the Census, 1991).

Awareness that the nature of the American family has changed can also be found in public opinion. Newsweek's special issue focusing on the changing American family cited the results of a survey which indicated that 75% chose "a group of people who love and care for each other" as the definition of a family, as compared with 22% who chose "a group of people who are related by blood, marriage, or adoption" (Newsweek, 1989). However, while 75% of Americans seem to know intuitively that what constitutes a family goes beyond relationships of blood, marriage, or adoption, it becomes much more difficult to write a definition of the relationship that is quantifiable and capable of being proven, for example, to claim employment benefits.

The legal definition of "family" was first expanded in a 1989 groundbreaking rent-control court case in New York, *Braschi v. Stahl Associates*. In this case, New York's highest court ruled that a gay couple is entitled to the same benefits as married couples under the state's rent control laws. In *Braschi v. Stahl*, the New York court outlined some useful and fair criteria for determining family status: (1) degree of emotional commitment and interdependence; (2) interwoven social life (presenting and thinking of selves as a couple/family, engaging in family activities such as visiting each other's families of origin, etc.); (3) financial interdependence (sharing household expenses and duties; joint arrangements such as checking or savings, power of attorney, life insurance, wills, etc.); (4) cohabitation; (5) longevity; and (6) exclusivity.

The National Center for Lesbian Rights (NCLR, 1992) suggested the following, more practical criteria: the domestic partners must be 18 years of age or older as a minimum age requirement, be unrelated by blood or marriage, and neither partner should be married to anyone else. In addition, the individual identified as a partner is to be the employee's "sole" or "principal" partner as verified by an affidavit signed by both the employee and the partner. In practice, some definitions of domestic partnerships have included a variety of other criteria, many of which are not required of individuals who claim marital status for their opposite-sex partner. The NCLR comments upon these typical criteria:

1. *Requirement that the individuals must live together.* This requirement is theoretically unfair to domestic partners because married couples are not required to share a residence in order to obtain benefits. Practically, however, living together is the most tangible indication of couplehood, and is verifiable through documentation such as a lease or property title executed in both individuals' names.

2. *Requirement of financial commitment and sharing basic living expenses.* This criterion is usually demonstrated by a signed affidavit, because a requirement to bring proof such as utility bills, joint checks, and other documentation becomes too unwieldy. Examples of basic living expenses include food and shelter. To maintain fairness in comparison to married employees, the same affidavit could be required of married employees in lieu of a marriage certificate.

3. *Waiting periods (coverage does not take effect for a specified period).* For health insurance and similar benefits, a reasonable waiting period—although unfair—does offer a practical and easily verifiable requirement that addresses concerns about fraud and abuse. When considering access to campus facilities and services, however, such a waiting period may result in more confusion and administrative costs than is saved by not immediately granting access.

4. *A specified length of time for the relationship.* This type of requirement is not recommended, unless it is used to make an exception to a waiting period. The requirement is inherently unfair if not applied to married partners. In addition, without same-sex marriage or domestic partnership registration, it may be difficult to measure and verify the length of a relationship.

5. *"Existence of a 'marriage-like' commitment" and "would marry if the law permitted."* Generally, these criteria are considered too vague, impossible to verify, and subject to problems in interpretation.

A poll of 7,800 gay and lesbian couples conducted by Overlooked Opinions determined that 56% were in monogamous relationships. Gay and lesbian partnerships tend to have an average longevity of 8.9 years, as compared with an average longevity of 7.1 years for opposite-sex marriages (Singer & Deschamps, 1994). Clearly, interest in long-term committed domestic partnerships is high among gays and lesbians. And those partnerships tend to be as long-term as those of the average opposite-sex married partners.

Domestic Partner Benefits: The Employee's Perspective

Depending upon the exact benefits offered, employment benefits currently are estimated by the U.S. Chamber of Commerce to constitute as much as 40% of total employment compensation. While most of these are individual benefits (for example, annual vacation), benefits for partners typically account for 5% of what an employee earns (Mickens, 1994). Annually, a gay or lesbian staff member whose salary compensation is $40,000/yr is estimated to receive $2,800 less total compensation per year than an opposite-sex married staff member.

Perhaps the most moving and powerful insight into the impact of not having domestic partner benefits, though, is found in the lives of those affected. Personal testimonies about the unavailability of employment benefits for same-sex partners at the University of Minnesota were collected in a campus-wide effort to evaluate the climate for gays, lesbians, and bisexuals at the university. Faculty and staff members reported severe financial hardship and added stress in their home life from the inaccessibility of benefits for same-sex partners (University of Minnesota, 1993). Stories included the following:

> *The University should honor its nondiscrimination policy statement by eliminating all policies that discriminate on the basis of sexual orientation. The University should recognize domestic partnership couples as they do married couples. I simply want for my family what a married employee can count on for his/her family. . . . As employees of the University, we should have the same treatment. Gays and lesbians employed by the University have been systematically excluded from benefits that have been provided to their heterosexual colleagues, with whom they work side by side, sometimes performing exactly the same work. . . . This has cost me dearly financially, and has sent me the message that who I love is not valued.* (p. 6)

> *It is very demoralizing to see the incredible benefits that my married colleagues (heterosexual) get. . . . My partner is self-employed and health coverage is astronomical. . . . In order to buy a plan similar to that at the U, it would cost us $5-7,000 per year. Since it's so costly, my partner does not have very good coverage and as a result I am very concerned about what would happen if a serious health crisis occurs. So I am not just losing the $1,500 or so the U would pay out to cover her because of the lack of recognition, I will have to pay $5-7,000 per year more than most of my colleagues.* (p. 8)

In addition to the financial inequity, lack of access to employment benefits routinely offered to opposite-sex married partners also contributes to a demoralizing feeling in the workplace:

*I feel discredited in all but the most professional sense since my
University will not acknowledge the centrality of my relationship with
my partner of 14-plus years. . . . My family life is erased and made
invisible by an institution of higher learning which touts acceptance of
diversity and pursuit of truth.* (p. 8)

Domestic Partner Benefits: What the Employer Gains

Many of the benefits that are available to an opposite-sex married
partner were initiated fairly recently, dating from the World War II era
when employers began to offer benefits such as health insurance and
pensions in lieu of wage increases. After the war ended, such benefits
spread through collective bargaining and competition for labor. The
practice of providing benefits to spouses and children was based upon
the then-prevalent concept that a man should be able to support an entire
family (Badgett, 1995).

Over time, employers have come to recognize the benefit to themselves
as employers when they offer health insurance and other employment
benefits to opposite-sex married partners. Employers have noted improved
productivity from employees who are not pre-occupied with thoughts of
partners who are ill and not receiving adequate medical care. Partner
benefits also relieve the stress in the home environment that may be
caused by tight finances when the costs of health care or insurance impact
monthly budgets. Employee loyalty and retention are also discussed as
reasons to offer benefits to partners (Badgett, 1995).

The Segal Company, called "one of the most prominent international
benefits consulting firms" analyzed the issue of benefits for domestic
partners for the Lotus Corporation. As a result of their research, not
only did Segal recommend adoption of domestic partner benefits by the
Lotus Corporation, the Segal Company itself also implemented domestic
partner benefits. Segal noted that most employers who have extended
domestic partners coverage have been motivated by more long-term
priorities, as compared with interest in holding down costs. These long-
term priorities include investment in human capital, commitment to
employees' diverse needs, and the ability to recruit qualified personnel
(Segal, 1993).

Segal noted that employers often have a public commitment to non-
discrimination and to providing equal pay for equal work. This is especially

true for colleges where the non-discrimination statement in many cases specifically includes sexual orientation—and usually marital status as well. Inconsistency between a non-discrimination policy and inequalities in a benefits compensation plan opens the institution to potential litigation for failure to abide by its own policies. Colleges and universities may also be required to provide domestic partner benefits under local non-discrimination ordinances (if a private institution) or statewide policy or statute in the states that have adopted such measures.

Most colleges today, like employers in the private sector, actively promote diversity in the workplace. Domestic partner benefits in the private sector are seen as a concrete example of how the employer is sensitive to employees' various needs. As for married partners, domestic partner benefits "cushion the impact of personal and family crises in order to reduce their adverse effect on an employee's job performance" (McNaught, 1993, p. 81). Colleges and universities capture the true essence of diversity education and support when tangible efforts, like domestic partner benefits, are included in the campus benefits plan. By so doing, the institution demonstrates an active commitment to enhancing the climate of diversity and respect.

Segal (1993) also cited employee recruitment as a strong incentive. As growth in the population of young, well-educated workers tapers off, corporations see having a domestic partner benefits program as an advantage in competition for the most highly qualified employees. Employers wish to make themselves as attractive as possible to the widest range of potential employees so the best candidates for employment will not have a reason to look elsewhere. Not only are gay, lesbian, and bisexual potential employees attracted to such employers, but so are those who are seeking an employer who is progressive and open to supporting diversity. Colleges will face this same competition for the best faculty and staff. Susan Jurow, executive director of the College and Universities Personnel Association, noted, "Some companies that offer this benefit use it as a recruitment and retention tool. It's a benefit that allows you to be competitive on an equal footing" (Israelson, 1997, Salt Lake City Tribune Website). In addition to competing with other colleges and universities for talented faculty and staff, many institutions also must consider intense competition from the non-academic labor market (Badgett, 1995).

Colleges have an additional reason related to their educational mission to extend domestic partner benefits. It has long been held that the presence of faculty and staff on campus enriches the college experience of students through increased interaction and contact (Baxter Magolda, 1992; King, 1996; Kuh, Schuh & Whitt, 1991). For minority students in particular, the presence and visibility of minority faculty and staff is seen to play an even more important role in contributing to retention and providing role models and mentors. To encourage and facilitate this presence and contact, many colleges permit faculty and staff to obtain tickets for campus events for an opposite-sex married partner at employee rates. Spouse and family discounts at athletic or recreational facilities are also provided in an attempt to encourage faculty or staff presence through family-centered participation. Some institutions offer on-campus apartments to faculty and maintain on-campus apartments for residence life staff to further increase such interaction. As is the case with opposite-sex partners, the ability to include one's gay or lesbian domestic partner facilitates on-campus presence. Perhaps even more importantly to gay or lesbian students, the presence on campus of gay or lesbian faculty or staff members and their domestic partners provides visible role models of successful gay or lesbian relationships not easily found in the student's non-college community.

Common Objections to Domestic Partner Benefits

Because extending employment benefits to domestic partners of gay and lesbian employees is a "new" idea when the question is first introduced on a campus, it is not surprising that many objections are raised when such benefits are proposed. But many of these objections have proved to be unfounded based upon actual experience with domestic partners benefits programs (Badgett, 1995).

Although theoretically costs should not be a factor when considering correcting inequalities, expenses of health insurance in particular are a concern when domestic partner employment benefits are considered. Early proposals for domestic partner benefits assumed that 10% of the workforce was gay, and utilized this percentage of employees in calculating the maximum number of employees who would take advantage of such a program. In reality, however, experience has shown that far fewer employees in both the private sector and at colleges have taken advantage of domestic partner benefits. This is believed to be due, in part, to the reluctance of some eligible faculty and staff to "go on the record" publicly in employment records as being gay or lesbian, wishing to remain closeted at work for personal reasons. In addition, the Internal Revenue Service has ruled that domestic partner employment benefits are taxable income, and there may be a tax savings incentive for some individuals to not claim benefits (Mickens, 1994c).

The University of Michigan conducted a survey (as cited in University of California, 1995) of eight institutions offering domestic partner benefits (Stanford, Chicago, Harvard, MIT, Columbia, Dartmouth, Iowa State, and the University of Iowa). This study found the average enrollment rate to be 0.29% (2.9 employees per thousand) for same-sex partners. Michigan's actual experience has been that of approximately 30,000 employees total, 80 employees have enrolled their same-sex domestic partners for benefits. Citing the Michigan survey of other institutions, a report prepared at the University of California concluded that costs to extend domestic partner benefits to same-sex partners for the UC system would range between $810,000 (based upon 0.29%) to $3.6 million if 3.0% of the 91,500 employees enrolled for same-sex domestic partner benefits. Harvard University expected its initial costs for domestic partner health insurance to be between $78,000, based upon 0.2%, and $390,000, based upon a high estimate of 1.0% taking advantage of such a program (City University of New York, 1993). Harvard's total medical and dental insurance costs for 10,400 active employees at the time was $45 million. In comparison, the cost of same-sex domestic partner benefits is negligible.

The cost of providing health insurance coverage to a pool of people who were at risk for AIDS, with its perceived greater health care costs, was also an initial worry that has proved unfounded. The *New York Times*, in a 1993 article on the trend towards domestic partners benefits, reported that AIDS-related claims are "no higher than the cost associated with other serious illnesses, such as cancer, kidney dysfunction, or heart disease" (Noble, 1993, p. F4). Similar results were reported by the Lotus Corporation in an analysis of the claims made under their program. A later report in the *Wall Street Journal* concluded: "The added benefits turn out to come surprisingly cheap. . . . And contrary to many firms' expectations, health care costs for gay partners are often less than those of heterosexuals, despite the corporate fears of footing the bill for more AIDS cases" (Jefferson, 1994, p. 1). In concluding remarks of a report at the University of Pennsylvania, it was noted, "It seems reasonable to conclude from the available information that the cost of extending medical coverage to domestic partners and their dependent children would not be burdensome" (University of Pennsylvania, 1994, p. 2). Richard Jennings, executive director of Hollywood Supports, noted that employers can "adopt a benefit that doesn't cost much of anything . . . (but that) sends an incredibly powerful message of a company's support of all its employees, regardless of sexual orientation" (Jefferson, 1994, p. 1).

An early concern often cited in denial of domestic partner benefits was the potential for fraud and abuse of the system—that employees would misstate their relationship with someone in order to secure health insurance for the individual. Lambda Legal Defense and Education Fund, a non-profit advocacy group for gay and lesbian civil rights, maintains there is no reason to assume there will be more fraud and abuse of domestic partner benefits than is currently found for married employees, who may have sham marriages and who are usually never asked to produce a marriage certificate in order to claim benefits (Lambda, 1994). The increased tax liability, the public record of identification as gay or lesbian, and other restrictions usually found in domestic partner benefits programs all contribute to minimize risk of fraud or abuse. Added tax liability is believed to be the major contributor to minimizing fraud and abuse. The Internal Revenue Service views domestic partner health insurance benefits as "imputed income" and part of taxable income, unlike health insurance for spouses. A spokesperson for a California company estimated that gay employees who enroll their partners in the company's premium health plan may pay as much as $1,000 in extra taxes each year (Jefferson, 1994).

Despite the demonstrated lack of fraud and abuse of domestic partner benefits, campus legal consultants sometimes have problems with domestic partner benefits in general, and with the definition of domestic partner used in decisions about eligibility for such benefits. At most institutions the campus legal advisor will point out that there are no legal mandates to offer domestic partner benefits. The exceptions are public institutions in Vermont that are required to offer domestic partner benefits through a decision of the Vermont Labor Relations Board (1993), and Ithaca College (Ithaca, NY), which lost a case based upon the city's non-discrimination statute. In a legal analysis rendered for the University of Maryland system, lawyer Terry Roach noted that domestic partnerships are difficult to verify without public records such as are available with marriage. Common criteria used may be seen as vague and containing arbitrary distinctions (Roach, 1995). Yet some combination of these criteria remain in use by institutions that offer domestic partner benefits (Wilson, 1999).

An increase in administrative time required to manage a domestic partners benefits program was frequently cited as an initial concern during consideration of the first domestic partners benefits programs. Personnel officers balked at the need to maintain files of domestic partnership affidavits, affidavits of dissolution of domestic partnerships, waiting periods, and other paperwork required to administer the program. With the small number of employees usually involved, however, this argument fades. Initial startup costs for a domestic partners benefits program would include costs of mailing to eligible employees and revisions of brochures and paperwork. Companies such as Levi Strauss have minimized ongoing administrative time and costs by integrating the program with benefits for opposite-sex married partners. For example, proof of domestic partnership in not required just as proof of opposite-sex marriage is not required to apply for benefits (Lambda Legal Defense and Education Fund, 1994). With such an approach, administrative cost per enrollee is minimized and is the same as for married partners.

A final objection and stumbling block to implementation of domestic partner employment benefits has been political and public relations considerations. State officials have threatened and taken budgetary action against colleges that have shown financial support for gays and lesbians. For example, as a result of legislative threats from a state senator, Indiana University decided to fund the campus Gay, Lesbian, Bisexual Student Support Center's $50,000 annual budget from non-state funds (Quest, 1994). Private colleges and other colleges that are heavily dependent upon alumni or capital campaign support may have concerns about donor or alumni reactions and decreased fundraising. The gay and lesbian faculty and staff group at the College of William and Mary in Virginia, for example, chose to fund domestic partner insurance benefits through a fundraising campaign directed towards and coordinated by members of the college's gay and lesbian alumni organization rather than attempt to use general college funds. Conservative Christian organizations such as the American Family Association, the Family Research Council, and others known for lobby attempts against gay/lesbian civil rights, have become involved when domestic partner benefits are under consideration. A common moral argument raised is that the employer is supporting the gay lifestyle and undermining marriage and the family. Brian McNaught, a consultant to corporations on gay issues in the workplace, offered the rebuttal that support is needed for both married partners and domestic partners. Paying a gay person in a committed relationship does not undermine marriage: "Are we assuming that if gay people are treated equitably that heterosexuals will decide not to marry? (Does someone) need to be discriminated against in order for a heterosexual to feel his or her marriage is valued?" (McNaught, 1993, p. 81).

Some colleges simply wish to avoid the media spotlight and a public relations controversy because they are concerned about the image of the college and the reactions of parents of prospective students. However, as of Spring 1995 no universities offering domestic partner benefits had reported any losses due to drop-off in alumni donations or political budgetary fall-out (Badgett, 1995).

Typical Employment Benefits for Partners

Employment benefits offered to opposite-sex married partners frequently vary from institution to institution. (See Table 1 for examples.) Usually, the human relations or personnel department will be able to identify most of the benefits that are available to married partners. The simplest approach to implementation of a domestic partners benefits policy is a brief policy statement that employment benefits normally available to spouses and children of married employees are also granted to domestic partners and children of gay or lesbian employees.

At a state institution, access to employment benefits plans is sometimes "state driven;" that is, they are controlled by a state personnel agency or by statute. An audit of employee benefits and privileges for academic and civil service employees at the University of Minnesota identified four state-driven benefits: spouse and dependent coverage under the health plan (including vision care); spouse and dependent coverage under the dental care plan; spouse and dependent life insurance under the state plan; and long-term disability insurance (civil service only) (University of Minnesota, 1993).

Other employment benefits at a state institution are "university driven"—they are controlled by the policies enacted by the college or university. The Minnesota audit listed the following university driven benefits: (a) ability to purchase group term life insurance; (b) retirement plan, and optional retirement plan; (c) mortgage program; (d) spousal hire programs; (e) leaves of absence for sickness and disability; parental leave; and family and personal leave without pay programs; (f) bereavement leave; (g) automatic access to a credit union; (h) athletic

Table 1
Examples of Typical Institutionally Driven Partner Benefits (Boden, et al, 1995)

Benefit	Discussion
Bookstore discounts	Some college bookstores extend to married spouses the the same discount on purchases that is extended to an employee.
College Unions	College unions generally extend access and discounted rates for various facilities such as the games room and services such as outdoor equipment rental to married spouses.
College Events	Discount ticket prices and admission fees are often available to spouses for various events on campus such as performing arts series, sports events, film series, lectures, etc.
Gym and Recreational Facilities	Many colleges permit married spouses to use facilities and programs at discounted rates, such as access to a weight room, aerobics classes, intramural sports, or summer children's programs.
Health and Counseling Services	Spouses and children are often able to access inexpensive health care and counseling services, including Employee Assistance Programs.
Library Access	Spouses and children may be permitted to check out books, use research services and facilities, computer labs and internet access.

Table 1 *(continued)*

Benefit	Discussion
ID Cards	ID cards for spouses and family members provide a means of access to many facilities and services. On campuses with heightened security concerns, they may even control access to a campus building to visit the office of a partner, or to a cafeteria.
Relocation Assistance	For some employees in highly recruited positions, a college may provide reimbursement of some moving costs and assist spouses in finding new employment in the community.
Day Care Services	While children of a married partner (from a former marriage) are often automatically eligible for access to subsidized day care provided by the college, the children of a partner may not necessarily be granted the same access.

and cultural events; (i) access to the university library; (j) access and spousal membership for campus recreational facilities; (k) membership in a campus club; (l) access to "family" housing (graduate students); (m) access to child care services; (n) alumni relations functions and services; and (o) availability of residency tuition benefits.

In many cases, decisions about access to these programs are made by an individual program director, by a manager, or by an advisory committee. These decisions are often guided by institutional policy and by current practice in the field.

Some employment benefits at a state institution may already be available to partners of employees through other means. For example, some states have statutes that permit any citizen of the state to utilize any library, including college libraries, at no cost. Tickets to athletic, cultural, or social events may be available to both the employee and the partner at the employee discount rate when purchased by the employee if the ticketing control policies or procedures are lax, or upon the discretion of the ticket seller. In many cases, guests visiting the college's campus center or attending free campus events are not required to show an identification card in order to gain access to facilities or programs. At a private college or university, all benefits are university driven and under control of the trustees or college officers.

Current Practice: The Domestic Partners Survey Project

The American College Personnel Association's Standing Committee for Lesbian, Gay, and Bisexual Awareness (SCLGBA) began a survey in 1993 to collect information about domestic partnership benefits at colleges and universities around the country (Leppo, 1995). The Domestic Partnership Project (DPP) is designed to assist student affairs professionals by providing profiles of individual institutions with information about the campus environment for gays, lesbians, and bisexuals. The Project also indicates which domestic partner benefits are offered (if any) and about campus policy and practice that regulates whether domestic partners may reside in on-campus staff apartments with those residence life professionals who are required to live on campus. Campus environment questions examine whether the institution has included sexual orientation in its non-discrimination and harassment policies, whether there are support organizations for gay, lesbian, and bisexual students or faculty/ staff, and other factors such as whether there is a gay, lesbian, bisexual student services office. A second purpose for the Domestic Partners Project is to provide lists of institutions offering domestic partnership benefits and permitting live-in domestic partners for those involved in attempting to change institutional recognition of domestic partners.

Methodology and Findings

The survey was developed from a research project in 1992 by Boden and Stenta. At that time, 250 institutions were surveyed via instruments mailed to senior housing officers. The survey received a response rate of

52% and the results were presented at the annual ACPA conference. The survey instrument was then revised and extended to include specific questions about benefits.

The SCLGBA began to administer the survey under the Domestic Partners Project. Information has been collected by the Project at annual conferences, and by mail or telephone contacts. Attendees and placement center employers at the annual conference are asked to complete the survey regarding their institution. A network of Project representatives in nearly 40 states have mailed surveys or contacted senior student affairs officers. Completed surveys were forwarded to the SCLGBA Resource Clearinghouse, which makes the information available to those who request it.

As of March 31, 1996, over 420 institutions had been surveyed by the Domestic Partners Project. Of these institutions, 23 (5%) offer policies that provide at least four out of the five main benefits including insurance (medical, dental, vision and life) and tuition waivers. Eight (2%) institutions offer at least four main benefits as a matter of practice. At least one benefit is offered as a policy by 32 (8%) institutions, and six (1%) colleges and universities provide at least one benefit by practice.

Access to campus events and facilities for domestic partners was assessed in this Project. The survey defined access to campus events and facilities as offering tickets to campus events and activities; use of library, gym or recreation center, and union; and a campus identification card. A total of 90 campuses (21%) provide access to events and facilities as a matter of policy or practice.

A total of 81 campuses (19%) provide some accommodations for domestic partner housing to live-in residence life staff. Of these 81 institutions, 26 offer this benefit as a departmental policy, while 55 provide this benefit as a practice. Twelve campuses offer a meal plan for the partner when a meal plan is provided to the residence life staff member. In addition, 29 campuses provide parking opportunities either by policy or practice.

Despite the fact that 216 (51%) institutions out of 420 include sexual orientation as part of their non-discrimination clauses, only 69 (16%) actually support their policy through extension of benefits.

The methodology of this Project has some limitations. Some information in the survey may be inaccurate due to the self-reporting nature of the survey method. At the conference, for example, the senior student affairs officer may not be the person responding to the survey. As a result, there may be some inaccurate or misperceived information. Changes in policy or practice may have taken place over time, and may affect the accuracy of the survey information if the institution's information has not been updated. Policies and practices are interpreted in different ways from institution to institution, and may provide some inconsistency in the results. Some survey information requires a subjective response (such as "Do you feel that your department or institution has actively recruited or hired gay, lesbian, and bisexual professional staff?") versus a quantitative answer (specific employment benefits, campus policies, or support organizations).

Change Process Considerations

The process to develop domestic partner benefits often begins with one individual asking if such benefits are available. One respondent in the Boden-Stenta survey commented:

> *Our policy changed one day when I went to our Human Resources office a few years ago and asked them why we did not have benefits for domestic partners at our college. He replied to me, "That's a good question. Let me ask the President (of the College)." The next day he called me back and told me that the policies would be changed to extend all benefits to all members of the college community effective immediately. We did not have a struggle.*

Ed Mickens reflects on a similar route to change in the workplace found in the corporate sector:

> *The real power in this movement (towards workplace equality) comes directly from the individual lesbians and gay men in the workplace, struggling to improve their own situations. . . . I see many cases of large companies where a single, brave queer takes a stand. Sometimes this person has influence; sometimes not. Sometimes others in the company are inspired by his or her actions, and begin to band together; sometimes not. Sometimes sympathetic, non-gay colleagues or managers will become allies; sometimes not. But it's these admirable gay and lesbian individuals who make all the difference.* (Mickens, 1994, p. 31)

On most campuses, however, the change process for domestic partner benefits becomes a long, heavily discussed and very political issue. Another Boden-Stenta respondent talks about the experience on his or her campus:

> *We have had one roadblock after another. Every time we take one step forward, we end up two steps back. The president and student affairs staff are very supportive. But the problem lies with a conservative Board of Trustees and state legislature. Everyone is worried about what the citizens of (state) will think. Well, most citizens probably don't care, and if they do, the concern will go away after a while. I am not sure what it will take to get (name of institution) to get some courage and do the right thing. I am almost embarrassed to work here.*

Some colleges and universities have taken steps to implement domestic partner benefits without a formal change in policy or an official policy being written. These institutions have, by informal adoption of the practice, extended some or all domestic partner benefits to same-sex partners. Generally these have been "no-cost" benefits, such as allowing domestic partners to live with residence life staff in campus housing. This method of change usually requires only a short time to implement, with few people being involved in the decision making. An informal arrangement with a supervisor, manager, or advisory committee will permit same-sex partners to enjoy benefits rather quickly. However, reliance upon such "good will" and informal accommodations can sometimes be a gamble. A change in leadership at any level of the institution can change an informal benefits program overnight if the new staff member does not agree with the policy, or if he or she is not adequately informed. Any constituent—student, staff, alumni, faculty, community member—could "blow the whistle" to create controversy and call attention to the practice, resulting in a "political" decision to stop the practice to quell the controversy. As a result, reliance upon informal practice can sometimes make a domestic partners benefit very transitory. Although a formal policy change process can be burdensome, frustrating, and worrisome, the change is usually more permanent when it occurs.

Although an individual will usually begin the formal policy change process towards domestic partner benefits, involving others in the effort will permit a sharing of the workload in researching, preparing, and presenting proposals to various individuals and governing bodies. As with most change efforts, coalitions and allies can be extremely helpful in the process. The initial starting point for an internal change process to secure benefits has been varied—some have begun with the institution's Affirmative Action and Equal Opportunity Officer; some campuses have advisory committees on employee benefits; and others have begun within the governance structure, such as a faculty/staff committee on benefits of the university senate or council.

An advantage of involving others in the effort to secure domestic partner benefits is that there will be additional individuals available to assist with the large amount of background research typically required in writing a proposal for domestic partners benefits. One of the first areas for research is to investigate the institution's non-discrimination clause to see if one's institution is among the many colleges and universities where sexual orientation is specifically mentioned. If not, does the statement mention non-discrimination on the basis of marital status? Although both forms of discrimination are operational when same-sex domestic partners are denied benefits, the choice of one or the other approach does have implications. Granting domestic partner benefits to avoid marital status discrimination usually means that unmarried opposite-sex partners will also become eligible for benefits. Using this approach could bring in valuable allies among heterosexual faculty and staff, but it could also increase costs—where only 1% of the average workforce will enroll same-sex domestic partners, the number rises to about 3% when opposite-sex domestic partners are eligible (Jefferson, 1994). In some states that permit common law marriage, the question becomes irrelevant because the state recognizes opposite-sex partners as married. At a private institution, community or statewide non-discrimination ordinances may also apply to the college as employer if the ordinance is written to apply to non-governmental employment.

Another area for research when considering domestic partner benefits is to determine who has decision-making authority about eligibility for the benefit. As previously discussed, some public institutions operate under a central state personnel agency or may offer some benefits under a state statute that defines eligibility. In research on domestic partner benefits at the University of Utah, for example, the human resources department identified 12 of 13 total benefits that could be extended to domestic partners without action by the state legislature, which controls pension benefits and limits the recipient of the benefit only to a spouse upon the death of an employee (Israelson, 1997). At the University of Minnesota, employees are reimbursed for the cost of insurance benefits because state statute defines criteria for eligibility for participation in the state insurance program (University of Minnesota, n.d.). Part of this research will require the identification of how the institution funds each benefit. If the institution is not self-insured and utilizes an insurance company, the university's insurance provider may need to become involved in the process. Although the first employers to offer health insurance benefits to domestic partners encountered resistance from insurers, fortunately more and more insurers have adapted to the changing demand from their institutional customers. Health insurance benefits for domestic partners are now frequently available from insurers at the same rate as for married same-sex partners.

In most efforts to obtain domestic partner benefits, an analysis of the fiscal impact will be required. The institution's human relations or personnel benefits office should be consulted to obtain information about the methods of funding insurance benefits, costs per individual insured, and other helpful data. Fortunately domestic partner benefits now have a "history" that documents enrollee statistics and overall costs to the employer for both public and private institutions. In some cases this information is available directly from the organizations—Levi Straus has been a corporate leader in sharing information about its domestic partners benefits program. (Reese Smith, Levi Strauss Director of Employee Benefits as cited in Lambda Legal Defense, 1994). Additional information has been compiled by lesbian and gay advocacy organizations such as Lambda Legal Defense and Education Fund, or the National Gay and Lesbian Task Force Policy Institute.

In a few cases when internal routes for change proved ineffective, individuals have chosen to pursue compensation equality through external, formal procedures. As noted previously, in some cases domestic partner benefits were won through litigation. This was the case at Ithaca College, where a judgment in favor of the employees was won in court (Ithaca College cited, 1994). In other cases, a labor-based approach was used. In Vermont, the state labor relations grievance board issued a favorable decision that affected all state employees (Vermont Labor Relations Board, 1993). In Oregon, the Oregon Public Employees Union negotiated a collective bargaining agreement with the State of Oregon which prohibited discrimination based upon sexual orientation for all state workers, including university employees (Lambda Legal Defense, 1990). However, this ruling was insufficient to obtain domestic partner benefits, even upon appeal to the state's employment board due to Oregon's state employee policy. A decisive court case filed by university employees found that the state's policy violated the equal protection clause of that state's constitution, and as a result all state employees are now eligible for domestic partner benefits (Guernsey, 1996).

Attempts to change domestic partner benefits at the statewide level— where a state statute and the legislature are involved, or where a central state personnel agency controls eligibility for benefits—have not yet proved successful, with the exception being the decision by the state labor relations board decision in Vermont. Gay and lesbian employee groups have attempted to unite all campuses of a multi-campus state system to pressure the state agency to grant benefits, because the university system is the largest state employer. This effort has not been successful to date.

Conclusion

Lesbian and gay faculty and staff in same-sex domestic partnerships face similar issues and financial needs as those who are married to opposite-sex partners. Recognition of domestic partnerships through a benefits program provides for equality in compensation, improved productivity, and competitive faculty/staff recruitment conditions. Colleges and universities provide domestic partner benefits also to be consistent with non-discrimination statements and with an institutional commitment to supporting a diverse campus. Initial concerns about expense and abuse of domestic partner benefits have proved unfounded, and an adequate track record now exists for both institutions of higher learning, as well as other private and public institutions. Although varied routes to achieving domestic partner benefits are used, the process usually begins with a single individual inquiring about such benefits because a real need is felt. Perhaps more important than the financial support and compensation, however, is that institutional recognition of domestic partners in employment communicates to the same-sex family the message that the institution also values and holds important their loving primary relationship.

References

Badgett, M. V. L. (1995, Spring). Domestic partner recognition: Doing the right—and competitive—thing. *SYNTHESIS: Law and Policy in Higher Education, 6,* 483-484.

Baxter Magolda, M. B. (1992). *Knowing and reasoning in college: Gender-related patterns in students' intellectual development.* San Francisco: Jossey-Bass.

Benefits for the Fringe. (1994, January 25). *The Advocate,* pp. 56-59.

Boden, S., Leppo, J., & Stenta, D. (1995). *Examples of typical institutionally driven partner benefits.* Unpublished manuscript.

Brooke, J. (1996, September 18). Denver extends health coverage to partners of gay city employees. *The New York Times,* p. 24.

Buehrens, J. (1996, September/October). HORIZONS . . . Reflections from the president of UUA. *The World,* p.4.

City University of New York. (1993, October). *The report of the CUNY study group on domestic partnerships.* Unpublished manuscript.

Dalton, J. C. (1996). Managing human resources. In S. R. Komives & D. B. Woodard (Eds.), *Student services: A handbook for the profession,* 3rd ed., (pp. 494-511). San Francisco: Jossey-Bass.

D'Emilio, J. (1996). *The marriage debate: NGLTF Task Force report Fall 1996.* Washington, DC: National Gay and Lesbian Task Force.

Fried, J. (1995). *Shifting paradigms in student affairs: Culture, context, teaching, and learning.* Washington, DC: American College Personnel Association.

Guernsey, L. (1996, September 6). Gay workers' partners win benefits in Oregon. *The Chronicle of Higher Education,* p. A-20.

Jackson, P. (1994, January 27). Ithaca College cited for discrimination. *The Ithaca Journal,* p.1.

King, P. (1996). Student cognition and learning. In S.R. Komives & D. B. Woodard (Eds.), *Student services: A handbook for the profession,* 3rd ed., (pp. 218-243). San Francisco: Jossey-Bass.

Kuh, G., Schuh, J. H., Whitt, E. J., & Associates (1991). *Involving colleges: Encouraging student learning and personal development through out-of-class experiences.* San Francisco: Jossey-Bass.

Ladner, G. (1994). Baehr v. Lewin: Will equal protection lead to the end of prohibitions on same-sex marriages? *Journal of Sexual Orientation Law, 1* (1), 127-135.

Lambda Legal Defense and Education Fund. (1994). *Negotiating for equal employment benefits: A resource packet.* Unpublished manuscript.

Leppo, J. (1995, Fall). Domestic partners project. *Xveritas,* p. 3.

MacDonald, E. (1993, May). Contract to love. *OUT Magazine,* pp. 83-86.

McEwen, M. K., & Roper, L. D. (1994). Incorporating multiculturalism into student affairs preparation programs: Suggestions from the literature. *Journal of College Student Development, 35,* 46-53.

McNaught, B. (1993). *Gay issues in the workplace.* New York: St. Martin's Press.

Mickens, E. (1994a, February 22). What good are partner benefits? *The Advocate,* p. 31-32.

Mickens, E. (1994b). *The 100 best companies for gay men and lesbians.* New York: Pocket Books.

Mickens, E. (1994c, April 19). The taxing problem of benefits. *The Advocate,* p. 33-34.

National Center for Lesbian Rights. (1994). *Recognizing gay and lesbian families: Strategies for obtaining domestic partner benefits.* Unpublished manuscript.

Noble, B. P. (1993, June 13). A quiet liberation for gay and lesbian employees. *The New York Times,* p. F4.

Poll shows gays and lesbians gaining acceptance. (1997, January 10). *Gay People's Chronicle,* p. 5.

Pope, R. L., & Reynolds, A. L. (1997). Student affairs core competencies: Integrating multicultural awareness, knowledge, and skills. *Journal of College Student Development, 38,* 266-277.

Roach, T. (1995, Spring). Definition of "domestic partner." *SYNTHESIS: Law and Policy in Higher Education, 6,* 485-486.

Quest (Queers United for Equal Social Treatment). (1994, September). *News release via the Internet.*

The Segal Company Executive Letter (1993). Vol.17, No. 1 & 2.

Singer, B. L., & Deschamps, D. (1994). *Gay & lesbian stats: A pocket guide of facts and figures.* New York: The New Press.

Special issue on the family. (1989, November). *Newsweek.*

Under surveillance. (1996, December 24). *The Advocate,* p. 12.

University of California. (1995). *Preliminary findings on the extension of health benefits to the domestic partners of U.C. faculty, staff, and students.* Unpublished manuscript.

University of Minnesota. (1993, January). *Interim report of the select committee.* Unpublished manuscript.

University of Minnesota. (n.d.). *How to access domestic partnership benefits at the University of Minnesota.* (Available from University of Minnesota Employee Benefits Department, Suite 210, 1313 Fifth Street SE, Minneapolis, MN 55411-4504).

University of Pennsylvania. (1994). *Statement on domestic partner benefits from the Division of Human Resources.* Unpublished manuscript.

U.S. Bureau of the Census. (1991). *Census of the population: 1970 and current population reports, marital status and living arrangements: March 1991.* Series P-20, No. 461.

Vermont Labor Relations Board. (1993, June) Docket No. 92-32, Grievance of B. M., B. B., S. S., C. M., & J. R.

Wilson, R. (1999, February 12). For gay academics, benefits for partners have a financial and emotional impact. *The Chronicle of Higher Education,* p. A10-A12.

Winfield, L., & Spielman, S. (1995). *Straight talk about gays in the workplace.* New York: American Management Association.

Wolfson, E. (1994). Crossing the threshold: Equal marriage rights for lesbians and gay men, and the intra-community critique. *New York University Review of Law and Social Change, 21,* 567.

Chapter 4

ഏരൂ

Religiously Affiliated Institutions and Sexual Orientation

HEIDI LEVINE AND PATRICK G. LOVE

Lesbian, gay and bisexual (LGB) people attend, teach and work at religiously affiliated institutions (RAIs). Writings that consider LGB issues at RAIs are quite scarce, paralleling the still small literature base on LGB issues in general. This dearth of literature perhaps reflects an underlying assumption that "those people" do not go to "those institutions" (Love, 1997). The scarcity of research makes it difficult to speak with scholarly "authority" on the topic, thereby implicitly communicating the message that there is, in fact, nothing to say. This absence of dialogue both points and contributes to the invisibility experienced by LGB students who attend RAIs. While some issues related to creating more accepting campus communities for LGB students (and faculty/staff) are universal, special considerations exist at RAIs. Attention must be paid to such issues as the stance of the affiliated denomination vis-a-vis homosexuality, characteristics of LGB students who choose to attend religiously affiliated schools, the critical role external constituencies play in the life of such institutions, and cultural conflicts that may exist within those campus communities.

Among the colleges and universities in the United States, an estimated 700 are religiously-affiliated (Sandeen, 1991). These RAIs vary tremendously, based on such factors as size, geographic location, degree of conservatism/liberalism, denomination, and the strength of affiliation with the founding denomination. While several of these variables also differentiate non-religiously-affiliated campuses, a common factor that joins RAIs and sets them apart from their fellow institutions is the fact that—to varying degrees—they are guided by the principles, traditions and dictates of the denomination or religion with which they are affiliated.

There are obstacles and barriers facing LGB students on all American college campuses. Additional barriers that may exist on many religiously affiliated college campuses include the invisibility of the issue of sexual orientation, the lack of a visible community of LGB people, an institutional culture that avoids conflict, the way in which institutions approach issues of sexuality, the negative messages coming from the sponsoring religious organization, and tacitly approved homophobia. Not all of these barriers exist on all religiously affiliated campuses and some exist on secular campuses as well; however, these particular barriers tend to be related to the religiously affiliated nature of the campus. Estanek (1996) identified sexual orientation as the most challenging issue facing Catholic institutions, and staff at both Methodist and American Baptist colleges have identified parallels in the conflict around this issue on their campuses and within their denominations.

While we are not theologians and do not intend to critique practices or doctrine of different religions, in this chapter we will explore some issues pertinent to lesbian, gay, and bisexual students at RAIs. Our focus is to provide a resource for the staff at RAIs who are seeking to make their institutions safer and more welcoming environments for LGB students. What we have to say is based both on the research that has been conducted on the subject (for example, Estanek, 1996; Gutierrez, 1987; Love, 1993, 1997) and our own experiences. One of the authors also solicited specific anecdotes and examples from colleagues at various institutions. We begin with a brief introduction to factors that may impinge on the climate of RAIs in general and specific barriers that face many lesbian, gay, and bisexual students, and end the chapter by providing suggestions for student affairs professionals interested in creating more welcoming environments on these campuses.

Climate and Barriers at RAIs

Institutional Culture

In any institution, culture helps determine what is held to be important and how business is carried out. The culture of an organization exists on multiple levels, which can be viewed in terms of its artifacts (rituals, stories and symbols), values (what is asserted to be important) and core assumptions (Kuh, 1990). The strength of the culture is dependent upon a number of variables, including the size, age, history and type of institution (Kuh & Whitt, 1988). Ideally, there is congruence among the various aspects and levels of culture, but inconsistencies can exist. It is possible, for example, for there to be discrepancies between the stated values of the institution and the behaviors of its members. In the case of RAIs, it can be between the values of the institution and its founding denominations (for example, love, mutual respect, and being nonjudgmental) and the tolerated behaviors and attitudes of some of its members (for example, homophobia).

For RAIs, the denominational assumptions, values and artifacts help define the campus culture. A statement of "core values" upon which institutional policies are based may grow out of and reflect the teachings and doctrine of the sponsoring religion. Beyond the development of policies and procedures, these values often implicitly (or explicitly) shape expectations about how individuals will deal with each other and respond to issues that emerge on campus. How liberal or conservative a denomination is, what it defines as "sin" and how it responds to "transgressors" all provide a lens through which issues and conflicts are viewed. And, again, there is potential for conflict to exist between these different aspects of culture.

A complicating caveat to this issue is that student affairs practice occurs within the context of the individual institution (American Council on Education, 1937; American College Personnel Association/National Association of Student Personnel Administrators, 1998). The values of student affairs and of the individual student affairs professional must then be incorporated into the institutional mission and the values implied by that mission. This can be a significant challenge, especially on extremely conservative campuses where some individuals may want the institution to "help" LGB students "change."

External or Typically Peripheral Constituencies

Several external or typically peripheral constituencies may play an important role for RAIs. While alumni, parents and trustees are influential groups on most campuses, the power they yield at RAIs is often greater than typically experienced at most secular institutions (though it may be similar to what is found at small, private, secular liberal arts colleges). In addition, denominational authorities such as dioceses or synods as well as the local religious community can be extremely important in influencing institutional priorities, policies and actions. While some RAIs have loose affiliations with denominational governing bodies, many have strong links that can determine the direction of institutional initiatives and approaches. As these connections to external constituencies become stronger, they not only set the tone for how potentially controversial issues will be handled, but may also have an impact on the leeway with which administrators can make decisions and provide leadership in addressing those areas.

The contexts of RAIs can serve as barriers to dealing with issues of sexual orientation; however, there are additional barriers facing LGB students on these campuses.

For example, one key dimension along which denominations differ relates to acceptance of controversy and disagreement with faith tenets. While many religions tolerate—or even encourage—questioning of beliefs, others leave little room for dissension. Especially in more fundamental and conservative institutions this aspect of the culture—a focus on a single, enduring, and universal "Truth"—suppresses disagreement and conflict. It discourages questioning of basic premises and encourages individuals to avoid bringing up difficult issues. At one Methodist institution, members of the board of trustees and some students spoke about wanting the difficult issue of sexual orientation and the beliefs related to LGB people "to just go away."

The unwillingness to deal with conflict or to explore multiple truths can be in conflict with some of the basic principles of the student affairs profession. For example, those professionals attempting to encourage students' development recognize that cognitive development theories describe a shift from cognitive or moral absolutism to a commitment to relativism (Perry, 1970) that may come into conflict with cultural expectations on campus. Other beliefs and values that have been identified as intrinsic to student affairs work include freedom, respect, compassion, human dignity, and equality (Pavela, 1995; Young & Elfrink, 1991). Young and Elfrink (1991) suggested that included in the value of equality is an appreciation of multiculturalism, and that "multiculturalism might be a superordinate value of current student affairs practice" (p. 51). If issues related to gay, lesbian, and bisexual people are considered to fall under the rubric of "multiculturalism," then the possibility for tension between the stated student affairs value and the value of a religion which labels homosexuality as "sin" is great.

Negative messages coming from the church or religious organization

Many messages about homosexuality and bisexuality coming from the churches and religious organizations that founded the college or university are negative. For example, in Catholicism's case homosexuality has been identified as an "intrinsic disorder" (Congregation for the Doctrine of the Faith, 1975). There are very clear and consistent beliefs about homosexuality at many *Bible* colleges and fundamentalist schools— it is a choice, it is wrong, it is immoral, and the *Bible* specifies homosexuality to be a sin (Maret, 1984). These beliefs pose a significant barrier to young people struggling with their sexual orientation.

Most issues of sexuality eventually relate to behavior and issues of choice facing students or the institution. These behaviors include premarital sexual relations, abortion, birth control, and availability of condoms on campus. Particular religions and religiously affiliated institutions have strictures about most of these practices. However, in the case of sexual orientation, one is speaking about a person's identity—who a person is, not what that person chooses to do. Despite protestations otherwise, one's sexual orientation is not a matter of choice (Money, 1988), and it should be pointed out that many mainline religions, such as Catholicism (American Bishops, 1976; Coleman, 1995; Ratzinger, 1986), now accept that one does not choose one's sexual orientation. There may be a choice about whether to act on one's feelings, but that is a different choice than the choices involved in the other behaviors listed above. For LGB students the choice appears to be between denying who they are and what they are feeling in order to remain good and upright, or exploring their sexuality and risk being labeled "intrinsically disordered" or sinful, thereby risking the loss of one's relationship with God and disconnection from the community.

Although the official line of many mainstream religions regarding homosexuality is one of tolerance and understanding of homosexuals (while condemning homosexual behavior), there are leaders in the spotlight who publicly condone homophobia (for example, Catholic Cardinal O'Connor in New York and Bishop Daley in Brooklyn). This tacitly approved homophobia contributes to the violence toward and harassment of LGB students. On individual campuses, students report that violence against and harassment of LGB students are not pursued to the same extent as other incidents of violence (Norris, 1992; Rhoads, 1994). In fact, Norris (1992) found at one historically liberal RAI that while people expressed support of LGB students, their actions often pointed toward feelings of ambivalence and outright homophobia. At one small Methodist college, LGB students who are out on campus experience verbal harassment despite institutional discussion about including sexual orientation in the college's anti-discrimination statement. There is a sense of understanding why people might want to hurt or harass homosexuals— "they do not belong on this campus anyway." And at many RAIs, LGB students are labeled "sinners" merely due to their sexual orientation. At one small suburban Catholic college, a faculty member complained to the president about a presentation on institutional homophobia where she heard the presenter state homosexuality is not a sin. The president then contacted the CSAO and suggested that such programming was not appropriate at this institution.

Invisibility of Sexual Orientation as an Issue on Campus

On many religiously affiliated campuses, and especially those that specifically condemn homosexuality as a sin, the issue of sexual orientation is invisible. There is no lesbian, gay, or bisexual organization and no educational programming, it is not dealt with in professional or student staff training, and it is not mentioned in any campus publications. The prevailing cultural assumption is that no one on campus is lesbian, gay, or bisexual or, as at one small Methodist college, there is an unofficial policy of "don't ask, don't tell." This is perhaps the greatest obstacle facing LGB students on these campuses. They are isolated and must deal with their feelings and thoughts by themselves, and, in fact, may believe that there are no other LGB persons on campus. They are unaware that there may be supportive and understanding people in the counseling center, in residence life, in campus ministry, or on the faculty. They have no way of knowing about any safe spaces, because speaking aloud about their feelings risks censure and ostracism. They hear only negative messages about sexual orientations other than heterosexual. LGB young people are more prone to suicide than heterosexual youth (Gibson, 1989) and the context that some students experience at RAIs intensifies the elements, such as isolation, self-hatred, fear, that contribute to suicidal gestures and attempts. Although no firm data exist, there is anecdotal evidence to indicate that these students tend to transfer from or drop out of these institutions at a higher rate than heterosexual students (Love, 1993). The silence and surface calm about issues of sexual orientation at many RAIs often mask a great deal of pain and suffering.

Lack of lesbian, gay, or bisexual community

Given the barriers listed above, it is no wonder that there would be a lack of a LGB community or subcommunities at many RAIs. In an environment where the issue is invisible, individuals are isolated and fear coming out, conflict is avoided, and those concerned about the needs of LGB students fear talking about issues of sexual orientation, there is little opportunity for the development of a lesbian, gay, or bisexual community. Communities are an important element in growth and development. It is through their communities that people learn how to act and behave in the various contexts in society. They learn how to communicate. They learn about themselves as reflected in the mirror of community. Heterosexual students learn what it means to be heterosexual in their family community, religious community, neighborhood communities, and school communities. Through her research on sexual identity formation, Cass (1979) pointed out the importance of a being a part of a *LGB* community on the ability of gays and lesbians to develop positive self-identities. Her point is that one cannot develop a positive self-identity in isolation. Given the invisible nature of homosexuality and bisexuality in the communities at most RAIs, LGB students who attend these institutions have no mirror through which they can learn what it means to be lesbian, gay, or bisexual. They only learn that it is wrong and that they are bad and sinful. The lack of community—the lack of connection with anyone related to issues of sexual orientation—also means there is no informal communication network through which students who are struggling with their sexual orientation can learn about supportive staff and faculty or external community resources.

Barriers Facing Student Affairs Professionals

For student affairs professionals seeking to meet the needs of LGB students at religiously affiliated institutions some significant barriers exist as well. Perhaps the most significant is the stigma associated with the topic of homosexuality. Related to stigma is the issue of when and where it is culturally appropriate to discuss sexual orientation on a religiously affiliated campus.

Stigma. Homosexuality has long been recognized as a stigmatizing agent in our society (Herdt, 1989). There is also evidence of courtesy stigma (Goffman, 1963)—the stigmatizing nature of being acquaintances or friends with stigmatized individuals (in this case homosexuals) (Gochros, 1985; Pfuhl, 1986; Sigelman, Howell, Cornell, Cutright, & Dewey, 1991). However, there is evidence that the stigma extends beyond interacting with stigmatized people to anyone who chooses to associate with a stigmatized topic—homosexuality (Love, 1993). Given the degree of heterosexism at typical RAIs, anyone concerned about the issue of sexual orientation or homophobia is often assumed to be lesbian, gay, or bisexual. Anyone who decides to address issues of sexual orientation or homophobia must also deal with the fact that culturally negative assumptions will be made about them. This is a barrier because the process of stigmatization is used by others to discount people's actions or motivations, thereby reducing their power and influence. Being stigmatized in this way may cause the individual to be less influential, and thus less effective, in other aspects of her or his job as well.

Addressing issues of sexual orientation. In a case study conducted at a small Catholic college, there were two culturally appropriate ways to discuss sexual orientation that protected an individual from being stigmatized: one was in an educational/academic context and the other was in a counseling situation (Love, 1997). Given the value of academic freedom, individual faculty could address the topic of sexual orientation in the context of their classes or an educational context, such as a debate or an institutionally sponsored educational program. Given the mission of the counseling center, counselors could work with LGB students, but could also address the college community about the mental health needs of LGB students. They could do that because it was seen as their job to "help" LGB students. At one Lutheran college, counselors experienced pressure from the campus community to help gay and lesbian clients "change."

Often any other mode of addressing the issue of sexual orientation means that it is becoming politicized. Political discussion challenges the underlying beliefs, values, and attitudes of a culture. Addressing the topic in the context of class intellectualizes it and removes it from the context of the institution and its culture. Dealing with it in the context of counseling means that it is being dealt with quietly and individually and that the symptoms (for example, depression, anger, frustration) are being addressed, but not all of the causes (such as oppression, being closeted, homophobic climate).

Lesbian, Gay and Bisexual Students at RAIs

A question one might ask is, "If most RAIs present climates for LGB students that are worse than those at secular institutions, why would LGB students choose to attend such an institution?" There are no data available to determine whether the percentage of LGB students attending RAIs is similar to or less than that at secular institutions. However, despite the assumptions of many who work at and attend RAIs, there are gay, lesbian, and bisexual students at these institutions. These students attend for a wide variety of reasons, including for some of the same reasons other students attend a particular RAI (for example, college reputation; perceived similarity in values; parents, siblings, or friends may have attended).

We know that the traditional college years (ages 18-22) are when many LGB students begin to actively explore their sexuality (D'Augelli, 1991). Therefore, some LGB high school students who are beginning to struggle with the inherent contradiction between their emerging sexual feelings and their religious upbringing may attend an RAI in order to avoid dealing with questions about sexuality. Some other LGB students may choose a college and enroll before they have come out to themselves and accept their sexual orientation (D'Augelli, 1991). The result is that LGB students who fit these two categories end up on campuses that are the least prepared and often least willing to help them deal with issues of their sexuality.

As we have outlined in this section, there are significant barriers related to dealing with sexual orientation at RAIs that face student affairs professionals and LGB students. In the final section of this chapter we will provide some strategies for challenging these barriers and, hopefully, creating more accepting and welcoming communities at religiously affiliated institutions for LGB students.

Strategies for Creating More Accepting and Welcoming Communities

There are at least two important questions that need to be addressed by student affairs professionals working at religiously affiliated institutions related to meeting the needs of LGB students. Can the institution deal with LGB people and issues in an accepting and supportive manner without compromising its religious identity? If not, then how can staff at such institutions better meet the needs of the LGB students who attend the institution? Each institution is unique, but for those at many religiously affiliated institutions the answer to the first question may be "no." The culture on campus and powerful external and typically peripheral constituents (for example, local religious leaders, the Board of Trustees, alumni, donors, parents of students, and parents of prospective students) exert significant influence on campus and in maintaining the religious identity of the institution. Many of these constituents will see action related to meeting LGB student needs as antithetical to the institution's mission and religious identity and resist these changes. Even at resistant institutions, however, it is possible to begin the work of meeting students' needs. It is important that student affairs professionals analyze and evaluate their own campus and consider the usefulness of the following strategies and suggestions for addressing issues of sexual orientation.

Work Within the Campus Culture

Part of considering one's individual campus is exploring and understanding the institution's history, mission, traditions, and culture. What is the stated purpose of the institution? What contribution did the founders envision the institution making? What are the values discussed in institutional planning and decision making? It is possible to concentrate on closely held values (e.g., love and compassion) and traditions (e.g., service to others) and focus them on the needs of LGB students. Those values will increase the sensitivity of some members who are actively striving to "live out the mission" of the institution.

For example, an institution may espouse and seek to enact the values of holistic student development, critical thinking, or care for the individual. Any one of these can be refocused on the needs of LGB students. In appropriate contexts (including staff meetings, planning meetings, student organization advising) it would be possible to ask, "How is our avoidance

of discussing sexual orientation adversely affecting the holistic development of our LGB students?" or "Wouldn't it be important to compare
the most recent research information about the lack of choice in one's
sexual orientation and our institution's assumption that it is a choice?" or
"Isn't it possible that our LGB students do not feel cared about on
campus?" Each one of these questions needs to be consciously and clearly
linked with an accepted aspect of the institution's culture. Only in that
way can an individual be seen as working from within the culture and not
as someone who is acting counterculturally.

Another example that might fit on most religiously affiliated campuses
is that it may be strategically more palatable to work against homophobia
than to adopt a pro-lesbian, gay, bisexual stance. It is hard to argue that
someone is working counter to the values of most RAIs when one is
working against hatred and fear. In that vein, encouraging the creation of
ally groups may be culturally more supportable than establishing LGB
organizations.

Begin Where it Is Safest and Most Culturally Appropriate

Related to working within the culture is beginning to address issues
of sexual orientation and the needs of LGB students where it is safest and
most culturally appropriate. Earlier in the chapter, we provided the
example of one campus where culturally appropriate ways in which to
address issues of sexual orientation were in an educational context or a
counseling context (Love, 1997). At this institution, conducting educational
programming on issues of sexual orientation, though not welcomed by
everyone, was still seen as legitimate by most institutional members.
Some sociology, psychology, and religious studies faculty addressed the
issue of sexual orientation in a positive manner in the context of their
courses. A faculty and staff group organized to fight homophobia ("People
Against Homophobia") specifically articulated an educational mission.
The director of the counseling center was one person on campus identified
as someone who could advocate for the needs of lesbian, gays, and
bisexuals without being discounted or assumed to be lesbian. At a southern,
Baptist college the initial efforts to break the silence took the form of a
LGB/straight alliance. Safe and culturally appropriate ways to address
issues of sexual orientation will vary from campus to campus and need to
be discovered by student affairs professionals working there.

Focus on Challenge and Support

Remembering the basic student development principle of "challenge and support" (Moore & Upcraft, 1990) can provide a valuable guide in working to create more welcoming campuses. In dealing with individual students, student groups and the institution as a whole, both aspects of this practice are essential. Initially, careful assessment of both the environment and specific issues that need to be addressed must be considered. Subsequent steps should be planned that are "one step ahead" of where the target group(s) is. If change is pushed too quickly the likely response is for people to feel threatened and fall back into their comfort zones, often expressing greater levels of homophobia than before. By utilizing lower levels of challenge—along with support for the efforts people have been making and for their basic values—members of the institution are more likely to stretch themselves to move to a new stage of comfort and acceptance. At one small Catholic college, for example, while the director of counseling encountered support for running a group for *LGB* students and presenting workshops on homophobia, it was made clear that "gay pride demonstrations" would not be acceptable.

Have Action Be Student Driven and Focused on Students' Needs

Part of the challenge for student affairs professionals at RAIs is to empower students to act on their own behalf. By empowering students, student affairs professionals are operating within a student development framework—teaching personal responsibility, encouraging openness to diversity, addressing social justice issues (Moore & Upcraft, 1990; Young & Elfrink, 1991). The work of empowerment includes encouraging heterosexual students, in addition to LGB students, to be concerned about issues of social justice and oppression. Students need culturally savvy advisors—professionals who can help students navigate the difficult and dangerous waters of cultural opposition. Students need support and assistance, but they also need to experience the subtle and not so subtle culturally resistant forces that exist in and around the institution. Also, any movement toward cultural change concerning the issue of sexual orientation may be more accepted coming from students than from staff. However, it is important for student affairs professionals not to hide behind students or use them as a tool to press forward in this area— students should be guided and advised, not forced and manipulated.

Campuses that are truly welcoming and affirming to gay, lesbian, and bisexual people will develop and implement policies that reflect this stance. Ideally, institutional non-discrimination statements will include sexual orientation, LGB student organizations will be officially recognized, and domestic partners of lesbian and gay employees will have access to the same benefits as spouses of heterosexual employees. While many campuses endure tremendous struggle and conflict to realize these goals, for most RAIs the barriers can be even more difficult to overcome. In the process of working to effect that level of institutional change it is vital to remain focused on student needs.

Resistance to institutional change at the policy level is likely to be vigorous, driven largely by the perception that such change cuts right to the heart of the institution and its values and heritage. Again, this resistance is most intense at those RAIs where the denomination holds negative beliefs related to homosexuality. Though also challenging many of the same tenets, a focus on program development and change specifically related to student needs tends to be somewhat easier to accomplish. An awareness that, fundamentally, "we are here for the students" and the presence of some form of a mission which supports students' development can make increased tolerance (and eventually acceptance) more tenable to resistant campus constituencies.

Break the Silence, Increase the Visibility

Beyond working within the culture, it is important to break the silence regarding sexual orientation and make the issue visible on campus. There are isolated individuals who are suffering and have no idea where or to whom to reach out for help. The topic can be made visible in multiple ways, including organizing a group of allies to fight homophobia, displaying signs and symbols in one's office (for example, pins, posters, books) to indicate to closeted students that one is safe and will be supportive, writing letters to the editor of the campus newspaper to discuss the contradiction between the institution's mission and homophobic acts and violence, or creating and advertising a counseling center-based (and, therefore, culturally appropriate) support group for LGB students. It is important to note about this last suggestion, that connecting LGB students with the counseling center, although culturally appropriate, may perpetuate a stereotype that homosexuality is an illness. In two situations (Gutierrez, 1987; Love, 1993), a counseling-based support group was an appropriate beginning, but in both cases as the students developed a sense of group, they moved the group out of the counseling center. Finally, increasing the visibility of the issue usually increases the visibility of supportive people and provides to closeted students avenues to resources and counteracts the sense of isolation and the belief that they are the only lesbian, gay, or bisexual persons on campus.

Incorporate Personal Beliefs and Values

As an advocate for change it is essential to know and incorporate one's own beliefs and values into one's work, all the while recognizing the primacy of the institutional mission. In the face of the resistance— and possible hostility—likely to be encountered when raising LGB issues, the importance of being clear about one's own motives and feelings cannot be over emphasized. The extent to which individuals understand themselves vis-a-vis the myriad points that will arise around this issue will determine how grounded and stable they are in their efforts, and thus how they are perceived. Individuals have the greatest potential for influence when they are clearly speaking out of their own, deeply held, convictions and spiritual beliefs.

Advocates of LGB students should have specific knowledge about the tenets of the institution's denomination in regard to sexuality and related issues. Particularly when an individual is in an "expert" position, such as a campus minister or professor of religion, this knowledge can also be a useful tool in responding to questions and challenges and, in turn, to challenging the prevailing cultural assumptions. "Lay" professionals are encouraged to understand the various biblically based arguments against homosexuality and the theological arguments that counter them. A resource list is included at the end of the chapter. One caveat is to be aware of the potential to be drawn into arguments about what the *Bible* does and does not say about homosexuality with individuals who are not truly open to hearing differing opinions.

Develop Ally Networks

It is difficult and tiring to work alone on the issue of sexual orientation in what may be a hostile climate. It is important to find other people who are concerned about the needs of LGB students and bring them together to pool energy and provide mutual support. When seeking allies, do not overlook groups on campus where there may be unsuspected (and powerful) support, such as campus ministry and religious studies departments. It could be seen as surprising that support and allies might be found in these places. One might expect these individuals to be the staunchest "defenders of the faith." Some people in campus ministry, however, typically are tied more closely to the pastoral mission of the institution and some of the ministers may be aware of the struggles, pain, and suffering LGB students are experiencing. Religious studies professors have a more in-depth understanding of the issue vis-a-vis theology, and often are aware of the official religious interpretation regarding sexual orientation (as opposed to the assumed official interpretation). Their understanding of the issues is much more sophisticated than the "it's wrong, it's sick, it's immoral, it's in the *Bible*" type phrase often used by people who use religious beliefs to fuel their homophobia. Other unlikely, though potential, sources for allies include alumni, parents, and the greater religious community. There are bound to be LGB alumni, though the challenge is in finding them. Seeking allies from areas traditionally supportive of issues of marginalization and oppression, such as other student affairs professionals and Women's Studies programs, is important. However, looking in unlikely places has an additional benefit—the more closely allies are tied to the institution and its religious mission, the less likely they will be viewed as countercultural or discounted as outsiders. A well-developed student development committee of the board of trustees also has the potential of being a powerful ally.

In dealing with the needs of LGB students, it is important that the issue of sexual orientation is a top priority for a number of people. Other than during cataclysmic events, culture change requires time and persistence. In addition to general resistance to change, individuals working to meet the needs of students and change attitudes and behaviors regarding sexual orientation at an RAI are faced with being stigmatized and discounted, and being influenced by cultural webs that extend far beyond the boundaries of the campus. Ally networks play an important role because people can get tired of fighting an uphill battle. LGB people may remain closeted or leave. Heterosexual allies can become comfortable with the status quo, where most homophobia is subtle or out of sight. Allies need to maintain an active network so that they can support one another and continue to keep this issue a high priority.

Be Realistic

It is easy to feel discouraged or hopeless when change either occurs slowly or does not seem to be happening at all. It can be very helpful at those times to remember the nature of the change process. Organizational culture change occurs slowly—even more so than individual change. The movement generally takes place in small steps, and not all of those are steps forward! Often after some movement has been made there will be a period of stasis or retrenchment. Though this may look and feel like back-sliding, often these "rest periods" are periods of reflecting on and internalizing the changes that have just been made. This is a necessary precursor to future and additional development. Similarly, "backlash" reactions or responses are often indicative of members of the community's traditional power base feeling threatened. At one Baptist school, alumni, in particular, were described as disgruntled over the "degree to which the college is falling away from its principles" when LGB issues began to be addressed. While such reactions are frustrating and potentially demoralizing, remembering that they can be pointing to the fact that previously unheard voices are now making an impact can be tremendously helpful. Another aspect of organizational change to bear in mind is that it rarely occurs from the top down—at least around controversial issues. The amount of grass-roots energy needed to help shift an RAI's stance on sexuality is great, and will require on-going effort from a large number of people.

Because it is so easy to get mired in the fear that things can not change, it is vital to celebrate the successes experienced and steps made. They do add up, and while the process is slow, culture-transforming change can occur! Signs of light are appearing at a number of RAIs. These include a Midwestern, Lutheran college where LGB and allies groups are recognized and funded by the Student Senate, sexual orientation has been added to the college's non-discrimination statement, and increasing numbers of faculty and staff are coming out on campus.

Our LGB students on all campuses need our support to help create climates that respect, honor and celebrate their lives and membership in our communities. At those RAIs where the challenges discussed in this chapter exist our call for action is of particularly vital importance. In addition to the suggestions we have presented, in Chapter 14 of this text DuMontier discusses issues related to faith development of GLB students that may also help us to deal with the special challenges that exist at many RAIs. Together these suggestions provide approaches that can aid us in initiating and maintaining the momentum needed to make religiously affiliated campuses more inclusive and welcoming places for the lesbian, gay and bisexual members of our communities.

Additional Resources

Coleman, G. D. (1995). *Homosexuality: Catholic teaching and pastoral practice*. New York: Paulist Press.

Estanek, S. M. (1996). A study of student affairs practice at Catholic colleges and universities. *ACCU Current Issues, 16* (2), 63-72.

McNeill, J. (1993). *The Church and the homosexual*. Boston: Beacon Press.

References

American College Personnel Association/National Association of Student Personnel Administrators (1998). *The principles of good practice in student affairs.* Washington, DC: ACPA/NASPA.

American Bishops (1976). To live in Christ Jesus: A pastoral reflection on the moral life. *Pastoral Letters, 14,* 170-195.

American Council on Education (1937). *The student personnel point of view.* Washington, DC: American Council on Education.

Cass, V. C. (1979). Homosexual identity formation: A theoretical model. *Journal of Homosexuality, 4,* 219-235.

Coleman, G. D. (1995). *Homosexuality: Catholic teaching and pastoral practice.* Mahwah, NJ: Paulist Press.

Congregation for the Doctrine of the Faith. (1975). *Declaration on certain questions concerning sexual ethics.* Rome: Vatican City.

D'Augelli, A. R. (1991). Gay men in college: Identity processes and adaptations. *Journal of College Student Development, 32,* 140-146.

Estanek, S. M. (1996). A study of student affairs practice at Catholic colleges and universities. *ACCU Current Issues, 16* (2), 63-72.

Gibson, P. (1989). Gay male and lesbian youth suicide. In ADAMHA, *Report of the Secretary's Task Force on Youth Suicide*, Vol. 3 (DHHS Publication No. ADM 89-1623). Washington, DC: U. S. Government Printing Office.

Gochros, J. S. (1985). Wives' reactions to learning that their husbands are bisexual. *Journal of Homosexuality, 11,* 101-113.

Goffman, E. (1963). *Stigma: Notes on the management of a spoiled identity.* Englewood Cliffs, NY: Prentice-Hall.

Gutierrez, F. J. (1987, March). *Managing the campus ecology of gay/lesbian students on Catholic college campuses.* Paper presented at the annual meeting of the American College Personnel Association, Chicago, IL. (ERIC Document Reproduction Service No. ED 324 612)

Herdt, G. (1989). Introduction: Gay and lesbian youth, emergent identities, and cultural scenes at home and abroad. *Journal of Homosexuality, 17,* 1-42.

Kuh, G. D. (1989). Organizational concepts and influences. In U. Delworth & G. R. Hanson (Eds.), *Student services: A handbook for the profession* (2nd ed., pp. 209-242), San Francisco: Jossey-Bass.

Kuh, G. D., & Whitt, E. J. (1988). *The invisible tapestry: Culture in American colleges and universities.* ASHE-ERIC Higher Education Report, No. 1. Washington, DC: American Association for Higher Education.

Love, P. (1997). Contradiction and paradox: Attempting to change the culture of sexual orientation at a small Catholic college. *Review of Higher Education, 20,* 381-398.

Love, P. (1993, November). *Organizational and individual factors in the establishment of a lesbian, gay, and bisexual organization at a church-related college.* Paper presented at the annual meeting of the Association for the Study of Higher Education, Pittsburgh, PA.

Maret, S. M. (1984). Attitudes of fundamentalist toward homosexuality. *Psychology Reports, 55* (1), 205-206.

Money, J. (1988). The development of sexual orientation. *The Harvard Medical School Mental Health Letter, 4,* 4-6.

Moore, L. V., & Upcraft, M. L. (1990). Theory in student affairs: Evolving perspectives. In L. V. Moore (Ed.), *Evolving theoretical perspectives on students* (New Directions for Student Services, No. 51, pp. 3-23). San Francisco: Jossey-Bass.

Norris, W. P. (1992). Liberal attitudes and homophobic acts: The paradoxes of homosexual experience in a liberal institution. In K. M. Harbeck (Ed.), *Coming out of the classroom closet* (pp. 81-120). New York: Harrington Park Press.

Pavela, G. (1995). *The power of association: Defining our relationship with students in the 21st century.* Washington, DC: NASPA.

Perry, W. G., Jr. (1970). *Forms of intellectual and ethical development in the college years: A scheme.* Troy, MI: Holt, Rhinehart & Winston.

Pfuhl, E. H., Jr. (1986). *The deviance process* (2nd ed.). Belmont, CA: Wadsworth.

Ratzinger, J. (1986). Letter to the bishops of the Catholic Church on the pastoral care of homosexual persons. *The Pope Speaks, 31,* 62-68.

Rhoads, R. A. (1994). *Coming out in college: The struggle for a queer identity.* Westport, CT: Bergin & Garvey.

Sandin, R. T. (1991). *HEPS profiles of independent higher education* (vol. 1, no. 1). Lake Forest, IL: Higher Education Planning Services.

Senate of Priests (1983). *Ministry and homosexuality in the Archdiocese of San Francisco.* San Francisco.

Sigelman, C. K., Howell, J. L., Cornell, D. P., Cutright, J. D., & Dewey, J. C. (1991). Courtesy stigma: The social implication of associating with a gay person. *Journal of Social Psychology, 131,* 45-56.

Young, R. B., & Elfrink, V. L. (1991). Essential values of student affairs work. *Journal of College Student Development, 32,* 47-55.

Chapter 5

෩ෞ

Issues for Lesbian, Gay, and Bisexual Students in Traditional College Classrooms

MARK CONNOLLY

*I*t was her introductory logic and reasoning class during her sophomore year that was Sophie's favorite. She especially liked it because the instructor often used real-life examples to illustrate complex philosophical concepts. During one class, the instructor noted that the class had not completely grasped the difference between a necessary and a sufficient condition. "Let me try this as an example," said the instructor. She walked down one of the rows of the classroom and, standing next to Sophie, asked her, "Sophia, what would you look for in a husband?"

Caught off guard but not wanting to say what was really on her mind, Sophie replied, "Uh, probably somebody who was thoughtful."

"Okay, great," said the instructor. "Now, would thoughtfulness be a sufficient or a necessary condition for your marrying someone? Anybody?" The instructor moved farther into the class and continued to develop her example with other members of the class. However, Sophie's thoughts

were far from logic and reasoning. Instead, her mind incessantly replayed the exchange with the instructor in her mind, asking "Did I say the right thing? Or will people suspect from that lame answer of mine that I'm a lesbian?"

That the climate of most college and university campuses is unfriendly and seldom nurturing for lesbian, gay, and bisexual (LGB) students is unfortunately all too commonplace (Rhoads, 1995; Tierney, 1992). LGB students regularly face acts of aggression in settings both public and private, on campus and off (Cage, 1993; Slater, 1993). However, perhaps because reports of physical violence against LGB students reveal that many of the most egregious acts tend to occur in students' residences, on campus grounds, and at off-campus locations, violence against LGB students is often considered a student life issue and left for student affairs offices to address. Although the involvement of student affairs offices is essential to creating a safe and just campus climate, student affairs administrators and practitioners often have no control and very little influence in ensuring the safety of LGB students in the most influential and commonly shared environment on the college campus: the classroom. Indeed, the curricular life of the campus and the faculty's role in shaping it may be the most important influences upon campus climate (Smith, 1990; Tierney & Bensimon, 1996).

Recent literature on LGB college students has covered a variety of important topics, including coming out experiences (Rhoads, 1994), legal rights (Liddell & Douvanis, 1994), the effectiveness of student affairs offices in serving the needs of LGB students (Croteau & Lark, 1995) and campus climate (for example, Herek, 1993; Yeskel, 1991). Evans and Wall's (1991) volume addressed lesbian and gay issues in campus environments such as residence halls (Bourassa & Shipton, 1991), fraternities and sororities (Hughes, 1991), and student groups and organizations (Scott, 1991). Despite efforts to make LGB students' experiences more visible and more important, little attention has been paid to their experiences in the classroom environment.

Considering the central role of the college classroom experience in students' educational achievement, why its role in influencing campus climate has been frequently overlooked remains a mystery. One hypothesis for why the classroom environment for LGB students is not explored with the same urgency as out-of-class environments is because the classroom setting is often considered to be a safe place, one that is value-neutral and carefully managed by well-trained and objective instructors (Sherrill & Hardesty, 1994).

Such assumptions of safety, neutrality, and objectivity, however, are ill-founded (Bensimon, 1994a; Halpern, 1994). The typical classroom perpetuates the same homophobic prejudices and heterosexist attitudes as the campus and society at large. And although the threat of physical violence to LGB students is greatly diminished in the classroom setting, they nevertheless are subjected to psychological violence that can result from being systematically silenced and misrepresented.

The purpose of this chapter, then, is to examine important issues for LGB students *qua* students. First, it examines the myth of the classroom as a value-neutral environment and how efforts to diversify the curriculum often neglect LGB perspectives. Second, it uses a continuum framework to name and organize classroom environments that tend to include or exclude the experiences of LGB students. Finally, it suggests how faculty and student affairs staff can transform the traditional classroom setting into one where LGB students feel safe, affirmed, and empowered.

Making Classrooms More Multicultural

Throughout the history of higher education in the United States, college and university students have engaged most often in learning activities in environments that might be described as *traditional classrooms*. Considering that college classes are taught in diverse environments ranging from lecture halls and laboratories to rehearsal rooms and faculty homes, traditional classrooms are not necessarily physical settings. Rather, they are characterized principally by a belief that both their curricular content (that is, what is taught) and instructional strategies (that is, how it is taught) are objective and value-neutral (Adams, 1992). Furthermore, it is assumed that because content and instruction are not culturally bound, students' cultural perspectives do not influence what they already know, what they need to know, and how they learn it. Consequently, in the traditional classroom, it is assumed that students' success in intellectual endeavors varies only according to the amount of effort they expend in academic activities such as writing papers and participating in class.

However, it has become more apparent in recent decades that the traditional classroom is indeed a manifestation of particular cultural beliefs and assumptions. According to Adams (1992), the traditional classroom embodies an "academic culture," derived mainly from European culture, imported and cultivated by nineteenth- and twentieth-century European descendants and immigrants. Despite a long-held and pervasive belief that the traditional college classroom is an equal opportunity environment, it excludes members of social target groups, such as women, persons of color, people with disabilities, and lesbians and gays, and privileges members of dominant social groups (for example, Whites, men, able-bodied persons, heterosexuals) whose background and prior schooling experiences may be most similar to established norms.

In addition to embodying academic culture, traditional classrooms also reflect a culture of power (Delpit, 1995). That is, classrooms are places where power imbalances between social groups are enacted and often replicated. As in society at large, the traditional classroom reflects the rules and norms of those who belong to dominant social groups. Those who hold social power (for example, men, Whites) are frequently least aware of—or least willing to acknowledge—its existence and the privilege it brings. Those with less power are often most aware of its existence (Delpit, 1995; McIntosh, 1995).

Colleges and universities have recently taken steps to offer students educational experiences that better incorporate human diversity (Carnegie Foundation, 1992; Levine & Cureton, 1992). However, most institutional efforts to include underrepresented perspectives in the classroom have focused primarily on improving the representation of women and people of color (Sherrill & Hardesty, 1994). In many cases, institutional definitions of multiculturalism used to direct campus policy implicitly or explicitly exclude lesbian, bisexual, and gay persons (Pope, 1995). Implicit exclusion suggests that although an institution may espouse the protection and inclusion of persons on the basis of sexual orientation, its actions instead reveal that its disenfranchised groups are configured in a "hierarchy of oppression" in which some—such as women or African Americans—are seen as more "legitimate" than lesbians, gays, and bisexuals.

Another explanation for why the curriculum has changed little to include issues of sexual orientation can be found in understanding the different approaches to curricular change. Bensimon (1994b) explained that the model used most frequently for creating an inclusive curriculum can be described as human relations multiculturalism (Sleeter & Grant, 1987). Although this approach is useful for its emphasis on understanding human difference and teaching tolerance, it overlooks conflict and tension among different groups and ignores the structures that perpetuate power imbalances. Because examination of differences in this model is largely limited to race and gender, sexual orientation is more likely to be ignored (Bensimon, 1994b).

To lesbian, gay, and bisexual students, the traditional classroom is a reflection of the power and privilege held in the United States by heterosexuals and the concomitant oppression of non-heterosexuals. Social norms suggesting that only male-female relationships are normal and same-sex relationships are abnormal constitute a culture of heterosexist power that is, in turn, unquestioningly enacted in traditional college classrooms. To the majority of students and instructors who benefit from heterosexual privilege, the enforcement of these norms is not evident in traditional classrooms. Yet, gay, lesbian, and bisexual students are acutely aware of the myriad ways in which pedagogy and curriculum collude to force their silence (DeSurra & Church, 1994; Lopez & Chism, 1993).

Because of the lack of understanding about the oppression and implicit violence that LGB students face regularly in the traditional college classroom (Slater, 1993), student affairs professionals and faculty need to know more about these unsafe settings and how they affect all students. That is, homophobic and heterosexist classrooms not only oppress LGB students but also send powerful messages to heterosexual students legitimizing institutionalized homophobia and heterosexism.

Constructing One's Identity in the Classroom

College is a time—particularly for traditional-age students—for exploring and defining identity (Lehman, 1978). For lesbian and gay students, the process of developing a sense of identity can be complicated even further by the process of coming out—to oneself, to family, to friends, to classmates (D'Augelli, 1994; Rhoads, 1994). Lesbian and gay students tend to reflect often about their identity, seeking to decide who they are, how they should represent themselves to others, and which battles they will fight (Lopez & Chism, 1993).

For lesbian and gay students, the classroom is yet another social setting in which they must constantly assess the level of risk they face and negotiate the extent to which they may self-disclose (Malinowitz, 1995). However, unlike the meaningful conversations that students typically encounter in other social settings (for example, a party or a work site), the discourse that occurs in a college classroom is often perceived as being more legitimate, more powerful. The college classroom is not simply a means of acquiring information, but it is also a highly influential social context in which students participate in the construction of knowledge—of others and of self—in the company of two groups that influence students most during college: peers and faculty (Pascarella & Terenzini, 1991). Because of the impact of the classroom experience and how it reflects or denies one's sense of identity, what occurs in the college classroom may have profound effects on how some lesbian and gay students experience coming out.

A Continuum of Classroom Experiences of LGB Students

In a study of the classroom experiences of lesbian and gay college students, DeSurra and Church (1994) described a "marginalizing-centralizing" continuum that represented the extent to which LGB students perceived messages that signaled whether LGB perspectives would be included or excluded in their classes. To further classify the respondents' experiences, DeSurra and Church indicated whether the messages that shaped the classroom environment were either explicit or implicit. The resulting continuum reflected the degree to which classroom environments were explicitly marginalizing, implicitly marginalizing, implicitly centralizing, and explicitly centralizing.

Using DeSurra and Church's (1994) continuum as a framework to move from the most hostile environments to the most nurturing, I will describe how LGB students may interpret messages experienced while participating in classroom activities, such as interacting with faculty and peers, scrutinizing course content, managing homework and research assignments, and so forth. In short, I will use the framework to describe how many LGB students encounter and respond to the three principal problems of the heterosexist academy: bigotry, ignorance, and silence (Tierney, 1992).

Explicit Marginalization

"Well, you might not think this is such a great poem if you knew that the poet wrote it with his 'butt buddy' in mind." [Comment by instructor about a gay poet.]

A classroom environment that is explicitly marginalizing is characterized by overt homophobic messages and behaviors from either the instructor or the students that go unchallenged. In some cases, such bigoted statements and threatening behaviors occur during class for all students to hear; in other circumstances, hateful remarks may be made in less public contexts, such as among a group of students in the back of the room or during a one-to-one interaction with the instructor. Regardless of the manner by which an LGB student is subjected to such bigotry, the intentions are unmistakably the same: to make it clear that bisexuals, lesbians, and gays are not safe—let alone welcomed—in this setting.

Another way in which LGB students can receive signals that they and their perspectives are being explicitly excluded from the classroom is through the use of instructional materials (such as books, articles, movies) that openly denigrate lesbians, gays, and bisexuals. For example, an instructor who uses a text in a religion class that proclaims that homosexuality is wicked and sinful provides all students in the class with the clear message that being gay is wrong and gay perspectives will not be easily tolerated in the classroom. Similarly, instructors send strong signals about the exclusion of LGB perspectives when they conspicuously omit LGB perspectives and issues from course materials or discussions that would typically warrant their inclusion (such as a human sexuality course).

This type of classroom environment, while not the most common, is certainly the most oppressive and threatening. Not only does its overt bigotry seek to intimidate and silence LGB students, but the unwillingness of instructors and classmates to interrupt or condemn such behavior reveals their complicity—either intentional or unintentional—in a conspiracy of hatred. Faced with such adverse circumstances, LGB students often enact a number of different responses. DeSurra and Church (1994) categorized student responses to messages received in classroom settings and suggested that how LGB students will respond is shaped by whether they are self-assured or self-conscious in their identity as lesbian, gay, or bisexual. Students who are more self-assured are more likely to respond to homophobic behaviors by saying something to repudiate the remark. However, students who are more self-conscious of their gay identity are more likely not to respond outwardly. As DeSurra and Church (1994) point out, a student's decision to remain silent does not suggest that she or he was not affected by the behavior; rather, the researchers' findings suggest that students who opt not to confront homophobic remarks are deeply affected, sometimes haunted by feelings of either failure for not responding or irritation for having had to endure such a hateful and painful experience. And, for some LGB students, the cumulative effects of oppressive classroom experiences lead them to drop out of the institution entirely. Although some LGB students may return when they feel more comfortable with themselves (that is, self-assured) and can concentrate more on their academic responsibilities (DeSurra & Church, 1994), others will never return.

Implicit Marginalization

On the first day of class, the professor had asked the students in his graduate seminar in school administration to propose topics they wished to explore during the semester. After two students suggested discussing working with parents and promoting teachers' professional development, one student, Colin, spoke up: "I'd like our class to talk about gay and lesbian adolescents and what our schools can do to support them."

A few of Colin's classmates contemptuously rolled their eyes; his bringing up "the gay thing" in every class was something they had come to expect. The professor's brow tightened as he said, "I'm not sure that's relevant to this class topic. Does anybody else think we should talk about this?" Everybody but Colin sat silently staring at the seminar table. After a few moments, the professor said, "Sorry, but it appears that nobody else is interested in this issue. Maybe you can bring it up in a different class."

Classroom environments that are implicitly marginalizing are characterized by subtle, indirect messages from both students and the instructor; that is, if explicitly marginalizing classrooms are outspokenly homophobic, then implicitly marginalizing classrooms are more subtle in their heterosexism. Despite the absence of outspoken hatred toward gays, the implicitly marginalizing classroom nevertheless employs a more covert language shared among heterosexuals that proclaims that heterosexuality is the norm, and although gays, bisexuals, and lesbians may not be evil, they are nevertheless abnormal, the "Other."

Classrooms that project implicit messages of oppression and marginalization are probably more commonplace than the more explicitly marginalizing classes mentioned above. Part of the reason why classroom homophobia takes this more covert yet similarly virulent form is because it appears to be less contentious. That is, LGB students do not encounter naked hatred that even heterosexuals students cannot overlook; rather, LGB students must withstand the invidious effects of indifference, ignorance, and "good" intentions—a death of a thousand cuts. Because oppression perpetuated by means other than outright aggression and hatred is less obvious, it is more difficult to identify and therefore confront (Yamoto, 1995).

Such classrooms are characterized most of all by invisibility and ignorance. While LGB issues are not openly criticized, they also are not acknowledged. Throughout the curriculum, whether it be in the fields of education, biology, or religious studies, little information about lesbians, bisexuals, and gays exists, and what does exist simply serves to reinforce stereotypes. For all intents and purposes, lesbian, gay, and bisexual sexual orientations are not considered to be topics worthy of scholarly examination except as examples of deviance.

The manner of instruction used in the classroom also conveys innumerable implicit messages about the worth of lesbian, gay, and bisexual people. The seemingly innocuous use of heterosexist examples and language perpetuate the notion that heterosexuality is the norm. And, should a student attempt to interject a gay perspective into the class discussion, such a remark in this type of classroom environment often will be barely acknowledged and subsequently ignored. Likewise, students who wish to pursue research topics or homework assignments with an LGB component or focus are frequently encouraged to study a "more meaningful" subject; to continue against the instructor's preferences means they run the risk of their work being graded down solely on the basis of its subject matter.

In this type of classroom, most faculty are not openly antagonistic but nevertheless ignorant of and indifferent to the concerns of LGB people. Their classroom behaviors signal their belief that they do not see the need to include oppressed perspectives. To run the class smoothly and effectively, they believe, it is necessary to avoid conflict, and avoiding conflict entails avoiding the controversial and non-mainstream perspective of gays, lesbians, and bisexuals.

In some cases, well-meaning faculty who believe gay students are present in their classroom will strive to teach in a less heterosexist manner. However, this strategy relies on the faulty assumption that the presence of lesbian, gay, and bisexual students will always be obvious to the instructor. Although these assumptions are sometimes justifiable, as when a student self-identifies as being bisexual, gay, or lesbian to the class or to the instructor in private, there are nevertheless many other times when lesbian, gay, and bisexual students will choose not to self-disclose in class. These students, then, will be assumed to be heterosexual and treated as such.

The practice of making the classroom gay-positive on an "as needed" basis rests on other dangerous but commonplace assumptions. First, faculty may assume that they can rely on their "ability" to identify lesbian, gay, and bisexual students based on stereotypical characteristics, such as their appearance or manner of speaking. When it does not appear that the classroom has any gay students, then the class may be taught as usual. Second, this practice also assumes that the only gay students worth defending, representing, and supporting are those who are out; those who are not out are essentially punished for their silence. Finally, the strategy does heterosexual students a gross disservice in that it fails to see that the use of non-heterosexist language and examples not only makes lesbian, bisexual, and gay students feel included, but it also educates heterosexual students and disallows them the heterosexual privilege of remaining oblivious to the marginalization of lesbians, bisexuals, and gays. Thus, because faculty in this type of classroom setting frequently place responsibility for decentering heterosexist norms upon LGB students and their allies, acknowledgment of sexual orientation issues will not occur when LGB students are not visible in the classroom.

In the implicitly marginalizing classroom, LGB students may feel less threatened than in the explicitly marginalizing classroom. But, because LGB topics are represented either incorrectly or not at all, LGB students frequently find they alone are willing to challenge heterosexist norms by breaking the silence and confronting ignorance and indifference. In such classrooms, LGB students soon discover the risks of speaking up. For example, students who bravely persist in turning the class's attention to marginalized perspectives may soon find that such efforts are seen as pushing a gay agenda in the class. Homophobic classmates will question why homosexuality has to be "shoved down their throats," and instructors will wonder aloud why gay students are so obsessed with bringing their sex life into the classroom. LGB students quickly discover that the exchange of such implicit messages as classmates rolling their eyes or an instructor's brush-off render this classroom environment as oppressive and excluding as nearly every other class they have had.

Some LGB students who must endure oppressive classroom environments are fortunate to locate other settings and activities that are more affirming. However, with their time and energy possibly torn between classes that deny their worth and other people who sustain their sense of identity, LGB students may struggle with academic work (Lopez & Chism, 1993). Unfortunately, from the view of the traditional academic culture, the lack of success of LGB students in fulfilling their academic responsibilities is often attributed to their lack of effort or ability rather than to their alienation in the classroom.

Implicit Centralization

"This guy in my class just kept yammering on about the importance of marriage as a social institution, family values, blah, blah, and I was ready to scream! Usually, I spend so much time rehearsing my response that the discussion has moved on and I miss my chance. This time, however, I took a deep breath and said my piece about how if marriage is so great then why can't gays and lesbians marry, and so on. After a pause that seemed like forever and I'm feeling like Wile E. Coyote hanging in mid-air before the inevitable fall, finally the professor said, "That's a very important point . . ." and then she proceeded to explore the issue. I just thought that was so cool that she kept the topic going." [Student in a sociology class.]

The continuum that DeSurra and Church (1994) used to locate messages that LGB students received in their classes can also include signals that the experiences and perspectives of lesbians, gay men, and bisexual women and men have moved from the social margins to the center of classroom discourse. As with the classroom environments that sought to marginalize these perspectives, centralizing classroom environments are also created through both implicit and explicit messages. Implicitly centralizing classroom environments are generally characterized by unplanned responses by the instructor. For example, whether to challenge an overtly homophobic comment by a student or disclose the heterosexist assumptions of a course reading, these responses make LGB students feel included and represented. However, the unplanned and unpredictable nature of such implicit messages reveals that significant structural changes in the course content and instructional strategies probably have not occurred. Nevertheless, LGB students are often grateful for these implicit messages, perhaps because they yet occur so infrequently (DeSurra & Church, 1994).

Explicit Centralization

"I've had one class that was simply like no other. The university offers a section of Composition 102 that is focused specifically on lesbian and gay themes. Most of the students are queer, but there are a couple of heterosexual women, too. I was a bit nervous at first, but now that the semester is nearly over, I feel like I can be myself in class, that I can write about what matters to me. I feel like I'm just beginning to find my voice. It's been difficult at times, but we've all had so much unlearning to do." [Student in a writing class.]

The explicitly centralizing classroom environment transmits messages that clearly inform students that subjugated knowledges and otherwise marginalized perspectives—including those of lesbian, gay, and bisexual voices—will be actively integrated throughout the course. In these classrooms, faculty are unequivocal in their efforts to bring subjugated perspectives to the center of class discourse. Language and examples used in this type of class not only refrain from using heterosexist terms but also actively seek to introduce examples of bisexuals, lesbians, and gays when possible (McNaron, 1991; Rofes, 1989). The instructor also seeks to reframe the course content to include LGB resources, perspectives, viewpoints, and so forth. Fields such as history, business, education, literature, and other disciplines in the social sciences, humanities, and fine arts seem to be most receptive to including marginalized perspectives (Crew, 1978). Although imagining how to make the content of a physics course more inclusive may be difficult, it is useful to bear in mind that the physical sciences have often served as exemplars of the traditional, academic culture, seeking to remain objective and removed from the realm of human "subjectivities." Thus, making science and math courses more inclusive is possible once instructors acknowledge the importance of introducing biographical information and applying concepts to social concerns (Lopez & Chism, 1993).

In short, this type of classroom, which is the most gay positive, is not characterized simply by a more inclusive type of instruction or taking care to mention that certain historical figures, for example, happened to be lesbian or gay or bisexual. Rather, an explicitly centralizing classroom employs a critical pedagogy, one that explicitly sees the purpose of education as the opportunity to critically interrogate privileged perspectives that are manifest in every discipline and move toward social action that corrects social injustice (Malinowitz, 1995). Through this process of subverting heterosexist norms, LGB students find their own voices and gain self-confidence from constructing a knowledge of themselves that is accurate and positive.

Explicitly inclusive classrooms exist not merely as an ideal; some faculty have begun to implement strategies for including LGB perspectives in a variety of classrooms and disciplines (for example, Aitken, 1993; Chapkis, 1994; Chesler & Zúñiga, 1991; D'Augelli, 1992; González, 1994; Malinowitz, 1995; Warshauer, 1993). Although some are taught by out lesbian and gay faculty (for example, Malinowitz, 1995), some are taught by heterosexual faculty who use their heterosexual privilege and power as instructors to serve as allies to LGB students and colleagues as well as to educate their fellow heterosexuals (Berg, Kowaleski, Le Guin, Weinauer, & Wolfe, 1994; Keating, 1994; Kitch, 1994; Winkler, 1996). Given the enormous number of courses taught in U.S. higher education, the number of such inclusive offerings is quite small, but they nevertheless serve as badly needed models of intellectual creativity and moral courage.

Suggestions for Creating Inclusive Classrooms

Studies of lesbian and gay students' perceptions of college classrooms reveal that faculty are the most important actors in shaping classroom environments, both oppressive and inclusive (DeSurra & Church, 1994; Lopez & Chism, 1993). In most cases, however, faculty treat LGB students with "benign neglect," failing to take any action (McNaron, 1991). The decision not to bring issues of sexual orientation into the center of class discourse in either implicit or explicit ways nevertheless marginalizes LGB students. That is, faculty inertia further feeds the problem (Sears, 1992).

For many faculty, the main obstacle in making their classrooms more inclusive for all groups is not seeing the necessity of change; rather, it is seeing the means to enacting such change in their own classrooms (Wilkerson, 1992). Those teachers who are willing to change yet lack a starting point might reflect upon the following recommendations (Abramson, 1986; Chism & Pruitt, 1995; Rhoads, 1995; Tierney, 1992; Tierney & Bensimon, 1996) for creating inclusive classrooms for LGB students:

1. *Don't assume all of the students in the class are heterosexual.* Although you may never be aware of their presence, lesbian, bisexual, and gay students may compose approximately 10% of your class roster (Fassinger, 1991).
2. *Address students' homophobic comments, even those ostensibly made in jest.* When a person makes a provocative comment in class, students will scrutinize the instructor's response—or lack of one—for clues to what is or is not accepted in the classroom setting. Although one course of action is to address the offensive comment directly, other options that are less confrontational yet still instructive include asking other students in the class to respond or directing class discussion to sexual orientation at a later time when emotions may not be running so strongly.
3. *Challenge heterosexist assumptions.* Traditional classrooms reflect heterosexist norms, and assumptions about heterosexual superiority that underlie such norms are difficult for heterosexuals to recognize, let alone challenge. Unless such assumptions are surfaced and challenged, heterosexual students will continue to believe heterosexuality is simply "the way things are." Be certain to regularly use examples and language that include lesbians, gays, and bisexuals. Turn the use of heterosexist statements into teachable moments.
4. *Be proactive in creating a safe classroom.* Rather than having to react to homophobic comments, communicate your intentions for making the classroom environment safe for LGB students from the outset. For example, if your institution has a statement of anti-discrimination, incorporate it into your syllabus.
5. *Do not rely exclusively on out students to provide "the" gay perspective.* Some LGB students are reluctant to come out in class because they fear being "the class queer," the one who always has to provide the gay perspective. Instructors should give LGB students the space to make choices about speaking up. Being out shouldn't mean having always to be "on."
6. *Educate yourself.* Although faculty have made a career of being life-long learners, they often neglect to employ those skills to teach themselves about the diversity of their students and innovative pedagogical practices. Take time to read about educational inequalities for lesbian and gay students. Encourage and participate in faculty development activities that teach faculty how to make their classrooms safer for LGB students.

7. *Encourage students to explore topics related to sexual orientation in homework and research assignments.* In an effort to help students focus their assignments, faculty often point students in the direction of which topics to examine; unfortunately, students who show an interest in LGB topics are sometimes directed away from them. The pursuit of LGB topics should not only be allowed, it should be represented as an important area of scholarly study and encouraged of all students, regardless of their sexual orientation.

8. *Consider both content and method.* Making classrooms more inclusive involves not only changing instructional techniques, such as using non-heterosexist examples to illustrate a point. Truly inclusive classroom environments require a corresponding transformation of curricular content, moving LGB perspectives from the margins to the center of the course when possible. Although attending to the tenor of class discussions is critical, making only cosmetic changes to class discussions while leaving the misrepresentation of lesbians, bisexuals, and gays in course texts unchallenged and intact will never create a classroom that will be truly inclusive of LGB students.

Dealing with Unresponsive Faculty

The recommendations above, of course, are of greatest use to those who wish to create explicitly centralizing classrooms for LGB students; they are offered with the assumption that some faculty have an interest in effecting substantive changes in how they teach and what their students learn. But, what about faculty who have no interest in the inclusion and visibility of LGB students? What can LGB students do when they must take classes with an instructor who has no interest in acknowledging the marginalization they experience regularly in the classroom?

Improving classroom climates under these conditions is much more difficult, for if faculty will not change of their own volition, impelling them to change how and what they teach will threaten the principles of academic freedom and autonomy that are core faculty values in higher education in the United States (Austin, 1990). In some cases, the solution for the student might be as simple as moving to a different class section in the hope that the new section's instructor will not be as homophobic. However, this strategy avoids the problem rather than addressing it. And, when LGB students are trapped in a required class, avoidance is not a viable option. Furthermore, the power imbalance between students and faculty may mean a student who complains will be punished in covert ways (for example, receiving lower grades on subjectively evaluated assignments).

Consequently, the decision to resist an oppressive and uncooperative faculty member should be considered carefully. An important factor to assess when making such a decision is the quality of the campus climate and the sources of support it provides for LGB students. For example, does the institution have campus offices or organizations, such as an LGB student center or a student advocate's office, that will help students organize a response? Are there out LGB faculty or faculty allies to consult for advice? Has the institution a history of responding to similar situations?

LGB students who enlist the assistance of others, both on and off the campus, may find they can achieve greater changes at a decreased personal expense. However, the absence of such sources of support and assistance does not portend the failure of an LGB student's efforts to resist an oppressive instructor. Indeed, the emerging history of lesbians and gays reveals that their subjugation does not ensure their silence and resignation; sometimes the force of conviction of just one person serves to bring an end to an oppressive condition and inspires others to take action. Although some LGB students will need and want the support and encouragement of others when taking a stand, many others need no assistance to exhibit the courage and perseverance of their LGB antecedents to enact social justice on their campuses and in their communities.

The Role of Student Affairs Professionals

This chapter's discussion of the issues lesbian, gay, and bisexual students face in traditional college classrooms has emphasized the role faculty play in shaping classroom environments. Although the formal curriculum is traditionally within the purview of faculty, focusing exclusively on faculty as change agents suggests indirectly and wrongly that student affairs professionals cannot or should not influence what occurs inside college classrooms. When student affairs professionals act as transformative educators, they play a crucial role in influencing the institutional culture and campus climate within which students learn and develop (Rhoads & Black, 1995), which in turn can affect how students learn and faculty teach.

One of the most influential ways for student affairs professionals to facilitate the development of inclusive classrooms is through helping faculty think about students with greater complexity. Whether through formal faculty development efforts or through informal consultation with an individual instructor, student affairs staff can share their expertise in promoting student development and learning to help faculty construct a more complete picture of their students. In addition to working directly with faculty, student affairs staff can also influence them by modeling gay-positive attitudes and practices. Of course, student affairs professionals play a valuable role in fostering more inclusive classrooms when they serve as allies to LGB students who encounter hostile or indifferent academic settings. Not only can student affairs staff offer students reassurance and encouragement, but staff can also help them identify other sources of support and explore ways of effecting positive change. Furthermore, student affairs professionals often have the opportunity to teach classes themselves (for instance, courses for resident assistants and peer helpers, seminars for first-year students). Using the recommendations above, student affairs professionals can establish explicitly centralizing classrooms and encourage both LGB and heterosexual students to think differently about themselves, one another, and the classroom setting they share. Finally, student affairs professionals can apply these recommendations to other educational settings, such as staff meetings, planned presentations, and so forth.

Concluding Thoughts

Because of their invisibility as a group, lesbian, bisexual, and gay students frequently experience classroom environments that are either directly or indirectly hostile towards them. In some classrooms, LGB students are subjected to overtly bigoted messages that lesbians and gays are morally and ethically deviant and deserve to be punished. In still other classrooms, LGB students receive signals about their lack of worth by what is not said about them. These oppressive conditions often persist at institutions that purport to celebrate human diversity. Despite their valiant efforts in the midst of educational neglect, LGB students may struggle in their development of an authentic sense of identity and experience difficulty succeeding academically.

Fortunately, the negative messages that constitute oppressive classroom environments can be counteracted to help LGB students establish a sense of belonging and worth as they make sense of themselves and other people. The key to transforming exclusive classrooms into inclusive classrooms is speaking out and refusing to allow lesbians, gays, and bisexuals—both in the classroom and in the canon—to remain invisible. Although acts of student resistance are crucial, the power to enact these changes lies primarily in those who teach and lead such classes. The act of curricular and pedagogical transformation requires bravery and dedication, but its central aim—naming and changing oppressive social structures—has the potential to create academic environments that are safe and inclusive for all students.

References

Abramson, A. (1986). *TA's guide for overcoming homophobia in the classroom.* Berkeley, CA: University of California.

Adams, M. (1992). Cultural inclusion in the American college classroom. In L. L. B. Border & N. V. N. Chism (Eds.), *Teaching for diversity* (New Directions for Teaching and Learning, No. 49, pp. 5-17). San Francisco: Jossey-Bass.

Aitken, J. E. (1993, November). *"Privileges": A student activity designed to increase interpersonal communication competence regarding gay and lesbian concerns.* Paper presented at the annual meeting of the Speech Communication Association, Miami, FL.

Austin, A. E. (1990). Faculty cultures, faculty values. In W. G. Tierney (Ed.), *Assessing academic cultures and climates* (New Directions for Institutional Research, No. 68, pp. 61-74). San Francisco: Jossey-Bass.

Bensimon, E. M. (Ed.). (1994a). *Multicultural teaching and learning: Strategies for change in higher education.* University Park: Pennsylvania State University, National Center on Postsecondary Teaching, Learning, and Assessment.

Bensimon, E. M. (1994b). Philosophical concepts: The contested meanings of multicultural education. In E. M. Bensimon (Ed.), *Multicultural teaching and learning: Strategies for change in higher education* (pp. 7-18). University Park: Pennsylvania State University, National Center on Postsecondary Teaching, Learning, and Assessment.

Berg, A., Kowaleski, J., Le Guin, C., Weinauer, E., & Wolfe, E. A. (1994). In L. Garber (Ed.), *Tilting the tower: Lesbians, teaching, queer subjects* (pp. 108-116). New York: Routledge.

Bourassa, D., & Shipton, B. (1991). Addressing lesbian and gay issues in residence hall environments. In N. J. Evans & V. A. Wall (Eds.), *Beyond tolerance: Gays, lesbians and bisexuals on campus* (pp. 79-96). Lanham, MD: American College Personnel Association.

Cage, M. C. (1993, March 10). Gay students face backlash of assaults and harassment. *Chronicle of Higher Education,* p. A22.

Carnegie Foundation for the Advancement of Teaching. (1992, January-February). Signs of a changing curriculum. *Change, 24,* 49-52.

Chapkis, W. (1994). Explicit instruction: Talking sex in the classroom. In L. Garber (Ed.), *Tilting the tower: Lesbians, teaching, queer subjects* (pp. 11-15). New York: Routledge.

Chesler, M. A., & Zúñiga, X. (1991). Dealing with prejudice and conflict in the classroom: The pink triangle exercise. *Teaching Sociology, 19,* 173-181.

Chism, N. V. N., & Pruitt, A. S. (1995). Promoting inclusiveness in college teaching. In W. A. Wright (Ed.), *Teaching improvement practices: Successful strategies for higher education* (pp. 325-345). Bolton, MA: Anker.

Crew, L. (Ed.). (1978). *The gay academic.* Palm Springs, CA: ETS Publications.

Croteau, J. M., & Lark, J. S. (1995). A qualitative investigation of biased and exemplary student affairs practice concerning lesbian, gay, and bisexual issues. *Journal of College Student Development, 36,* 472-482.

D'Augelli, A. R. (1992). Teaching lesbian/gay development: From oppression to exceptionality. In K. M. Harbeck (Ed.), *Coming out of the classroom closet: Gay and lesbian students, teachers, and curricula* (pp. 213-227). New York: Harrington Park.

D'Augelli, A. R. (1994). Identity development and sexual orientation: Toward a model of lesbian, gay, and bisexual development. In E. J. Trickett, R. J. Watts, & D. Birman (Eds.), *Human diversity: Perspectives on people in context.* San Francisco: Jossey-Bass.

Delpit, L. (1995). *Other people's children: Cultural conflict in the classroom.* New York: The New Press.

DeSurra, C. J., & Church, K. A. (1994, November). *Unlocking the classroom closet: Privileging the marginalized voices of gay/lesbian college students.* Paper presented at the annual meeting of the Speech Communication Association, New Orleans, LA.

Evans, N. J., & Wall, V. A. (Eds.).(1991). *Beyond tolerance: Gays, lesbians and bisexuals on campus.* Lanham, MD: American College Personnel Association.

Fassinger, R. E. (1991). The hidden minority: Issues and challenges in working with lesbian women and gay men. *The Counseling Psychologist, 19,* 157-176.

González, M. C. (1994). Cultural conflict: Introducing the queer in Mexican-American literature classes. In L. Garber (Ed.), *Tilting the tower: Lesbians, teaching, queer subjects* (pp. 56-62). New York: Routledge.

Halpern, D., & Associates (Eds.). (1994). *Changing college classrooms: New teaching and learning strategies for an increasingly complex world.* San Francisco: Jossey-Bass.

Herek, G. (1993). Documenting prejudice against lesbians and gay men on campus: The Yale sexual orientation survey. *Journal of Homosexuality, 25*(4), 15-30.

Hughes, M. J. (1991). Addressing gay, lesbian, and bisexual issues in fraternities and sororities. In N. J. Evans & V. A. Wall (Eds.), *Beyond tolerance: Gays, lesbians and bisexuals on campus* (pp. 97-116). Lanham, MD: American College Personnel Association.

Keating, A. (1994). Heterosexual teacher, lesbian/gay/bisexual text: Teaching the sexual other(s). In L. Garber (Ed.), *Tilting the tower: Lesbians, teaching, queer subjects* (pp. 96-107). New York: Routledge.

Kitch, S. (1994). Straight but not narrow: A gynetic approach to the teaching of lesbian literature. In L. Garber (Ed.), *Tilting the tower: Lesbians, teaching, queer subjects* (pp. 83-95). New York: Routledge.

Lehman, J. L. (1978). Gay students. In J. Crew (Ed.), *The gay academic* (pp. 57-63). Palm Springs, CA: ETS Publications.

Levine, A., & Cureton, J. (1992, January-February). The quiet revolution: Eleven facts about multiculturalism and the curriculum. *Change, 24,* 25-29.

Liddell, D. L., & Douvanis, C. J. (1994). The social and legal status of gay and lesbian students: An update for colleges and universities. *NASPA Journal, 31,* 121-129.

Lopez, G., & Chism, N. (1993). Classroom concerns of gay and lesbian students: The invisible minority. *College Teaching, 41,* 97-103.

Malinowitz, H. (1995). *Textual orientations: Lesbian and gay students and the making of discourse communities.* Portsmouth, NH: Boynton/Cook.

McIntosh, P. (1995). White privilege and male privilege: A personal account of coming to see correspondences through work in women's studies. In M. L. Andersen & P. Hill Collins (Eds.), *Race, class, and gender: An anthology* (2nd ed., pp. 76-87). Belmont, CA: Wadsworth.

McNaron, T. (1991, Winter). Making life more livable for gays and lesbians on campus: Sightings from the field. *Educational Record, 72*(1), 19-22.

Mittler, M. L., & Blumenthal, A. (1994). On being a change agent: Teacher as text, homophobia as context. In L. Garber (Ed.), *Tilting the tower: Lesbians, teaching, queer subjects* (pp. 3-10). New York: Routledge.

Pascarella, E. T., & Terenzini, P. T. (1991). *How college affects students: Insights and findings from twenty years of research.* San Francisco: Jossey-Bass.

Pope, M. (1995). The salad bowl is big enough for us all: An argument for the inclusion of lesbians and gay men in any definition of multiculturalism. *Journal of Counseling and Development, 73,* 301-304.

Rhoads, R. A. (1994). *Coming out in college: The struggle for a queer identity.* Westport, CT: Bergin & Garvey.

Rhoads, R. A. (1995, January 27). The campus climate for gay students who leave "the closet." *The Chronicle of Higher Education,* p. A56.

Rhoads, R. A., & Black, M. A. (1995). Student affairs practitioners as transformative educators: Advancing a critical cultural perspective. *Journal of College Student Development, 36,* 413-421.

Rofes, E. (1989). Opening up the classroom closet: Responding to the educational needs of gay and lesbian youth. *Harvard Educational Review, 59,* 444-453.

Scott, D. (1991). Working with gay and lesbian student organizations. In N. J. Evans & V. A. Wall (Eds.), *Beyond tolerance: Gays, lesbians and bisexuals on campus* (pp. 117-130). Lanham, MD: American College Personnel Association.

Sears, J. T. (1992). Educators, homosexuality, and homosexual students: Are personal feelings related to professional beliefs? In K. M. Harbeck (Ed.), *Coming out of the classroom closet: Gay and lesbian students, teachers, and curricula* (pp. 29-79). New York: Harrington Park.

Sherrill, J., & Hardesty, C. A. (1994). *The gay, lesbian, and bisexual students' guide to colleges, universities, and graduate schools.* New York: New York University Press.

Slater, B. (1993). Violence against lesbian and gay male college students. In L. C. Whitaker & J. W. Pollard (Eds.), *Campus violence: Kinds, causes, and cures* (pp. 177-202). New York: Haworth.

Sleeter, C. E., & Grant, C. A. (1987). An analysis of multicultural education in the United States. *Harvard Educational Review, 57,* 421-444.

Smith, D. G. (1990, December). Embracing diversity as a central campus goal. *Academe, 76,* 29-33.

Tierney, W. G. (1992, March-April). Building academic communities of difference: Gays, lesbians, and bisexuals on campus. *Change, 24,* 41-46.

Tierney, W. G., & Bensimon, E. M. (1996). Supporting diversity through campus culture. In R. J. Menges, M. Weimer, & Associates (Eds.), *Teaching on solid ground: Using scholarship to improve practice* (pp. 337-362). San Francisco: Jossey-Bass.

Warshauer, S. C. (1993, April). *Rethinking teacher authority to counteract prejudice in discussions of gay/lesbian/bisexual representation: A model of teacher response in the networked computer classroom.* Paper presented at the annual meeting of the Conference on College Composition and Communication, San Diego, CA.

Wilkerson, M. B. (1992, January-February). Beyond the graveyard: Engaging faculty involvement. *Change, 24,* 59-63.

Winkler, B. S. (1996). Straight teacher/queer classroom: Teaching as an ally. In K. J. Mayberry (Ed.), *Teaching what you're not: Identity politics in higher education* (pp. 47-69). New York: New York University Press.

Yamoto, G. (1995). Something about the subject makes it hard to name. In M. L. Andersen & P. Hill Collins (Eds.), *Race, class, and gender: An anthology* (2nd ed., pp. 71-75). Belmont, CA: Wadsworth.

Yeskel, F. (1991). *The consequences of being gay: A report of the quality of life for lesbian, gay, and bisexual students at the University of Massachusetts at Amherst.* Amherst: University of Massachusetts, Amherst, Office of the Vice Chancellor for Student Affairs.

Chapter 6

ঔ෩ళ

Assessing Campus Environments for the Lesbian, Gay and Bisexual Population

WALLACE EDDY AND DEANNA S. FORNEY

> Just as feminist visions of involvement are rooted in women's particular experience, so gay and lesbian students defend their right to declare who they are without being attacked, excluded, or defamed. At most campuses, hostile students routinely tear down or deface posters for their events. Gay men living in dorms are repeatedly harassed with menacing phone calls, and messages like "die fags" and "queers get out" are written on their doors. Western Michigan's Alliance for Gay and Lesbian Rights had its office broken into six times in a single year. Gay groups at some schools even feel compelled to meet off campus, so members cannot be identified unless they choose to be. (Loeb, 1994, p. 218)

The picture drawn of college and university campuses in the above quotation seems bleak as it pertains to the lesbian, gay and bisexual population. Since college often represents the formative time for developing a stable sexual identity (D'Augelli, 1992) and the first coming out and sexual experiences for lesbian, gay and bisexual people often occur in college (D'Augelli, 1991), it is important that institutions of higher education provide environments for optimal identity formation.

In this chapter, we examine the elements necessary in an environment for lesbian, gay, and bisexual identity development to occur. This examination will include theoretical bases for identity development and a review of related literature regarding campus environments as experienced by lesbians, gays, and bisexuals. The main purpose of this chapter is to introduce a measurement tool to assess the campus environment that is based on the reviewed theory.

It may be helpful to begin by looking at what is meant by environment. Heubner (1989), citing Kaiser, defined environment as "a set of stimuli occupying consciousness in any given moment" (p. 175). Heubner went on to explain that "environment, in this construction, is active and evocative and calls forth a response from consciousness" (p. 175). It is this active orientation that allows the work of student affairs educators to influence the student development experience by manipulating the elements in the environment.

Understanding the environment is the first step in improvement of campus climate for lesbians, gays, and bisexuals. To understand the environment, information must be gathered about how that environment is experienced. Gathering this information provides an understanding of environmental press that is "inferred from the aggregate of self-reported perceptions or interpretations of the environment" (Heubner, 1989, p.169). Our approach for gathering information is to provide a framework that allows individuals to reflect upon their experiences and provide feedback and examples. In this model, practitioners take on the role of campus ecology manager as defined by Banning (1989).

The campus ecology model has as its underlying tenet the need for environmental assessment and understanding of "fit" between the student population and the environment. Banning (1989) described applications of the campus ecology model, two of which apply directly to the assessment tool described later in this chapter. They are: a) studying specific groups; and b) studying events and issues. Banning went on to describe one of the key steps in the ecosystem design process as measuring students' perceptions of the environment. The assessment tool discussed in this chapter was designed specifically to identify perceptions of the nature of the environment for the lesbian, gay, and bisexual population.

Developmental Theory and LGB Students

Information from identity development theory can be helpful in increasing understanding of potential experiences, issues, and perspectives that lesbian, gay, or bisexual individuals may encounter at higher education institutions. This understanding can, in turn, provide an awareness of some important considerations in assessing campus climates and designing supportive environments.

As Chickering and Reisser (1993) noted in their updated presentation of Chickering's psychosocial theory, college students typically are confronted with a variety of developmental tasks: developing competence, managing emotions, moving through autonomy toward interdependence, developing mature interpersonal relationships, establishing identity, developing purpose, and developing integrity. Therefore, establishing a lesbian, gay, or bisexual identity is a developmental task likely to be encountered by the individual in a context of also dealing with several other developmental issues. As Evans and Levine (1990) have noted, addressing this aspect of identity development may overshadow or compete for attention with other developmental concerns as well as with other environmental demands and expectations (for example, academic). Consequently, the developmental process for lesbian, gay, or bisexual college students is likely to be even more complex and challenging than for heterosexual students. Appropriate environmental supports to aid students in dealing with developmental issues related to sexual identity are crucial.

Levine and Evans (1991) have pointed out that all definitions of gay identity have in common a shift in the perception of self as a member of the majority to self as a member of the minority. Relatedly, development of a lesbian, gay, or bisexual identity has been described as predominantly an internal psychological process involving re-definitions of values and acceptable behaviors. Given the prevalence of heterosexism and homophobia in our society, addressing the standard developmental question of "Who am I?" can involve some additional self-esteem issues and feelings of isolation for lesbian, gay or bisexual individuals, as Wall and Evans (1991) indicated. To complicate this identification process, this sense of isolation may be intensified by the various levels of self-identification within the lesbian, gay, and bisexual community on campus (Gose, 1996).

Often cited because of its comprehensive scope and research base, Cass's (1979, 1984) model of sexual identity formation provides support in understanding how the developmental process may proceed. Stage 1, Identity Confusion, centers around an awareness that some feelings, thoughts, or behaviors may be viewed as homosexual. Identity Comparison, Stage 2, involves an increasing awareness of self as possibly homosexual, accompanied by feelings of alienation from others. Stage 3, Identity Tolerance, is characterized by increased contacts with the gay community, but a homosexual identity is tolerated rather than accepted. Identity Acceptance, Stage 4, involves a continuing validation and normalization of the individual's homosexual identity. Stage 5, Identity Pride, includes heightened pride in one's gay identity as well as heightened anger at heterosexual society. In the final stage, Identity Synthesis, similarities and differences with both homosexual and heterosexual others are acknowledged.

Cass's model has been criticized for its linearity (Evans & Levine, 1990). Clearly, development may not occur in neat, distinct stages, so such models need to be used tentatively rather than prescriptively. The potential for gender differences in the development process (Brown, 1995; Gonsiorek, 1995) should also be kept in mind. Gonsiorek emphasized individual differences within the populations of lesbians and gay men, while also noting that the external pressures encountered can bear some similarities for everyone. Relatedly, while Zinik (1985) has suggested that bisexual identity may develop in stages similar to Cass's, Fox (1995) has asserted that the bisexual identity formation process differs from models of lesbian and gay identity development in its absence of both linearity and a fixed outcome. Additional considerations in responding to individual differences include the heightened feelings of isolation that can characterize bisexual identity development (D'Augelli & Garnets, 1995) and the potential need to address multiple issues of oppression for lesbian, gay, and bisexual students of color (Wall & Washington, 1991). Finally, as Wall and Evans (1991), citing Westfall, have commented, gender, age, cultural background, and experience represent four factors which can produce very distinctive sexual identities. In conclusion, recognition of the potential for individual differences is a prerequisite for intelligent use of any identity development model. At the same time, such models can be of great assistance as empathy and design tools.

Miranda and Storms (1989) found a relationship between sexual identity development and psychological adjustment. Self-labeling and self-disclosure were two developmental processes which were linked to psychological adjustment. However, as both Cain (1991) and Rhoads (1994) have cautioned, self-disclosure or coming out can also put the individual at risk. As a result, environmental factors can impede the developmental process for lesbian, gay, or bisexual individuals or exact a toll from those individuals who undertake the developmental task of coming out in a climate of fear, harassment, and violence. The need for sensitivity on the part of individuals seeking to assist lesbian, gay, and bisexual students with this process and the need for environmental supports are both underscored.

The Campus Environment for LGB Students

The campus environment for lesbians, gays and bisexuals has been discussed in the literature. Several emergent themes are evident: lesbian, gay and bisexual students' fear for their safety; harassment and violence targeted at lesbian, gay and bisexual individuals; and negative attitudes toward lesbian, gay and bisexual people and/or issues.

While attitudes toward lesbians, gays and bisexuals are improving (Hogan & Rentz, 1996; Loeb, 1994; Pratte, 1993), much of the literature cites negative attitudes toward this population on campus (Croteau & Lark, 1995; D'Augelli & Rose, 1990; D'Emilio, 1990; Engstrom & Sedlacek, 1997; Kurdek, 1988; LaSalle, 1992; Malaney, Williams, & Geller, 1997; McNaron, 1991; Piernick, 1992; Simoni, 1996; Young & Whertvine, 1982). Negative attitudes often lead to negative behaviors. "From a gay vantage point, something is still wrong in the academy" (D'Emilio, 1990, p. 17).

The negative behavior is expressed as harassment and violence against the lesbian, gay, and bisexual population. This harassment and violence has been documented by researchers and writers who provide both research-based and anecdotal information (D'Augelli, 1992; Good, 1993; Liddell & Douvanis, 1994; Loeb, 1994; Tierney, 1992). Living under the fear of violence and harassment exhausts energy better used in academic pursuits and identity exploration and development.

The fear expressed by the lesbian, gay, and bisexual population has also been documented in the literature (Cain, 1991; Lopez & Chism, 1993; Reynolds, 1989; Tierney, 1992). This fear is antithetical to one of the basic tenets of psychosocial development as characterized by Erikson (1968), namely, freedom from excessive anxiety.

In order to provide an environment facilitative of sexual identity development for lesbians, gays, and bisexuals, the context in which the negative experiences of this population have occurred must be understood (Reynolds, 1989). The environment has a direct impact on lesbian, gay, and bisexual identity development (Cass, 1979; Evans & Levine, 1990; Zinik, 1985). By examining the environment the implicit may be made explicit: McNaron (1991) has stated that it is hard to pin down the feeling on campus, but the ethos for the lesbian, gay, and bisexual population is perceived as negative and this is not an environment that is conducive to learning.

Finally, exploring environmental issues will lead to a better understanding of the discomfort felt by heterosexual students. Peers have an important impact on the development of identity (Chickering & Reisser, 1993) and peers are more uncomfortable with lesbian, gay, and bisexual issues than educators (Geller, 1990; LaSalle, 1992). In turn, this discomfort leads to harassment and violence (D'Augelli, 1992) which interferes with the identity development of lesbian, gay, and bisexual students. For many years, students, if they came out to staff who weren't sure what to do or how to deal with this emerging identity, were likely to be sent to the counseling center. This was considered to be the most logical place for referral since homosexuality was considered a clinical issue (Hudson & Ricketts, 1980; Strickland, 1995).

To put this discussion in context, much has changed in our culture with regard to the treatment of lesbians, gays, and bisexuals. In reading the popular gay press such as *The Advocate*, it is clear that many members of that population would say there is still a great distance to go, yet the distance already traveled must not be overlooked. While it is true that, as of 1998, only 10 states and the District of Columbia had specific protections for the lesbian, gay, and bisexual population (National Gay and Lesbian Task Force, 1998), at no other time in history has the topic of sexual orientation made the headlines as frequently as today. Were there lesbians, gays, or bisexuals serving in cabinet-level positions in the White House in the past? If so, they certainly were not "out" or open about their sexual orientation and therefore not part of recorded history. Now there is lesbian, gay, and bisexual representation in our governance systems and in the mainstream media, often with positive connotations attached and not the derisive language used to describe this subgroup in the past.

These changes mark the beginnings of a paradigm shift in our culture in terms of dealing with the issue of sexual orientation. College and university campus constituents consider themselves the bastions of free thought and expression. If educators are to live up to this ideal, they must be sure that their campus environments are safe for all members of their communities to learn, grow, and express themselves. Because campus environments are not safe for all members of their communities, D'Augelli (1991) stated that "student development professionals must provide leadership in creating a more supportive campus climate so that young lesbians and gay men can meet the routine challenges of college life" (p. 145). We would extend this call to leadership to all members of the campus community with influence and power to make a difference.

Assessing Campus Environments

In order to complete a paradigm shift, educators must begin to examine the environment, rather than the individual, from a clinical perspective. Hudson and Ricketts (1980) have previously suggested this notion. The support the individual needs is how to cope with and navigate the potentially homophobic environment. In considering strategies to assess the environment, we began by articulating a concept that would address the various points where faculty and administrators could be intentional in the influencing, changing, and designing of environments. The concept used was "philosophy to policy to practice" or APPP" for short. This model is cyclical and multidirectional in nature.

Philosophy allows educators to formally espouse their values. In statements of philosophy reference is made to the freedom to learn and other educational equity language is used. Philosophy leads to the creation of policies. It is often at this stage that faculty and administrators may have an impact. The policies created should reinforce the values expressed in philosophy statements. Otherwise educators are being hypocritical and students will notice. As McNaron (1991) noted, "lesbian and gay students at more and more colleges and universities have begun to pressure their institutions to bring their practices more nearly in line with their rhetoric" (p.19). Practice, the last part of our intervention model, is where policies are applied. Are educators doing what they say they do? As Pace and Stern (1958, cited in Reynolds, 1989) explained, "implicit press and explicit objectives should reinforce one another, [because] an institution should operate in reality the way it means to operate in theory" (p. 276).

Educators must be mindful that their practices are an honest application of their policies, and likewise that their policies support their philosophies. If educators cannot trace a direct relationship among these three, then they must examine their environment. One way to assess whether or not a campus supports the "PPP" concept is to reflect upon the experiences and perceptions of the population under consideration. We have designed such an assessment called the Reflective Assessment Tool.

Development of the Reflective Assessment Tool

The main objective in the development of the Reflective Assessment Tool (RAT) was to provide structure and guidance for reflection on the campus environment as it affects the lesbian, gay, and bisexual population. The RAT is based on the work of Erik Erikson (1968) and Widick, Parker and Knefelkamp's (1978) reading and interpretation of his ideas. In their understanding of Erikson's (1968) conceptualization of psychosocial development, Widick, Parker and Knefelkamp (1978) extrapolated five elements that are necessary in an environment for identity resolution (development) to occur. These five elements are freedom from excessive anxiety, time for reflection and introspection, the experiencing of choice, experimentation with varied roles, and meaningful achievement.

Erikson's (1968) work was chosen as a basis for the RAT because, as the "parent" of psychosocial theory, Erikson is likely to be familiar to many members of the campus community. Since Erikson is widely recognized outside of the field of student affairs, there is a potential for credibility with faculty across the disciplines. If student affairs educators want their focus on lesbian, gay, and bisexual concerns to be taken seriously, they must be sure they are communicating in a language their intended audience can understand and identify with as valid.

By including attention to the environment as well as a life span developmental focus, Erikson's work has a broad scope. It is not as limited as some student development theories focused either on the 18-22 year old age group or only on students and not other members of the campus community. We concerned ourselves with the entire campus community in designing the RAT since every member has potential to affect the environment either positively or negatively. We found Erikson's psychosocial framework most useful as it attempts to explain the interaction of the individual and the environment in its most basic form—regardless of the cohort group to which one belongs.

Wall and Evans (1991) cautioned that educators must be careful in applying existing psychosocial theories to the lesbian, gay and bisexual population since "most of these theories are based exclusively on the experiences of White heterosexual men" (p. 25). They also noted that this tendency is changing and go on to examine the "applicability of various developmental concepts to nonheterosexual populations" (p. 25). The development of the RAT furthers this effort by re-evaluating the heterosexist assumptions underlying Erikson's work pointed out by Wall and Evans (1991). Our attempt at refocusing and examining the broader application of Erikson's work to the lesbian, gay, and bisexual population is accomplished by pulling out the five basic constructs of environmental impact (freedom from excessive anxiety, time for reflection and introspection, the experiencing of choice, experimentation with varied roles, meaningful achievement) and designing an assessment to address these constructs as they are experienced by the lesbian, gay, and bisexual population.

Attitudes and actions directed at the lesbian, gay, and bisexual population could hinder these five facilitative factors. After considering the literature related to identity development, lesbian, gay, and bisexual issues, and campus environmental impact, we designed a set of reflective thought questions for each of the five environmental elements (facilitative factors) as outlined by Widick, Parker and Knefelkamp (1978). To increase validity, during the development of the RAT individuals considered highly knowledgeable in the area of lesbian, gay, and bisexual identity development were asked to review items for their appropriateness relating to the various identity development elements. We also placed at the end of each section a note asking respondents to create any questions that may reflect additional environmental considerations on their particular campus. This technique allows the users to gather information most relevant to their campus (see Appendix A).

In addition, the RAT asks the respondent to assess which campus constituency(ies) have control over, or the ability to have an impact upon, the area explained in the question. This information, once analyzed, is useful in creating an action plan since it points the user toward the constituency(ies) with the power and influence to make a difference.

The action plan is the second part of the RAT and moves the user from assessment to development of an approach for improving the campus environment for the lesbian, gay, and bisexual population. After the user has gone through all the reflective thought questions and noted well-considered responses backed up with behavioral (observable) evidence, the next step is to go back to each of the five environmental elements and list the campus's strengths and challenges as related to that specific environmental element. Once a list of the strengths and challenges has been generated, the user returns to the columns where those who have control over the content of the reflective thought questions were noted. By comparing the challenges and control columns the user can decide the best approach to overcoming the campus challenges while keeping political (control and reaction) considerations in mind. The strengths column may help provide some answers in overcoming the challenges and also serves to keep proper perspective; it can be too easy to condemn the campus environment when coming from the perspective of a nondominant subculture. The last section of Part 2 of the RAT is a space for writing notes related to developing the action plan for each element.

In designing the RAT, we were mindful of the need, as demonstrated by developmental theory, to recognize the development of a gay, lesbian, or bisexual identity as a continuing process calling for different forms of support at different stages and allowing for individual differences in how the process unfolds. Therefore, the RAT has included environmental components intended to anticipate and respond to the different needs students are likely to have based on where they are developmentally. A key underlying concept is the importance of providing supports that can aid in the process of one's becoming aware of a minority sexual identity, exploring this identity, and accepting and acting on it as the individual deems appropriate. For example, numerous items in the "time for reflection and introspection" element (items 2-7) and "the experiencing of choice" element (items 1-4) of the RAT represent potential forms of support for individuals who are becoming aware of a minority sexual identity and/or those wishing to explore this identity. In regard to accepting and acting on this identity, several items in the "experimentation with varied roles" element (items 1, 2, 5) and in the "meaningful achievement" element (items 2 and 4) can be viewed as representing forms of support (see Appendix A).

Specific environmental components mentioned in the RAT also reflect areas of concern cited in the literature related to the lesbian, gay, and bisexual population on campus. For example, the need for inclusive campus policies has been noted (D'Emilio, 1990; Liddell & Douvanis, 1994; Tierney, 1992). Items such as 1 and 2 in the "freedom from excessive anxiety" element of the RAT address this issue (see Appendix A). Relatedly, attention to the academic/curricular arena has been advocated (Lopez & Chism, 1993; Rhoads, 1994; Tierney, 1992). Items such as 1 in "time for reflection and introspection" and 4 in "meaningful achievement" have this focus (see Appendix A). Finally, the need for campus programs and services that both educate the heterosexual population (student and staff) and support the lesbian, gay, and bisexual population is evident (Bourassa & Shipton, 1991; Burkholder & Dineen, 1996; Croteau & Hedstrom, 1993; Croteau & Lark, 1995; D'Augelli, 1989; D'Emilio, 1990; Eldridge & Barnett, 1991; Elliott, 1993; Good, 1995; Hughes, 1991; Piernik, 1992; Rhoads, 1995; Schreier, 1995; Washington & Evans, 1991). Items that relate include: 5 and 7 in "freedom from excessive anxiety"; 4, 5, and 7 in "time for reflection and introspection"; 4 in "the experiencing of choice"; and 1, 2, and 4 in "experimentation with varied roles" (see Appendix A). In assessing and designing campus environments, the importance of providing varied supports throughout the campus structure to respond to differing developmental needs cannot be overemphasized.

Use and Application of the RAT

The two most useful applications of the RAT are information gathering and developing action plans for improving the environment on campus with regard to lesbian, gay, and bisexual identity development. Clearly, these applications complement each other, and should be used in tandem for the most credible and positive result.

Since the focus is on the campus environment, anyone interested in lesbian, gay, and bisexual issues and how this population experiences the campus environment can use the tool. Its design is based on specific developmental constructs, but no knowledge of these constructs is necessary for use since the content areas are illustrated clearly by the reflective thought questions. The three groups who may find particular use for the RAT are educational advocacy groups, ad hoc study groups, and senior management groups.

Campus educational advocacy groups are frequently at the forefront of disseminating information regarding the discrimination, harassment, and negative experience of lesbians, gays, and bisexuals. By using the Reflective Assessment Tool, these groups may collect qualitative data to support their concern for the identity development of lesbians, gays, and bisexuals. These groups must, as we pointed out in a previous section, include a wide variety of voices in their use of the RAT to gather information in order to understand the breadth of perspectives on campus. It would be of little use to only gather information from those who agree with the group's opinions. As Loeb (1994) pointed out, "Participants in even the strongest communities of concern need to maintain ties to some larger social fabric, to connect them with individuals for whom politics is not necessarily the sole central priority of their lives. They need it as well to be full human beings, with dimensions of their lives beyond political activism" (p. 227). Again, we stress the use of the RAT as a means of increasing inclusiveness of thought, perspective, and impressions of the campus environment.

Ad hoc study groups formed with the purpose of assessing the campus environment as it affects the identity development of lesbians, gays, and bisexuals may also attain inclusiveness of perspective. These groups may be designated by senior management groups, concerned faculty, or as a specially focused sub-group of an educational/advocacy group. When forming such a group, it is important to keep in mind the necessity of a wide representation of campus constituencies—including diverse sexual orientations and levels of power. The wide variety of opinion is likely to hinder the efficiency (speed) of work but the richness of data can override this concern.

Senior management groups often have the power to make changes that result in an improved environment on campus. Those concerned with lesbian, gay, and bisexual issues embrace senior managers who champion their concerns. The RAT allows senior managers to understand the environment of their campus as it is experienced by those in less privileged positions and by those of minority sexual orientation. By remaining in touch with the campus environment as various constituencies experience it, senior managers show their empathy for the overall educational efficacy of their institution and demonstrate their commitment to educational equality.

Information Gathering

Information gathering is achieved by collecting responses to the reflective thought questions. For the most comprehensive understanding of campus climate, the RAT should be administered to a wide range of campus constituency representatives.

In gathering information the RAT can be used either as a discussion generator or qualitative research tool. Using the RAT as a discussion generator allows more depth of responses since the user may ask follow-up questions to clarify responses given to the reflective thought questions. Using the RAT as a research tool requires creating worksheets to gather responses to the questions and the perceptions of control. An analysis may be done by grouping the responses in categories such as: sexual orientation, campus constituency group, and identification with an educational/advocacy group dealing with lesbian, gay and bisexual issues. Emerging patterns of responses may then be noted and documented in report form. We wish to point out that this form of inductive coding is an arduous task, but such a global assessment and analysis can be done as was evidenced in a pilot study conducted by the authors.

As a discussion generator, the RAT may be used in much the same way—if discussants are willing to identify their sexual orientation, campus constituency group and membership status with an educational advocacy group. The RAT may also be used to promote discussion of lesbian, gay, and bisexual issues without a formal analysis being performed. It is probably most useful to have two individuals administering the RAT; one facilitating discussion while the other makes notes that will be useful in developing action plans to improve the campus environment. Areas to be addressed in discussion are: a) responses to each reflective thought question; b) perceptions of control/political ramifications of these perceptions; c) the open/additional questions generated by the respondents and why they are relevant; d) campus strengths; e) campus challenges; and f) strategies for improvement. Once discussion has taken place for each developmental area, a general discussion may take place with the focus on setting goals to overcome campus challenges by prioritizing them and by generating an action plan.

We wish to stress the desirability of including a wide variety of voices when using the RAT. Including members of as many campus constituencies and sexual orientations as possible is crucial in assessing the campus environment accurately and completely. Also, due to potential violence (either real or perceived) against respondents, it may be important that respondents are assured anonymity so they will feel free to be honest and provide the most useful information. As well, the work of Loeb (1994) demonstrates that some students want to be supportive but do not want to get visibly involved.

By documenting discussion as generated by the RAT (especially the behavioral/observable evidence), the user will have data to support the action plan when presenting it to those with the power and influence to make change. Without some data/evidence to back up claims, there will be little credibility and the user may have difficulty in convincing others that an action plan is necessary for the benefit of the lesbian, gay, and bisexual population.

Developing an Action Plan

There are many approaches to developing an action plan. Here we present one way of accomplishing this task. There are six components listed below in outline form and in the order that makes sense to us. These steps (and order) should be modified as necessary by the user to be more useful to the specific situation.

1. Prioritize areas of concern based on RAT responses.
2. Brainstorm possibilities (including using campus strengths section of RAT) and evaluate how realistic they are after brainstorming.
3. Identify obstacles to overcome (both institutional and personnel).
4. Formulate plan (with measurable outcomes).
5. Have those allies with a sense of history about campus politics look over the plan as a final reality check.
6. Present plan to those who have the power to implement and ask for a response to the plan and the likelihood of implementation.

A final note about the development of an action plan: be realistic. If the campus is perceived to be highly homophobic and officials have been reluctant in the past to engage in discussion about the viability of various sexual orientations, an action plan calling for an immediate 180 degree change in position is unlikely to be feasible. The action plan should have incremental phases so small victories can be celebrated and the positive energy generated from those victories can motivate those involved. Perseverance is a key ingredient in effecting change.

Final Thoughts

In working to effect change and improve the campus environment for lesbians, gays and bisexuals, change agents must be mindful of the insidious nature of all forms of oppression. Recognizing the connections among various forms of oppression, educators are encouraged to see the commonalities and build coalitions between various marginalized groups.

By improving the environment for lesbians, gays, and bisexuals, educators create a climate where identity may be explored and developed with a sense of safety. As gay, lesbian, and bisexual students become more visible on campus, a human face is attached to the phenomenon of homosexuality. This "personalization of the phenomenon" has been shown to lessen homophobic attitudes on campus (Burkholder & Dineen, 1996; Geasler, et. al., 1995; Geller, 1991) when the environment is such that an open exchange of ideas and experiences may take place.

The Reflective Assessment Tool is one means to improve the environment for lesbians, gays, and bisexuals. The RAT, grounded in environmental theory, developmental theory, and the literature on lesbian, gay, and bisexual issues, is intended to serve as a vehicle for assessing and improving campus environments. In this capacity, the RAT can be a stimulus and resource for moving forward the process of attempting to provide a climate that supports both the growth and development of all students and the differing needs of a diverse staff. As a formal assessment instrument or an informal discussion facilitator, the RAT is meant to provide a structure that aids in taking stock and making further progress.

Appendix A
The Reflective Assessment Tool

Identity Development Element: freedom from excessive anxiety

Reflective Thought Questions (keep in mind behavioral evidence):

	Who has control?		
students	admin.	faculty	other	uncertain

1. Is sexual orientation included in the campus non-discrimination policy?

2. What protections/grievance procedures are offered students and staff should they be harassed or assaulted because of their sexual orientation?

3. How sensitive is the student affairs division to these issues?

4. What is the campus lore about past harassment due to sexual orientation and the way in which the incidents were handled?

5. What kind of climate exists in the residence halls and within student organizations for the LGB population? Are residence life (professional and paraprofessional) and student activities staff sensitized and trained in LGB (or diversity/oppression) issues?

6. How visible are "allies" on your campus (organization and individuals)?

7. How is the heterosexual population educated about LGB issues?

8. Knowing your campus, what additional questions, would you ask relevant to this identity development element?

Campus Strengths: Campus Challenges: Strategy for Improvement:

Identity Development Element: time for reflection and introspection

Reflective Thought Questions (keep in mind behavioral evidence):

Who has control?

students admin. faculty other uncertain

1. How does the shape of the curriculum (content *vs.* process issues) affect time for reflection and is there anything in the curriculum to support the needs of LGB students?

2. What support groups on campus encourage and facilitate taking time for reflection and introspection with regard to LGB identity issues?

3. What campus or local organizations are available to students which provide a forum for "rap" sessions and help students gain some focus in their reflection and introspection?

4. How able/willing are religious affairs staff to talk with students about sexual identity/orientation and religious beliefs?

5. How available are student affairs staff to be "sounding boards" for LGB students, e.g., providing a "safe space" for reflection and introspection?

6. What active outreach is undertaken by student affairs staff toward the LGB population?

7. What resources personnel are available to LGB students to explore their sexual identity within the context of individual cultures from which they come?

8. Knowing your campus, what additional questions would you ask relevant to this identity development element?

Campus Strengths: Campus Challenges: Strategy for Improvement:

Identity Development Element: the experiencing of choice

Reflective Thought Questions (keep in mind behavioral evidence):

Who has control?

students   admin.   faculty   other   uncertain

1. How accepted on campus is discussion of the viability of various sexual identities/orientations?

2. What environmental issues/concerns exist that would affect a student's comfort level in choosing to experiment and discover his or her true sexual identity?

3. How available are role models for the LGB population on campus? Are there any "out" faculty or staff who can provide support to these students?

4. What resources are available to students on campus (periodicals, videos, texts) to show the various lifestyles experienced by LGB individuals and the "normalcy" of these varied roles? Where are these resources located? Counseling Center, Library, Individual Departments? What message does location send?

5. Knowing your campus, what additional questions would you ask relevant to this identity development element?

Campus Strengths: Campus Challenges: Strategy for Improvement:

Identity Development Element: experimentation with varied roles

Reflective Thought Questions (keep in mind behavioral evidence):

Who has control?

students   admin. faculty other uncertain

1. What freedom and support do students have to create their own organizations which might support the LGB population?

2. What possibilities exist for students to become peer helpers for the LGB population?

3. What kind of training would be offered for LGB peer helpers? Are there staff members qualified to offer such training?

4. What support is provided to LGB students seeking internship or external study positions which might enhance their identity development? Who provides this support?

5. How connected is the institution to LGB community organizations such as switchboards, hotlines, or resource centers where students can be involved in the LGB community in a variety of ways?

6. Knowing your campus, what additional questions would you ask relevant to this identity development element?

Campus Strengths: Campus Challenges: Strategy for Improvement:

Identity Development Element: meaningful achievement

<u>Reflective Thought Questions</u> (keep in mind behavioral evidence):

	Who has control?		
students	admin.	faculty	other	uncertain

1. What role can LGB students play in the governance structure of the institution? How responsive are the "powers that be" to listening to diverse groups' input? How free are LGB students in governance roles to express concerns with issues of sexual orientation?

2. How supportive are campus officials in helping students get involved in meaningful LGB community activities such as pride festivals, rallies, and political coalition meetings?

3. How open would campus officials be to working with LGB students to organize a conference, drive-in workshop, etc. that dealt with LGB issues? Where would financial and personnel support come from?

4. Where are LGB issues addressed in the curriculum so that a student may explore these issues intellectually?

5. Knowing your campus, what additional questions would you ask relevant to this identity development element?

Campus Strengths:　　　　Campus Challenges:　　　　Strategy for Improvement:

References

Banning, J. H. (1989). Creating a climate for successful student development: The campus ecology manager role. In U. Delworth & G. R. Hanson (Eds.), *Student services: A handbook for the profession* (2nd ed., pp.304-322). San Francisco: Jossey-Bass.

Bourassa, D., & Shipton, B. (1991). Addressing lesbian and gay issues in residence hall environments. In N. J. Evans & V. A. Wall (Eds.), *Beyond tolerance: Gays, lesbians and bisexuals on campus* (pp. 79-96). Alexandria, VA: American College Personnel Association.

Brown, L. S. (1995). Lesbian identities: Concepts and issues. In A. R. D'Augelli & C. J. Patterson (Eds.), *Lesbian, gay, and bisexual identities over the lifespan* (pp.3-23). New York: Oxford University Press.

Burkholder, G. J., & Dineen, A. (1996). Using panel presentations to increase awareness of experiences of gay, lesbian, and bisexual people. *Journal of College Student Development, 37,* 469-470.

Cain, R. (1991). Stigma management and gay identity development. *Social Work, 36* (1), 7-73.

Cass, V. C. (1979). Homosexual identity formation: A theoretical model. *Journal of Homosexuality, 4,* 219-235.

Cass, V. C. (1984). Homosexual identity formation: Testing a theoretical model. *Journal of Sex Research, 20,* 143-167.

Chickering, A. W., & Reisser, L. (1993). *Education and identity* (2nd ed.). San Francisco: Jossey-Bass.

Croteau, J. M., & Hedstrom, S. M. (1993). Integrating commonality and difference: The key to career counseling with lesbian women and gay men. *Career Development Quarterly, 41,* 201-209.

Croteau, J. M., & Lark, J. S. (1995). A qualitative investigation of biased and exemplary student affairs practice concerning lesbian, gay, and bisexual issues. *Journal of College Student Development, 36,* 472-482.

D'Augelli, A. R. (1989). Homophobia in a university community: Views of prospective resident assistants. *Journal of College Student Development, 30,* 546-552.

D'Augelli, A. R. (1991). Gay men in college: Identity processes and adaptations. *Journal of College Student Development, 32,* 140-146.

D'Augelli, A. R. (1992). Lesbian and gay male undergraduates' experiences of harassment and fear on campus. *Journal of Interpersonal Violence, 7,* 383-395.

D'Augelli, A. R., & Garnets L. D. (1995). Lesbian, gay and bisexual communities. In A. R. D'Augelli & C. J. Patterson (Eds.), *Lesbian, gay and bisexual identities over the lifespan* (pp. 293-320). New York: Oxford University Press.

D'Augelli, A. R., & Rose, M. L. (1990). Homophobia in a university community: Attitudes and experiences of heterosexual freshmen. *Journal of College Student Development, 31,* 484-491.

D'Emilio, J. (1990). The campus environment for gay and lesbian life. *Academe, 76,* 16-19.

Eldridge, N. S., & Barnett, D. C. (1991). Counseling gay and lesbian students. In N. J. Evans & V. A. Wall (Eds.), *Beyond tolerance: Gays, lesbians and bisexuals on campus* (pp. 147-178). Alexandria, VA: American College Personnel Association.

Elliott, J. E. (1993). Career development with lesbian and gay clients. *Career Development Quarterly, 41,* 210-226.

Engstrom, C. M., & Sedlacek, W. (1997). Attitudes of heterosexual students toward their gay male and lesbian peers. *Journal of College Student Development, 38,* 565-576.

Erikson, E. H. (1968). *Identity: Youth and crisis.* New York: Norton.

Evans, N., & Levine, H. (1990). Perspectives on sexual orientation. In L. V. Moore (Ed.), *Evolving theoretical perspectives on students* (New Directions for Student Services, no. 51, pp. 49-58). San Francisco: Jossey-Bass.

Fox, R.C. (1995). Bisexual identities. In A. R. D'Augelli & C. J. Patterson (Eds.), *Lesbian, gay and bisexual identities over the lifespan* (pp. 48-86). New York: Oxford University Press.

Geasler, M. J., Croteau, J. M., Heineman, C. J., & Edlund, C. J. (1995). A qualitative study of students' expression of change after attending panel presentations by lesbian, gay, and bisexual speakers. *Journal of College Student Development, 36,* 483-492.

Geller, W. W. (1990). *Students and educators: Attitudes on gay and lesbian matters* (ERIC Document Reproduction Service No. ED 330 914)

Geller, W. W. (1991). *Attitudes towards gays and lesbians: A longitudinal study* (ERIC Document Reproduction Service No. ED 340 970)

Gonsiorek, J. C. (1995). Gay male identities: Concepts and issues. In A. R. D'Augelli & C. J. Patterson (Eds.), *Lesbian, gay, and bisexual identities over the lifespan* (pp. 24-47). New York: Oxford University Press.

Good, R. T., III (1993). Programming to meet the needs of the lesbigay community. *Campus Activities Programming, 26* (2), 40-44.

Gose, B. (1996, February 9). The politics and images of gay students. *The Chronicle of Higher Education,* p. A33-34.

Hogan, T. L., & Rentz, A. L. (1996). Homophobia in the academy. *Journal of College Student Development, 37,* 309-314.

Hudson, W. W., & Ricketts, W. A. (1980). A strategy for the measurement of homophobia. *Journal of Homosexuality, 5,* 357-372.

Huebner, L. A. (1989). Interaction of student and campus. In U. Delworth & G. R. Hanson (Eds.), *Student services: A handbook for the profession* (2nd ed., pp. 165-208). San Francisco: Jossey-Bass.

Hughes, M. J. (1991). Addressing gay, lesbian and bisexual issues in fraternities and sororities. In N. J. Evans & V. A. Wall (Eds.), *Beyond tolerance: Gays, lesbians and bisexuals on campus* (pp. 97-116). Alexandria, VA: American College Personnel Association.

Kurdek, L. A. (1988). Correlates of negative attitudes toward homosexuals in heterosexual college students. *Sex Roles, 18,* 727-738.

LaSalle, L. A. (1992). *Exploring campus intolerance: A textual analysis of comments concerning lesbian, gay, and bisexual people* (ERIC Document Reproduction Service No. ED 349 497)

Levine, H., & Evans, N. J. (1991). The development of gay, lesbian, and bisexual identities. In N. J. Evans & V. A. Wall (Eds.), *Beyond tolerance: Gays, lesbians and bisexuals on campus* (pp. 25-38). Alexandria, VA: American College Personnel Association.

Liddell, D. L., & Douvanis, C. J. (1994). The social and legal status of gay and lesbian students: An update. *NASPA Journal, 31,* 121-129.

Loeb, P. R. (1994). *Generation at the crossroads: Apathy and action on the American campus.* New Brunswick, NJ: Rutgers University Press.

Lopez, G., & Chism, N. (1993). Classroom concerns of gay and lesbian students. *College Teaching, 41* (3), 97-103.

Malaney, G. D., Williams, E. A., & Geller, W. W. (1997). Assessing campus climate fpr gays, lesbians, and bisexuals at two institutions. *Journal of College Student Development, 38,* 365-375.

McNaron, T. (1991). Making life more livable for gays and lesbians on campus: Sightings from the field. *Educational Record, 91,* 19-22.

Miranda, J., & Storms, M. (1989). Psychological adjustment of lesbians and gay men. *Journal of Counseling and Development, 68,* 41-45.

National Gay and Lesbian Task Force. (1998). NGLTF Home Page [web page]. URL http://www.ngltf.org *[1999, February 27].*

Piernik, T. E. (1992). Lesbian, gay and bisexual students - Radically or invisibly at risk. *Campus Activities Programming, 25* (6), 47-51.

Pratte, T. (1993). A comparative study of attitudes toward homosexuality. *Journal of Homosexuality, 26* (1), 77-83.

Reynolds, A. J. (1989). Social environmental conceptions of male homosexual behavior: A university climate analysis. *Journal of College Student Development, 30,* 62-69.

Rhoads, R. A. (1994). *Coming out in college: The struggle for a queer identity.* Westport, CT: Bergin & Garvey.

Rhoads, R. A. (1995). Learning from the coming out experiences of college males. *Journal of College Student Development, 36,* 67-74.

Schreier, B. A. (1995). Moving beyond tolerance: A new paradigm for programming about homophobia/biphobia and heterosexism. *Journal of College Student Development, 36,* 19-26.

Simoni, J. M. (1996). Pathways to prejudice: Predicting students' heterosexist attitudes with demographics, self-esteem, and contact with lesbians and gay men. *Journal of College Student Development, 37,* 68-78.

Strickland, B. R. (1995). Research on sexual orientation and human development: A commentary. *Developmental Psychology, 31* (1), 137-140.

Tierney, W. G. (1992). Building academic communities of difference: Gays, lesbians, and bisexuals on campus. *Change, 24* (2), 41-46.

Wall, V. A., & Evans, N. J. (1991). Using psychosocial theories to understand and work with gay and lesbian persons. In N. J. Evans & V. A. Wall (Eds.), *Beyond tolerance: Gays, lesbians and bisexuals on campus* (pp. 25-38). Alexandria, VA: American College Personnel Association.

Wall, V. A., & Washington, J. (1991). Understanding gay and lesbian students of color. In N. J. Evans & V. A. Wall (Eds.), *Beyond tolerance: Gays, lesbians and bisexuals on campus* (pp. 67-78). Alexandria, VA: American College Personnel Association.

Washington, J., & Evans, N. J. (1991). Becoming an ally. In N. J. Evans & V. A. Wall (Eds.), *Beyond tolerance: Gays, lesbians and bisexuals on campus* (pp. 195-204). Alexandria, VA: American College Personnel Association.

Widick, C., Parker, C. A., & Knefelkamp, L. (1978). Erik Erikson and psychosocial development. In L. Knefelkamp, C.Widick, & C. A. Parker (Eds.), *Applying new developmental findings* (New Directions for Student Services, no. 4, pp. 1-17). San Francisco: Jossey-Bass.

Young, M., & Whertvine, J. (1982). Attitudes of heterosexual students toward homosexual behavior. *Psychological Reports, 51,* 673-674.

Zinik, G. (1985). Identity conflict or adaptive flexibility?: Bisexuality reconsidered. In F. Klein & T. J. Wolf (Eds.), *Two lives to lead: Bisexuality in men and women* (pp. 7-19). New York: Harrington Park Press.

PART III

INTERVENTIONS IN STUDENT AFFAIRS

Chapter 7

ഇൗരു

From the Trenches: Strategies for Facilitating Lesbian, Gay, and Bisexual Awareness Programs for College Students

VERNON A. WALL, JAMIE WASHINGTON,
NANCY J. EVANS, AND ROSS A. PAPISH

Picture this. A 19-year-old college sophomore attends a one-day student leadership conference. At the conference, there are several program sessions offered at concurrent times. As our student scans through the sessions offered, there is one program that looks particularly interesting: "Someone you care about is gay: Understanding and supporting your fellow lesbian, gay, and bisexual students." Hmm . . .

"Why is this program offered at a leadership symposium?"

"What will happen at the program?"

We wish to thank Scott H. Reikofski and William Matthews for their contributions to this chapter.

"If I attend, will someone think I'm gay?"

"Will the presenters try to make me think a certain way?"

"Who's presenting this program anyway?"

"Will it be a big battle like I see on the Jerry Springer Show?" Whew . . .

As one can see, even before an awareness program on gay/lesbian/ bisexual issues begins, there can be much anxiety and apprehension. This chapter is written to introduce effective strategies for facilitating programs for college students focusing on lesbian/gay/bisexual concerns. The chapter addresses six components of successful LGB awareness programs: Assessment/Ground Rules, Awareness, Knowledge, Skills, Action, and Closure/Evaluation. At the end of this chapter, examples of activities and exercises are presented. Special attention is paid to programming for Greek social organizations. Credits have been cited whenever possible; however, some materials have been "passed down for generations" making it difficult to credit all. The authors of this chapter have been involved in facilitating awareness programs for college students for over ten years each and much of the material included is based on their work. It is important, however, that the following individuals be acknowledged for their contributions to this chapter: Warren J. Blumenfeld, Jay Scott, Kathy Obear, Maura Cullen, and Doug Cureton. All are excellent trainers and all have contributed to the authors' learning.

Assessment/Ground Rules

Griffin and Harro (1997) state that one of the most important challenges to facilitators is the task of constructing an educational experience that acknowledges the complexity of the issues involved without overwhelming students who bring a variety of experiences to the session. Some students will be talking about these issues for the first time. Others might be questioning their sexual orientation. For some, addressing heterosexism and homophobia requires them to challenge basic and deeply held religious beliefs or personal fears about lesbian, gay, and bisexual people. Griffin and Harro (1997) believe that with this challenging mix of participants it is essential to construct a learning environment in which students have control over how much of their personal experiences and sexual identities they choose to disclose as part of the session's activities.

Not enough can be said about the importance of what is done before the program begins. Assessment not only includes learning about the audience, but also learning about the climate. Listed below are some questions that facilitators might wish to ponder:

- What is the current campus climate concerning LGB issues?
- What stories have been in the media recently concerning LGB issues?
- What is known about the group to whom the program will be presented with regard to such issues as gender breakdown, ethnicity, organizational purpose and goals?
- Is this a required session for the participants?
- Was the program developed as a result of a specific incident?
- What is the awareness level of the participants?

In addition to understanding the group with which they are working, programmers must also carefully consider their own role as a facilitator. The following LGB workshop considerations are listed in a *Handbook of Structured Exercises and Experiences* (1993) published by the American College Personnel Association for a traveling workshop on lesbian, gay, and bisexual awareness. This list is a compilation of observations and insights from experienced presenters who have identified common issues in workshops.

1. Facilitators must decide at what point their own sexual orientation should be disclosed to the group or not at all. For many presenters, this can be a strategic decision for impact regarding participants' stereotypes, attitudes, and beliefs.
2. The sexual orientation of the individuals in the group should not be assumed. Careful attention should be paid to the directions, information and insights shared, and the language used. An entire group can be lost if the facilitator does not think before speaking.
3. Facilitators must be ready for the opposite opinion. They must be prepared to encourage the exploration of diverse viewpoints in a constructive, proactive manner. The most teachable moments in workshops often come from taking a participant through the various stages of information and accepting the challenge of their viewpoints.

4. Facilitators must be aware of any "out" lesbian, gay, or bisexual individuals in the group.

5. Presenters should bring humor and laughter into the workshop whenever possible to balance the anxiety. Creative thought and openness to new ideas should be encouraged. Incorporating stories, videotapes of situational comedies and comedians, or personal anecdotes helps to underscore points and validate feelings.

6. Individuals have different learning styles. Facilitators should recognize that not all people learn the same way and that they need to balance the workshop with lecture, discussion, panels, interactive exercises, simulations, multimedia presentation, games, props, toys, food, and any other multi-sensory stimulus that will activate the participants' potential for learning. Facilitators should always have handouts and overheads to allow participants to focus on the presentation. Too much note taking can take away from the experiential learning process.

7. Presenters need to be aware of the balance of messages and representation of all groups affected by the topic.

8. It is important to be cautious of the balance of information and discussion regarding sexual orientation issues, sexual behavior/practice issues, and sexuality issues. LGB workshops should include all three issues and not necessarily in that order.

9. Facilitators need to decide the extent to which they can include the breath and depth of sexuality in their presentation.

Facilitators must never overlook the importance of a solid workshop title. Titles with current themes seem to work the best with students. Some examples are:

- Little Boy Birds, Little Girl Birds (from Whoopi Goldberg's comedy sketch)
- Someone You Know is Gay
- I Have Something to Tell You . . .
- If You're Straight, Does That Mean I'm Crooked?
- Straight Answers to Queer Questions

Each of these titles could be used with an additional line that reads something like: "Understanding Lesbian, Gay, and Bisexual Students" or "Combating Heterosexism on Campus" or "The Gay, Lesbian, Bisexual Experience at _____ University."

Prior to beginning any workshop experience on diversity/multicultural issues, it is important to establish some guidelines for participants to reduce anxieties and minimize conflicts. The following list are some of the more common recommendations but are not fully inclusive of all issues:

1. Accept others where they are. No two individuals have the exact same background and experiences. Accept that a person's perspective may be valid and true for that individual.

2. Listen actively. Don't just hear what someone is saying— LISTEN FOR UNDERSTANDING. Practice good listening skills such as posture, silence, and summarization of meaning.

3. Understand that each participant is a student and a teacher. Many individuals have experiences and backgrounds that can greatly enhance the workshop. Encourage active participation from all participants by inviting their insights.

4. Respect individuals' opinions and their willingness to share them. Some participants may not wish to actively participate in discussions or exercises and it is important to establish that verbal participation is not required. However, it is important to encourage individuals to participate at their own levels of comfort and to challenge themselves to stretch and grow. Encourage passive participation by asking participants to think about what is occurring for them.

5. When individuals do share their feelings and opinions, request that they speak for themselves and not as representatives of particular groups. Encourage use of "I believe . . ." and "For me . . ." statements and be ready to focus individuals back on track if a generalization statement is made.

6. Discourage the use of absolute statements such as "All people from this group do . . ." or "It has never happened that . . ." Such statements often lead to the polarization of individual attitudes and split groups into "us versus them" camps.

7. Insure confidentiality of the content and information discussed in the workshop. Ask participants to respect the decision of

members to share information with each of them and to not bring any of the information outside of the experience without the permission of the individuals involved.

It is important to engage the audience in developing these guidelines and ground rules. Participants may be asked to add to the list—or even challenge or ask questions about anything listed. One question that might assist in accomplishing this task is: "What do you need from either me or the people in this room that would help you get the most out of this session?"

Awareness

Blumenfeld (1992) stated that he sees workshops addressing LGB issues as "providing a space where heterosexuals can begin the process of purging early heterosexist conditioning, which has contained them and compromised their humanity" (p. 277). The awareness component of any workshop is designed to help individuals begin the process of understanding the information and misinformation with which they have grown up. Most students do not realize that they have been "taught" many things about lesbian, gay and bisexual people. Recognizing those things is the first step in the "unlearning" process. One helpful exercise is known as the "Guided Journey." Several variations of this exercise exist, each of which takes participants through an experience that usually involves "walking a mile in a gay person's shoes." These journeys can take the form of being heterosexual in a gay world or actually being gay and experiencing rejection, fear, and community. An additional awareness exercise, the Critical Events Inventory, is provided in Appendix A at the end of this chapter.

Griffin and Harro (1997) state that the diversity among lesbian, gay, and bisexual people and the increasing complexity of issues of concern result in conflicts within their communities. As a facilitator, it is important to recognize this dynamic and develop activities and exercises that encourage dialogue on the diversity that exists in the lesbian, gay, bisexual, and transgender community. In the past few years, bisexual men and women; transgender people; lesbians and gay men of color; working class and poor lesbians, gays and bisexuals; lesbian, gay, and bisexual people with disabilities; and others have expanded the boundaries of issues and identities that need to be addressed and included when we discuss homophobia and heterosexism (Griffin & Harro, 1997; Sears, 1994). These inclusive conversations help to strengthen our discussions on oppression and justice generally.

Knowledge

Once an awareness base is established, the group is ready to focus on increasing their knowledge. One of the facilitator's first steps is to define terms that are used in discussing LGB issues. One must never make the assumption that the meaning of certain words is known or understood by all. Definitions of words used also differ from person to person. It is important to acknowledge this reality while providing a forum for participants to begin the process of individual understanding. See Appendix B at the end of this chapter for an example of selected definitions.

Topics that can be discussed during the knowledge section of the program include: the components of sexuality (included in Appendix C), the "coming out" process and identity development models (see Levine & Evans, 1991), sexual orientation research (see Chapters 1 and 2 in this volume), the sharing of personal stories and campus climate issues (see Rankin, 1998).

A favorite exercise designed to increase knowledge is modeled after a traditional "bingo" game. Participants use a specially designed card to talk with fellow participants and find someone who: "can name a gay or lesbian author," "knows what college formed the first lesbian sorority in 1988," or "knows what an upside down pink triangle represents."

Skills

During the "skills" component of programs, participants are asked to take the information they have become aware of and make the transition toward action. This goal is accomplished by acknowledging the skills that one possesses to identify and interrupt homophobia and heterosexism. Listed below are questions that could be asked during a brainstorming session on skill-building.

1. What if you're sitting with a group of friends, and a couple of them make an obnoxious comment about LGB people—what could you do?

2. What's hard about some of these responses?
3. What's the trade-off? What will you gain if you confront them?
4. What could you do if a friend tells you a "rumor" that a floor member is supposedly gay?
5. We do a lot of programming and activities in the halls and most of it is designed for heterosexuals without considering the interests or needs of LGB students. What activities do we have that in some way could exclude LGB students or at least not recognize their needs and interests?

Hearing other students' responses to such questions allows students' to see that they are not alone in wanting to confront homophobic and heterosexist actions and gives them options they may not have thought of on their own. The discussion can be taken further to consider the implications of taking active steps in support of gay, lesbian, and bisexual persons and how to handle possible negative reactions. The information contained in Chapter 15 can be very helpful in structuring a discussion of how to develop the skills needed to be an ally.

Action

The action component is a crucial piece. Participants should leave a program with some feeling that they can make a difference—that they can work to fight oppression and benefit from that fight. Defining the term ally, listing the costs and benefits of being an ally, and brainstorming "ally-like" behaviors is a good start. (Refer to Chapter 15 for a more in depth discussion on the role of the ally in combating homophobia and heterosexism.) A set of open-ended questions may begin the thought process for a group. For example:

1. What are some of the attitudes and behaviors of others that get in the way of our working together?
2. What are some of the attitudes and behaviors of others that help us to work together?
3. What are some of your attitudes and behaviors that get in the way of our working together?
4. What are some of your attitudes and behaviors that help us to work together?

5. What do you want and need from others so you can better work with this group to meet the needs of gays, lesbians, and bisexuals on campus?
6. What are you willing to do to support others as we work together?
7. What are some of your unique contributions that will help to meet the needs of lesbians, gays, and bisexuals on campus?

Washington (1991) presented eight stages for responding to heterosexist attitudes and actions in a presentation during the 1991 ACPA Conference. The actions move from being extremely homophobic or heterosexist on the left end of the continuum to extremely anti-homophobic and anti-heterosexist on the right side of the continuum. These stages, which could be shared in the action section of a workshop, are found in Appendix D.

Closure/Evaluation

Closure exercises should be quick, precise and upbeat, sending the participants away with positive messages about the future and their role in shaping it. "Read arounds" are very effective. They make use of quotes from scholars, leaders, celebrities, and the audience to empower people to play an active role in educating others and confronting homophobia and heterosexism. Video clips from television shows that depict gay characters are also effective.

As with any program, it is important to gather feedback in some way. The facilitator should know what has worked and what needs to be re-worked. Focused discussion questions, a short Likert-type questionnaire, or several written open-ended questions could be used for this purpose.

Programming in Greek Organizations

As the body of literature addressing issues of concern to gay, lesbian, and bisexual students has slowly expanded over the last several years, a void still remains related to the needs of gay, lesbian, and bisexual students in men's and women's Greek letter social organizations. Hughes (1991) enumerated a number of issues needing the profession's attention, including the problems facing the LGB chapter member who is pressured to deny personal experience and conform to group norms by the distinctly heterosexual nature of chapter activities. The need for sexual orientation awareness programming in fraternities and sororities is paramount (Matthews & Reikofski, 1998). Included in Appendix E at the end of this chapter are exercises that will serve as a resource in developing effective interventions for the Greek community.

From the Trenches . . .

This chapter has provided a framework for developing programs and activities on sexual orientation issues. Listed below are some final "words of wisdom."

1. Always remember that there will be participants in the audience who are gay, lesbian, and bisexual or unsure of their sexual orientation. They should be given a safe space to "come out" if they choose to but also be informed that it is okay if they choose not to.
2. Be aware of what the current issues are in the world and on the campus as the presentation is developed. If the president has recently made a statement on gays in the military; if there has been a gay bashing incident on campus; if the sitcom Roseanne aired an episode the night before the program with a gay character in it; that's what the students will be talking about. Be current!
3. Encourage participants to move beyond arguing over specific points and toward a general understanding of all the issues involved and the complexity of those issues.
4. Remember that if it took these students at least 18-21 years to learn heterosexist attitudes, they will not unlearn them in 2 hours attending a program (no matter how wonderful it is). The facilitator's goal should be to heighten awareness.
5. Be prepared to discuss how other "ism's" are related to homophobia and heterosexism. For some students, using examples of sexism, ableism, or racism may help them make connections with lesbian, gay, and bisexual students.

6. In developing a program, the diversity within the lesbian, gay, and bisexual community should be taken into consideration. Reference should be made to different cultural and ethnic groups. Experiences differ for each person.
7. Many programs related to sexual orientation issues tend to neglect discussions on bisexuality and transgender issues. Facilitators should learn as much as possible about these subjects and be honest when they do not have enough information to respond to a question. More dialog is needed around the subjects of bisexuality and transgender issues.
8. Be prepared to answer the question: "What's in it for me?" Heterosexual students must begin to understand that homophobia and heterosexism affects everyone!
9. Be current. Be thought provoking and be entertaining. Utilize video, music, visuals—you name it! Not only will this make the program more interesting, it can also help to relax participants, allowing greater participation.
10. Be aware of "trigger words"—words and phrases that are in the media that evoke emotion; for example: "special rights," "it's a choice," "gay agenda," "religious right." These words and phrases can be potentially explosive and are fueled by the media. Students may not know the implications of these words but they have heard them so much that they repeat them sometimes without thinking.

Picture this. Our 19-year-old student wanders out of his first gay/lesbian/bisexual awareness program a little dazed—but the wheels are turning. New things were learned. A vow has been made to continue investigating this intriguing population. Let us hope that through programming efforts such as those described in this chapter, more students will begin the journey from awareness to action. This work is vitally important.

Appendix A
Critical Events Inventory

PURPOSE: To begin to identify some early learning about sexual identity and our experiences with differences in sexual orientation.

DIRECTIONS: For each question, try to think of a specific event or experience the day, place, and circumstances, if possible. As you review each situation please try to answer the following questions:

1. When did it occur?
2. How old were you?
3. How did you feel about the situation?
4. How did the situation influence your attitudes, values, or beliefs about sexual orientation and heterosexism/ homophobia?

QUESTIONS:

1. When was the first time, or a significant time, when you became aware that people had a sexual orientation different from you?
2. When was the first time, or a significant time, when you became aware that people were treated differently because their sexual orientation was different from yours?
3. When was the first time, or a significant time, when you became aware that your sexual orientation affected the way you are and would be treated in this society?
4. When was the first time, or a significant time, in which you felt angry about homophobia/heterosexism in our society?
5. When was the first time, or a significant time, in which you were challenged about your beliefs or attitudes regarding sexual orientation?
6. When was the first, or a significant time, in which you felt ashamed, guilty, or embarrassed of your sexual orientation?
7. When was the first, or a significant time, which you felt proud of your sexual orientation?
8. When was the first, or a significant time, in which you felt helpless as an individual in creating change regarding homophobia/ heterosexism in our society?
9. When was the first, or a significant time, that you decided to actively resist homophobia/heterosexism?

Appendix B
Defining a Common Language

Sexism	The societal/cultural, institutional, and individual beliefs and practices that privilege men, subordinate women, and denigrate women-identified values.
Heterosexism	The societal/cultural, institutional, and individual beliefs and practices that assume that heterosexuality is the only natural, normal, acceptable sexual orientation.
Sexual Orientation	The desire for intimate emotional and sexual relationships with people of the same gender (lesbian, gay), the other gender (heterosexual), or either gender (bisexual).
Homophobia	The fear, hatred, or intolerance of lesbians, gay men, or any behavior that is outside the boundaries of traditional gender roles. Homophobia can be manifested as fear of association with lesbian or gay people or being perceived as lesbian or gay. Homophobic behavior can range from telling jokes about lesbian and gay people to physical violence against people thought to be lesbian or gay.
Biphobia	The fear, hatred, or intolerance of bisexual men or women.
Heterosexual Privilege	The benefits and advantages heterosexuals receive in a heterosexist culture. Also, the benefits lesbians, gay men, and bisexual people receive as a result of claiming heterosexual identity or denying homosexual or bisexual identity.
Heterosexual Ally	Heterosexual people who confront heterosexism, homophobia, and heterosexual privilege in themselves and others out of self-interest, a concern for the well-being of lesbian, gay, and bisexual people and a belief that heterosexism is a social justice issue.
Gender Identity	One's psychological sense of oneself as a male or female.

Gender Roles	The socially constructed and culturally specific behavior and appearance expectations imposed on women (femininity) and men (masculinity).
Biological Sex	The physiological and anatomical characteristics of maleness or femaleness with which a person is born.
Transsexual	A person whose biological sex does not match their gender identity and who, through gender reassignment surgery and hormone treatments, seeks to change their physical body to match their gender identity. Transsexuals' sexual orientation can be heterosexual, homosexual, or bisexual.
Transgender Person	A person whose self-identification challenges traditional notions of gender and sexuality. Transgender people include transsexuals and others who do not conform to traditional understandings of labels like male and female or homosexual and heterosexual.
Cross-dresser	A person who enjoys dressing in clothes typically associated with the other gender. Also called a transvestite. Many cross-dressers are heterosexual married men.
Queer	Originally a derogatory label used to refer to lesbian and gay people or to intimidate and offend heterosexuals. More recently this term has been reclaimed by some lesbians, gay men, bisexual people, and transgender people as an inclusive and positive way to identify all people targeted by heterosexism and homophobia. Some lesbians and gay men have similarly reclaimed previously negative words such as "dyke" and "faggot" for positive self-reference.
Pedophile	An adult who is sexually attracted to children. Pedophiles can be male or female and heterosexual or homosexual. Most pedophiles are heterosexual men attracted to female children. Some pedophiles are attracted to children of either gender. It is a myth that most gay men are pedophiles. Police statistics show that well over

	90 percent of all reported cases of child molestation involve heterosexual adult males and female children.
Drag Queen	A gay man who dresses in clothes, typically flamboyant and glamorous styles, associated with female movie stars or singers, all with theatrical intent and sometimes with the intention of poking fun at gender roles.

Reference: Adams, M., Bell, L. A., & Griffin, P. (Ed.). *Teaching for diversity and social justice*. New York: Routledge, 1997.

Appendix C
Components of Sexuality

Growing up in America has provided most people with an overly simplistic understanding of sexuality. It is this factor that contributes to the lack of understanding of homosexuality and heterosexuality. This component of training is designed to provide a more in-depth look at some of the complexities of sexuality as we see it today.

Sexuality can be explored by using the following seven components (Washington, 1991):

Biology/Physiology – This component speaks to one's biological and physiological make up. Genetics, genitalia, and chromosomes are variables in this component.

Biology/Physiology Identity Congruence – This component speaks to the extent to which one experiences cognitive and affective identity congruence with his/her bio/physio make up.

Gender – This component speaks to one's masculine and feminine characteristics or traits. It is important to note that masculinity and femininity are social constructs and therefore fluid. However, these constructs have a major impact on how individuals see themselves and how they are seen by others.

Sexual/Affectional Orientation – This component refers to one's natural capacity to fall in love with and connect with another at a romantic level.

Sexual Behavior – This component speaks specifically to one's sexual behavior. This can include, but is not limited to partner choice/ preferences, with whom one actually has sex, whether one chooses to have sex or not, different sexual practices, and frequency.

Sexual Orientation Identity – This component refers to how one names and sees him/herself (i.e., bisexual, lesbian, heterosexual, asexual, just a person, and so forth). It is important to note that the way one self-identifies is often influenced by how he or she behaves. While that identification may not be accurate because of oppression, one's self-identity is another critical component in understanding the complexities of sexuality.

How Others See and Identify a Person – This last component is important in a world where people often "judge a book by its cover." Specifically, if one looks or acts in a manner that society has come to associate with homosexuality or bisexuality, then that is the way others will see and name the person. For this reason, persons will often act or behave in ways that will protect them from being seen as bisexual, lesbian, or gay.

These seven components are the basis for a discussion of the complexities of sexuality. They reflect the often missing and biased information that most people receive in their socialization. A key concept to share during this information piece is that people have been socialized to believe that these seven components should, and do fall into a nice neat little package. However, that is an inaccurate assumption. These components are independent and may have little to no congruence with each other. The discussion of sexuality is extremely value laden. Therefore it is important to provide this type of information without judgment about what is right or wrong. The audience should be allowed to decide for themselves.

Appendix D
Stages of Responding to Heterosexist Attitudes and Actions

1. **Actively Participating**. This stage of response includes actions that directly support lesbian/gay oppression. These actions include laughing at or telling jokes that put down lesbians or gays, making fun of people who don't fit the traditional stereotypes of what is masculine or feminine, discouraging others and avoiding personal behavior that is not sex-stereotyped, and engaging in verbal or physical harassment of lesbians, gays, or heterosexuals who do not conform to traditional sex-role behavior. It also includes working for anti-gay legislation.

2. **Denying or Ignoring**. This stage of response includes inaction that supports LGB oppression coupled with an unwillingness or inability to understand the effects of homophobic and heterosexist actions. This stage is characterized by a "business as usual" attitude. Though responses in this stage are not actively and directly homophobic or heterosexist, the passive acceptance of these actions by others serves to support the system of gay and lesbian oppression.

3. **Recognizing, But No Action**. This stage of response is characterized by a recognition of homophobic or heterosexist actions, and the harmful effects of these actions. However, this recognition does not result in action to interrupt the homophobic or heterosexist situation. Taking action is prevented by homophobia or a lack of knowledge about specific actions to take. This stage of response is accompanied by discomfort due to the lack of congruence between recognizing homophobia or heterosexism yet failing to act on this recognition. An example of this stage of response is a person hearing a friend tell a "queer joke," recognizing that it is homophobic, not laughing at the joke, but saying nothing to the friend about the joke.

4. **Recognizing and Interrupting**. This stage of response includes not only recognizing homophobic and heterosexist actions, but also taking action to stop them. Though the response goes no further than stopping, this stage is often an important transition from passively accepting homophobic or heterosexist actions to actively choosing anti-homophobic and anti-heterosexist actions. In this stage a person hearing a "queer joke' would not laugh and would tell the joke teller that jokes that put down lesbians and gays are not funny. Another

example would be a person who realized that s/he is avoiding an activity because others might think s/he is lesbian or gay if s/he participates in it, and then decides to participate.

5. **Educating Self**. This stage of response includes taking action to learn more about lesbians, gays, heterosexism, and homophobia. These actions can include reading books, attending workshops, talking to others, joining organizations, listening to lesbian or gay music, or any other actions that can increase awareness and knowledge. This stage is also a prerequisite for the last three stages. All three involve interactions with others about homophobia and heterosexism. In order to do this confidently and comfortably, people need first to learn more.

6. **Questioning and Dialoguing**. This stage of response is an attempt to begin educating others about homophobia and heterosexism. This stage goes beyond interrupting homophobic and heterosexist interactions to engage people in dialogue about these issues. Through the use of questions and dialogue, this response attempts to help others increase their awareness of and knowledge about homophobia and heterosexism.

7. **Supporting and Encouraging**. This stage of response includes actions that support and encourage the anti-homophobic and anti-heterosexist actions of others. Overcoming the homophobia that keeps people from interrupting this form of oppression even when they are offended by it is difficult. Supporting and encouraging others who are able to take this risk is an important part of reinforcing anti-homophobic and anti-heterosexist behavior.

8. **Initiating and Preventing**. This stage of response includes actions that actively anticipate and identify homophobic institutional practices or individual actions and work to change them. Examples include teachers changing a "Family Life" curriculum that is homophobic or heterosexist, or counselors inviting a speaker to come and discuss how homophobia can affect counselor-client interactions.

Appendix E
Sample Intervention Exercises for Fraternity and Sorority Populations

These intervention exercises are only a sampling of those that were collected by Scott Reikofski and William Matthews. While these exercises can be utilized with any population, the authors found them most effective with Greek community members.

Exercise One

Name: Over the Line

Goals: To encourage dialogue and information sharing

Number of Participants: Minimum 12 participants; Maximum 34 participants.

Type of Participants: Activity works well with both student groups and staff member groups.

Time Needed: 30 minutes to 40 minutes, depending on size of the group and discussion needed.

Materials: No outside materials are needed. However, the facilitator should have a copy of the questions prepared. Room should have enough space for entire group to stand up and move around.

Activity: Participants should be standing in two lines, one facing the other. Participants should be facing each other with a large enough space in the middle to also have two additional lines. Facilitator should ask the group a question and provide for time for each person to respond by physically moving into the space allowed. When a statement is read the members should self-select if the statement applies to them. If the statement applies to them they are asked to stand in the middle between the two lines of people and look around. They should be encouraged to think about how they feel being in the middle, who is in the middle with them, who is not in the middle, what do the people who are not in the middle look like. This reflection should not last any more than 45-60 seconds. For groups with less than 20 participants they should have one line and have the people in the middle turn around and look at the line of people.

Facilitator Questions/Discussion Items: The following statements are examples of statements used in the past. The difficulty/level of discussion will depend on the types of statements used. These examples are for a high level discussion. Facilitators should be reminded that these statements can provoke some emotion in the participants. You should also notice the use of terms like "believe," "feel," and "am" versus "think." This activity is designed to avoid abstract discussions and focus in on personal feelings and emotions.

1. I am proud of being an African American.
2. I am proud of being a Latino.
3. I am proud of being an American.
4. I am proud of being a White American.
5. I am proud to be gay/lesbian or bisexual.
6. I feel it is difficult being proud of being White.
7. I feel our campus is a comfortable place for all students.
8. I do not feel our campus is a comfortable place for students like me.
9. I am proud of being a Native American.
10. I am proud of being multi-racial.
11. I believe racism exists on our campus.
12. I believe homophobia exists on our campus.
13. I believe I have worked to remove racism on our campus.
14. I believe I have confronted homophobia on our campus.
15. I have not contributed in removing racism from our campus.
16. I believe myself to be an ally to students who are not in the majority

Contributed by Dawn Mays & Sandra Vonniessen-Applebee of D/S Productions, 1064 Varsity Square West, Bowling Green, OH 43402, telephone 419.372.2343.

Exercise Two

Name: Concentric Circles

Goals: This activity is designed to give all participants the chance to talk on a one-to-one basis about several different topics. The goal is to provide participants a non-threatening opportunity to reflect on their past experiences with bisexual, lesbian, and gay people and issues. Participants will also have the opportunity to verbally explore their own values toward lesbian, gay, and bisexual individuals.

Number of Participants: minimum 12, maximum 50-60.

Time Needed: 20-25 minutes, depending on length of time facilitator allows for each question and how many questions s/he uses.

Materials Needed: No outside materials are needed. However, facilitator should have a copy of the questions prepared. Room should have enough space for entire group to stand up and move around.

Instructions: Divide the group in half, forming group a and group b. Inform both groups that they each will be forming a circle. Instruct group a to form a circle with the participants standing shoulder to shoulder and facing away from the center of the circle. Instruct group b to pick a partner by approaching and shaking hands with a member of group a. At this point, you should have two circles each facing the other—an inner circle and an outer circle.

Instruct the group that you will be giving them a phrase or question to discuss with their partner. Individuals on the inner circle respond first and the outer people will listen. After about 30 to 45 seconds, the outer group will respond.

For the next question, instruct the group to change partners as follows: (for example). "everyone in the outside circle move two people to your left", or "everyone in the inside circle move one person to your right". Give them the second question or topic to discuss with their new partner, and continue in the same manner for 10 to 15 minutes.

A note on listening: Those who are listening are asked not to speak while their partner is speaking. Even in silence, they are asked to simply wait for the next question or instruction. This allows room for those who do not normally speak so easily to do so!

Discussion Items:

1. What is your first memory of dealing with the issue of homosexuality?
2. What did you learn when you were growing up about homosexuality from your parents? your place of worship? TV or other media?
3. What kinds of words do people use to describe gay men? lesbians? bisexuals?
4. What are some of the stereotypes of lesbians? bisexuals? gay men?
5. How do you think it feels to grow up in a heterosexual culture knowing you are not heterosexual?
6. Why do some gay, lesbian, or bisexual people choose not to come-out publicly?
7. How are lesbian, bisexual, or gay people treated in your fraternity or sorority? How do you think they would be treated if they come out?
8. What do you do to support gay, bisexual, and lesbian students on campus? in your fraternity or sorority?

Contributed by Daniel Watts, University of Rochester, and Tammy Lou Maltzan, University of Colorado—Boulder.

Exercise Three

Name: Guided Journey

Number of Participants: At least ten participants are needed to complete this activity so that the sound effects have an impact.

Type of Participants: This is a high level challenge exercise. Only participants who are comfortable with low and medium level challenge should participate in this activity, otherwise participants will walk away frustrated and confused. (Meeting participants where they are is important.)

Materials: The guided journey story. You may want to write your own guided journey. Guided journey experience have been used in reference to childhood experiences for understanding some of the challenges possibly faced by gays, lesbians, and bisexuals, African Americans, and Native Americans. Other items needed are small slips of paper for participants. It is best if it can be done in a room that can be darkened.

Activity: See the directions that are on the actual guided journey. The actual guided journey is NOT handed out to participants, the participants should only have their slips of paper. Before you begin reading the guided journey, ask the participants to get comfortable and ask them to close their eyes. If people choose not to close their eyes, ask that they fixate their eyes on a particular object; barring both of those ask that those who do not want to participate remain silent throughout the entire activity (it will not have the same effect if people begin to talk). It is helpful if you have two facilitators for this activity—one to read and one to walk around the room and collect cards. After you read each passage and instruct the participants to hold up their card, walk around collecting the cards and with as much force as you can either tear up or crinkle the cards as you walk around collecting them for added effect. This story is based on actual incidents that have happened.

Facilitator Questions / Discussion Items: Before processing or asking any questions, allow 2-3 minutes for the whole concept to sink in. It is also important to discuss that not every gay, lesbian, or bisexual person may have experienced these issues. The purpose of this activity is not to stereotype but rather to give some examples of true stories in hopes of increasing awareness and understanding of the challenges of members of underrepresented populations.

1. Does anyone want to share anything about that activity? How did you feel about that?
2. How was that significant or not significant for you?
3. Did it disturb you?
4. Do you think it was realistic?
5. Do you think any of your friends may have had some of these experiences?
6. Does this make you think about any issues?
7. What might we draw from this experience?

8. What can we do to make change happen?—Even though we are only one person, remember Rosa Parks was only person . . .

Guided Journey: Gay/lesbian/bisexual persons
Directions: Distribute to each participant five slips of paper and a writing instrument. Have participants number the slips from 1-5 and then write on the corresponding slip:

1. Participant's favorite book as a child
2. Participant's best friend in elementary school
3. Participant's favorite activity in high school
4. The name of participant's first love
4. Participant's most fond memory of college
5. A dream participant has for the future

Read/told to the participants: "Your imagination is the key instrument in this exercise of guided journey. We will be taking a chronological journey through your mind's eye of what your life might be like if you were growing up as a gay man. You may experience a variety of feelings, but try not to let your feelings distract you from participating in this exercise. Please understand that my intent is not to manipulate your feelings, but the goal is to help you understand some of the feelings and experiences that someone who is a gay man might feel. Many of the experiences are based on true stories. The experiences that I am about to take you through are not universal but several of the themes presented are somewhat common."

"As you undertake this imaginary journey, think about the personal meaning of what you have written. Imagine how you would feel if any or all of these things were suddenly no longer there for you."

"Let's go back to your early childhood. Choose an age at which you have your earliest consistent memories. Perhaps you'll be five or six. Your mother is reading your favorite book to you. As you look through the pages of the book you realize that the characters may look like you but may not be like you. It is as if you could not exist in the world. You wonder why you are different. Is something wrong with you? When you watch t.v. or go to the movies, the only people you see who seem like you are characters portrayed as very effeminate men, men who are made fun of, or men who only dress like women. Hold up the card of your favorite book. You cannot identify with it, you feel as if you do not belong. You wish you were straight."

"You are now in grade school. You are good friends with a student who seems quite popular; his name is Chuck. You and Chuck hang out during school and are in lots of classes and project together. You are best friends, he has met your family, come over for dinner, and even spent the night. Your parents are so glad you have found such a good friend. One day you run back to your locker because you have forgotten something and you overhear Chuck say to a group of guys—"yeah he's such a fag—you know, one of THOSE (and makes a gesture with a limp wrist). I bet he even wears his sisters dresses at home, and has his own set of Barbie dolls! My mom told me that he will never be a real man and that I shouldn't play with him, that I might develop a swish, too" (which he demonstrates with a flamboyant walk down the hall). All of the boys laugh. Hold up the card of your best friend in elementary school—you will never be best friends—you realize he is not really your friend."

"It is your first year of high school and you are so excited. After the first semester of class you go to see your guidance counselor about the classes he has placed you in. As you begin to explain to him that you are failing your gym class because you are too slight of build, and the other boys are significantly bigger than you are, they pick on you and make fun of you, calling you "sissy," "fag," "queer." You expect him to be supportive but instead he looks at you and says "I can't believe this—you are supposed to be a man by now. Your family must be ashamed of you, especially your dad—no man wants to have a scrawny queer for a son." You are scared of embarrassing your family. You begin to wonder if you should be in that club you just joined, so you drop out of it so you can work out and eat more to get bigger. Hold up the card of your favorite activity in high school—you are no longer involved in that because you need to devote all your time to proving that you are normal so that your dad doesn't disown you or leave the family because of you."

"They say you never forget your first love—there is something magical about the first time that you have that kind of connection. You remember back that it was odd for you that it was a guy, and it built up without you really noticing it for a while, but it was love, just the same. The excitement, the butterflies, the thrill of the first kiss. You enjoyed being together, exploring each other's bodies, getting to know each other's dreams and what gets you turned on. Then on the news, you see that even the President of the United States, who has been supportive of gays up to this point, publicly states that your relationship has no place in our society and that the love you feel should not be legitimized through legal means. Churches, civic groups, and other government leaders are all speaking out and claiming that there should never be support for romantic, affectionate love between two men. Hold up the card of the name of your first love—society won't support the relationship and coming out proves to be too much for him, so he suddenly disappears—not a word to you, his family or friends, anyone."

"You are now a freshman in college. You made it! On World AIDS Day, you pass a group of demonstrators yelling about queers. They have set up a booth with signs that say that AIDS is God's answer to homosexuality—AIDS exists to kill of the queers and faggots in the world, to rid society of their repulsive ways. They are chanting that "God made Adam and Eve, not Adam and Steve," and that "No queers deserve to live." A tear comes to your eye because you have known several people who have suffered horrible deaths from HIV related illnesses that were contracted either from loving someone or from a blood transfusion. You have volunteered at the hospital caring for babies born with AIDS to drug addicted mothers. Hold up the card of your most fond memory of college. It has been overshadowed because no matter what, this is the image you will remember the most."

"You have just graduated from college and been accepted into a prestigious, Ivy League medical school in Philadelphia. You have just arrived in Pennsylvania and you are sitting outside in a park downtown enjoying a warm afternoon. You are excited because you are embarking on an education and a career with a lot of promise. You will not face the same financial restraints as your parents and you are excited by the possibility that you will be able to repay them and take care of them, and give them a lifestyle they have not experienced. You are daydreaming about repaying them for all of the sacrifices they have made for you, and the first vacation you will send them on. As you sit in the park you notice a group of youth approaching you, it looks like about 15 people. You are a bit shy so you put your head down so they do not think you are starring, when you realize they are approaching you. As they get closer they start shouting at you "faggot," "queer," "cocksucker," "womanhater." Hold up the card with your dream for the future. It doesn't matter that you had this dream. You have been beaten to death by the mob of youth."

Adapted from exercise contributed by Dawn Mays & Sandra Vonniessen-Applebee of D/S Productions, 1064 Varsity Square West, Bowling Green, OH 43402, telephone 419.372.2343.

Exercise Four

Name: The Closet Game: Part I

Purpose: The purpose of this activity is to show you what it's like to live in the closet (in other words, what it's like to have to keep your sexual orientation secret).

Number of Participants: Any number of participants. Large groups may be broken into smaller groups for discussion, sharing, and processing.

Time Needed: Part I—about 10 minutes, Part II—20-45 minutes.

Materials: Closet Game sheet, scoring on a separate sheet, one of each for each participant.

Activity: If you are heterosexual, most of the items listed below are things you probably do all the time to advertise the fact that you are attracted to persons of the opposite sex (both affectionally and sexually). Add up the number of points shown in each case for all the things you have done in the past year and the past month.

Name: The Closet Game: Part 2

If you had to keep your heterosexuality secret, all of the activities listed in part 1 would be extremely dangerous. In fact, if you lived in a "heterophobic" society (one that condemned heterosexuality), most of the activities would carry heavy penalties. To find out what might happen to you in such a society for "carrying on" as you have during the past year/month, find your score below and follow the instructions.

Scoring Instructions

1 – 10   `Keep up the good work. You are relatively discreet about your heterosexuality. Select any two penalties from list A below.

11 – 40   Oops: You need some practice in covering up your heterosexual lifestyle. Select three penalties from list A below and one from list B.

41 – 70   You are a real "flaunter." Select three penalties from list A below and two from list B.

71 – 100 You obviously can't keep a secret, and the future doesn't look too good for you. Select four penalties from list A below and three from list B.

List A

1. Several of your friends refuse to see you anymore because you are heterosexual.
2. Your best friend becomes very cool toward you and states flatly that she/he never wants to meet your spouse.
3. Your family disowns you.
4. Your supervisor at work tells you to stop "flaunting" your lifestyle, or she/he will have to let you go.
5. Someone scratches the word "straight" into the finish of your car.
6. Someone in a passing car shouts "heterosexual!" and screams obscenities at you.
7. The other members of your church shun you because they think it is immoral and sinful for you to act upon your heterosexual feelings.
8. (If you were dancing in public) the bouncer at a local nightclub throws you out.
9. Your reputation is ruined when someone starts a "whisper" campaign to spread the word that you are heterosexual.
10. Since it is against the law to sell alcohol to known heterosexuals, a local bartender refuses to serve you.

List B

1. Your boss fires you from your job.
2. State court denies you custody of your children.
3. Four teenagers shouting "Heterosexual trash!" beat you up and throw you off a bridge into the river.
4. Your landlady evicts you because she considers you an "undesirable."
5. It becomes clear that you will not get the promotion you had expected (and that you deserve) because you are heterosexual.

6. The bank denies you and your spouse a loan because you are in a heterosexual relationship.
7. The Navy discharges you even though you have always received high performance ratings. Since you are two years away from retirement, you lose all of your benefits.
8. You lose your governmental security clearance at work because (since you are heterosexual) you are considered a security risk.
9. (If you were holding hands in public) you are arrested and booked on a charge of disorderly conduct.
10. After joining a new church that ministers specifically to heterosexuals, you are seriously burned in an arson attack on the church sanctuary.

Discussion Questions

1. What factors influenced you in selecting the penalties you chose?
2. The above activity compares what might happen to you in a "heterophobic" society with what actually happens to lesbians and gay men in our society today. Do you feel this is a legitimate comparison to make? Why or why not?
3. If you actually lived in a heterophobic society, what changes would you have to make in your life in order to survive?
4. Do you feel the above activity has given you a better understanding of the difficulties lesbians and gay men face in our society? Why or why not?

Contributed by Daniel Watts, University of Rochester, and Tammy Low Maltzan, University of Colorado—Boulder.

Closet Game Sheet

Action	Year (1 point)	Month (5 points)

1. Held hands in a public space with someone of the opposite sex.
2. Put your arm around someone of the opposite sex in public.
3. Kissed (either on the lips or cheek) a person of the opposite sex in a public place.
4. Said "I love you" (or anything else affectionate) to a person of the opposite sex within the hearing of others.
5. Said anything publicly to indicate that you are attracted to someone of the opposite sex ('Wow, she's a great looking woman!" or "Isn't that a gorgeous guy?" etc.).
6. Told another person that you have a "special friend" of the opposite sex.
7. Told another person that you are engaged to someone of the opposite sex.
8. Told another person that you are married to someone of the opposite sex.
9. Shown a photo of your "special friend" or fiancee to another person.
10. Shown a photo of your spouse to another person.
11. Worn an engagement or wedding ring in public.
12. Been seen frequently (enough to make people wonder) in the company of a "special friend," fiancee, or spouse.
13. Been seen entering or leaving the place where you reside with another person in a heterosexual relationship (married or otherwise).

14. Been seen entering or leaving a hetero-
    sexual singles bar (either alone or with a
    person of the opposite sex).
15. Danced in public with someone of the
    opposite sex.
16. Been seen frequently in the company of
    known or admitted heterosexuals.
17. Been seen purchasing a magazine such as
    Playboy or Playgirl (which ever is appro-
    priate).
18. Carried or read a book in public that had a
    heterosexual theme (romantic novel,
    psychological study of heterosexuals, etc.).
19. Displayed a tattoo in public showing the
    name of a person of the opposite sex (on
    your arm or elsewhere).
20. Done anything else you can think of that
    might make people suspect that you are
    heterosexual.

Total
    Add up points. Month = 5 points, year = 1 point

References

Blumenfeld, W. J. (Ed.). (1992). *Homophobia: How we all pay the price*. Boston: Beacon.

Beyond tolerance: Gays, lesbians, bisexuals on campus. (1993). (A handbook of structured experiences and exercises for training and development, developed for the Beyond Tolerance Roadshow). Washington, DC: American College Personnel Association.

Levine, H., & Evans, N. J. (1991). The development of gay, lesbian, and bisexual identities. In Evans, N. J., & Wall, V. A. (Eds.), *Beyond tolerance: Gays, lesbians and bisexuals on campus* (pp. 1-24). Alexandria, VA: Amercian College Personnel Association.

Griffin, P., & Harro, B. (1997). Heterosexism curriculum design. In M. Adams, L. A. Bell, & P. Griffin (Eds.), *Teaching for diversity and social justice* (pp. 141-169). New York: Routledge.

Hughes, M. J. (1991). Addressing gay, lesbian, and bisexual issues in fraternities and sororities. In N. J. Evans & V. A. Wall (Eds.), *Beyond Tolerance: Gays, lesbians and bisexuals on campus* (pp. 97-116). Alexandria, VA: American College Personnel Association.

Rankin, S. (1998). Campus climate for lesbian, gay, bisexual, and transgendered students, faculty, and staff: Assessment and strategies for change. In R. Sanlo (Ed.), *Working with lesbian, gay, and bisexual students: A guide for administrators and faculty* (pp. 203-212). Westport, CT: Greenwich.

Reikofski, S., & Matthews, W. (1998). *Homosexuality and men's and women's fraternities*. Unpublished manuscript.

Sears, J. (Ed.). (1994). *Bound by diversity*. Columbia, SC: Sebastian Press.

Washington, J. E. (1991). *Beyond tolerance: Toward understanding, appreciation and celebration*. (Handout developed for an ACPA Conference presentation, available from the author).

Chapter 8

ᔕᔕᔕ

Group Counseling for Lesbian, Gay, and Bisexual Students

Ruperto M. Perez, Kurt A. DeBord,
and Kathleen J. Brock

Group counseling has increasingly become an effective and efficient way to address the various concerns of people seeking counseling services. The effectiveness of group counseling rests, in large part, with the experiences and dynamics shared by and among group members. As a result, group counseling provides clients with repeated opportunities to address issues that vary widely in content, including such diverse topics as relationships, depression, anxiety, family issues, career issues, and other life transitions (Conyne, 1997). Notably, group counseling is playing an increasingly significant role in providing counseling services to students at universities and colleges. Group counseling can prove to be a rewarding experience for college students as they encounter a number of life transitions, experiences, and decisions (Archer & Cooper, 1998).

Clearly, the college years can be a time of intense inter- and intrapersonal exploration for many students. Group counseling provides a means by which students can express and explore their concerns within the context of a supportive and therapeutic environment. For many students, the college experience allows for an increased awareness of personal issues, one of which is sexual/affectional orientation (Archer & Cooper, 1998). For students who are lesbian, gay, or bisexual (LGB), this increased awareness can lead them to seek support, understanding, and insight related to their newfound awareness.

Unfortunately, a number of societal forces may prevent LGB students from receiving the appropriate services for their needs. As a "hidden minority" (Fassinger, 1991), LGB students are subjected to varying degrees and types of societal oppression that can have a significant impact upon their psychosocial adjustment. LGB students may encounter effects of heterosexism and homophobia unique to a college or university environment. For example, LGB students may be denied such things as access to married student housing, funding for LGB student groups, and protection under university non-discrimination policies. Heterosexism and homophobia force many LGB students to hide or deny their sexual orientation. As well, students may cope with discrimination or homohatred in potentially damaging ways, such as isolating themselves, abusing substances, or even attempting suicide. Indeed, for many LGB students, college may not be the best years of their lives as illustrated in these words of a gay college student:

> I didn't ask to be gay. It is not a decision that one makes. It is not a trivial matter. It is not a lifestyle choice . . . I guess I've always known that I was gay. Well actually, I've always known that I was different . . . Knowing all this, I went on with my life, denying what I felt in my heart to be the real me from showing. I had gone on so long with this charade of sorts that it became a part of my life. What I felt was not something that I discussed with others, I had accepted as yet another burden in my life. . . . Coming to grips with my identity was without a doubt the most important thing I could have accomplished while at college. Yet until my time was right, I was content with keeping it my own little secret. (A former client, Author's files, January, 1993).

The concerns of gay, lesbian, and bisexual college students have only recently been widely addressed. Works by Dworkin and Gutierrez (1992) and Evans and Wall (1991) have been instrumental in bringing these issues to light. Recent research has begun to examine therapists' attitudes towards clients who are lesbian, gay, or bisexual (Hayes &

Gelso, 1991; Rudolph, 1988). In addition, Iasanza (1989) has highlighted the importance of incorporating sexual orientation issues into counselor training curricula. Few studies have explored the importance of providing group counseling to LGB students (Westefeld & Winkelpleck, 1983), and practical models for providing services to LGB students are still needed (Betz & Fitzgerald, 1993; Fassinger, 1991).

The purpose of this chapter is to explore the theoretical and practical issues in developing and offering group counseling for LGB college students. In this chapter, we discuss the basic tenets of group counseling theory and their application to LGB groups. We also address the potential goals of LGB groups and describe three group formats designed to meet different goals. Further, we discuss the pragmatics of offering such groups and offer suggestions regarding group content, format, and facilitator characteristics.

The phrase "lesbian, gay, and bisexual (LGB)" and the term "queer" are used interchangeably in this chapter to convey uniqueness as well as inclusiveness. Specifically, our use of the word "queer" is meant to reflect and represent a consistent positive, unifying, and political affirmation of all those claiming a lesbian, gay, or bisexual identity (Rhoads, 1994). As such, the term "queer" in this chapter also serves to challenge the confining forces of heterosexism and homophobia, a goal which we consider both admirable and desirable.

Group Counseling

Group counseling can be especially beneficial for those students who are motivated to change, open to learning about themselves, have limited social supports, or who have limited opportunities to express their concerns to others (Archer & Cooper, 1998; Yalom, 1985). Conversely, students who may not benefit from a group experience are those who are not motivated to change and who may have difficulty adhering to group norms and expectations (for example, confidentiality).

The purpose of group counseling is to provide a therapeutic environment in which individuals may gain awareness and insight into their concerns by exploring various issues with other group members who may or may not share the same experiences. The therapeutic nature of the group lies in its ability to act as a therapeutic change agent by providing what Yalom (1985) has described as "therapeutic factors."

We have summarized these factors in Table 1. These therapeutic factors can facilitate members' exploration and awareness of a number of individual concerns such as family issues, interpersonal relationships, stress management, career indecision, and personal growth. Because of the range of possible concerns that groups can readily confront, groups are often offered in various forms and designs that specifically focus on one or more of these concerns.

A number of group formats exist that address the issues that students experience. In general, three types of groups may be offered: 1) psychoeducational, 2) structured/semi-structured, and 3) unstructured or process (Archer & Cooper, 1998). Psychoeducational groups are designed to offer information concerning specific topic areas such as drug and alcohol use, safe sex, and cultural diversity. These groups are beneficial in imparting important information in a concise and understandable way (Archer & Cooper, 1998).

Structured and semi-structured groups are typically offered as a way to effectively address such topics as stress management, anger control, coping skills, social skills training, and vocational and career exploration (Archer & Cooper, 1998). Structured groups are typically arranged in a sequential order such that each previous session provides information and skills that are then used in subsequent sessions. Semi-structured groups also often adopt a sequential format, and may also allow for more temporal flexibility as well as incorporating elements of support or psychotherapeutic processing. The advantage of these groups is their ability to provide both information and awareness in a brief period of time. Overall, both structured and semi-structured groups can be a beneficial therapeutic alternative for time-limited counseling and therapy.

Process groups are designed to explore core issues that underlie a person's presenting concern (Archer & Cooper, 1998; Yalom, 1985). In process groups, members are encouraged to bring their concerns to the group and express them openly. Interaction between group members is highly encouraged and is seen as essential to the functioning of the group. This interaction allows for a free-flow exchange of information and learning from others. Relationship issues among group members are often talked about and processed during the group as they reflect individual concerns. Process groups can be especially helpful for exploring various issues such as family concerns, relationship and interpersonal difficulties, and personal growth.

Table 1
Summary of group therapeutic factors (adapted from Yalom, 1985)

1. **Installation of Hope** – mutual support gives members a sense of optimism.
2. **Universality** – the awareness by members that they are not alone in experiencing their concerns.
3. **Sharing Information** – members benefit from receiving information and advice from group members and group facilitators.
4. **Altruism** – group members gain a sense of confidence and beneficence in helping others in the group.
5. **Re-enactment of Family Dynamics** – group experience provides an environment in which family dynamics and experiences are reenacted facilitating awareness and resolution of issues.
6. **Developing Socializing Techniques** – group allows for learning and trying different social skills within a safe environment.
7. **Group Cohesiveness** – members experience a sense of closeness and interpersonal sharing with each other.
8. **Catharsis** – the group experience allows its members the opportunity to express their feelings openly to others in the group.
9. **Existential Factors** – the group raises an awareness of existential issues and experiences for members.

Overall, group therapy can be a valuable therapeutic tool for a number of reasons. First, group counseling can allow students to openly express and talk about their concerns with others in a way that can feel safe and supportive (Archer & Cooper, 1998). In this way, issues are explored openly and processed within the group setting. Each member benefits from other members' feedback and experiences as shared in the group.

Second, group counseling can provide an opportunity and a setting to try out new behaviors and ways of relating to others in a supportive and safe environment. Third, group counseling can also be an important adjunct to individual counseling and can enhance a client's insight and awareness. Fourth, group counseling can be a beneficial means for providing counseling within a prescribed time frame (Archer & Cooper, 1998; Yalom, 1985). As most counseling centers, counselors, and psychologists become aware of the impact of managed care and session limits, group counseling can provide a means through which a number of concerns can be addressed in a time-efficient, productive, and therapeutic manner (Seligman, 1995).

In sum, the benefits of group counseling are many. Its usefulness in addressing certain issues is clear. By engaging in group counseling, clients are able to focus on issues, receive information, and gain awareness and insight. Each type of group (that is, psychoeducational, structured/semi-structured, process) is uniquely suited to meet particular goals and has its unique benefits. Each type of group can be an important adjunct to individual counseling as well as providing therapeutic services in a matter that is timely and conducive to promoting insight, awareness, and individual growth.

Group Counseling With Lesbian, Gay, and Bisexual Students

Little information is currently available about providing group counseling to LGB students (Chojnacki & Gelberg, 1995). In this section, we attempt to address a number of important considerations that counselors, psychologists, and therapists are likely to face within the areas of group structure, policy, and content in planning group counseling for LGB students. Additionally, we provide a variety of goals, content ideas, and conclusions derived from our experiences in conducting LGB student groups.

Because most college social activities are heterosexually based, LGB students can have difficulty finding peer and community support. Many experience difficulty in facing "typical" developmental challenges while simultaneously struggling with painful feelings of isolation and stigmatization (Browning, 1987; Wall & Evans, 1991). Claiming an identity, exploring social and romantic relationships, separating from parents, and developing self-esteem can be made all the more difficult by the negative biases facing LGB students.

For those students who have claimed a gay, lesbian, or bisexual identity, regular experiences with homophobia or homohatred on campus can wear on their emotional and physical wellbeing. In one recent study, 29% of first year students reported that the university would be a better place without lesbians and gay men (D'Augelli & Rose, 1990). Another study indicated that 65% of LGB college students, staff, and faculty had experienced verbal insults; 25% had been threatened with physical violence, and 12% had been sexually harassed or assaulted (Herek, 1993). Herek (1993) concluded that many LGB members of college communities live in a world concealing their sexual orientation and fearing both discrimination and verbal or physical abuse. Students may also feel invisible as their experiences fail to be addressed again and again in courses and classroom materials (Stoller, 1994). Additionally, intolerance and isolation, along with internalization of negative attitudes are primary reasons why LGB students seek help (Eldridge & Barnett 1991). As institutional biases, these forces represent examples of institutionalized heterosexism that, left untreated, can result in LGB student attrition from universities and colleges (Kitzinger, 1990). To avoid this manifestation of heterosexism, the need for support for LGB students is paramount.

Establishing a Group: Student Needs, Group Goals, and Format

Group counseling provides a particularly effective way to meet some of the unique needs of LGB college students. Overall, group therapy can be a valuable therapeutic tool for LGB students in that group therapy can allow LGB students to experience deeper intimacy with others than ever before, primarily because they may have never before felt safe enough to openly discuss their sexual orientation. The supportive group setting can allow LGB students to openly explore and process their concerns with others in the group in a manner that can be safe and supportive. Indeed, such groups are imperative in working to create a non-homophobic campus environment to make the college experience safer and more positive for LGB students (Stoller, 1994). While this is not to say that all LGB students are in need of counseling—group, individual, or otherwise—group counseling can serve as a safe place in which LGB students can begin or continue to explore significant areas in their lives. Group counseling can be an important means through which LGB students can also improve interpersonal functioning or decrease unhealthy coping patterns such as substance abuse (Conlin & Smith, 1994).

One of the first and most substantial decisions that faces LGB group facilitators is determining what type of group to promote. At times, the needs of LGB students may seem overwhelming, and a successful group is one whose goals are clearly defined at the outset. One way to determine what kind of group is most appropriate on a given campus is to conduct a needs assessment. Such an assessment may be accomplished by informally surveying members of Queer student organizations, LGB clients, or counselors of LGB students at the campus counseling center or mental health center. By performing a needs assessment, counselors and therapists can gain a good sense of what important needs should be addressed and how they can develop the specific goals and strategies by which to best meet those needs.

Decisions regarding the content and structure of a group can also depend on the nature and extent of other resources available on a given campus. For example, facilitators may decide to offer a group focused on clarifying sexual identity or "coming out." However, a coming out group may be too limited in scope to meet the needs of all Queer students. Students who are already "out" as gay, lesbian, or bisexual may also need the social support a group can provide. In some cases, facilitators may recognize the need for a psychoeducational group (for example, "Queer 101") to help LGB students develop a sense of their own history and to challenge their own stereotypes about Queer individuals. However, at the rare schools that offer Queer History or Queer Studies courses, counseling resources might be better utilized offering an interpersonally oriented process group in which LGB students can extensively explore their relationship hopes, dynamics, and personal histories. Alternately, facilitators may decide that providing a support group format with an emphasis on community building would best serve their campus. In sum, facilitators must be familiar with existing campus resources and student needs in order to make decisions about the best services to offer to LGB students.

In developing specific goals for counseling groups, it is important to note the type of group that will be offered and how the group will attempt to meet particular needs for LGB clients. Several of the following goals may serve as primary focus for an LGB counseling group. Many of these goals, and the strategies that they encompass, overlap; and each has implications for the nature of the group offered (for example, format, duration, screening).

Primary goals for LGB student groups may include: 1) identity clarification and "coming out," 2) increased self-esteem and Queer pride, 3) increased healthy coping, 4) decreased isolation and increased support, 5) community building, and 6) relationship enhancement. Membership in an LGB student group may accomplish some of these goals in and of itself. That is, a group can decrease social isolation for LGB students and help to establish a more Queer affirmative support system. A natural mixture of members at different levels of "outness" or identification can facilitate identity development as members and facilitators serve as role models for the group. Facilitators can devise specific strategies and activities to meet other specified goals for their group. These specific goals will be explored in a subsequent section.

For the purposes of this chapter, we focus on our experiences as group facilitators in two types of groups for LGB clients: process-oriented and semi-structured groups. Process-oriented groups describe those counseling groups that are unstructured and focus on interpersonal dynamics and issues. In these groups, a number of concerns and group dynamics are examined, such as coming-out, family of origin, relationships, and interpersonal styles. In these groups, it is the responsibility of group members to be actively engaged in the group and with one another as concerns are addressed and interpersonal relationships are examined.

Semi-structured groups refer to those in which certain themes and activities are chosen for weekly meetings and time allowed for more unstructured discussion related to themes. For these groups, weekly themes are developed with input from group members and group facilitators coordinate the activities. Semi-structured groups are flexible to accommodate relevant current experiences in members' personal lives or on campus or in society. The semi-structured groups described here contain a significant psychoeducational component as well, based on the belief that providing information can serve to deconstruct harmful stereotypes and myths and to instill a sense of group history.

Group Membership

Among the host of decisions that face group facilitators at the beginning stages of group development are those regarding membership and member characteristics (for example, same-sex or mixed-sex), attendance policies, and the timing of accepting new members. Although many of these issues may be resolved with member input, it is important that facilitators have a clear determination of the group's characteristics in order to best meet the goals for a particular group.

Membership considerations should include the varying degrees of outness or stages of identity development group members will embrace (see Levine & Evans, 1991). Chojnacki and Gelberg (1995) suggested that LGB groups may be most helpful for students in particular stages of identity development. Specifically, persons in the initial stages of self-identifying as LGB (or cycling back through this stage as development is not necessarily linear) might be unwilling to associate with a group of negatively valued others. To an extent, as it becomes more important for students to self identify as LGB, the more visible they are in their eagerness to commit to an LGB group. Therefore, students in most other stages of development will likely gain from group contact with other LGB students, experiencing the decreased isolation, the increased support, and the normalization that occur in the group. It is also suggested that students in the "identity pride" stage may be unwilling to attend a group facilitated by a non-LGB counselor or may be intolerant of the hesitancy of other group members to identify as LGB (Chojnacki & Gelberg, 1995). In our experience, groups composed primarily of the "out and proud" students can prove challenging as these students tend to be intensely immersed in their Queer identity and may be perceived as threatening by other group members who are just beginning to explore their LGB identity.

Another decision of group membership is determining whether the group will be open to same-sex clients or whether the group will be open to both men and women. The decision as to whether or not to offer same-sex or mixed-sex groups can be difficult and will likely depend on student needs and facilitator experience and training. However, once again, campus resources may be the primary determinant of this decision. We have found that there are different benefits to each type of group. For example, mixed-sex groups provide consistent opportunities for men and women to recognize commonalties in their experiences. Such recognition, in turn, serves to enhance feelings of a unified Queer community. Further, the intersection of sexism with homophobia and biphobia is more readily apparent in mixed-sex groups, allowing for more in-depth, interpersonal exploration of these issues. However, women in particular may not wish to have to confront sexism in the group that may provide their only support and validation. For this reason, same-sex groups sometimes provide a safer context in which to discuss the complexity of sexual identity, gender socialization, and sexism for women.

While Queer self-identification can unify a group, unchallenged member or facilitator biases or blind spots can destroy group cohesion. For these reasons, group discussions regarding race and ethnicity, age, class, and transgender issues are an imperative and productive component of any LGB group, regardless of membership composition. Additionally, biphobia and issues unique to bisexuality should be addressed in every group, again regardless of composition. These issues can typically provide thought provoking and insightful group discussions. While these issues pertain to group content and counselor training as well as member diversity, we mention them here because facilitators should consider at the group's outset the manner in which these concerns will be addressed in the group. Clearly, it should not be the responsibility of group members to take a didactic role regarding these issues. Facilitators must be alert for oppressive attitudes held by group members (such as racism) and must be sure they consider the ways in which being gay, lesbian, or bisexual can differ depending on other aspects of a person's identity. Such consideration will make it more likely the group will be a truly safe place for all potential members.

Group Screening, Attendance, and Duration

Once a decision has been made regarding the goals, format, and membership of the potential group, the remaining decisions related to screening of group members, attendance, and duration may be clearer. Pre-group interviews, or group screenings, of potential members can be an important first step in selecting group members. Screenings serve primarily to determine whether member needs/wants are congruent with group goals. As well, screenings may even serve to determine group goals based on pre-group interviews.

In the case of a process group, thorough pre-group screening of potential group members is important in order to determine whether they are psychologically facile enough to engage in the interpersonal process of group and gain insight from their experience. Alternatively, the screening criteria of a semi-structured group may vary according to the themes and goals of the group. For example, if the success of a semi-structured group is likely to depend on the ability of its members to share emotional intimacy, then screening for that skill is logical. If a group is primarily psychoeducational, minimal participant screening may be necessary.

In addition, the group format and goals will in part determine the duration and attendance requirements of the group. For example, students in the initial stages of adopting an LGB identity may be apprehensive about committing to meet weekly with a group, fearing that such a commitment is tantamount to proclaiming a Queer identity. For this reason, other group formats may be available, such as establishing a group with a "drop-in" format. This type of format allows new members to join the group at any time during the semester with no further expectation of attending future groups, provided they are willing to adhere to the mission statement adopted by the group. This type of group policy may resolve a number of attendance problems while still permitting a significant degree of intimacy among members.

A process-oriented group will likely be most successful if it runs consistently for a time period with the same composition of group members in order to facilitate group cohesiveness and interpersonal dynamics. The addition of new members to the group must be considered carefully and introduced with member consensus. Process groups work best with consistent attendance and over a regular given period of time (for example, one or two semesters). Process groups permit an on-going therapeutic relationship with a core group of members who, over time, begin to develop their own sense of trust, understanding, and relationship to one another.

Finally, no single solution addresses all attendance considerations. However, there is no substitute for consensus among group facilitators and member input in decisions regarding attendance policy and membership in producing group cohesiveness and achieving group goals.

Group Content and Activities

Group content and activities follow closely from both the goals and format of the group (for example, process-oriented or semi-structured). Facilitators can devise strategies and activities aimed at meeting the group's goals in a number of areas. Specific key goals include: 1) identity clarification and coming out, 2) self esteem and Queer pride, 3) healthy coping, 4) increased support and community building, and 5) relationship enhancement.

Increasing member self-esteem underlies and flows from many of the other goals for LGB groups. Again, simply being in an LGB group can provide the beginnings of increased self-esteem as members receive validation, normalization, and support for themselves, their values, and their relationships. Facilitators can provide positive messages about being LGB, and, if Queer themselves, can serve as role models of healthy, productive, happy Queer adults. Facilitators can help group members explore and examine the family and cultural messages they received about being LGB. In addition, facilitators should be alert for indications of internalized homophobia and shame, and should plan ways to counteract these.

Group esteem (that is, Queer pride) can be enhanced by providing material for discussion about Queer history and political activism. In addition, the role of "play" and fun centered around being LGB should not be underestimated. Such activities communicate that being Queer is not simply an oppression—it's a wonderful way of living! The sharing of Queer culture through books and videos can also create a sense of belonging and broader community for members.

Providing support to LGB students is often a primary goal of group facilitators, and this goal, too, is often accomplished with little effort on the part of facilitators. As members share experiences, feelings, hopes, fears, and other members respond, support is accomplished. Members, perhaps for the first time, realize that they are not alone. In addition, being in a group often provides members with useful resources to further increase social support. Facilitators and members can identify campus and community resources and events at which members might expand their friendship networks. Members may also, depending on the nature and the policies of the group, develop friendships or social relationships with one another that continue after the group ends. Facilitators can also promote exploration of the relationship between coming out and gaining social support.

In a group whose goals include sexual identity clarification and decision-making about coming out, several psychoeducational interventions (or "mini-lectures" by facilitators) can be useful starting points for discussion. Students may benefit from information regarding a continuum

of emotional-erotic attachment, the social construction of sexual identity, or the relationships between sexual identity and gender identity.
Personal exploration of feelings, attitudes, and experiences related to
being LGB within the safety of the group can be beneficial, as can the
sharing of personal histories and coming-out experiences. Facilitators
can assist members to analyze risks and benefits, costs and rewards of
coming out to self and others, as well as the costs and rewards of "passing." When these issues hold the group's focus, leaders should watch for
pressure from the more out or political members on the members not
wishing to claim a Queer identity. Exploration of the different meanings
that being LGB holds for each group member is critical. In a process-
oriented group, members can receive direct feedback from one another
regarding how they are viewed and how being LGB contributes to those
views and self-perceptions.

Many LGB groups aim to help members devise more healthy ways
of coping with homophobia, heterosexism, and life stress. Some of these
will not differ from helping any other client or group accomplish healthy
coping (for example, time management, positive self-talk, and so forth),
but others will be specific to LGB students. Facilitators can encourage
discussion of member experiences with homophobia and homohatred
and allow members time to process their emotional reactions to such
events. Group members can share strategies for responding to and coping
with such events or can even role-play a range of possible responses.
Facilitators should help members to analyze potential consequences of
member responses.

Community building can be defined in various ways. Goals might
include helping LGB students to feel a part of the group, a campus
community, or a wider regional, national, or international community.
Alternately, goals might include helping LGB students see the commonalities in their experiences such that they experience themselves as "being
on the same side." Some leaders may want to incorporate aspects of
coalition-building as well, helping LGB students to see the benefits of
working against other forms of oppression. Again, psychoeducation
regarding historical events and the fluidity and social construction of
sexual identity can be helpful in allowing members to honor both their
similarities and their differences in an appropriate context. Member
discussion about attitudes towards bisexuality can be shaped by leaders
to decrease biphobia.

The interaction, support, challenge, and conflict inherent in process-oriented groups provide the optimal environment for enhancing members' relationship skills and interpersonal functioning. Simultaneously, semi-structured and psychoeducational groups can provide unique insight and relationship enhancement for LGB students. Of course, traditional interventions involving communication style and active listening, can be utilized. Facilitators can also plan discussion of the unique joys and challenges of same sex relationships (for example, gender socialization factors or managing relationships with ex-lovers).

Pragmatics: Promoting the Group and Ensuring Its Safety

A number of remaining decisions face facilitators of LGB groups. Of these, the major decisions include: 1) how to recruit new members, 2) where to find potential members, 3) where to conduct the group, and 4) how to ensure confidentiality and safety for group members. As with other foundational decisions regarding the group, a facilitator's conclusions regarding member recruitment will likely depend upon the type of group.

Process and semi-structured support groups can flourish by relying solely on referrals from already existing student services (such as a wellness center or women's center). Finding members for some LGB groups requires advertising and other creative recruitment strategies. Publicizing the group through newspaper and radio advertisements typically requires only a phone call and a completed form; however, some papers and radio stations do not provide such service announcements for free. Depending upon the available finances, it may be possible to place large advertisements in school or LGB newspapers, places where LGB student readership is likely to be high.

Advertising admission to an LGB group through flyers placed on campus is another effective way of promoting such a group. But special measures may be necessary if this is the promotional plan. Depending upon the pervasiveness of homophobia and biphobia on campus, weekly flyer posting may be necessary to attain adequate publicity and to prevent/deter their removal by other students, faculty, or staff. Relatedly, depending on the campus and community climate, the safety of facilitators should be considered as well as group safety when promoting the group. One way to help ensure group safety is to avoid publishing the exact location of the group in flyers or advertisements. Including only the meeting time, the theme of the group, and a contact telephone number on flyers should provide adequate and useful information.

In addition to placing flyers on campus, local merchants may be encouraged to post group announcements. This strategy can result in regular rewarding opportunities to discover and foster public alliances between local business people and the LGB group. The visibility of group advertisements in local establishments can also create a more affirming atmosphere surrounding the campus for LGB students as well. The placement of flyers in LGB businesses (such as bars and bookstores) is another effective use of this advertising medium. Finally, as mentioned earlier, posting flyers and promoting the group in ways that are sensitive to and encouraging of the participation of individuals from a variety of racial and ethnic groups is essential in establishing a group that is beneficial to all of its members.

A final important consideration regarding group promotion is that the more opportunistic and creative the facilitators are, the more likely it is that word will spread about the availability of the group. By participating on classroom panels, granting interviews to radio and newspaper reporters, presenting at national conferences, and consistently advertising the group at all local Queer functions, student awareness of the availability of groups can be greatly increased. In all, the success of many LGB groups relies heavily upon the priority and time given to their promotion in their early stages of development.

Confidentiality must be explicitly and thoroughly addressed in groups. Safety of members and respect of each individual's level of disclosure or nondisclosure to others is imperative. In groups where membership changes regularly, group members must agree to keep confidential the names and identities of other members as well as the content of the group's discussions. As well, it is recommended that facilitators lead discussions of how to handle unexpected encounters with group members outside of the group and problematic dual relationships (for example, a group member is friends with another member's lover). Facilitators must know that even at large universities, the Queer community may be quite small and highly interconnected. More than with other groups, boundary issues and confidentiality issues must be addressed and dealt with before group work will be productive (Holahan & Gibson, 1994).

Finally, the possibility of alerting campus police to the potential of student harassment of the group's members should be considered. Undoubtedly, the psychological and physical safety of LGB group members must be something would-be facilitators consider seriously before beginning to arrange for an LGB group.

Counselor Considerations

Group facilitators must have insight and awareness into the experiential world of their clients, as well as a keen awareness of their own experiences while working with clients. This is especially true in counseling gays, lesbians, and bisexuals. Recent research has begun to examine counselors' attitudes towards clients who are gay or lesbian (Hayes & Gelso, 1991; Rudolph, 1988). In their landmark contribution, the American Psychological Association (APA) Task Force on Lesbian and Gay Concerns (APA, 1990; Garnets et al., 1991) provided substantial information on counselor bias and attitudes towards lesbian and gay clients. Iasenza (1989) concluded that it is important that counselors be insightful of their own biases, values, and "-isms" when working with gays and lesbians.

Much has been written about counselor characteristics necessary for effective and ethical group and individual counseling with LGB clients (Clark, 1977; Chojnacki & Gelberg, 1995; Conlin & Smith, 1994; Corey, Corey, & Callahan, 1990; Eldridge & Barnett, 1991; Holahan & Gibson, 1994; Rochlin, 1994). These suggestions will be highlighted briefly here.

Although many people assume that an LGB group is best led by at least one LGB therapist (Conlin & Smith, 1994), others such as Schwartz and Hartstein (1986) disagree noting, "sexual orientation per se neither qualifies one to lead a gay therapy group nor disqualifies a therapist from doing so" (p. 171). Rochlin (1994) suggested that therapists' attitudes are the most important determining factor in their appropriateness to lead LGB groups. According to Rochlin, regardless of sexual orientation, homophobic or heterosexist therapists cannot be helpful to LGB group members. The leader of an LGB group must possess attitudes that are "beyond tolerance." Tolerance is not an affirmative enough stance from which to help LGB students to establish positive identities, increase their self-esteem, or decrease internalized homophobia. Leaders must be able to express true admiration and appreciation of Queerness and, if Queer themselves, must be able to express genuine joy at being so.

Based on the work of Schwartz and Hartstein (1986), we suggest that effective counselors (regardless of sexual orientation) must possess the following knowledge base of the diverse experiences of LGB students. First, counselors must be familiar with various theories of LGB identity development. This information is essential in understanding client experience and guiding therapeutic goals and interventions. Second, counselors must also be aware of the challenges facing gay, lesbian, or bisexual people of color (Dworkin & Gutierrez, 1992; Greene, 1994; Wall & Washington, 1991) in order to be effective in gaining a cultural awareness of these clients. Third, counselors should be familiar with LGB events, resources on campus and in the wider community (for example, social events, sports teams, affirmative churches, where to buy Queer books, magazines, and music) and current legal and political issues facing the Queer student community. In addition, awareness of homophobia and heterosexism on individual, cultural, and institutional levels is necessary. Fourth, counselors should be comfortable with LGB people and their choices, and should be able to discuss sexual aspects of LGB relationships. As well, counselor knowledge of LGB individuals should not be limited to clinical experience but should also include self-initiated and continued education regarding recent LGB topics and research.

LGB Facilitators. It is widely recognized that role models provide an important ingredient in effective counseling and also widely recognized that LGB people frequently lack positive role models (Rochlin, 1994). The unique benefit offered by proud, active LGB counselors is that such people can serve as role models to group members (Conlin & Smith, 1994). In addition, having two LGB co-therapists can highlight the diversity within Queer culture with regard to values, attitudes, and lifestyle choices. Conlin and Smith (1994) suggested that LGB counselors should be in late stages of coming-out, having worked through disclosure to friends, family, and colleagues to the extent that this is possible. Depending on the nature of the group, the extent of counselor self-disclosure, and the counselor's visibility on campus, group members might interpret the counselor's hiding or "passing" (as heterosexual) behavior on campus as a mirror for their own shame. Passsing behavior could interfere with the group leader's perceived trustworthiness and thus the effectiveness of the group.

Non-LGB Facilitators. On many campuses there may be no self-identified gay, lesbian, or bisexual counselor available to lead an LGB group. However, non-LGB counselors who have conducted such groups on their campuses report that they have had success in conducting groups by taking care to think through all of the issues discussed above. As well, non-LGB facilitators of LGB groups are likely to experience concerns about being "politically correct," a desire to be liked and a wish to not offend group members with subtly or overtly homophobic statements, and fear of being a target of members' rage at heterosexist society (Chojnacki & Gelberg, 1995; Holahan & Gibson, 1994).

For non-LGB counselors, issues of internalized homophobia/biphobia, socialized biases, and myths can have dire effects and consequences within the group. As a result, the counseling relationship between an LGB client and non-LGB counselor may present unique dynamics within the counseling relationship and issues for the counselor. Counselors who are unaware of their internal beliefs and feelings about working with LGB clients have the potential of creating a counseling relationship in which the client's personal growth is hindered. These issues and others must be worked through in supervision or consultation with one who has significant knowledge of LGB issues.

Finally, based on previous studies (Chojnacki & Gelberg, 1995; Holahan & Gibson, 1994), we strongly recommend that non-LGB counselors disclose their sexual orientation during screening interviews to avoid member feelings of betrayal later and to allow members to make an informed decision about working with a non-LGB group leader. Openness, respect, and willingness to examine one's own heterosexual privilege will allow these group facilitators to become true allies of the LGB students they serve.

Conclusions and Recommendations

Group counseling provides a unique opportunity for campus counseling and mental health services to facilitate creating peer and community support for LGB students. Indeed, for many LGB students, group counseling may initially provide the only safe place in which they can talk about their lives and explore concerns and relationships.

An assessment of existing campus resources and unmet student needs can enable facilitators to determine the best approach to offering LGB group counseling on their campus. The needs of students can help determine group format, goals, and content. Although issues will be addressed differently within various group formats (such as process, structured, and psychoeducational groups), each type of group can contribute to achieving a number of important goals for LGB students including identity clarification and coming out, developing individual self-esteem and Queer pride, facilitating healthy ways of coping, increasing support and community building, and enhancing relationships with others.

And while unique challenges face both heterosexual and LGB counselors conducting an LGB group, all potential facilitators should, at minimum, have an awareness of and familiarity with models of identity development, the impact of individual, cultural, and institutional heterosexism and homophobia, as well as events and resources available in the community. Additionally, group facilitators must also have an awareness of their own strengths and limitations and be comfortable in aiding group members to explore and discuss all aspects of being lesbian, gay, or bisexual.

There are a number of existing and potential benefits for LGB students who choose to participate in group counseling. However, in the end, perhaps the most important accomplishment achieved by an LGB counseling group is creating a collective atmosphere of confidentiality, mutual support, safety, affirmation, and openness to being in genuine relationships with others.

References

American Psychological Association, Committee on Lesbian and Gay Concerns. (1990). *Final report of the task force on bias in psychotherapy with lesbian women and gay men*. Washington, DC: Author.

Archer, J., & Cooper, C. (1998). *Counseling and mental health services on campus*. San Francisco, CA: Jossey-Bass.

Betz, N. E., & Fitzgerald, L. F. (1993). Individuality and diversity: Theory and research in counseling psychology. *Annual Review of Psychology, 44,* 343-381.

Browning, C. (1987). Therapeutic issues and intervention strategies with young adult lesbian clients: A developmental approach. *Journal of Homosexuality, 14,* 45-52.

Chojnacki, J., & Gelberg, S. (1995). The facilitation of a gay/lesbian/bisexual support therapy group by heterosexual counselors. *Journal of Counseling and Development, 73,* 352-354.

Clark, D. (1977). *Loving someone gay*. Berkeley, CA: Celestial Arts.

Conlin, D., & Smith, J. (1994). Group psychotherapy for gay men. In J. Gonsiorek (Ed.), *A guide to psychotherapy with gay and lesbian clients* (pp. 105-112). New York: Harrington Park.

Conyne, R. K. (1997). Group work ideas I have made aphoristic (for me). *Journal for Specialists in Group Work, 22,* 149-156.

Corey, G., Corey, M., & Callahan, P. (1990). Role of group leader's values in group counseling. *Journal for Specialists in Group Work, 15,* 68-74.

D'Augelli, A. R., & Rose, M. L. (1990). Homophobia in a university community: Attitudes and experiences of heterosexual freshman. *Journal of College Student Development, 31,* 484-491.

Dworkin, S. H., & Gutierrez, F. J. (Eds.). (1992). *Counseling gay men and lesbians: Journey to the end of the rainbow*. Washington, DC: American Counseling Association.

Eldridge, N., & Barnett, D. (1991). Counseling gay and lesbian students. In N. J. Evans & V. A. Wall (Eds.), *Beyond tolerance: Gays, lesbians and bisexuals on campus* (pp. 147-178). Washington, DC: American College Personnel Association.

Evans, N. J., & Wall, V. A. (Eds.). (1991). *Beyond tolerance: Gays, lesbians and bisexuals on campus*. Washington, DC: American College Personnel Association.

Fassinger, R. E. (1991). The hidden minority: Issues and challenges in working with lesbian women and gay men. *The Counseling Psychologist, 19,* 157-76.

Garnets, L., Hancock, K. A., Cochran, S. D., Goodchilds, J., & Peplau, L. A. (1991). Issues in psychotherapy with lesbians and gay men. *American Psychologist, 46,* 964-972.

Greene, B. (1994). Lesbian women of color: Triple jeopardy. In L. Comas-Diaz & B. Greene (Eds.), *Women of color* (pp. 389-427). New York: Guilford.

Hayes, J. A., & Gelso, C. J. (1991). *Male counselors' discomfort with gay and HIV-infected clients*. Presented at the Conference of the North American Society for Psychotherapy Research, Panama City, FL.

Herek, G. (1993). Documenting prejudice against lesbians and gay men on campus: The Yale sexual orientation survey. *Journal of Homosexuality, 25,* 15-30.

Holahan, W., & Gibson, S. (1994). Heterosexual therapists leading lesbian and gay therapy groups: Therapeutic and political realities. *Journal of Counseling and Development, 72,* 591-594.

Iasenza, S. (1989). Some challenges of integrating sexual orientations into counselor training and research. *Journal of Counseling and Development, 68,* 73-76.

Kitzinger, C. (1990). Lesbians in academe. In S. S. Lie & V. E. O'Leary (Eds.), *Storming the tower: Women in the academic world* (pp. 163-172). East Brunswick, NJ: Nichols.

Levine, H., & Evans, N. J. (1991). The development of gay, lesbian, and bisexual identities. In N. J. Evans & V. A. Wall (Eds.), *Beyond tolerance: Gays, lesbians and bisexuals on campus* (pp. 1-24). Washington, DC: American College Personnel Association.

Rhoads, R. A. (1994). *Coming out in college: The struggle for a queer identity*. Westport, CT: Bergin & Garvey.

Rochlin, M. (1994). Sexual orientation of the therapist and therapeutic effectiveness with gay clients. In J. Gonsiorek (Ed.), *A guide to psychotherapy with gay and lesbian clients* (pp. 21-29). New York: Harrington Park.

Rudolph, J. (1988). Counselors' attitudes toward homosexuality: A selective review of the literature. *Journal of Counseling and Development, 67,* 165-168.

Schwartz, R., & Harstein, N. (1986). Group psychotherapy with gay men: Theoretical and clinical considerations. In T. Stein & C. Cohen (Eds.), *Contemporary perspectives on psychotherapy with lesbians and gay men* (pp. 157-177). New York: Plenum.

Seligman, M.E. (1995). The effectiveness of psychotherapy: The Consumer Reports study. *American Psychologist, 50,* 965-974.

Stoller, N. (1994). Creating a nonhomophobic atmosphere on a college campus. In L. Garber (Ed.), *Tilting the tower* (pp. 198-207). New York: Routledge.

Wall, V. A., & Evans, N. J. (1991). Using psychosocial development theories to understand and work with gay and lesbian persons. In N. J. Evans & V. A. Wall (Eds.), *Beyond tolerance: Gays, lesbians and bisexuals on campus* (pp. 25-38). Washington, DC: American College Personnel Association.

Wall, V. A., & Washington, J. (1991). Understanding gay and lesbian students of color. In N. J. Evans & V. A. Wall (Eds.), *Beyond tolerance: Gays, lesbians and bisexuals on campus* (pp. 67-78). Washington, DC: American College Personnel Association.

Westefeld, J. S., & Winkelpleck, J. M. (1983). University counseling service groups for gay students. *Small Group Behavior, 14,* 121-128.

Yalom, I. D. (1985). *The theory and practice of group psychotherapy.* New York: Basic Books.

Chapter 9

৪০০৪

Shattered Pride: Resistance and Intervention Strategies in Cases of Sexual Assault, Relationship Violence, and Hate Crimes Against Gay, Lesbian, Bisexual, and Transgender Students

CLAIRE N. KAPLAN AND SANDY L. COLBS

Victimization of sexual minorities through physical and sexual violence is on the rise, and colleges and universities are not protected from this tragedy. Herek (1993), D'Augelli (1989), Waterman, Dawson, and Bologna (1989), and Norris (1992) have all documented cases of anti-gay/lesbian violence and harassment on college campuses. Gay, lesbian, bisexual, and transgendered (LGBT) students are no less vulnerable to sexual, domestic, or hate-motivated violence than they would be if they

Many thanks to Kris Raab of Gay Men and Lesbians Opposing Violence (GLOV), Los Angeles Commission on Assaults Against Women, and Rape Aggression Defense Systems, Inc. for information on resistance strategies.

were out in the "real" world and on their own. Like women who are targets of violence by significant others as well as total strangers, LGBT people are victimized by total strangers and by people known to them— sometimes by their partners. College and university administrators, faculty, and staff have an obligation to face this problem in order to lessen its frequency and impact on victims.

Any response to sexual and hate-motivated violence requires a multi-disciplinary approach, involving all areas of the institution that may have contact with victims. Thus, both education to reduce the rate of violence and intervention for victim/survivors must be on the agenda. We first discuss prevention/risk reduction strategies, and then address the question of serving sexual minority victim/survivors.

Resistance Strategies

Is it possible to prevent sexual and hate-related violence against lesbian, gay, bisexual, and transgendered people? With a combination of strategies, the frequency of violence could be reduced, and perhaps stopped. Borrowing from the wellness model that stresses educational programs that affirm positive self-image and healthy relationships, primary prevention should begin well before an individual develops the potential for acting violent toward others. What works against this intention is the sad fact that by the time students arrive on campus, they have already learned a great deal about sexuality, relationships, intolerance, and may already be survivors—or perpetrators—of sexual assault or relationship violence (Koss, 1989). This pattern should not prevent educators from making their best effort. Working to halt the process of victimizing or victimization is the goal.

Institutional support of LGBT students is paramount—support that goes beyond lip service. By this we mean: administrative statements declaring a zero tolerance of hate-motivated violence of any kind, including against sexual minorities; visible support through benefits for life partners of students, staff and faculty equal to those available to heterosexual married couples; as well as employment of a student affairs professional whose job it is to support LGBT students; access to funds and facility space by LGBT student and employee groups; visible faculty/staff organizations; and visits to campus by out queer scholars. In the event that hate crimes do occur, campus administrators must take a strong stand in opposition to such violence. Publishing advertisements in student papers, issuing letters to students, and holding forums or town hall meetings are all community-based strategies that the institution may wish to implement. If violence is the extreme of intolerance, these suggestions are the minimum requirements necessary to creating a campus community that adheres to a zero tolerance of violence.

But whether or not an institution is so evolved that these services are in place, there is much that can be done. What role do student affairs professionals and their colleagues have in tackling these issues? Unlearning homophobia workshops, fostering tolerance and acceptance, and creating an environment where it is safe for sexual minority people to come out to themselves and others is the baseline of prevention. This form of prevention is on the wider community level and has been addressed in Evans and Wall's (1991) book, *Beyond Tolerance: Gays and Lesbians on Campus,* and elsewhere, but more can be done. Violence de-escalation workshops and self-defense courses specifically set up for sexual minority students and funded by student affairs are examples, and may already be offered by campus women's centers, sexual assault education programs, or similar departments. While many campuses offer self-defense classes for women, of which lesbians frequently take advantage, they are not always open to gay, bisexual, or transgendered men. The need exists, however, and such workshops could be taught by the same instructors who offer women's classes. Additionally, whether grievances between students are heard by student or administrative judicial boards, visible involvement by LGBT students or administrators is essential so that victims feel some degree of safety if they choose an internal hearing to resolve a complaint of hate violence.

Prevention v. Risk Reduction v. Resistance

"Prevention" is a common yet controversial term, for it is the perpetrator who is ultimately responsible for preventing an assault, while most educational programs target potential victims. Anti-sexual assault activists argue that use of this word fosters victim-blaming if an assault occurs. The term "risk reduction" is not a great improvement either, for it implies that potential victims are powerless to do anything other than lower the chances of assault. An alternative term is resistance. Someone who defends her or himself with verbal and physical self-defense, or other less-intense techniques, such as avoidance and safety strategies, is actively resisting an assault. The term gives agency to the potential victim while recognizing that the violence belongs to the assailant(s) alone. We will henceforth refer to safety strategies as "resistance" and the participants as "resistors."

Until the world is recreated such that acts of violence against another are unthinkable, potential targets must develop specific resistance strategies. As unfair as it seems, the burden lies on sexual minorities to enhance their own safety, just as women are faced with resisting rape, even while allies join in the effort to decrease both rates and prevalence of dating/domestic and hate-induced violence. Resistance strategies for someone being abused in a relationship are somewhat different from those one uses on the street. And in all cases, speaking out about any anti-gay violence or harassment may mean coming out of the closet. When considering methods and forms of violence resistance, it is important to discuss both violence within and outside the LGBT community. Mental preparedness for stranger or acquaintance assault varies, even if resistance techniques are similar, so we will discuss them separately.

Resistance strategies are largely borrowed from those developed by feminist self-defense instructors, who recognize that the realities of people's lives do not fit convenient "do and don't" safety lists. For example, "Don't go out late at night alone" seems quite sensible. However, a single working mother who discovers that the milk has gone bad will have to go out at 11:00 p.m. to the market. By the same token, in a climate where the closet remains the only perceived option for many gay men and lesbians, there are few options for meeting potential mates other than bars or clubs that may be frequented by acquaintance rapists or staked out by violent homophobes. Oppression, too, exacts its toll; a victim of domestic violence might remain in a partnership for all the reasons many women stay in battering relationships—fear of retribution, internalized homophobia (I deserve this because I'm gay; God is punishing me), fear of being alone or not meeting any other gay people, or for financial reasons.

What Gay, Lesbian, Bisexual Students Need to Know About Dating/Domestic Violence

Sexual minorities may be intimately acquainted with violence and yet be quite unaware of the patterns and forms that assaults may take, such as domestic violence and same-sex sexual assault in dating relationships. Lesbians have been discussing the latter for several years, and several books are in print on this issue, written by lesbians who have been active in the anti-rape and domestic violence movements. For example, Kerry Ann Lobel's (1989) *Breaking the Silence: Lesbian Battering*, and Claire Renzetti's (1992) *Violent Betrayal: Partner Abuse in Same Sex Relationships* are widely used resources. Resources for gay men are now available in greater numbers as well, such as Michael Scarce's (1997) *Male on Male Rape: The Hidden Trauma of Stigma and Shame*.

Yet there is still a general lack of awareness of the behaviors and patterns exhibited by lesbian, gay, or bisexual rapists or batterers. There is the general feeling that only straight people commit this kind of violence (a myth that is especially pervasive among women), a view that is typical of an oppressed group that is loathe to air its dirty laundry for fear that the oppressor will take advantage of such knowledge. It is easier to consider the threat of a stranger who harbors hatred toward the entire community than to accept that one of "our own" might be repeatedly assaulting his mate. And yet, resistance techniques are useless without a serious discussion of these issues.

There are various forms of dating violence, including emotional, physical, sexual, or economic abuse. In any given relationship, any or all of these forms may appear, given the individuals involved. When educating sexual minority students about dating/domestic violence, it is essential to provide them detailed information. Tools such as the Domestic Violence Project, Inc.'s "Power and Control Wheel" (see Figure 9.1) are extremely useful models for illustrating the nature of violent relationships, particularly when used in conjunction with descriptions of abuse in relationships as cyclical or in an increasing spiral.

Stranger Assault

Among the LGBT community, stranger assaults against women take on various forms. First, there are the type of assaults committed against lesbians merely because they are women; the rapist may not be aware of her lesbian/bisexual/transgendered identity and yet that identity is part of her even as she is raped and it will impact her response and healing. But most often, it isn't clear if the assailant knew or not, especially if the crime was committed during a robbery, or in a venue such as a parking garage near the survivor's place of employment and she happened to wander into the situation at the wrong time.

VIOLENCE

Using Existing Isolation and Heterosexism

Since the victim may know few, if any, other lesbians or gay men, the batterer reminds the partner that she/he will be alone, that no one will believe her/him, that the police won't take the situation seriously, and that seeking help will bring the victim "out".

Threats of "Outing"

Threatening to expose the partner and bring her/him "out of the closet" if she/he leaves or seeks help...to children or an ex-spouse (loss of custody)...to an employer (loss of job)...to straight friends, church, or family (loss of support systems.)

GAY & LESBIAN POWER & CONTROL WHEEL

Sexuality and Emotional Abuse

Using the victim's own internalized homophobia against her/him... Calling partner "deviant", "pervert", "sick", and "unnatural"...Suggesting that whatever happens is because of this, even God's will...Forcing partner into sado-masochistic role and then using this as a weapon.

Denying Reality, Blaming the Victim

Batterer assumes the "victim" stance, even going so far as to present him or herself at a shelter for services, calling police, or getting a restraining order. Describes any self-defensive behavior on the part of the victim as abuse.

VIOLENCE

Figure 9.1. Domestic Violence need not take the form of physical violence to be abusive. The threat of physical violence is enforced by the forms of abuse described in the wheel's spoke area. If the non-physically violence control strategies are no longer effective, then physical violence reasserts the abuser's power and control over the victim/survivor.

"Gay and Lesbian Power & Control Wheel" modeled after the "Power & Control and Equality Wheels" developed by the Domestic Violence project, Inc., 3556 Seventh Avenue, Kenosha, WI, 53140. 414/656-3500. Revised and reprinted with permission.

The second kind of stranger assaults that women experience are because they are lesbians: rape by men who may be staking out lesbian bars or clubs, who may be stalking a specific woman and be aware of her sexual orientation, or who may simply assume that a woman is a lesbian (whether or not she is) because of her dress or behavior. The latter type of assault falls into the legal definition of a hate crime, although there are many people who view any attack on a woman because she is female to be a hate crime as well. This type of assault nearly always involves rape or other kinds of sexual assault, perhaps other forms of violence, and sometimes results in murder. A lesbian's appearance is not always a factor, although cross-dressing women ("butches" or "drag kings") particularly threaten certain groups of men. But there are no rules: butch or femme, plain or traditionally beautiful, strong or weak lesbians and straight women have been targeted for homophobic violence. Men who attack lesbians in this way aim to punish, but their language is that of "teaching a lesson"—"I'll show you what a real man is," "what you need is a good fuck," etc.—in other words, language of "conversion." In teaching resistance, one can never emphasize enough that women's sexuality is not defined by male sexuality—even in the case of hetero-sexuality.

Gay, bisexual, or transgendered men are rarely assaulted by strangers because they are men; rather, they are assaulted because they also are sexual transgressors. These transgressions include not only having sex with other men, but also challenging gender roles that undermine the meaning of masculinity in society. The most blatant examples are cross-dressers (transvestites) and transsexuals. The latter group at any point during a gender reassignment are quite vulnerable to attack. The great irony here is that, like women, men who are victimized by hate-motivated violence are not always gay—their assailants simply think they are. Regardless of the sexual identity of the victims, sexual/hate-motivated violence against men typically is extremely violent. Men who commit hate crimes against other men may presume that they need to employ a greater level of force to overcome resistance. They are much clearer in their communication that this is a punishment for traitorous behavior against the male gender. Also, because some studies indicate that anti-gay sentiments may be linked to suppressed homoerotic feelings, the perpetrators may be punishing something within themselves (Herek, 1995).

Violent crime perpetrated by groups is an incredibly frightening scenario. It is helpful for students to understand that people who form these mobs are rarely well organized. Any means of drawing attention to assailants, or of targeting the ring leader for active resistance, can result in a disintegration of group cohesion. As any woman who has resisted multiple-assailant rape can attest, it is shocking how disorganized these people really are. And yet, one must again employ a range of resistance strategies—and only if this is something a person feels she or he can do. Anyone in a threatening situation must assume that the attackers mean to do the worst.

The good news is that street patrols and other forms of community/coordinated resistance are effective against hate-motivated violence. Whether in urban or rural areas, coordination between local and campus police and anti-violence projects of this kind may not only reduce hate crimes, but can also develop community cohesion and solidarity.

Putting Gender Back Into Anti-Gay Violence

The relationship of gender to hate/sexual violence must be addressed in any educational program pertaining to sexual, dating, or hate-induced violence in the lesbian, gay, bisexual, and transgendered community. This takes the form of a discussion of sexual oppression and how it relates to sexism and patriarchy as a whole. Jenness and Broad (1994) criticized anti-violence projects' "activist strategies and 'collective action frames'" (p. 403) that view homophobia as a product of institutionalized heterosexism without addressing "how gay men and lesbians, as gendered beings, are differentially located at the intersection of gender—and homophobic—motivated violence" (p. 414). The unique issues of lesbians of color also go unaddressed. By ignoring the complexity of this issue, many anti-violence projects may be missing a key element in educating members of the sexual minority community about the roots of sexist oppression, which in turn might limit the creative possibilities for resisting violence.

In addition, according to Jenness and Broad, many of these projects do not provide advice concerning whether or not a lesbian should report to the hate crimes hotline, a rape hotline, or both. "Thus, violence against lesbians as women is omitted from the work of gay and lesbian-sponsored anti-violence projects" (p. 414).

In part it is because of the gendered nature of anti-woman violence that feminist self-defense instructors are wary of "Do and Don't" lists, so prevalent in gay and lesbian anti-violence projects. This is due to the implication that if one strayed from the list and was assaulted, the victim would be to blame for her own assault. Lists serve to further oppress women, rather than empowering them to resist violence.

And yet, lists can be useful. Most suggestions offered by groups such as Gays and Lesbians Opposing Violence in Washington, DC are practical, "doable" strategies. If such lists are distributed, they should contain a caveat: as long as we live in a sexist society in which gays and lesbians threaten cultural assumptions about gendered behavior, any lesbian or gay man is a potential target. And any lesbian might be targeted because she is a lesbian and/or a woman.

Resistance: From the Individual to the Community

Feminist self-defense educator Py Bateman (1991) has developed the concept of three levels of resistance to sexual violence: personal, community, and global. She advocates first educating the individual, then the community. From the community, the ripples extend outward to the rest of the world. And, Pauline Bart (1987) found that the more resistance strategies employed, the greater the success of resistance. Therefore, it is important not to rely solely on safety lists, or whistle campaigns, or any other single strategy, but to develop a range of possibilities, which must include self-defense and assertiveness training.

In the case of acquaintance assault that occurs outside the context of a relationship, students need encouragement to listen to their instincts, their "inner voices," and not to trust someone simply because he or she is a "member of the congregation." The types of strategies employed by women to avoid acquaintance assault are all applicable to LGBT people as well.

Any physical self-defense curriculum must have an assertiveness component. If it does not, the instructor needs to revise the curriculum to include this material or invite a guest instructor in to teach students these techniques. Much of what is called "self-defense" are actually basic awareness and assertiveness techniques. When employed during possibly threatening situations (whether the potential assailant is known or a stranger), they are highly effective and may allow a potential victim to escape or avoid harm without ever lifting a finger to physically resist.

Along with these practical applications, inclusion of a discussion of the roots of homophobia and sexism is critical, including a discussion of internalized homophobia, and the characteristics of violent relationships. Resources provided must address not only the needs of survivors of stranger assault, such as a local sexual assault crisis center, but also of individuals in abusive same-sex relationships. It is dangerous to assume, however, that battered women's shelters are prepared to handle gay and lesbian survivors. Thus it is important to query the local shelter staff regarding their policies pertaining to LGBT survivors before distributing resource information to students.

Practical Strategies

Any police department or self-defense program has developed a list of practical safety strategies that can be modified to fit the needs of LGBT students. Additionally, anti-violence organizations such as GLOV (see Resource Information at the end of this chapter), readily provide their lists to those who inquire. A more active way to encourage students to think in terms of their own safety is to conduct a "brainstorm" session with them, inviting police, rape prevention specialists, and any other concerned individuals to participate. One result of this type of discussion may be a clearer picture of how people's lives rarely fit neatly into the kinds of styles for which these lists are universally applicable. But the positive side is that people begin to think and plan on a more regular basis, as well as look out for one another.

A safety plan must also include resources and steps to take if one witnesses an incident. Heroism is not necessarily the best approach, yet there are many ways to help someone in danger. In this case, engaging law enforcement officers in developing a cooperative plan will not only empower students to take productive action if needed, but enhance the relationship between the police and the LGBT community. Just as individuals may learn new ways to resist violence, a community may organize itself in a similar manner.

Community Resistance

Street/neighborhood/campus patrols. Student affairs professionals can be instrumental in establishing coordinated community resistance to violence. For example, organizations have formed in most major cities in response to anti-LGBT hate-induced violence as well as to confront violence in gay and lesbian relationships. If there is no anti-violence project in an area or on a campus, students can be helped to mobilize themselves into coordinated resistance "cells." These are not vigilante groups, but watch and alert groups. It is important to work with local or campus crime prevention officers to develop a plan to alert the police to violent situations, creating a collaboration that will benefit all those involved, including the likely improvement of attitudes by police officers toward LGBT people.

Campus and community police departments must work with LGBT student organizations to improve working relationships if they are not already smooth, and to collaborate on how best to address violence from both the grassroots and criminal justice perspectives. Again, coordinated actions could be facilitated by student affairs professionals, just as they should be with students of color.

The National Coalition of Anti-Violence Projects is a resource that provides referrals to local groups that can provide training to concerned campus groups. Most women's self-defense organizations with experience in working with survivors of sexual assault and domestic violence can also be helpful.

Whistle campaigns. Many colleges and universities have implemented whistle campaigns for women's safety. The funds for purchasing whistles may be provided by the university administration or student activities offices. Whatever the source, whistle campaigns are only effective if the whole community embraces the plan, and even in this case, there are major limitations. Whistles, screechers, or any other non-violent external defense systems work only if the perpetrator responds as hoped, or if a bystander hears the noise and calls for help or comes to assist. It is important for people to know what to do if they recognize the whistle as a call for assistance; and if there is no response, the person under attack must be aware of other options for resistance and escape.

If whistles are distributed, information should also be provided about how to use them safely. (For example: "Don't keep them in your mouth; use it only when you are more than punching distance from the attacker so he can't slap you in the mouth and injure you. Don't wear them around your neck, the cord can be used to choke you. Use it only if you mean it.") Also, alert the media when the whistles are handed out so that others will also know their purpose.

Other Strategies. Street patrols aren't the only form of resistance to hate-motivated violence. Organizing groups to write letters or op-ed pieces for the student paper are effective activities for student organizations. Faculty and administrators can participate as well by holding teach-ins and self-defense classes. Faculty, administrators, and students may join forces to start a speakers bureau or engage faculty in discussing the issue in the classroom. The possibilities are limitless. Above all, these strategies must be conducted in coalition with other target groups. Hate-motivated violence warrants strong and vocal response by both LGBT and straight people even when they are not the direct targets of these crimes. No one group can fight hate-induced violence alone.

Anti-gay violence will only end if the entire community—LGBT and straight people—engage in a dialog about diversity, acceptance, and the meaning of sexual oppression in our culture. An open, public discussion along these lines also sends a message to sexual minority students: that they matter; that their concerns are concerns of heterosexuals as well, and the administration in particular. In so doing, an environment can be fostered that will hopefully reduce violence and also allow survivors of violence to seek help from student affairs and other campus professionals as they work through the healing process.

General Considerations When Offering Intervention for LGBT Victims

Sexual assault and violence perpetrated against LGBT students impact victim/survivors on multiple levels. In order to provide sensitive and effective intervention, student affairs professionals must be able to understand and assess the many ways in which students are affected. Identity formation, psychological well being, social functioning, academic functioning, and spiritual development may be impacted by an experience of sexual assault. Understanding students from a developmental perspective facilitates an in-depth understanding of the impact of sexual assault on the sexual minority student. Student affairs professionals are, therefore, uniquely qualified to offer effective intervention.

Student affairs professionals sometimes refer LGBT students to an expert on sexual minority issues, arguing that their lack of familiarity, comfort, or specific knowledge of LGBT issues renders them ineffective in intervening with this population of students. Often this expert is an openly gay or lesbian staff member who may or may not actually have the necessary knowledge and skills to intervene effectively. This approach is less than optimal for several reasons.

First, the number of campuses who have on their student affairs staff a self-avowed expert on LGBT issues is limited. Homophobia in the academic environment keeps many sexual minority professionals closeted, and those who are out may or may not be experts beyond their own individual experience. Homophobia also prevents heterosexual professionals from learning about LGBT issues. Few choose to specialize in the needs of sexual minority students because of fear of being perceived as gay or lesbian or because the field as a whole has been marginalized.

To assume because someone is LGBT that he or she is an expert on the needs of the sexual minority student is to falsely assume that all sexual minority people are alike and that therefore the individual's personal experience necessarily translates into knowledge about sexual minority issues. Also, to assume that an openly LGBT professional has an interest in specializing in working with sexual minority students is insulting to that professional who, like most student affairs professionals, is multifaceted in interests, talents, and skills.

Second, even if the student affairs staff includes an expert on LGBT student concerns, that person(s) may not be qualified to address sexual assault or other types of violence. Knowledge of both the student and the situation is necessary.

Third, the mechanisms for intervention in cases of sexual assault or other violence involves contact with many individuals and agencies at all times of the day or night. The sensitivity of those initial contacts in the intervention system is critical for the student who has been victimized. Those students who perceive those initial contacts as insensitive or homophobic are less likely to follow through with necessary medical or psychological intervention, and may be less willing to continue to work within the system to press charges or pursue other legal remedies.

Expecting that only the experts on this type of student will provide intervention is unrealistic and unnecessarily limiting. All professionals in the intervention system need to be prepared to handle these situations.

Finally, sexual minority students are often quite sensitive to being pigeonholed and may perceive being referred only to an "out" professional as stigmatizing. They may feel this implies that their experience of having been assaulted is somehow more shameful and must therefore be discussed only within the secrecy of the gay community. This sense of stigmatization enhances the already existing sense of shame experienced by a sexual assault survivor. While contact with a professional who is openly LGBT can be an empowering and effective component of intervention after an assault, this should not be the sole focus of an intervention, nor should it be the preferred intervention for all LGBT students.

Effective intervention with LGBT students who have experienced sexual assault or violence requires knowledge of the needs of these students as well as knowledge of effective intervention for sexual assault in general. General knowledge of the impact of sexual assault and effective intervention is a necessary, but not sufficient, foundation. Such basic information is vital, but is beyond the scope of this chapter. Rather than try to summarize this literature, this section will focus on the unique aspects of the sexual assault experience for LGBT students. The reader is referred to the resource lists at the end of this chapter for additional references.

Identity Development, Internalized Homophobia, and Sexual Assault

An assessment of the student's identity development and the responses of the significant people in their lives to their coming out process is important when intervening with an assault survivor. Many of the students who will need intervention are traditional age college students. These students are dealing with the full range of normal developmental issues for the late teens or early 20's. The work of Chickering and Reisser (1993), Gilligan (1982) and others is, therefore, a helpful foundation for understanding all of the factors affecting a student at the time of the assault. In addition, traditional age college students often struggle with issues of sexual orientation or sexual identity. Levine and Evans (1991) provided an overview of theories of sexual identity development.

LGBT students who are just beginning to deal with questions of sexual orientation may interpret a sexual assault by someone of the opposite gender as reinforcement of their same-sex orientation or conversely, depending on their spiritual background, as punishment for thinking about same-sex sexual contact. Students who are more comfortable with their sexual identity may not question that identity after an assault and may be more easily able to see the assault as a violent act rather than as a judgment of their sexuality. The exact meaning of an assault will vary by the individual, but the sexual identity development serves as a lens through which sexual minority students will view the experience of having been assaulted.

It is also important to examine the role of internalized homophobia when working with sexual minority students who have been sexually assaulted. Because a crisis situation challenges the coping resources of the individual, it is not unusual for that person to revert to previously held beliefs or values. Just as some persons generally reject religion or spirituality until they are faced with their own mortality, persons who have been traumatized tends to cling to their earliest beliefs about themselves or about the world as an anchor in a world that has been turned upside down by the traumatic event.

In the case of a sexual assault, early beliefs about personal sexual identity will often emerge, even if individuals have come to a different present understanding of this aspect of their identity. For LGBT persons who have experienced sexual assault, deeply ingrained stereotypes and values about sexuality and sexual identity and expression are likely to emerge, even when individuals have discarded these beliefs. It is not uncommon, therefore, for even fully integrated sexual minority students to re-question their sexual orientation or gender expression after an incident of sexual assault.

Additionally, students who have not reached a point of feeling positively about their sexual orientation may perceive a connection between their assaults and their orientations even when a connection does not exist. Students who, for example, are struggling with internalized homophobia, may view the assault as happening to them because they are LGBT. While some sexual assaults of LGBT students are actually hate crimes focused on the student's sexual minority status, others are random acts committed by strangers, acquaintances, or partners.

Openness to the questioning of a survivor about the connection between the assault and their sexual identity is a critical component of effective intervention. For example, a lesbian may wonder if she would have been protected from violence if she had a boyfriend. Feeding on the cultural myths about appropriate gender behavior (e.g., a female should not attend an evening event without a male escort), the student may begin to question her lesbianism or question if society might be right. On the other hand, if the student has developed her sexual identity to a more integrated level, and has a strong support system, she may be less likely to link the assault to her norm-breaking behaviors. The counselor needs to be able to suspend his or her own attitudes and beliefs about the connection between the student's sexual identity and the assault in order to allow a full processing of these questions.

Vulnerability and Self-Disclosure after Sexual Assault

The issue of disclosure is another unique dimension for LGBT students who have experienced sexual assault. All students who have been assaulted face questions about whether or not to disclose the incident to police, to friends, to family, to health care providers, and others. For LGBT students, these decisions are often complicated by the question of whether or not to concurrently disclose their sexual orientation. These questions increase the stress for the student, sometimes forcing the disclosure of sexual orientation or gender expression at a particularly vulnerable time and in very public settings. The sense of shame or embarrassment that is a common reaction to sexual assault may be compounded by disclosure of sexual orientation that is developmentally premature for that individual.

In addition to internal pressures around these issues, external factors may also come into play. For example, internalized homophobia has contributed to a need for the LGBT community to hide their dirty laundry and present a positive image to the heterosexual community. A LGBT student who has been assaulted by a date or a partner may therefore be reluctant to disclose the nature of the relationship to the police or health care providers in order to protect the reputation of the sexual minority community.

While disclosure of sexual identity may be an important factor in treatment of or intervention with assault providers, students may be far from ready to disclose this information to traditional social support systems, such as family. In fact, for many sexual minority students, the primary social support network is a family of friends rather than the family of origin. Disclosure to health care providers, counselors, residence hall staff, and others may be too risky, particularly if the student is aware that standard practice includes informing parents of emergency situations. The student's social support system may include heterosexual friends who are not aware of the student's sexual minority status. Some of the typical environmental intervention strategies (for example, meetings with roommates or family members to offer support to the survivor) may not be appropriate if the student is not "out" to everyone. Students may feel pressured to disclose their sexual orientation or gender expression in a negative context. When students come out in the context of disclosing about a sexual assault or other negative event (for example, discovering HIV+ status), those hearing the disclosure are more likely to respond negatively.

In addition to possible negative social consequences to disclosure, identity disclosure in the context of seeking help after an assault can result in job loss, loss of parental rights, loss of child custody, or isolation from the sexual minority community. Being "outed" in the context of seeking assistance can be particularly devastating for LGBT persons of color because of the possibility of ostracism from the entire community of color as well as by employers, family, and friends (Waldron, 1996).

Homophobia in the Intervention Systems

The general levels of homophobia on campus and in intervention systems are also important factors to consider when assisting LGBT sexual assault survivors. It is not uncommon for one agency to be more sensitive to the needs of sexual minority students than another. Proper intervention requires a coordinated effort with clear boundaries and respect for confidentiality in all agencies and systems. When one agency or office in the intervention system is homophobic, this coordinated intervention effort is compromised.

Homophobia in intervention agencies and systems is likely to be expressed through blaming the victim, and is rarely overtly expressed as a homophobic response. Attempting to build trust with the student who has been assaulted can be difficult when one intervention agent cannot trust another to be respectful of the survivor due to sexual orientation or gender expression. Blatant or subtle homophobic response by intervention systems constitutes a secondary victimization. This situation is parallel to the problems faced in assisting heterosexual women who have often been blamed for the assault not only by the perpetrator, but by the intervention agents (through comments such as, "she was asking for it by wearing that dress out in public", etc.). While campus environments have worked hard to eradicate sexist expressions of blaming the victim, work on addressing homophobia on campus is less evolved.

Types of Sexual Violence and Considerations for Intervention

In addition to a strong foundation of understanding of the sexual minority students' development and the impact of homophobia on intervention systems and responses, it is important to understand the different types of violence perpetrated against LGBT students. As in work with heterosexual students, the impact of a sexual assault varies depending on the nature of the assault, the identity of the perpetrator, and the gender of the survivor.

This section will examine three categories of sexual violence: relationship violence, assault by strangers, and hate crime assaults, and will discuss the impact on both male and female survivors.

Relationship Violence in LGBT Couples

While the literature dealing with relationship violence in sexual minority couples is limited, several studies have been reported that examine the prevalence of violence in these relationships. In a number of research studies reviewed by Elliott (1996), prevalence of same-sex domestic violence ranged from 17% to 46% of couples surveyed. Elliott concluded that despite limited research in this area, incidence rates are probably comparable to those for heterosexual couples. Incidence rates for sexual violence or rape in sexual minority couples have not been researched, nor has research on relationship violence focused specifically on the experiences of LGBT students. Anecdotal evidence suggests that for men in particular, sexual assault is common in early dating experiences, particularly violence perpetrated by older men against younger men.

Several myths about LGBT people, some of them well-intentioned attempts to minimize homophobia, can cloud our understanding of same-sex relationship violence. First, the belief that the partners in a same-sex relationship are equal to one another in power, while affirming of the attempts same-sex couples have made to create egalitarian relationships, may mask the reality of violence in the relationship (Elliott, 1996). Members of the couple or those intervening may assume that relationship violence is mutual, when in fact that is not always the case. As in heterosexual relationship violence, one partner may be the primary aggressor while the other may strike out in self-defense. It is important to remember that power and control are the primary issues in relationship violence. Simply being the same gender does not assure equal levels of power and control in the relationship.

Second, intervention agents may assume that the batterer in a same-sex relationship will always be the more masculine or physically larger partner. Power and control are again the key elements, which may or may not be linked to body type or gender expression. Merrill (1996) has argued that the traditional feminist model for understanding domestic violence as linked to oppression of women is insufficient to explain same-sex relationship violence. Power and control in a relationship are not automatically ascribed to the more masculine or physically stronger partner.

Understanding the complex social or psychological power dynamics in the relationship is more helpful than limiting an understanding of power to issues such as money, status, access to resources, or gender. These dynamics manifest in the power to intimidate through guilt, anger, jealousy, or fear as well as attacks on self-esteem.

A third assumption based on homophobic understandings of same-sex relationships is that it is easier for an individual to leave an abusive relationship with a same-sex partner. This false assumption is based on viewing people in same-sex relationships as not really married or likely to break up anyway. While society is not yet granting recognition of same-sex partnerships in most formal institutions, same-sex relationships are primary relationships, regardless of legal status. Leaving such a relationship may involve untangling of joint financial commitment, child custody and child visitation issues, and deeply felt emotional commitments. In addition, the threat of blackmail around disclosure of sexual orientation may, in fact, make leaving an abusive partner more difficult for the abuse survivor.

Intervention with male survivors of relationship violence. Intervention with gay, bisexual, or transgendered men who have been assaulted by their dates or partners requires an understanding of the psychological impact of sexual assault on men in general. Gender sex role stereotyping and cultural pressures on men to be macho make sexual assault of men a particularly humiliating and shame-filled experience. Men are taught that they should be able to defend themselves. This sex role norm is enforced through homophobia and sexism. Because of the sexism in our culture, accusing a man of being like a woman is the worst possible insult. Most of the homophobic language used against gay and heterosexual men who violate the macho sex role accuses men of being like women (e.g., sissy, queen, girl). Men who are victimized often feel intense shame not only in having been hurt, but also in having been overcome physically by another man. If a man is still struggling with his sexual identity, he may feel that he has been emasculated, which in turn can create intense ambivalence about being gay, bisexual, or transgendered. Internalized homophobia may lead men to think, for example, "If I were straight and a real man, this would never have happened to me." For these reasons, gay men often do not report sexual assault in dating relationships.

Interventions with female survivors of relationship violence. For women, a different, but equally damaging sex role stereotype comes into play. In response to homophobic and sexist accusations that lesbian women are like men, the lesbian feminist community has developed a cultural myth that lesbian women have escaped the patriarchal norms and are by nature nonviolent, nurturing, and egalitarian in their relationships. This belief, while an admirable ideal, is not the reality in many relationships between women, and is certainly not true for women in abusive relationships. A lesbian or bisexual woman is, therefore, breaking a community norm in speaking out about having been assaulted by another woman.

Because of ostracism by the community at large, lesbian women may find seeking assistance for domestic violence very difficult. Speaking out about abuse experiences within the lesbian community may feel like a betrayal of that community. Her need to maintain her social network may lead a survivor to maintain secrecy about her abusive relationship. Even when the violence in the relationship is disclosed to friends, these friends may prefer to blame the victim rather than risk the fracturing of the community by facing the reality of a batterer in their midst.

Assault of LGBT Students by Strangers

In this section, assault by a stranger with no known hate crime motive will be discussed. Heterosexual men most often perpetrate sexual assault by a stranger. Homophobia may contribute to blaming the victim of an assault of a sexual minority student. For male survivors, false assumptions about the promiscuity of gay men may lead some to doubt the survivor's report of an assault. If the perpetrator was encountered in a gay bar, or in locations commonly known for cruising, those intervening may falsely assume that the survivor was asking for it in similar ways to how heterosexual women have often been disbelieved. The additional sexist belief that men should be able to defend themselves may strengthen the phenomenon of blaming the male victim.

Homophobic beliefs about lesbian and bisexual women can also contribute to the tendency to blame the victim. Those who believe that lesbians antagonize and hate men may disbelieve the female survivor. A deeply rooted cultural belief that women should be accompanied by male escorts at all times may lead some to question the judgment of a female survivor (of any sexual orientation) who has chosen to travel alone or in the company of other women.

Hate Crimes against LGBT Students

National data indicate that reported hate crimes against LGBT people have increased dramatically in number and in intensity over the past ten years (Virginians for Justice, 1997). In the current reporting systems developed by the National Coalition of Anti-Violence Programs, an anti-gay incident is defined as one in which there are sufficient objective facts to lead a reasonable person to conclude that the offender's actions were motivated in whole or in part by the offender's bias against LGBT persons (Virginians for Justice, 1997, p. 1). Hate crimes of a sexual nature are particularly traumatic for LGBT students because they link the violation of self with a direct attack on sexual identity and/or gender expression. Any doubts rooted in internalized homophobia are realized in their full ugliness as the perpetrator makes clear that the individual is being assaulted because of being LGBT. In this sense a sexual assault hate crime is a personal, physical, psychological, and political assault.

The LGBT community may respond with outrage, organizing, and media attention when a hate crime is publicized. While important to the cause of ending oppression of sexual minorities, the publicity generated by this response may be quite threatening to the survivor. Disclosure of an assault to family, friends, and intervention systems is difficult in and of itself. Disclosure to the general public increases the sense of vulnerability.

Survivors may feel guilty if they choose not to report the assault to the legal authorities because they may feel that they have let down their community in making such a choice. A survivor may also incorrectly characterize an assault as a hate crime, in an honest search for an explanation of such an unfair event. Depending on the student's level of identity development, the sexual assault incident may galvanize the coming-out process. If a student is in Cass's (1979) Identity Pride stage at the time of an assault, he or she may use the hate crime as proof of the inherent badness of heterosexuals and may frame institutional response as homophobic when, in fact, that may not be the case.

These incidents are particularly sensitive for student affairs professionals who strive to meet the needs of the individual student, but also need to attend to the perception of the services by the general student body. The need to maintain confidentiality for a gay assault survivor while attending to the concerns of the sexual minority student organization, for example, demand careful attention to boundary issues and empathic understanding of the response of adolescents to injury.

Considerations for Student Affairs Offices and Programs

Sexual assault intervention systems often include several different college or university offices and programs. While the response of each agency is important, the coordination of efforts is crucial to effective response to survivors. While some might argue that intervention be centralized to one office or program, the multidimensional impact of sexual assault requires deep levels of expertise by many different types of service providers. While it is beyond the scope of this chapter to address each point of contact and intervention in depth, this section will explore some of the unique dimensions of intervention for specialists in several university service areas.

Counseling Centers: Counseling center staffs are uniquely qualified to address the emotional and psychological sequelae of sexual assault of a LGBT student. Counseling center staff should become familiar with the literature on trauma and should be well versed in assessing the sexual identity development of assault survivors. It is also important for counseling center staff to assess the social support system for the survivor, using the framework of that individual, which may include considerations of the family of friends or chosen family. Confidentiality concerns are vitally important, particularly in negotiating the sensitive boundaries between response intervention systems. It is likely to be most effective if counseling center staff remove themselves from the advocacy role so as to keep clearer boundaries around the counseling relationship. Counseling center staff should, however, participate actively in the development and training of persons to serve as advocates for sexual assault survivors. Assessment of general psychological functioning should not be ignored when counseling a LGBT sexual assault survivor. While the assault and/ or the coming out process may affect functioning in ways that mimic mental disorders, some LGBT students are dealing with mental illness in addition to facing the developmental challenges raised by the coming-out process and/or by an incident of sexual assault.

Student Health Services: Student health clinics are often the first point of contact for sexual assault survivors who are either (1) physically injured in the assault or (2) present with concerns about sexually transmitted diseases or pregnancy. While it is always important for student health services to be sensitive when providing examinations related to sexuality, in the aftermath of a sexual assault, concerns about privacy and confidentiality are critical. In addition, it is important for health care professionals to recognize that the student may experience the physical exam process itself as a recapitulation of the assault. Many assault survivors refuse to undress or be touched following an assault, and the physical exam may be the first experience of being touched since the assault occurred. Also, the involuntary aspects of being touched by a person in power (that is, the doctor or nurse), can make the student feel quite vulnerable, and may elicit feelings connected to the assault itself. Providing survivors with as much control as possible over the exam process and being extra careful to tell the student exactly what will be done before it happens will help to prevent these types of reactions.

In working with lesbian or bisexual women, it is important to recognize that the pelvic exam itself may be a new experience. Lesbians are less likely than heterosexual women to seek regular gynecological care, PAP smears, etc. (Denenberg, 1992; Simkin, 1993). For women with no history of sexual contact that includes penetration, the physical exam may be anxiety provoking and/or physically painful. Lesbian women may also lack knowledge of sexually transmitted diseases and of pregnancy considerations, and may need educative interventions that providers may assume are unnecessary with sexually active heterosexual students (of course, this is not a particularly valid assumption to make with any student).

Sexual minority assault survivors may not disclose their sexual orientation when seeking assistance. They may also withhold information about the details of the assault, fearing that disclosure of a particular detail of the assault (e.g., anal penetration) might reveal their identity. As with any sexual assault survivor, a thorough physical exam is important, recognizing that the sexual activity preferences of the survivor have no relationship to what may or may not have occurred in an assault situation.

Campus Police: Concern about homophobic responses by police is a frequently cited reason for sexual minority assault survivors not reporting assaults. Unfortunately, the cultural history of sexual minorities includes unfair treatment by police, including the bar raids of the pre-gay civil rights era (Katz, 1992), and poor response by police to sexual minority victims of violence and hate crimes. Sensitive and thorough responsiveness to assault survivors by campus police helps to create a general atmosphere of acceptance and support for sexual minority students. On many campuses, sexual minority students find one another and the gay grapevine is notorious. Positive response to a single survivor will become part of the cultural knowledge of sexual minority students. Likewise, perceived homophobia on the part of campus police (as with any other office on campus) will spread through the grapevine and will deter other students from reaching out for help. Of course, in some instances, this will, in turn, prevent a repeat offender from being apprehended.

Inclusive and nonhomophobic attitudes should also be reflected in crime prevention programming. As with other minority groups, sexual minority students will listen closely for evidence of inclusion and sensitivity. These students are seeking their safety zone and must do so quietly by listening closely. Use of gender nonspecific language and inclusion of examples of hate crimes in prevention programs lets students know that the campus police (1) know that there are sexual minority students on campus and (2) are sensitive in their responsiveness to crimes against sexual minority students.

Residence Education and Residence Life: The residence hall environment can be both an important source of support and a source of increased stress for the LGBT student who has been sexually assaulted. Effective responses to these students depends on a clear understanding of their sexual identity development, as well as their degree of "outness" to roommates, suite-mates, etc. The residence hall setting tends to magnify all aspects of any situation, including sexual assault. While support from roommates, suite-mates and residence hall staff can be provided in a way that commuting students may not experience, the crucible of a residence hall can magnify negative reactions of others, as well as put pressure on the assault survivor to talk about the incident.

For the student who has been assaulted by another member of the residence hall community, the social pressures of seeing the perpetrator and possibly continuing to interact with that person socially are very difficult. In some colleges and universities, sexual minority students may request adjacent housing in the residence halls. Pressure in this small community within a community to keep the peace and to maintain an oasis against the harshness of the broader community can negatively impact the survivor who needs to limit contact with the perpetrator and work through anger.

Residence hall staff and administrators need to emphasize safety for the survivor while recognizing that moving the student to another floor or hall for safety may also mean removing the student from an oasis of support and send a message of tacit support for the alleged perpetrator. On the other hand, taking action against the alleged perpetrator in the absence of a conviction (and often in the absence of charges being filed) is very difficult.

While there are no easy answers to these questions of intervention in the residence hall environment, residence hall staff can act proactively to promote a safe living environment for sexual minority students. A clear message of civility should pervade all orientation programs, printed materials, and staff training. Residence hall advisors should be trained specifically to work affirmatively with sexual minority students, and all direct and indirect harassment of sexual minority students should be handled swiftly and without hesitation. Once this atmosphere of support and acceptance is developed, the LGBT sexual assault survivor is much more likely to respond favorably to intervention efforts following an incident of assault.

Conclusion

Effective resistance strategies and intervention for sexual minority students in the area of sexual assault and sexual violence require that student affairs professionals view the world through multiple lenses. First, they must have a solid background and understanding of resistance strategies. Effective resistance involves both the individual and the community, and engages every member of that community in the process of creating a safe space for potential victims to believe in their right to stand up for themselves. In addition, survivors of assault must feel they can seek assistance from college or university administrators in the process of healing. Each professional must become familiar with appropriate intervention approaches. Most importantly, however, campus administrators must be knowledgeable and sensitive to the unique aspects of this work that come into play when working with LGBT students. In so many ways, these students are just like heterosexual students. If, however, the additional developmental, social, political, and psychological pressures that impact sexuality minority students are disregarded or forgotten, administrators are at risk of failing to meet their needs appropriately. The student development models in common use will serve student affairs professionals well in sharpening their skills, and in providing inclusive, sensitive, affirming, and respectful prevention and intervention with this population.

Resource Information

National Coalition of Anti-Violence Programs, Anti-Violence Empowerment Committee, P. O. Box 2206, Ventura, CA 93002. 805-650-9546 (Phone).

Committee on Lesbian, Gay and Bisexual Concerns, American Psychological Association, 750 First Street, N. E., Washington, DC 20002-4242. (202) 336-6041 (Phone). Contact Person: Clinton Anderson.

Los Angeles Commission on Assaults Against Women, 6043 Hollywood Blvd., Suite 200, Los Angeles, CA 90068. 213-462-1281 (Phone), 213-462-8434 (Fax), 213-462-8410 (TTY).

National Coalition Against Domestic Violence, PO Box 18749, Denver CO 80218-1852. 303-839-1852 (Phone).

National Coalition Against Sexual Assault, 125 N. Enola Drive, Enola, PA 17025. 717-728-9764 (Phone).

Office for Victims of Crime (U.S. Dept. of Justice), 800-627-6872 (Phone).

National Hate Crime Reporting Line, 800-2-JUSTICE (Phone).

References

Bart, P., & O'Brien, P. (1985). *Stopping rape: Successful survivor strategies.* New York: Pergamon Press.

Bass, E., & Davis, L. (1992). *The courage to heal.* New York: Harper Collins.

Brannock, J. C., & Chapman, B. E. (1990). Negative sexual experiences with men among heterosexual women and lesbians. *Journal of Homosexuality, 19* (1), 105-110.

Cass, V. C. (1979). Homosexual identity formation: A theoretical model. *Journal of Homosexuality, 4,* 219-235.

Chickering, A. W., Reisser, L. (1993). *Education and identity* (2nd ed.). San Francisco: Jossey-Bass.

D'Augelli, A. R. (1989). Lesbians' and gay men's' experiences of discrimination and harassment in a university community. *American Journal of Community Psychology, 17,* 317-321.

Denenberg, R. (1992, Spring). Invisible women: Lesbians and health care. *Health/PAC Bulletin,* 14-17.

Dickie, B. (Director). (1991). *Sandra's garden: Women and incest.* [Videotape]. (Available from Women Make Movies, Inc., 462 Broadway, Suite 501, New York, NY 10013)

Evans, N. J., & Wall, V. A. (1991). *Beyond tolerance: Gays, lesbians and bisexuals on campus.* Alexandria, VA: American College Personnel Association.

Elliott, P. (1996). Shattering illusions: Same-sex domestic violence. *Journal of Gay and Lesbian Social Services, 4* (1), 1-8.

Funk, R. (1993). *Stopping rape: What men can do.* Philadelphia: New Society.

Giggans, P. O., Hill, R., & Sutherland, J. I. (1987). *Self-defense: A complete guide to assault prevention.* Los Angeles: L. A. Commission on Assaults Against Women.

Gilligan, C. (1982). *In a different voice: Psychological theory and women's development.* Cambridge, MA: Harvard University Press.

Harvey, M., & Koss, M. (1991). *The rape victim: Clinical and community interventions.* Newbury Park, CA: Sage.

Herek, G. (1989). Hate crimes against lesbians and gay men: Issues for research and policy. *American Psychologist, 44,* 948-955.

Herek, G. (1993). Documenting prejudice against lesbians and gay men on campus: the Yale sexual orientation survey. *Journal of Homosexuality, 25* (4), 15-30.

Herek, G. M. (1995). Psychological heterosexism in the United States. In D'Augelli, A. R., & Patterson, C. J. (Eds.), *Lesbian, gay, and bisexual identities over the lifespan* (pp. 321-346). New York: Oxford University Press.

Hickson, F. C. I., Davies, P. M., Hunt, A. J., Weatherburn, P., McManus, T. J., & Coxon, A. P. M. (1994). Gay men as victims of nonconsensual sex. *Archives of Sexual Behavior, 23,* 281-294.

Jeness, V., & Broad, K. (1994). Antiviolence activism and the (in)visibility of gender in the gay/lesbian and women's movements. *Gender and Society, 8,* 402-423.

Katz, J. (1992). *Gay American history: Lesbians and gay men in the U. S. A.: A documentary history.* New York: Meridian.

Koss, M. P. (1989). Hidden rape: Sexual aggression and victimization in a national sample of students in higher education. In: M.A. Pirog-Good and J.A. Stets (Eds.), *Violence in dating relationships* (pp. 145-168). New York: Prager.

Langelan, M. J. (1993). *Back off!: How to confront and stop sexual harassment and harassers.* New York: Simon & Schuster.

Levine, H., & Evans, N. J. (1991). The development of gay, lesbian and bisexual identities. In N. J. Evans & V. A. Wall (Eds.), *Beyond tolerance: Gays, lesbians and bisexuals on campus* (pp. 1-24). Alexandria, VA: American College Personnel Association.

Levy, B. (1991). *Dating violence: Young women in danger.* Seattle: Seal.

Lobel, K. A. (1989). *Breaking the silence: Lesbian battering.* Seattle: Seal.

Merrill, G. 5. (1996). Ruling the exceptions: Same-sex battering and domestic violence theory. *Journal of Gay and Lesbian Social Services, 4* (1), 9-21.

Norris, W. P. (1992). Liberal attitudes and homophobic acts: The paradoxes of homosexual experience' in a liberal institution. In K. Harbeck (Ed.), *Coming out of the classroom closet* (pp. 81-120). New York: Haworth.

Poore, G. (Director). (1996). *Voices heard, sisters unseen.* [Videotape]. (Available from Women Make Movies, Inc., 462 Broadway, Suite 501, New York, NY 10013).

Renzetti, C. M. (1992). *Violent betrayal: Partner abuse in same sex relationships.* Newbury Park, CA: Sage.

Sanday, P. R. (1990). *Fraternity gang rape: Sex, brotherhood and privilege on campus.* New York: New York University Press.

Scarce, M. (1997). *Male on male rape: The hidden trauma of stigma and shame.* New York: Plenum.

Simkin, R. J. (1993). Unique health care concerns of lesbians. *Canadian Journal of Ob/Gyn and Women's Health Care,* 5, 516-522.

Virginians for Justice. (1997). *Anti-lesbian, gay, bisexual and transgendered violence in 1996.* Richmond, VA: Author.

Waldron, C. M. (1996). Lesbians of color and the domestic violence movement. *Journal of Gay and Lesbian Social Services, 4,* 43-51.

Waterman, C. K., Dawson, L. J., & Bologna, M. J. (1989). Sexual coercion in gay male and lesbian relationships: Predictors and implications for support services. *Journal of Sex Research, 26* (1), 118-124.

PART IV

DIVERSITY WITHIN THE LGBT COMMUNITY

Chapter 10

ॐ

Bisexuality: Identities and Community

LEAH ROBIN AND KARL HAMNER

"I wasn't gay until I met her." Uttered by Ellen's lover Anne Heche during their appearance together on "Oprah," these words would have passed unnoticed except they offended some members of the lesbian and gay communities. As was reported in *Newsweek* ("Chasing Anne" May 19, 1997, p. 6), some felt the comment reinforces stereotypes that gays and lesbians "convert" heterosexuals to become homosexual. In the end the comment went largely unnoted because it captures a fundamental misconception most of us hold about sexuality: that it is a dichotomy. A person is either gay or straight. Heche clearly thought that: she feels she was straight, then she was gay. Her critics appear to believe that, too, although their take is probably different from Heche's. If they object to the idea that she could have changed from straight to gay then they probably believe Heche was a lesbian all along.

Why didn't Heche, or DeGeneres, or Oprah, or *Newsweek* or anyone else it seems, suggest Heche might be neither gay nor straight? That she might be bisexual? It was not suggested because our fundamental misconception of sexuality as a heterosexual-homosexual dichotomy precludes bisexuality. Current theory and research views sexuality as a continuum from exclusively heterosexual to exclusively homosexual (Kinsey, Pomeroy, & Martin, 1948; Kline, 1993). However, the middle of this continuum—the many gradations of bisexuality—is not an option considered by most people who are attracted in whatever degree to someone of the same sex. The dominance of this dichotomous view leads many to erroneous conclusions about themselves: straight people are attracted to people of the opposite gender. I am attracted to people of the opposite gender, but I am also attracted to people of the same gender. Therefore, I must be gay. Because bisexuality is not part of the common parlance of sexuality, people attracted to both sexes typically do not know how to handle being in the middle of the continuum so they force their self-conceptions to one end or the other.

This misconception is not just part of popular culture, it is also common in the professional community, even among the counselors, therapists, educators, and researchers who deal directly with issues of sexuality. Because college remains a key arena for the ongoing negotiation of sexual identities for young people, we address professionals working on college campuses. By increasing their awareness and understanding of bisexual behavior, identity, and community, we hope to provide the tools they need to help others come to terms with being bisexual and to promote greater recognition and inclusion of bisexuality in social and academic arenas.

Definitions

In order to understand the complex phenomena and processes surrounding bisexual identities and communities, we must first consider the meanings of these terms. We will clarify them by focusing on what bisexuality is not through considering the common stereotypes about bisexuality. Addressing what bisexuality is not is as important as defining what it is, especially for those professionals and volunteers finding themselves in a position to help young bisexuals come to terms with who they are.

Bisexuality

At first the answer to the question "What is bisexuality?" seems readily apparent: bisexuality is the attraction of someone to both women and men. In reality, however, the answer is not so simple. Many who engage in sexual activity with both men and women do not identify as bisexual, while many self-identified bisexuals focus their sexual activity exclusively on one gender. People's desires, expectations, and conceptions of themselves may be at odds with the way they actually behave.

Bisexuality is romantic and sexual interest in or attraction to both men and women. These interests and attractions can include friendships, political and social commitments, and sexual behavior. Researchers have proposed many definitions of bisexuality. Morrow (1989) reported that bisexuality has been defined in four ways: as a state of being, as a desire, as a behavior, and as a personal identity. It is important to note here, however, that bisexuality does not mean non-monogamy or promiscuity. Sexual orientation and monogamy are separate issues. Although bisexuals are frequently portrayed as promiscuous, there is no population-based evidence to support the perception that bisexuals are more likely than heterosexuals or homosexuals to have multiple partners.

Another stereotype of bisexuality is that it is a "transitional" identity. Bisexuals are really just straights who are questioning their sexual identities, or gays and lesbians who have yet to fully embrace their "true" identities. Although this is sometimes the case, the reverse, in fact, appears to be more often true. Many bisexuals report adopting straight, gay, and lesbian identities as transitional, only later to adopt enduring bisexual identities (Fox, 1995). Sexual identities may change as people's experiences and conceptions of themselves change. Bisexuals are more likely to report change in sexual identity than straights, gays, or lesbians (Weinberg, Williams, & Pryor, 1994), although bisexuals may retain stable identities for long periods of time (Fox, 1995; McKirnan, Doll, & Burzette, 1995; Stokes, McKirnan, & Burzette, 1993). The lack of attention in sexuality research to change in sexual orientation over time may result in less visibility for bisexual behavior and identities (Fox, 1995).

Like bisexuality and non-monogamy, bisexual behavior and identity are also not synonymous. Bisexual behavior may be contextual rather than stemming from personal identity. When potential sexual partners of one's preferred sex are not available for some reason, sex partners of the other sex may be chosen. People in some cultural contexts may engage in bisexual behavior without identifying as bisexual. In cultures that promote dominant gender roles for men, such as Arabic and Hispanic cultures, it is not uncommon to find heterosexually-identified men having sex with same-sex partners. As long as a man is not the passive (receptive) partner, such sex is defined as consistent with a heterosexual identity (Ross, 1991).

Identity

Identity is also a complex issue. There are two kinds of identities: individual and group. Individual identity is who people believe they are and what their characteristics are. Thus, when people believe themselves to be gay, lesbian, straight, or bisexual, this characterization is part of their individual identity. Group identity is the extent to which people see themselves as belonging to a group of people, and believe themselves similar to others in that group.

Whether or not an identity (group or individual) is chosen can have a powerful effect on the way others react to it. For example, people who believe Human Immunodeficiency Virus (HIV) is the result of voluntary behavior characterize people with HIV as less deserving than people with other illnesses (Weiner, 1995). Involuntary, or ascribed, identities can reflect characteristics that people believe are inborn, such as gender, or can result from something over which a person has no control, such as becoming a paraplegic after an injury. Voluntary, or achieved identities, result from the intentional efforts of an individual. A person's profession is an example of an achieved identity.

The question of choice is central to the debate around sexuality. The belief that sexuality is ascribed, called the essentialist perspective, portrays sexual orientation as immutable and unchanging. This view of sexual identity reinforces the notion that sexuality is a dichotomy, leaving no space for bisexual identity (Udis-Kessler, 1996). The constructionist perspective, on the other hand, suggests that sexuality is achieved, and is subject to interpersonal, cultural, and historical situations and interpretations. Counselors and other student affairs professionals need to know that this latter view is more consistent with current research.

Identity is complicated because each person has multiple identities, reflecting his or her individual and social characteristics. And identities are not always consonant: they may pose conflicting demands and expectations. Some people resolve such conflicts. Others compartmentalize their behavior situationally, retaining identities that conflict with one another (Nichols, 1994). Some bisexuals may experience such conflicts and compartmentalize their identities in "two closets": passing as gay or lesbian in some situations and as straight in others. Others may establish a bisexual identity independent of the expectations that they will be either straight or gay.

Community

Group identities give people a sense of belonging, of similarity with others, and are often linked to communities. In a community, group members interact with each other within common spaces and social networks, including an infrastructure allowing for the dissemination of various resources (D'Augelli & Garnetts, 1995), such as food, money, or information. Individually identified bisexuals are also adopting group identities as bisexual communities grow around the nation (Garber, 1995). Common social networks for bisexuals are growing through social and political organizations, publications, and internet forums.

Resisting Bisexual Identities

Having defined identity, the question remains as to why bisexual identity is so much less common than bisexual behavior (Laumann, Gagnon, Michael, & Michaels, 1994). The answer lies in the resistance in our society to bisexuality as an identity. Bisexual identities are resisted in two ways. First, bisexuality is made invisible, either by denying its existence, or by appropriating it into straight, gay, and lesbian categories. Second, straights, lesbians, and gay men stigmatize bisexuality.

Invisibility

Straights, gays, and lesbians are dubious about the existence of bisexuality, and even some self-identified bisexuals doubt that bisexuality truly exists. Rust (1995) in a study of bisexual women and lesbians found that 1 in 4 lesbians expressed serious doubts that bisexuality existed, and studies of bisexual women and men in San Francisco (Weinberg et al., 1994) and bisexual women in London (George, 1993) reveal similar patterns. Bisexuality is often redefined to place bisexuals firmly within one category or another, characterizing them as either straights experimenting with same-sex sexuality, or gays or lesbians in denial of their fundamental homosexuality (Udis-Kessler, 1996).

Even when bisexuality is acknowledged as a viable sexual identity, it is often treated as identical to gay or lesbian identities. In the past decade, many gay and lesbian campus organizations have added "bisexual" to their titles, but include few bisexuals and do little programming that targets them. Similarly, researchers conducting studies in which bisexuals are not specifically excluded often add "bisexual" to titles of research papers without considering the range of diversity among bisexuals, nor how bisexuality differs from homosexuality (for example, McKee, Hayes, & Axiotis, 1994).

Research into the formation of sexual identities has also neglected bisexuality. While empirical studies of the development of gay and lesbian identity may include bisexual respondents, no study to date has focused specifically on the development of bisexual identity in adolescence (D'Augelli, 1996). The milestones in the development of gay and lesbian identities include disclosure to others about one's sexual orientation and contact with the gay and lesbian communities (D'Augelli, 1996; Schneider, 1991; Troiden, 1988; Troiden, 1989). It seems likely that the development of bisexual identities differs from that of gay and lesbian identities since bisexuals must come out in both heterosexual and homosexual contexts and may be stigmatized in both communities.

Stigma

The stigma our society attaches to non-heterosexual identities (Herek, 1992) contributes greatly to the invisibility of bisexuality. Studies of gay, lesbian, and bisexual adolescents and young adults find they disproportionately experience feelings of isolation, emotional distress, suicidality, life on the streets, dependence on alcohol or drugs, and violence by peers and family members (D'Augelli, 1996; Garnets, Herek, & Levy, 1992; Gonsiorek, 1993; Hamner, 1993; Herek, 1993; Hunter, 1990; McKee et al., 1994; Rosario, Rotheram-Boras, & Reid, 1996; Rotheram-Borus, 1995). These negative outcomes for gay, lesbian, and bisexual youth are attributed to the stress of coming out in homophobic settings, as well as active prejudice and discrimination aimed at gay, lesbian, and bisexual youth.

Bisexuals are subjected to both the many negative stereotypes attributed to homosexuality (generally termed homophobia), and to a unique set attributed to bisexuality (biphobia). This is a key factor that professionals working with bisexuals must grasp. Straights, gays, and lesbians may all stigmatize bisexuals, and bisexuals may hold stigmatizing beliefs about themselves (Rust, 1995). This latter factor is of particular concern when helping bisexuals come to terms with themselves. In addition to coping with attractions proscribed by the straight, gay, and lesbian communities, bisexuals have to come to terms with being in the middle. Not belonging to a clearly defined social category increases the likelihood of feelings of isolation and deviance.

A small body of research supports the existence of stigmatizing stereotypes about bisexuals and their negative effects. In a study of lesbian and bisexual women's attitudes about sexuality, Rust (1995) found that 56% of lesbians surveyed felt bisexual women were afraid to admit they were really lesbians, and 42% felt bisexual women were pretending to be heterosexual. Bisexual women were also perceived by lesbians to be uncommitted to the lesbian community, and likely to leave female lovers. George (1993) found that 56% of bisexual women in her sample felt they were not a part of the lesbian community. Weinberg et al. (1994) found that bisexual men and women were more likely than straights, gays, or lesbians to attribute social isolation to their sexual orientation.

Student affairs professionals should be aware that there is some indication that biphobia is more of a problem in the lesbian than the gay community. One ethnographic study suggests that bisexual women are rejected by lesbians when they are involved with men and taken "back into the fold" when they are involved with women (Esterberg, 1997). Udis-Kessler (1996) argued that this reaction results from how lesbians have come to define themselves. By the end of the 1970s, "rather than being a woman-loving woman, a lesbian [became defined as] a woman who did not sleep with men" (p. 23). When lesbian identity is viewed in this manner, bisexuality poses a political threat to the lesbian community. Gay men also resist bisexuality because of the challenge it poses to the dualistic notion of sexuality that is at the core of community building for gays and lesbians (Highleyman, 1995).

Biphobia also results from the association between bisexuality and HIV. Some individuals believe that bisexual men are vectors for HIV from the gay to straight communities, and bisexual women are vectors for HIV from straight to lesbian communities. HIV researchers have noted that sexual behavior, rather than identity, is the critical factor in the spread of HIV and other sexually transmitted diseases. Weinberg et al. (1994), who studied attitudes toward bisexuals before and after the HIV epidemic emerged, concluded that the characterization of bisexuals as disease vectors intensified already existing stigma against bisexuals. Farajajé-Jones (1995) noted that bisexuals have even been frequently portrayed as intentionally transmitting HIV.

Given the marginalized status of bisexuals, it is understandable that surveys have found fewer individuals identifying as bisexual than as gay or lesbian (Laumann, et al., 1994). Bisexuality is still seen by many people as a myth, which undermines the ability of bisexual youth to form both individual and group identities. Homophobia and biphobia may serve as further obstacles to the formation of bisexual identity and community (Weatherburn & Davies, 1993).

Stigma is likely to result in negative outcomes for bisexual youth. Unfortunately we know very little about bisexuals' experiences with harassment and violence because, as has occurred in other areas of research, bisexuals have either been omitted or sidelined. Many studies of harassment and violence, for example, do not report having any bisexual respondents (Berrill, 1992; Comstock, 1991; Dean, Wu, & Martin, 1992). Others report having bisexual respondents, but do not examine their experiences separately from those of lesbians and gays (D'Augelli, 1996; McKee et al., 1994; Rosario, et al., 1996; Rotheram-Borus, 1995).

Clearly, bisexual individuals have faced formidable barriers to building their sexual identities. In spite of this, visibility and organization among bisexuals has increased in the last decade. Such efforts have taken place in collaboration with straights, gays, and lesbians, and have also taken place as bisexuals organized and developed politicized notions of bisexual identity.

Building Bisexual Identities and Communities

The emergence of bisexuality as a social identity in the United States began in the 1970s (Trnka & Tucker, 1995). The first national bisexual organization, the National Bisexual Liberation Group, was formed in New York in 1972. But the real growth of the bisexual community has occurred in the past 10 years, through a boom in bisexual activism and a concomitant increase in awareness of bisexuality. Bisexuals have begun to build affirmative identities and communities in three ways: (1) through inclusive coalition-building in the "queer movement;" (2) through politicizing bisexual identities, and (3) through building local communities of bisexuals and increasing the number and visibility of bisexual organizations.

Coalition Building

Bisexual organization and network building has been accompanied by attempts to build alliances with gay and lesbian communities through the queer movement. These coalitions have increased the visibility of bisexuals, intensifying debate about how gay, lesbian, and bisexual interests intersect and differ. Colleges and other youth forums have been at the center of the movements pushing bisexuality to the fore, creating environments where young people can feel comfortable coming out however they may define themselves (Trnka & Tucker, 1995).

Politicizing Bisexual Identities

The political controversy around bisexuality focuses on bisexual identity, rather than sexual behavior. This is understandable because the behaviors of bisexual men and women are not particularly different from those of gays and lesbians. Rust (1992) found lesbians and bisexual women reported the same amount of opposite-sex and same-sex experience, but that their interpretations of those behaviors differed. Lesbians were likely to discount or downplay attractions to, and involvement with, men while bisexual women were more likely to consider them important. Studies find that the timing of same-sex and opposite-sex behaviors may differ between bisexuals and homosexuals. Weinberg et al. (1994) found that bisexual women and men were more likely than lesbians or gays to engage both in early and recent opposite sex relationships.

Bisexual identities have become politicized through writings and the rise of political, social, and support organizations building a bisexual social movement (Garber, 1995; Udis-Kessler, 1996). Bisexual activists argue that in addition to partner gender, other dimensions of sexuality, such as attraction to only one gender (monosexuality versus bisexuality), one's role in sex acts (active versus passive), and attraction based on how people display their gender socially need to be examined politically and scientifically.

Building Bisexual Communities

Bisexual organizations and social networks have emerged in urban areas such as Boston, Seattle, Washington DC, and Chicago in the last decade. National and international organizations, publications, conferences, and Internet resources have broadened local efforts to build bisexual communities. Preliminary evidence (Rust, 1997) indicates bisexual activism and community building may have increased bisexual women's belief in the authenticity of their sexual orientation, and their beliefs that bisexuals are socially and politically trustworthy. It seems likely that the growth of bisexual communities has strengthened the individual and group identities of at least some bisexuals.

Debate among bisexual activists about whether or not a bisexual community does, or even should, exist has been on-going. In some places it seems clear that bisexuals perceive themselves as part of a group with common interests, having geographic, social, and organizational space in which to congregate, and having established an infrastructure allowing for a distribution of resources such as information and social support. Weise (1996) argues that the debate about bisexual community should change its focus. Instead of focusing on whether bisexual communities exist, bisexuals must ask to what extent they are inclusive of the wide variety of people identifying as bisexual and how well these communities address their needs.

The barriers faced by bisexuals and their response to them have implications for bisexuals on campus. We can take the broader lessons learned from research on bisexuality and use it in the campus context to shape an environment responsive to the needs of bisexuals.

Implications for Bisexuals in Higher Education

Given the identity issues faced by college students in an often hostile environment, it is critical to provide student services that, as D'Augelli (1996) wrote, are affirmative of students' sexualities. Bisexual students will encounter both barriers to the development of bisexual individual and group identities and the emerging political and community-based understandings of bisexuality. On campus, the politicization of bisexual identity and the growth of communities have increased bisexual visibility, sparking debate about where bisexuals fit into university groups and services. In order to provide useful services for bisexual students, we make the following recommendations:

•   **Develop and implement policies prohibiting discrimination and harassment on the basis of sexual orientation, including bisexuality, for students, staff, and faculty**. Such policies help to provide an affirmative and secure campus environment for gays, lesbians, and bisexuals (D'Augelli, 1996), as well as indicating an unambiguous institutional stance against bias on the basis of sexual orientation. Grievance procedures and personnel should be set in place to enforce such policies.

- **Assume you don't know anyone's sexual orientation unless they tell you**. Even though bisexuality is often invisible and sexual orientation and behavior do not always match, student affairs professionals may assume that students with same-sex partners are gay or lesbian, and students with opposite-sex partners are straight. Such assumptions are misplaced, and contribute to the invisibility of bisexuality. Do not make assumptions about students' sexuality on the basis of their partners' gender, especially in providing counseling, health, or student psychological services.

- **Design services specifically for bisexuals**. Bisexuals are likely to face both homophobia and biphobia, and therefore service providers must address the unique situations of bisexuals on campus. Services for bisexuals should not simply be treated as "add-ons" to gay and lesbian services. Active outreach to bisexual students is required, rather than assuming that they will make use of gay and lesbian resources.

- **Recognize that bisexuals have a diverse set of needs**. Service providers should not base services on stereotypes about bisexual students and should expect them to be in various stages of identity formation, alliance with gay and lesbian communities, and in monogamous and multiple relationships. In order to accommodate the spectrum of needs and situations among bisexual students, it may be necessary to conduct in-service training to educate staff and faculty about bisexuality and the needs of bisexual students.

- **Acquaint yourself with local, regional, and national bisexual resources**. There are an increasing number of specifically bisexual resources which may be found in *The Bisexual Resource Guide* (Ochs, 1997), as well as on the Internet and in gay and lesbian yellow pages. Additionally, service providers should be aware of which organizations geared toward gays and lesbians (such as Parents and Friends of Lesbians and Gays) are bi-inclusive and bi-friendly.

- **Address the tensions between bisexuals and gays and lesbians on campus clearly**. Services and groups including bisexuals as well as gays and lesbians should specifically address conflicts on the basis of gender and sexual orientation. This effort should include clear policies for inclusion on the basis of sexual orientation, and ground-rules to resolve disputes when they arise.

- **Integrate bisexual issues where relevant into academic curricula**. The establishment of bisexual studies courses is a good first step for the inclusion of bisexuals. Additionally, educators should make efforts to integrate material specific to bisexuals into relevant curricula; preferably drawn from literature which does not conflate the needs or interests of bisexuals with those of gay men and lesbians.

These guidelines provide a starting-point to address the needs of bisexual students and may help them find a place in the emerging voices and communities of bisexuals around the world. As the national dialogue around Ellen DeGeneres and sexuality has demonstrated, we tend to think of sexuality in an "either/or" fashion. Bisexuals may be hidden from view because of our sexual assumptions, or their orientation may be actively stigmatized. Student affairs professionals are an important resource to help students whose sexuality does not fit into either end of the continuum.

References

Berrill, K. T. (1992). Anti-gay violence and victimization in the United States: An overview. In G. M. Herek & K. T. Berrill (Eds.), *Hate crimes: Confronting violence against lesbians and gay men* (pp.19-45). Newbury Park, CA: Sage.

Comstock, G. D. (1991). *Violence against lesbians and gay men.* New York: Columbia University Press.

D'Augelli, A. R. (1996). Enhancing the development of lesbian, gay, and bisexual youths. In E. D. Rothblum & L. A. Bond (Eds.), *Preventing heterosexism and homophobia* (pp. 124-150). Thousand Oaks, CA: Sage.

D'Augelli, A.R., & Garnets, L.D. (1995). Lesbian, gay and bisexual communities. In A. R. D'Augelli & C. J. Patterson (Eds.), *Lesbian, gay, and bisexual identities over the lifespan* (pp. 293-320). New York: Oxford University Press.

Dean, L., Wu, S., & Martin, J. L. (1992). Trends in violence and discrimination against gay men in New York City: 1984-1990. In G. M. Herek & K. T. Berrill (Eds.), *Hate crimes: Confronting violence against lesbians and gay men* (pp. 46-64). Newbury Park, CA: Sage.

Esterberg, K. G. (1997). *Lesbian and bisexual identities: Constructing communities, constructing selves.* Philadelphia: Temple University Press.

Farajajé-Jones, E. (1995). Fluid desire: Race, HIV/AIDS, and bisexual politics. In N. Tucker (Ed.), *Bisexual politics, theories, queries, and visions* (pp.119-130). New York: Harrington Press.

Fox, R. C. (1995). Bisexual identities. In A. R. D'Augelli & C. J. Patterson (Eds.), *Lesbian, gay, and bisexual identities over the lifespan* (pp. 48-86). New York: Oxford University Press.

Garber, M. (1995). *Vice versa: Bisexuality and the eroticism of everyday life.* New York: Simon & Schuster.

Garnets, L., Herek, G. M., & Levy, B. (1992). Violence and victimization of lesbians and gay men: Mental health consequences. In G. M. Herek & K. T. Berrill (Eds.), *Hate crimes: Confronting violence against lesbians and gay men* (pp. 201-226). Newbury Park, CA: Sage.

George, S. (1993). *Women and bisexuality.* London: Scarlett Press.

Gonsiorek, J. C. (1993). Mental health issues of gay and lesbian adolescents. In L. D. Garnets & D. C. Kimmel (Eds.), *Psychological perspectives on lesbian and gay male experiences* (pp. 469-485). New York: Columbia University Press.

Hamner, K. M. (1992). Gay-bashing: A social identity analysis of violence against lesbians and gay men. In G. M. Herek & K. T. Berrill (Eds.), *Hate crimes: Confronting violence against lesbians and gay men* (pp. 179-190). Newbury Park, CA: Sage.

Herek, G. M. (1992). The social context of hate crimes: Notes on cultural heterosexism. In G. M. Herek & K. T. Berrill (Eds.), *Hate crimes: Confronting violence against lesbians and gay men* (pp. 89-104). Newbury Park, CA: Sage.

Herek, G. M. (1993). Documenting prejudice against lesbians and gay men on campus: The Yale sexual orientation survey. *Journal of Homosexuality, 25* (4), 15-30.

Highleyman, L. A. (1995). Identity and ideas: Strategies for bisexuals. In N. Tucker, (Ed.), *Bisexual politics, theories, queries, and visions* (pp. 73-92). New York: Harrington Press.

Hunter, J. (1990). Violence against lesbian and gay male youths. *Journal of Interpersonal Violence, 5,* 295-300.

Kinsey, A. C., Pomeroy, W. B., & Martin, C. E. (1948). *Sexual behavior in the human male*. Philadelphia: Saunders.

Kline, F. (1993). *The bisexual option* (2nd ed.). New York: Haworth Press.

Laumann, E. O., Gagnon, J. H., Michael, R. T., & Michaels, S. (1994). *The social organization of sexuality: Sexual practices in the United States*. Chicago: University of Chicago Press.

McKee, M. B., Hayes, S. F., & Axiotis, I. R. (1994). Challenging heterosexism in college health service delivery. *Journal of American College Health, 42,* 211-216.

McKirnan, D. J., Doll, L., & Burzette, R. G. (1995). Bisexually active men: Social characteristics and sexual behavior. *Journal of Sex Research, 2,* 65-76.

Morrow, G. D. (1989). Bisexuality: An exploratory review. *Annals of Sex Research, 2,* 283-306.

Nichols, M. (1994). Therapy with bisexual women: Working on the edge of emerging cultural and personal identities. In M. P. Mirken (Ed.), *Women in context: Toward a reconstruction of psychotherapy* (pp.149-169). New York: Guilford Press.

Ochs, R. (1997). *The bisexual resource guide*. Cambridge, MA: Bisexual Resource Center.

Rosario, M., Rotheram-Borus, M. J., & Reid, H. (1996). Gay-related stress and its correlates among gay and bisexual male adolescents of predominantly black and hispanic background. *Journal of Community Psychology, 24,* 136-159.

Ross, M. (1991). A taxonomy of global behavior. In R. Tielman, M. Carballo, & A. Hendriks (Eds.), *Bisexuality and HIV/AIDS: A global perspective*. Buffalo, NY: Prometheus Books.

Rotheram-Borus, M. J. (1995). Prevalence, course, and predictors of multiple problem behaviors among gay and bisexual male adolescents. *Developmental Psychology, 31,* 75-85.

Rust, P. C. (1992). The politics of sexual identity: Sexual attraction and behavior among lesbian and bisexual women. *Social Problems, 39,* 366-386.

Rust, P. C. (1995). *Bisexuality and the challenge to lesbian politics: Sex, loyalty, and revolution.* New York: New York University Press.

Rust, P. C. (1997, August). *From biphobia to bipride: Changes in self-identified bisexual women's attitudes toward themselves during a decade of growing bisexual political activism.* Paper presented at the annual meeting of the Society for the Study of Social Problems, Toronto, Canada.

Schneider, M. (1991). Developing services for lesbian and gay adolescents. *Canadian Journal of Community Mental Health, 10,* 133-151.

Stokes, J. P., McKirnan, D. J., & Burzette, R. G. (1993). Sexual behavior, condom use, disclosure of sexuality and stability of sexual orientation in bisexual men. *The Journal of Sex Research, 30,* 203-213.

Trnka, S., & Tucker, N. (1995). Overview. In N. Tucker (Ed.), *Bisexual politics, theories, queries, and visions* (pp. 9-11). New York: Harrington Press.

Troiden, R. R. (1989). The formation of homosexual identities. *Journal of Homosexuality, 17,* 43-73.

Troiden, R. R. (1988). Homosexual identity development. *Journal of Adolescent Health Care, 9,* 105-113.

Udis-Kessler, A. (1996). Challenging the stereotypes. In S. Rose & C. Stevens (Eds.), *Bisexual horizons: Politics, history, lives* (pp. 45-56). London: Lawrence & Wishart.

Weatherburn, P., & Davies, P. (1993). Behavioral bisexuality among men. In L. Sherr (Ed.), *AIDS and the heterosexual population* (pp. 153-166). New York: Harwood Academic.

Weinberg, M. S., Williams, C. J., & Pryor, D. W. (1994). *Dual attraction: Understanding bisexuality.* New York: Oxford University Press.

Weiner, B. (1995). *Judgments of responsibility: A foundation for a theory of social conduct.* New York: Guildford Press.

Weise, B. R. (1996). The bisexual community: Viable reality or pipe-dream? In S. Rose & C. Stevens (Eds.), *Bisexual horizons: Politics, histories, lives* (pp. 303-313). London: Lawrence & Wishart.

Chapter 11

ℰᴐᴑᴙ

Transgenderism and College Students: Issues of Gender Identity and its Role on our Campuses

Kᴇʟʟʏ A. Cᴀʀᴛᴇʀ

A number of specific assumptions guide the college student affairs profession, one being the concept of the "whole student." By definition, the goal of student development is promoting the growth of the whole student in both the cognitive and psychosocial domains (Brown, 1989; Rogers, 1989). The awareness of identity as a part of social and personal development is apparent in many developmental theories used in the student affairs profession. For example, "identity versus role confusion" is one of Erikson's (1950, 1968) eight stages of development. This stage occurs while traditional students are attending college. Chickering also recognized the importance of identity development (Chickering, 1969; Chickering & Reisser, 1993). Other theories of majority and minority student development directly focus on identity awareness (Cass, 1979; Cross, 1991; Helms, 1990; Sue & Sue, 1990).

When we think of students establishing their identities, we rarely think of gender identity as an issue. We might think of specific male identity issues, "What does it mean to be a real man?" (Levinson, 1986) or specific female identity issues, "What does it mean to be a professional woman?" (Levinson, 1996). But an issue that faces some students is their actual gender identity, "Am I a man, woman, or something else?" (Feinberg, 1998). Sometimes this question arises due to physical vagueness: having both male and female genitalia. More often, students struggle with their assigned gender. Some students may feel more comfortable functioning outside of their gender roles either part-time or full-time. For others, the identity issue is even more pressing: they experience discomfort with their physical body. Some may question if, cognitively and emotionally, they truly are the other gender. A few students question if they are yet another gender, neither male nor female. All of these students can be considered transgendered (Feinberg, 1998).

Students with these identity issues bring a number of concerns to their college or university settings. On issues of gender, most of our society functions dualistically (Lips, 1997) and as a microcosm of society, so does higher education. Not only are our living facilities and rest rooms segregated by gender, but so are many student groups, athletic teams, and even our daily language. Tinto (1987, as cited in Love, Jacobs, Boschini, Hardy, & Kuh, 1993) recognized that, "students who identify with marginal or loosely connected groups (e.g., commuters on a residential campus) usually feel less connected to the overall student culture; those who feel unconnected are less likely to graduate" (p. 60). Marginalized transgendered students across the nation have been demanding comfortable living space, representation in organizations, and support from higher education administration and staff (Reitz, 1995; B. Zemsky, personal communication, November 15, 1996). Student affairs professionals, who are responsible for the development of all students, must see that the needs of transgendered students are met.

In order to understand transgendered students and their issues, four major topics must be addressed. First, educators must understand common terminology and the issues surrounding the use of various terms. Second, they must be familiar with the history of the phenomena surrounding transgenderism. Third, the psychology of transgenderism needs to be reviewed to eliminate stereotypical misconceptions. Fourth, the relationship between LGB issues and transgenderism needs to be discussed.

Terminology

Agreement on a common language or vocabulary would be helpful in communicating about transgender issues. The transgender movement is relatively new, however, and many transgendered individuals are still deciding how they want to define themselves. Feinberg (1996) raised a concern that many publications produced in the early stages of the movement will soon be outdated, due to changed vocabulary. There are some generally accepted terms, but understandably there are criticisms associated with these terms as well.

Originally the term *transgenderist* was meant to refer to a person who lives full time as the other gender, but who has not made any anatomical changes. Virginia Prince, a pioneer gender researcher, coined the term to refer to people like herself (Feinberg, 1996; MacKenzie, 1994). While many still use the word with Prince's intent, the community at large now views the term *transgendered* more generally, meaning an individual who bends or blends gender. It encompasses terms such as cross-dresser, transvestite, transsexual, and intersexual (Ekins & King, 1996; Raymond, 1996). Feinberg (1996) noted that the term *trans* is increasingly being used in an uniting way to make the term *transgenderist* available for those who are still identifying as such. In this chapter, *transgender* will be used as an umbrella term.

The terms *cross-dresser* and *transvestite* are often used interchangeably (Brown & Rounsley, 1996; Hirschfeld, 1910/1991; King, 1996), although some writers assert a distinction (Feinberg, 1996; MacKenzie, 1992). Many entirely reject the term transvestite due to its clinical origin (Garber, 1992). Others claim that both terms are legitimate, but have different meanings. These critics would claim the distinction lies in causality. A cross-dresser is motivated by social results, while a transvestite has a genuine emotional need to cross-dress. Most sources agree that the term cross-dresser refers to anyone who wears the sex role clothing of another gender, generally on a part-time basis. While cross-dressers tend to be very diverse, Brown and Rounsley (1996) asserted that a typical transvestite is heterosexual, married, and well educated. Benjamin (1953) proposed a continuum of cross-dressing that encompassed issues of causality, ranging from transsexuals to part-time cross-dressers. Rothblatt (1995) claimed that most modern women could certainly be referred to as cross-dressers because some wear clothing that was originally intended for males (such as pants, jeans, and even blazers and ties). In this chapter, the term *cross-dresser* will be used to indicate persons who wear clothing identified with a gender other than their own, regardless of the reason.

Gender dysphoria is a clinical label coined by Fisk in 1974 to refer to a gender identity crisis (Fisk, 1974). It has been incorporated into the *Diagnostic and Statistical Manual of Mental Disorders-IV* (American Psychiatric Association, 1994), a guidebook used by psychologists and psychiatrists to identify disorders exhibited by their clients. Although *gender dysphoria* is rejected as a social identity label, because few people are aware of any language associated with gender identity issues, the clinician's office is often the first place persons learn terminology and this label may be the first one they apply to themselves.

Transsexualism is yet another clinical term, although it is more widely used as an identity label. The term was first used in 1953 by Benjamin. Transsexuals identify a distinct difference between their physical sex and their internal sense of gender. Bolin (1988) described the male-to-female transsexuals in her study as "women who have male genitals...not hyper-feminine in gender identity or role" (p. 2, xii). Some transsexuals choose to undergo hormone therapy, often, but not always, followed by sex reassignment surgery (SRS). Those who have decided to undergo SRS, but haven't yet, or are in the process of transition, are considered *pre-operative*. Transsexuals who have completed SRS are considered *post-operative*. Some are either content with no physical alterations or cannot afford the change and are thus referred to as *non-operative* or *no-op*. Some in the latter group, such as Virginia Prince, prefer to be called *transgenderist*.

Consideration of physical versus emotional phenomena leads to the question: What determines sex and gender? Is there a difference? Feinberg (1996) and Lips (1997) explained that *sex* refers to physical make up. There are three criteria that distinguish an individual's sex: genitalia, chromosomes, and hormone levels. Some examples of sex are male, female, or *intersexual*. An *intersexual* is one whose genitalia, chromosomes, and hormone levels are not congruent with each other. Intersexuality does not occur in only one way; therefore there are many sexes. Some people have both male and female genitalia, while others may have vaguely defined genitalia matched with vague chromosome pairings such as XXY. By contrast, the term *gender* refers to internal identity (Bolin, 1988; Feinberg, 1996; Grimm, 1987; Lips, 1997). Some genders include masculine, feminine, and androgynous. Because gender is an internal identity, some transsexuals have defined their own gender.

Therefore there are endless variations on gender as well. Arguably, every individual could represent a unique gender.

When making the distinction of which way a cross-dresser is dressing or with what gender a transsexual identifies, the terms *female-to-male (F to M)* and *male-to-female (M to F)* are often used, the first word being their sex and the second being the gender they present or with which they identify. There are two strong criticisms of these terms. MacKenzie (1992) asserted that if the second term refers to one's gender then better terminology would be female-to-man and male-to-woman. Feinberg (1996) also noted that "terms like cross-dresser, cross-gender, male-to-female, and female-to-male reinforce the idea that there are only two distinct ways to be—you're either one or the other—and that's just not true" (p. xi).

As one of Hirschfeld's (1910/1991) mottoes states, "There are more emotions and phenomena than words" (p. 17). A major point to remember when using terminology is that people are free to identify as they choose. Understanding existing phenomena and associated terminology is necessary, however, if student affairs professionals are to learn more about how these issues can affect their students and their institutions.

Why Does "Gender Blending" Make Us Uncomfortable?

Transgenderism does make people uncomfortable. It is important to acknowledge that nearly every person raised in this nation, including those who are transgendered, was socialized to believe in the existence of only two sexes: male and female. A distinction between sex and gender is rarely made. Children are not born with the ability to distinguish what is male and what is female. Society works very hard to teach children the differences and by age three the goal is usually met (Lips, 1997).

Most people also are given fairly strict guidelines within which the two sexes function. Feminist rhetoric suggests that these rigid expectations are a result of sexism in the culture of this and other countries (Raymond, 1996). Certain emotions, communication styles, careers, and clothing choices are socially limited to one sex or the other. Violations of the social rules have serious implications. Picture a career-oriented male engineer wearing a smart tailored skirt with his jacket and tie to an interview. Even optimists who hope he would have a shot at the job know that bias will definitely be at work during his interview. Family, schools, media, and/or culture have taught gender role rules to nearly every American. Some people are actively attempting to unlearn them, but the socialization is strong. It is this socialization plus the prevalence of two commons myths that perpetuate discomfort with transgender issues. The two myths are that (1) transgenderism is a new fad and (2) transgendered people are crazy.

History of Transgenderism

Many people believe that transgenderism is a new topic and perhaps the newest fad in sexuality development. This myth has been fueled by the increasing visibility of transcending celebrities: Michael Jackson, Madonna, David Bowie, Annie Lennox, RuPaul, and Dennis Rodman. Because of the relatively recent origin of the transgender movement, it is tempting to believe that these phenomena are new and that this issue is trendy and will soon pass. In fact, the concept of gender bending is as old as gender roles themselves. The transgender phenomena can be accounted for in nearly every culture throughout history. Some societies and cultures even accounted for more than two gender roles (Feinberg, 1996).

During mid-3000 BCE (before the common era) in parts of Europe, the Middle East, northern Africa, and western Asia, male to female transsexual priestesses were reported as having important religious roles. These priestesses served as liaisons to a goddess most often called the Great Mother. This Great Mother has been described as an intersexual deity. The priestesses would castrate themselves and wear women's clothing (Besnier, 1993; Feinberg, 1996).

Many Greek mythological heroes and gods cross-dressed at one time or another and others even changed their sex. Intersexuals are represented in Greek mythology and Greek art (Feinberg, 1996; Herdt, 1993). One example is Eros the god/dess of love, whose parents were Hermes and Aphrodite. Their names are the source of the word hermaphrodite, an outdated term meaning intersexual. Cupid is the Roman equivalent of Eros. The Greek gods or heroes Dionysus, Athena, Achilles, Theseus, and Heracles were all reported to have cross-dressed at some time (Feinberg, 1996).

Although there are many accounts of the Amazons, no two seem to be quite the same. Most sources agree that these women were brave warriors either defending their territory or invading others' lands. Some accounts tell of male slaves who attended to domestic responsibilities and occasionally helped with procreation. Sources have placed them in numerous locations, including the north side of Asia Minor, Syria, Benin, and the banks of the Baltic Sea (Feinberg, 1996, Hirschfeld 1910/1991; Wheelwright, 1989). One source historically places their existence at around 1050 AD (Hirschfeld 1910/1991). According to Greek legend, Amazons were paired up in battles with such warriors as Achilles, Theseus, and Heracles. The Greeks made reference in their writings to an androgynous race they encountered during travels in Abomey, Benin in western Africa. These people were believed to also be the Amazons. In 1576, a Spanish explorer, Pedro de Magalhaes, wrote about a culture in northeastern Brazil in which the women lived as men and were accepted as such. It was he who named the "Amazon River" after the Amazons he had read about (Feinberg, 1996).

During the Byzantine Empire (200s-1100s), eunuchs were fairly common in eastern Europe. Eunuchs were men who chose to withdraw from the world and refused to procreate; thus the term means something more than just a castrated male. Some men chose to engage in these actions for religious reasons while others wanted to achieve status through court positions that were usually reserved for eunuchs. Others did not have a choice; they became sterile through illness, birth defect, or accident. Some peasant families had their infant sons castrated so they could be sold into slavery. The castration of men was an early form of sex reassignment surgery. The physiology of a woman was defined in relation to the male physiology (without a penis), hence the eunuch was viewed by many as a woman. However, most often in the Byzantine Empire, castration was performed by the mutilation of the testicles (removal, crushing, or tying off). In many cases, then, eunuchs were viewed as neither male nor female, just eunuchs. But the Roman society did not include a language for such a third sex option, so the masculine pronoun was applied to eunuchs. Eunuchs castrated in adulthood retained most of their secondary sex characteristics, and continued to be sexually active. Eunuchs castrated as boys never experienced puberty and therefore lacked body hair, musculature, and a deep voice (Ringrose, 1993).

Legend speaks of a female Pope Joan or John Anglicus during the mid-800s. She attended university with her lover, disguised as a man. She so loved the knowledge and critical thinking she was exposed to, that she never stopped passing as a man. "She recognized that her intellect was strong and she was drawn by the sweetness of learning" (Hotchkiss, 1996, p. 75). Joan pursued a career in the church and was elected as pope unanimously by the voting body. During a ceremonial procession Pope Joan dropped to the ground and gave birth. Stories say she died in childbirth or was killed by the mob there. Her reign was said to have lasted two years, seven months, and four days. To this day, the pope does not proceed down the alleyway where Pope Joan is said to have died (Dekker & van de Pol, 1989; Feinberg, 1996; Garber, 1991; Hotchkiss, 1996).

The story of Joan of Arc is well known. Born in the early 1400s, she came from a French peasant family and wore men's clothing. She became a warrior and was instrumental in leading other peasants in defending France against the English in the Hundred Years War. The peasants deemed her a sacred figure, while the French ruling class and church abhorred her heroism. As a peasant she accomplished what the people in power could not. For this reason the French aristocracy sought to execute her. They arrested her on charges of paganism and cross-dressing. The paganism became hard to prove, so they prosecuted her for cross-dressing. Because there were no laws against cross-dressing, they had her sign an agreement to never wear men's clothing again. However, as the French ruling class knew, Joan was illiterate and did not understand what she was signing. Since she continued to cross-dress, they executed her based on disobedience. It is evident in the accounts of her trial that Joan's decision to wear men's clothes was a spiritual one. When Joan had to make a decision of whether to burn alive tied to a stake at the age of 19 or wear women's clothing, Joan said "Not for anything would I take an oath not to arm myself and wear men's clothing in order to do our Lord's pleasure!" (Trask, 1996, p. 122). Her spirituality was evident to the French; some thought of her as a witch who used her powers for evil while others considered her a messenger from god (Dekker & van de Pol, 1989; Hotchkiss, 1996; Trask, 1996).

Dekker and van de Pol (1989) cited 119 cases of female to male cross-dressing in western Europe between the years of 1550 and 1839. They noted, "Whatever the personal motives for dressing as a man, an important consideration was that the women knew that they had predecessors, that other women had made the same decision" (p. 100).

In the 1700s, European seafarers recorded information about transgendered Polynesians. Journals noted boys being raised as females with and by women. Other times seafarers noted being attracted to a girl dancer who later turned out to be a young boy. Besnier (1993) cited examples in contemporary Polynesia of transgendered men taking on female roles in various societies. He also reported some cross-dressing, especially during festive occasions. There is no known religious connection for the transgendered Polynesians (Besnier, 1993).

In modern day India the hijras are considered neither male nor female. Hijras are vehicles of divine power to Bahuchara Mata, a version of the Mother God. A hijra is considered man plus woman. Born as intersexual or transsexual, hijras feel a calling to Bahuchara Mata. "It is by virtue of their sexual impotence (with women) that men are called on by Bahuchara Mata to dress and act like women and undergo emasculation" (Nanda, 1993, p. 373).

"Berdache" is an American anthropological word that was coined in the 1600s. Feinberg (1996) noted that many Native people consider the term offensive. Europeans used the word in a derogatory way to describe any Native person who did not fit narrow European definitions of gender. Feinberg used instead the respectful term, "Two-Spirit." The role of the Two-Spirit person is documented in nearly 150 North American societies. Roscoe (1993) explained three major roles of the Two-Spirit people: specialized production, supernatural sanction, and gender variation. "Berdaches were accepted and integrated members of their communities, as their economic and religious reputations indeed suggest...In a few cases they were feared because of the supernatural power they were believed to possess" (p. 335). Gender roles are loosely defined in many Native cultures and the Two-Spirit tradition continues today (Bolin, 1993; Feinberg, 1996; Katz, 1976; Roscoe, 1993).

Psychology of Transgenderism

The question of pathology verses identity comes up quite often when modern day transgendered media characters are considered. Two predominant stereotypes persist. Either transgendered people are introduced for comic relief (*Mrs. Doubtfire, Tootsie,* and *The Bird Cage*) or portrayed as being pathologically crazy (*Silence of the Lambs*). With such images in the media, it is easy to believe that transgendered people have a psychological disorder. But these images come from an even more powerful place. As noted previously, strict gender roles have been extremely influential in setting up norms for people's behaviors. Once any behavioral norm is violated, the person is labeled as abnormal and consequently mentally unhealthy (Lips, 1997).

Even though the concept of transgenderism has been known since antiquity (Dekker & van de Pol, 1989; Feinberg, 1996; Herdt, 1993; Hotchkiss, 1996), it wasn't until 1830 that Friedreich first described the condition in the medical literature. In 1980, the American Psychiatric Association included under psychosocial disorders a section on gender identity disorders in its third edition of the *Diagnostic and Statistical Manual of Mental Disorders* (DSM-III). Three different types of diagnoses were outlined: *transsexualism, non-transsexualism type*, and *not otherwise specified*. This was the first time the medical literature listed the transgender phenomena as a psychological disorder. This listing required insurance carriers to cover any services rendered to such persons, from psychotherapy to sex reassignment surgery (SRS).

Since 1980 there have been two more editions of the DSM: DSM-III-R (American Psychiatric Association, 1987) and DSM-IV (American Psychiatric Association, 1994). Within these newer documents, gender identity disorders (GID)) have been rearranged into various categories and even given a category of their own. Diagnoses and treatments vary as well.

Opinions within the transgender community vary greatly as to whether these identities should be included in the DSM. Some transgendered people believe that the inclusion is important to maintain insurance coverage. As long as gender identity disorders are included, there will be financial support for therapy, hormones, and full sex reassignment surgery (Pauly, 1992). However, many insurance companies refuse to cover costs regardless of the DSM inclusion of transgendered identities (Knox, 1989; Millenson, 1989).

Others argue that in order to have treatments covered, a person would have to be documented as having a mental illness. This labeling can be traumatic on many levels, but perhaps the most damaging is the cost to one's career (Goodavage, 1994; Johnson, 1994; Mazanec, 1993; Paddock, 1994; Pratt, 1995). Job discrimination against transgendered people in the United States is prohibited in only one state and three cities: Minnesota, Santa Cruz, Seattle, and San Francisco (Feinberg, 1996; Goodavage, 1994; Johnson, 1994; Paddock, 1994).

Many individuals believe that having a transgendered identity is not a mental disorder. A transsexual protester at an American Psychological Association meeting in 1993 said, "Transsexuality is not a disease. I am not crazy. It is who I am" (Olezewski, 1993, p. 13). Pressure to remove gender identity disorders from the DSM has been compared to the 1973 removal of homosexuality as a mental illness classification (Olezewski, 1993; Pauly, 1992).

During the early 1970s, research was based on the dualistic question, are transsexuals mentally sound or do they suffer from a psychopathological conflict? Two early studies (Finney, Bransdsma, Tondow, & Lemaistre, 1975; Stinson, 1972) showed a correlation between male-to-female transsexualism and a significant ego deficit, which implied some degree of psychopathology. Other researchers (Roback, McKee, Webb, Abramowitz, & Abramowitz, 1976; Rosen, 1974; Tsushima & Wedding, 1979) studied male-to-female transsexual mental health in relation to other psychiatric populations. They found that mental health adjustment is an issue; however, there was no evidence of a correlation to psychopathology (Johnson & Hunt, 1990).

As every dualistic question is investigated, gray areas are discovered. Research shifted to an investigation of variables that may predict psychiatric adjustment depending on the type of transsexuals being considered. Studies in the 1980s (Freund, Steiner, & Chan, 1982; Green, 1987; O'Gorman, 1982) focused on determining two separate etiologic tracks leading to transsexualism: male transsexuals whose gender orientation was rooted in a heterosexual cross-dressing fetishism and male transsexuals who first identified as gay men with feminine ideologies. Correlation was sought between the length of time the transsexuals spent in the feminine role and their mental health. O'Gorman (1982) theorized that late onset of transsexualism is correlated with a history of psychiatric illness. O'Gorman also assumed that late onset was correlated with heterosexual cross-dressing fetishism. Hence he theorized that transsexuals whose identity proceeded from heterosexual cross-dressing fetishism are more prone to psychiatric illness.

A study by Johnson and Hunt (1990) included 25 male-to-female transsexuals who were either post-operative or in the process of transition. They found a low correlation between the two typological features and psychological disturbance. The study also revealed that transsexualism manifests itself in both heterosexuals and homosexuals around the same time.

Bloom (1994) discussed two studies. The first involved a psychological test aimed at revealing a person's feelings of masculinity and femininity. The study compared female-to-male transsexuals before hormone therapy to genetic females. Findings showed that the transsexuals "tested high masculine/low feminine before the treatment and afterward as well-adjusted men who accept their feminine side" (p. 46). A second study compared the psychological personality of female-to-male transsexuals with genetic men and women. The transsexuals before treatment are not too far from the norm for women; but after treatment, they are completely in the normal range for men.

In November of 1995, headlines hit the world's papers, "Possible Transsexual Brain Trait Found" (Suplee, 1995). Dr. Dick F. Swaab and some of his colleagues in the Netherlands conducted a biological study of the brain. They looked at corpse brains of male-to-female transsexuals, heterosexual genetic men, homosexual genetic men, and heterosexual genetic women. A region of the hypothalamus, called the central division of the bed nucleus of the stria terminalis (BSTc), is thought to be responsible for sexual behavior. This area is 44% larger in men than in women, yet all 6 transsexual brains observed had female-sized BSTc. The researchers discovered that this area said nothing about sexual orientation, as the gay men's BSTc was the same size as the straight men's and the transsexuals varied in sexual orientation. (In an earlier study, LeVay, 1991 discovered another part of the hypothalamus that seems to be related to sexual orientation.) Further research into possible biological links to transgenderism is needed to confirm these findings.

With a better understanding of the history and psychology of transgenderism as a base, the implications of the transgender movement for LGB communities will be considered. What does gender identity have to do with sexual orientation?

Implications for the Lesbian, Gay, and Bisexual Communities

Although, by definition, gender identity and sexual orientation are two completely different issues, there are elements of each that bring them together. Gender identity refers to whether one is a man, woman, or person who transcends gender. Sexual orientation concerns the gender of the object of one's affections, such as heterosexual, gay, lesbian, or bisexual. Three concerns unite sexual orientation and gender identity in distinct ways: overlapping identities, mistaken identities, and the sexual orientation of transgendered people.

Individually, as transgendered people begin to define themselves, many first identify as lesbian, gay, or bisexual. They know that their life experience is different from others. Either lack of information about transgendered identities or internalized oppression can prevent transgendered people from embracing the accurate terminology. Many transgendered people find an accepting community among LGB people under the premise that they "belong" (Bloom, 1994). After identifying as transgendered, however, some people have been ostracized by their previously supportive LGB community.

While some individuals make a distinction between their sexual orientation and their gender identity, there is some overlapping of identities as well. An example is a drag queen, a cross-dressing man. Some men impersonate females only for the purpose of entertaining others, some cross-dress for comfort on occasion, and others incorporate women's clothing into their everyday wardrobe. Most drag queens are gay. There are LGB-identified people who identify as transgendered as well (Burana, Roxxie, & Due, 1994). Some post-operative transsexuals have reported experiencing attraction to the sex that they have transitioned to, and therefore identify as lesbian or gay (Bornstein, 1994).

Based on our popular culture stereotypes of LGB people (Lips, 1997), transgendered people are often mistakenly assumed to be the same as LGB people. Transgendered people are perhaps more vulnerable to random homophobic attacks than LGB people. Even though many members of the transgender community are not readily identifiable on the street, some are. As a male-to-female cross-dresser walks down the street in women's apparel, the shouts out of the passing car are not, "Hey, freaky transgendered guy." The shouts are most likely fueled by homophobia, like, "Faggot!" When a pre-operative female-to-male transsexual walks out of a store, the group who pulls him into an alley and beats him is not doing so because this person has transcended gender. This person is perceived as gay or lesbian, and is being gay bashed. It's not only strangers who attack transgendered people. Those who are not clearly identified have been attacked as well by people they have trusted and to whom they have acknowledged their identity. Contrary to media portrayal, transgendered people are quite often the victims of assaults and rarely are the perpetrators (Denny & Schaffer, 1992). Many transgendered people feel a connection to the LGB communities because they are all targets of the same hate—homophobia.

If gender identity concerns an individual's gender and sexual orientation concerns the gender of the object of one's affections, what happens when a transgendered person is involved in an affectionate relationship? What is the sexual orientation of the transgendered person? What is the sexual orientation of the person who is attracted to a transgendered person? Currently, there is no answer to that question. The premise upon which the transgender movement is based is freedom from gender, and yet when individuals identify their sexual orientation a rigid definition of gender is required. With limited options in our language many have become creative, using terms such as omnisexual or transdyke. However, these terms are by no means universal. The critical point to remember is that when the intent is to include all sexual orientations, the sexual orientations of transgendered people and the objects of their affections must be included. The safest way to accomplish this is to include the term transgendered when referring to all sexual orientation minorities; i.e., lesbian, gay, bisexual, and transgendered, or LGBT.

In summary, the transgender movement has the following implications for the LGB communities: (a) Some transgendered people have identified themselves, or currently identify themselves, as gay, lesbian, or bisexual; (b) Transgendered people are also targets of homophobia; and (c) Transgendered sexual orientation should be included when referring to all minority sexual orientations. The LGB movement and the transgender movement, although not the same, have too much in common to ignore.

Implications and Recommendations for Student Affairs

After reviewing the facts around two common myths about transgendered people (that transgenderism is a new phenomena and that transgendered people are crazy) and the relationship between transgendered individuals and LGB people, implications for the field of student affairs can now be discussed in an informed manner. Practitioners need to know what sort of incidents involving transgender issues are occurring on college campuses and how to proactively address potential issues.

Some practitioners may question whether transgender issues are prevalent enough within higher education to even warrant concern. Although transsexuals who seek sex reassignment surgery make up less than .01% of the population in Europe and the United States, "experts say that it is reasonable to assume that there are scores of unoperated cases for every operated one" (Brown & Rounsley, 1996, p. 9). Given that transsexuals are only part of the transgendered spectrum, it is likely that at least a few transgendered students will be found on most college campuses. If transgender issues are prevalent at all, they are relevant enough to address. There are three primary ways for student affairs administrators to address the needs of transgendered students: work towards an elimination of administrative gender division, provide support resources that specifically target transgendered students, and educate the university community about transgender issues.

Any segregation of students by gender presents a problem for individuals who transcend gender. Restrooms, sports teams, and some student organizations are segregated by gender. Daily language, including use of pronouns, demands that assumptions be made about the individuals people are talking to or about. In addition, society has normative expectations about men and women that, when violated, have serious social implications. Student affairs departments face these types of questions: Where does college housing assign a preoperative female-to-male transsexual? Which rest room is he allowed to use? For which track team does a male-to-female transsexual run, women's or men's? Is a cross-dressing male able to be admitted into a sorority? Can a cross-dressing student be dismissed from a classroom for being a disturbance? How should university records for transsexual students who change their names reflect these changes? In addition to these administrative questions, questions of support exist: Do LGB student resources also provide support for transgendered students? What will be the reaction of university officials who are asked to console a beaten cross-dresser? Does the university's definition of diversity include gender diversity? Which pronouns are to be used when staff speak to transgendered students? Does the university have certain expectations of each gender, behaviorally or otherwise?

Idealistically, once gender classification is eliminated from society, all of these questions will be resolved. During a talk given after her performance, "Opposite Gender Is Neither," at the Pennsylvania State University, Kate Bornstein explained her theory that there is absolutely no reason to categorize gender other than to discriminate and oppress (personal communication, April, 4, 1995). She sees a future where gender is chosen, and there are so many genders that oppression will not be an option. Rothblatt (1995) also argued against the necessity for gender definition. She equated gender categorization with racial apartheid.

While doing away with gender categorization seems fantasy-like and at best only a future solution, there are measures that can be taken now toward that end. Consider that co-educational housing, single occupancy rooms, unisex rest rooms, and open admission policies for all student groups are measures that many institutions are presently practicing (Winston, 1993). However, even if an institution of higher education established an intention to do away with all divisions based on gender, the school would still exist in a dualistic society and schools do not function independently of societal norms.

Despite this limitation, policies and common practices should be examined. Any gender segregation that can be eliminated, should be eliminated. If a policy, such as visitation restrictions, cannot be changed due to the politics or values of the institution, student affairs practitioners need to think about the implications of the policy for their transgendered student population. How would a school with a visitation policy react if a male-to-female cross-dresser walked into a women's residence hall after hours? Is there a procedure in place? How can the transgendered student be supported in such an environment? Being unprepared for such a situation can leave student affairs practitioners fumbling for an appropriate response. Institutions should identify the policies that transgendered students would find the most challenging to navigate around. Proactive measures, such as anticipating potential problems and appropriate responses (with regard to the student and the institution) would be helpful when and if the need arises.

For an institution of higher education realistically to meet the developmental needs of its transgendered students, support services must be provided. Any resources on campus that address LGB students' needs can be expanded to include transgendered students' needs as well. This effort should entail more than a name change for the established programs and offices. Staff members must be introduced to the meaning of terms and the issues of transgendered students. Some institutions have broadened the mission of their LGB student centers to include addressing the needs of their transgendered student population (Barnett, 1997) but many others have yet to consider this step.

To improve the campus climate, not only should support services be extended to transgendered students, but the college or university community must be educated on issues of transgenderism. In order for transgendered students to function comfortably, all students, faculty, staff, and administrators need to understand the concept that people have a right to be free from gender. This challenge extends beyond higher education environments and into the very core of society.

At the University of Minnesota, the mission of the Gay, Lesbian, and Bisexual Programs Office is to educate the university community. Director Beth Zemsky (personal communication, November 15, 1996) defines the problem as the campus climate, not the transgendered community. The University of Minnesota deals with a large open transgender community in comparison with many other universities due to the inclusion of gender identity in Minnesota's state civil rights law and the location of many clinics and services for transgendered people in Minneapolis. When the Gay, Lesbian, and Bisexual Programs Office opened in 1993, one of its the first goals was to educate the community about the meaning of "transgender." In January 1995, a planning committee made up of transgendered people from the university community put together a week of programming focused on transgender issues. The tone of the week's activities was, "Let's look at deconstructing gender; let's learn about ourselves!" (B. Zemsky, personal communication, November 15, 1996). Zemsky felt that this effort reached out to the transgender community and established the institution as an ally.

Language remains one of the biggest challenges. Even if society could accept freedom from gender, pronouns demand definition. The word "people" can be used in place of "men and women." Many gendered words can be neutralized; however, pronouns provide a limitation. In general, it is good practice to refer to people as the gender they are presenting. For example, a male-to-female cross-dresser would be referred to as "she" only when cross-dressing. However, the *best* practice is to respect the wishes of the person to whom one is referring. It is helpful to remember the advice given to allies of LGB people: don't assume the gender of the object of the person's affections. The same could be said for transgendered people: don't assume their gender identity.

There is absolutely no research on transgendered students. The size of the transgendered student population has not been determined. There is no documented method for recording incidents of harassment involving transgendered victims. While theorists and researchers have examined the identity development of LGB individuals (Cass, 1979; Zinik, 1985) there has been little research on the development of a transgendered identity. Bolin (1993) did study the psychosocial development of male-to-female transsexuals and proposed a four-stage model of development.

However, male-to-female transsexuals make up a very small part of the transgendered population. For practitioners interested in the study of gender identity development, it would seem advantageous to study people who function on both sides of the dichotomous gender line. After talking to a few transsexuals, it is obvious that there is more to gender than social roles. One person compared the feeling to that of a phantom limb. They feel something that physically just isn't there. For a greater understanding of all transgendered identities, further research is needed.

But institutions cannot wait for definitive research to address the needs of the transgendered student population. Transgendered students are attending colleges and universities and deserve consideration in the development of policies and in the provision of services. If student affairs professionals ignore this population that are failing to carry out their role as educators and advocates for all students.

References

American Psychiatric Association. (1980). *Diagnostic and statistical manual of mental disorders* (3rd ed.). Washington, DC: Author.

American Psychiatric Association. (1987). *Diagnostic and statistical manual of mental disorders* (3rd ed., rev.). Washington, DC: Author.

American Psychiatric Association. (1994). *Diagnostic and statistical manual of mental disorders* (4th ed.). Washington, DC: Author.

Barnett, D. (1997, January 24). *LGBT campus resource centers* [On line]. Available: http://www.uic.edu/orgs/lgbt/LGBT directors_list.html

Benjamin, H. (1953). Transvestism and transsexualism. *International Journal of Sexology, 7,* 12-14.

Besnier, N. (1993). Polynesian gender liminality though time and space. In G. Herdt (Ed.), *Third sex, third gender: Beyond sexual dimorphism in culture and history* (pp. 285-328). New York: Zone Books.

Bloom, A. (1994, July 18). The body lies. *The New Yorker,* pp. 38-49.

Bolin, A. (1988). *In search of Eve: Transsexual rites of passage.* South Hadley, MA: Bergin & Garvey.

Bolin, A. (1993). Transcending and transgendering: Male-to-female transsexuals, dichotomy and diversity. In G. Herdt (Ed.), *Third sex, third gender: Beyond sexual dimorphism in culture and history* (pp. 447-486). New York: Zone Books.

Bornstein, K. (1994). *Gender outlaw: On men, women, and the rest of us.* New York: Routledge.

Brown, M. L., & Rounsley, C. A. (1996). *True selves: Understanding transsexualism—for families, friends, coworkers, and helping professionals.* San Francisco: Jossey-Bass.

Brown, R. D. (1989). Fostering intellectual and personal growth: The student development role. In U. Delworth & G. R. Hanson (Eds.), *Student services: A handbook for the profession* (2nd ed., pp. 284-303). San Francisco: Jossey-Bass.

Burana, L., Roxxie, & Due, L. (1994). *Dagger: On butch women.* Pittsburgh, PA: Cleis Press.

Cass, V. C. (1979). Homosexual identity formation: A theoretical model. *Journal of Homosexuality, 4* (3), 219-235.

Chickering, A. W. (1969). *Education and identity.* San Francisco: Jossey-Bass.

Chickering, A. W., & Reisser, L. (1993). *Education and identity* (2nd ed.). San Francisco: Jossey-Bass.

Cross, W. E., Jr. (1991). *Shades of Black: Diversity in African-American identity.* Philadelphia: Temple University Press.

Dekker, R. M., & van de Pol, L. C. (1989). *The tradition of female transvestism in early modern Europe.* London: MacMillan.

Denny, D., & Schaffer, M. (1992, April 21). Do transgender issues affect the gay community? *Advocate: The National Gay & Lesbian Magazine,* p. 114.

Ekins, R., & King, D. (1996). Blending genders—an introduction. In R. Ekins & D. King (Eds.), *Blending genders: Social aspects of cross-dressing and sex-changing* (pp. 1-4). New York: Routledge.

Erikson, E. H. (1950). *Childhood and society.* New York: Norton.

Erikson, E. H. (1968). *Identity: Youth and crisis.* New York: Norton.

Feinberg, L. (1996). *Transgender warriors.* Boston: Beacon Press.

Feinberg, L. (1998). *Transliberation: Beyond pink or blue.* Boston: Beacon Press.

Finney, J. C., Bransdsma, J. M., Tondow, M., & Lemaistre, G. (1975). A study of transsexuals seeking gender reassignment. *American Journal of Psychiatry, 132,* 962-964.

Fisk, N. (1974). Gender dysphoria syndrome. In D. Laub & P. Gandy (Eds.), *Proceedings of the second interdisciplinary symposium on gender dysphoria syndrome* (pp. 7-14). Ann Harbor, MI: Edwards Brothers.

Freund, K., Steiner, B. W., & Chan, 5. (1982). Two types of cross gender identity. *Archives of Sexual Behavior, 11,* 49-63.

Garber, M. (1992). *Vested interests: Cross-dressing and cultural anxiety.* New York: Routledge.

Goodavage, M. (1994, December 19). San Francisco tough on transgender protection. *USA Today,* p. 7A.

Green, R. (1987). *The "Sissy Boy Syndrome" and the development of homosexuality.* New Haven, CT: Yale University Press.

Grimm, D. E. (1987). Toward a theory of gender. *American Behavioral Scientist, 31,* 66-85.

Helms, J. E. (1990). *Black and white racial identity: Theory, research, and practice.* New York: Greenwood.

Herdt, G. (1993). *Third sex, third gender: Beyond sexual dimorphism in culture and history.* New York: Zone Books.

Hirschfeld, M. (1991). *Transvestites: The erotic drive to cross-dress* (M. A. Lombardi-Nash, Trans.). Buffalo, NY: Prometheus Books. (Original work published in 1910)

Hotchkiss, V. R. (1996). *Clothes make the man: Female cross-dressing in medieval Europe.* New York: Garland.

Johnson, C. (1994, December 13). 'Transgender' bias is banned in S. F.: Supervisors create a new civil right. *San Francisco Chronicle,* pp. A15, A18.

Johnson, S. L., & Hunt, D. D. (1990). The relationship of male transsexual typology to psychosocial adjustment. *Archives of Sexual Behavior, 19,* 349-360.

Katz, J. (1976). *Gay American history: Lesbians and gay men in the U.S.A.* New York: Thomas Y. Crowell.

King, D. (1996). Gender blending: Medical perspectives and technology. In R. Ekins & D. King (Eds.), *Blending genders: Social aspects of cross-dressing and sex-changing* (pp. 79-98). New York: Routledge.

Knox, R. A. (1989, March 17). Transsexual blames insurer for plight. *Boston Globe,* pp. 15, 16.

LeVay, S. (1991). A difference in hypothalamic structure between heterosexual and homosexual men. *Science, 253,* 1034-1037.

Levinson, D. J. (1986). *The seasons of a man's life.* New York: Alfred A. Knopf.

Levinson, D. J. (1996). *The seasons of a woman's life.* New York: Alfred A. Knopf.

Lips, H. M. (1997). *Sex and gender: An introduction* (3rd ed.). Mountain View, CA: Mayfield.

Love, P. G., Boschini, V. J., Jacobs, B. A., Hardy, C. M., & Kuh, G. D. (1993). Student culture. In G. D. Kuh (Ed.), *Cultural perspectives in student affairs work* (pp. 59-79). Lanham, MD: ACPA.

MacKenzie, G. O. (1994). *Transgender nation.* Bowling Green, OH: Bowling Green State University Popular Press.

Mazanec, J. (1993, February 12). Transsexual joins ban on gays fray. *USA Today,* p. A3.

Millenson, M. L. (1989, May 25). Transsexual twilight zone. *Chicago Tribune,* section 5, pp. 1,4.

Nanda, S. (1993). Hijras: An alternative sex and gender role in India. In G. Herdt (Ed.), *Third sex, third gender: Beyond sexual dimorphism in culture and history* (pp. 373-418). New York: Zone Books.

O'Gorman, E. C. (1982). A retrospective study of epidemiological and clinical aspects of twenty-eight transsexual patients. *Archives of Sexual Behavior, 11,* 231-236.

Olezewski, L. (1993, May 24). Transsexuals protest at psychiatry meeting. *San Francisco Chronicle,* p. 13.

Paddock, R. C. (1994, December 26). S. F. targets anti-transgender bias. *Los Angeles Times,* pp. A3, A46.

Pauly, I. B. (1992). Terminology and classification of gender identity disorders. In W. O. Bockting & E. Coleman (Eds.), *Gender dysphoria: Interdisciplinary approaches in clinical management* (pp. 1-14). New York: Haworth.

Pratt, C. (1995, June 18). The perilous times of transgender youth. *New York Times,* p. CY7.

Raymond, J. (1996). The politics of transgenderism. In R. Ekins & D. King (Eds.), *Blending genders: Social aspects of cross-dressing and sex-changing* (pp. 215-224). New York: Routledge.

Reitz, J. E. (1995, January 24). Proposal to add 'transgender' to LGBSA debated, voted down. *The Daily Collegian* (The Pennsylvania State University), p.1.

Ringrose, K. M. (1993). Living in the shadows: Eunuchs and gender in Byzantium. In G. Herdt (Ed.), *Third sex, third gender: Beyond sexual dimorphism in culture and history* (pp. 85-110). New York: Zone Books.

Roback, H. B., McKee, E., Webb, W., Abramowitz, C. V., & Abramowitz, S. L. (1976). Comparative psychiatric status of male applicants for sexual reassignment surgery, jejunoileal bypass surgery, and psychiatric outpatient treatment. *Journal of Sex Research, 12,* 315-320.

Rogers, R. F. (1989). Student development. In U. Delworth & G. R. Hanson (Eds.), *Student services: A handbook for the profession* (2nd ed., pp. 117-164). San Francisco: JosseyBass.

Roscoe, W. (1993). How to become a berdache: Toward a unified analysis of gender diversity. In G. Herdt (Ed.), *Third sex, third gender: Beyond sexual dimorphism in culture and history* (pp. 329-372). New York: Zone Books.

Rosen, A. C. (1974). Brief report of MMPI characteristics of sexual deviation. *Psychological Reports, 35,* 73-75.

Rothblatt, M. (1995). *The apartheid of sex: A manifesto on the freedom of gender.* New York: Crown.

Stinson, B. (1972). A study of twelve applicants for transsexual surgery. *Ohio State Medical Journal, 68,* 245-249.

Sue, D. W., & Sue, D. (1990). *Counseling the culturally different: Theory and practice* (2nd ed.). New York: Wiley.

Suplee, C. (1995, November 2). Possible transsexual brain trait found. *The Washington Post,* p. A3.

Trask, W. (1996). *Joan of Arc: In her own words.* New York: BOOKS & Co.

Tsushima, W. T., & Wedding, D. (1979). MMPI results of male candidates for transsexual surgery. *Journal Personality Assessment, 43,* 385-387.

Wheelwright, J. (1989). *Amazons and military maids: Women who dressed as men in the pursuit of life, liberty, and happiness.* London: Pandora.

Winston, R. G. (1993). *Student housing and residential life: A handbook for professionals committed to student development goals.* San Francisco: Jossey-Bass.

Zinik, G. (1985). Identity conflict or adaptive flexibility? Bisexuality reconsidered. In F. Klein & T. J. Wolf (Eds.), *Bisexualities: Theory and research* (pp. 7-19). New York: Haworth.

Chapter 12

ℰℛ

Addressing Issues of Multiple Identities for Women of Color on College Campuses

ANGELA D. FERGUSON AND MARY F. HOWARD-HAMILTON

C ampus organizations and student groups are frequently established based on a single identity without recognition or discussion of the multiple characteristics many students embrace. Oftentimes, students identify with others based on immutable or visible characteristics relative to gender and race. For example, it is not uncommon to have student groups on campuses that focus on women's issues, African American issues, Latino issues, or international students' concerns and issues. Although these groups serve the needs of many college students, they are generally based on the assumption that their members represent a homogeneous group and that all members share common concerns. Group members may indeed share common concerns; however, discussions of or attention to diversity issues within organizations and social groups may not occur.

Henry Louis Gates (1996) cogently stated that people "speak as if race is something blacks have, sexual orientation is something gays and lesbians have, gender is something women have, ethnicity is something so called 'ethnics' have" (p. 3). Thus, if persons do not fit "neatly" into the aforementioned categories, they are not acknowledged as sharing group membership in any particular group. Moreover, if they do not openly identify with the above categories, people assume they do not have any worries about the various identities. This conclusion is far from true because everyone in our society is part of the multicultural salad bowl (Pope, 1995). Gates (1996) argued for an inclusive definition of multiculturalism of which gay, lesbians, and bisexuals are a part because: (a) the identity stages that racial groups must attain are comparable for sexual minorities; (b) multicultural counseling skills are transferable; (c) there is a cultural environment among lesbians and gays; and (d) the impact of oppression on gays and lesbians as well as the majority culture affects their careers, psychosocial development, and overall life.

In this chapter we discuss the issues specifically related to African American lesbian and bisexual women and how the integration of race, gender, and sexual orientation forms a confluence of characteristics that should be addressed to enhance sensitivity among student affairs practitioners, faculty, and students. Multicultural theoretical perspectives are discussed to provide a base for examining these issues. Strategies for inclusion related to training and interventions are presented.

Multicultural Perspectives in Student Affairs

Multicultural theoretical perspectives have their "roots in the racial civil rights movement of the 1960's and early 1970's" (Helms & Richardson, 1997, p. 62). Along with providing credibility for African American rights (Hutnik, 1991), this movement helped increase awareness of other undervalued, hidden, multiply oppressed groups of people in American society. The growing presence of women, men and women of color, openly LGBT students, and non-traditional students on college campuses has helped to serve as a catalyst in challenging earlier theoretical concepts of student development and their application to human behavior and mental health (Chickering & Reisser, 1993).

Early multicultural theoretical and empirical literature began changing traditional frameworks of understanding individuals by including the exploration of racial identity development (Atkinson, Morten, & Sue, 1998; Cross, 1991; Helms, 1993) This literature helped mental health and student affairs professionals gain an understanding of important characteristics and psychological dynamics involved in developing a non-White racial identity. Racial identity models that have focused specifically on non-European American individuals have examined the sociopolitical dynamics of each group's race, how racial issues are perceived and dealt with (Carter, 1995), and how social consequences of oppression and prejudice impact self-esteem.

Gender identity development models have surfaced since the emergence of the feminist movement. Gender role identity varies within and among cultural groups, and many cultures, including European American, continue to value stereotypic gender expectations and ideologies (Fassinger & Richie, 1997), particularly when intense and pervasive patriarchal values are embraced (Greene, 1994). Many women of color perceive their family as the primary social unit and a source of emotional refuge from racism in the dominant culture (Greene, 1994). Consequently, many lesbians of color may choose not to jeopardize connection with family members and with the ethnic community system by identifying themselves as lesbian. Kanuha (1990) stated that due to racism and the need for people of color to form alliances against it, "lesbians of color are inextricably bound to their racial-ethnic communities and therefore to men of color" (p. 172).

Several sexual orientation models (Cass, 1979; Coleman, 1982; Troiden, 1989) have appeared in the psychological literature. They outline the developmental tasks by which the individual comes to accept her or his sexual orientation. These models have also been useful in understanding the complex and all too often misunderstood development of a non-heterosexual identity. However, these approaches have been criticized for their insensitivity to diverse groups in terms of race/ethnicity, age, gender, and those who exhibit a bisexual orientation (McCarn & Fassinger, 1996). Tremble, Schneider, and Appathurai (1989) noted that "the study of the gay and lesbian experience in North America has been most often the study of the White, middle-class experience. Until recently, the impact of ethnic and racial differences among gay males and lesbians has remained largely unexamined" (p. 253).

Issues Impacting Lesbian and Bisexual Women of Color

Many college students struggle to adapt to a very new environment, one that may appear indifferent to and rejecting of their individuality, race, and culture. Many are also in the process of learning about and understanding issues related to sexuality and intimacy (Evans & D'Augelli, 1996), and are generally unfamiliar with the issues related to sexual orientation (Eldridge & Barnett, 1991). Moreover, many cultures have religious and/or familial values and principles that are not similar to traditional American dating rituals thereby restricting the individual's awareness and expression of sexuality relative to the culturally dominant groups on campus.

Developing a lesbian, gay, or bisexual relationship may be "a more complex process than achieving an intimate heterosexual relationship because of the invisibility of lesbian and gay couples in our society" (Evans, Forney, & Guido-DiBrito, 1998, p. 97). Consequently, many gay men, lesbians, and bisexual students have not had the opportunity of dating or developing romantic relationships with same-sex partners. This developmental task of developing and forming intimate relationships may be more challenging for lesbian and bisexual women of color due to the complexity of race, gender, and cultural factors.

As a group, lesbian and bisexual women of color include ethnically and culturally diverse individuals. African American, Black American of Caribbean descent, Latina, Asian American, Native American, Asian Indian, and Pacific Islander women comprise a few of the ethnic groups that may be considered "women of color." Cultural values and practices, belief systems, and gender values vary among the large group of women who consider themselves lesbian (Greene, 1994). Sexual orientation to date does not have a uniform definition and is not perceived similarly by the heterosexual community or the gay, lesbian, or bisexual communities (Ferguson, 1995). Definitions of sexual orientation may vary, in part, due to the fact that many cultures have a wide range of perceptions and attitudes about sexual behavior (Espin, 1984; Smith, 1997) depending on factors such as gender, religion, and social status. Moreover, Greene (1997) noted that sexuality is contextual and that ". . . what it means to be a gay man or a lesbian will be related to the meaning assigned to sexuality in the culture" (p. 218). Gender roles and expectations are significantly impacted by cultural and religious values, customs, and beliefs.

Lesbian and bisexual women of color are often attempting to integrate at least three social identities that have historically been stigmatized and oppressed: race, gender, and sexual orientation. The effects of race, ethnicity, and gender may differentially affect lesbian and bisexual women of color's coming-out process. For some women who are in the process of developing racial, ethnic, and gender identities while at the same time coming out, the effects of racism, homophobia, and sexism may uniquely impact their cognitive, emotional, and behavioral transitions relative to developing any one of their identities (Ferguson, 1995). Additionally, Morales (1989) noted that throughout their lives, ethnic gay and lesbian individuals have to relate to three different reference groups: "the gay/ lesbian community, the ethnic community, and the predominantly heterosexual White mainstream society" (p.22). The lesbian and bisexual woman of color on college campuses is visible and invisible in multiple ways. Many of her peers are typically focused on one or perhaps two of her social identities: race/ethnicity and gender, with little attention to the possibility of her having a non-heterosexual identity. As a result, her race/ethnicity is often the primary visible identity to heterosexual White and racial/ethnic communities, as well as to White gay, lesbian, and bisexual communities. She is invisible in that her sexual orientation can be minimized or ignored by the same communities. This visibility/ invisibility continuum presents lesbians of color with unique challenges on college campuses in terms of self-identity, group membership, group identification, and community inclusion/exclusion. Integrating themselves on a college campus is therefore more complex than simply experiencing "adjustment issues" to a new environment.

Issues Impacting Lesbian and Bisexual African American Women

The paramount issue facing bisexual and lesbian African American women is inclusion. Where do I belong and who will support me and my identity? Within certain lesbian movements, some African American lesbians and bisexuals have felt that the espoused belief in justice for all women was not inclusive of women of color (Louise, 1989). For African

American lesbians in particular, it is often difficult to find acceptance among the African American population because lesbianism is largely incompatible with female role expectations based on traditional African American values (Loiacano, 1989). Moreover, many African American lesbians and bisexuals perceive the African American community as very homophobic and rejecting of them (Mays & Cochran, 1988). Yielding to social pressure, many lesbians and bisexual women of African descent attempt to follow social expectations by marrying. An early study found that 47% of African American lesbians and 13% of African American gay males have been married a least once (Bell & Weinberg, 1978). More recently, Ferguson (1995) surveyed 181 women of African descent who identified as lesbian and found that approximately 67% of the women had been in a committed relationship with a man at some time in their lives. Additionally, approximately 39% of the women reported that they have children. Greene (1994) summarized that African American lesbians may ". . . have continued contact with men and with heterosexual peers to a greater extent than their White counterparts" (p. 246). African American lesbians' adherence to gender roles (for instance, marriage, children, commitment to men) may allow them to perceive themselves as part of their cultural and ethnic community, rather than feeling separated and isolated because of their sexual orientation (Ferguson, 1995).

Sexual attraction to men and forming a family have been embedded in the heterosexual community to mean that a woman is "normal" (Greene, 1994). Developmentally, African American women are attempting to negotiate teenage and adult expectations, as well as the meaning of womanhood for themselves and with their peers. Feeling "abnormal" may significantly prevent women from developing confidence, leadership skills, and socially visible roles on campus. Consequently, the question of belonging to which group(s) often poses a salient dilemma for many African American women who embrace a "non-heterosexual" sexual orientation.

Garnets and Kimmel (1993) found several themes relevant for understanding cultural influence on the identity of lesbians and gays. These themes are:

1. **Religion** – The African American community rallies around the church, which brings about racial pride in identity and solidarity among its members. However, the religious community often ostracizes African American gays and lesbians.

2. **Gender roles** – It is difficult for women to carry out androgynous or nontraditional roles.
3. **Family structure** – Coming out to family may mean the loss of a major support system. Many individuals therefore remain closeted.
4. **Identity formation** – Integration of multiple identities (race, gender, and sexual orientation) may engender a conflicting value system not only about themselves but what they may teach to others.
5. **Integration into the majority culture** – This may mean "an ongoing management of conflicting allegiances between those groups that represent the expression of intimacy and those that provide ethnic foundation" (Garnets & Kimmel, 1993, p. 334).

Strategies for Inclusion

Where does the woman of color who embraces a lesbian or bisexual identity go for support on campus? Student affairs faculty and practitioners are in a position to help create and implement curricular changes, programs, and services to be more inclusive of this population.

The authors of the *NASPA Perspective on Student Affairs* (1987) presented several assumptions and beliefs that shape the student affairs profession. In the belief that "each student has worth and dignity" (p.10) administrators were reminded that:

It is imperative that students learn to recognize, understand, and celebrate human differences. Colleges can, and indeed must help their students become open to the differences that surround them: race, religion, age, gender, culture, physical ability, language, nationality, sexual preference [sic], and lifestyle. These matters are learned best in collegiate settings that are rich with diversity and they must be learned if the ideals of human worth and dignity are to be advanced. (p. 10)

Addressing Multicultural Issues in Student Affairs Preparation

Based upon this philosophy, student affairs graduate preparation programs should be helping students understand and embrace the dramatic

changes in the demographic complexion of the student population on
college campuses (Talbot, 1996). Talbot examined current graduate
training programs and found that many of the students define and view
diversity narrowly. Populations that they included in their definitions
were "women, African Americans, and adult learners" (p. 174). The
students rarely mentioned other racial/ethnic groups or lesbians, bisexuals,
or gay men. Additionally, Talbot stated that "several students indicated
that gay, lesbian, and bisexual issues were almost 'taboo'; bringing up
the topic usually caused tension" (p. 174). Many instructors assert that
they lack the knowledge, interest, or time to prepare appropriate literature
and information that is inclusive of diversity (Vazquez, 1997). The students
interviewed in Talbot's (1996) study stated that in-class discussions about
multiculturalism were promoted by the students rather than being faculty
generated. These findings are alarming because the faculty who teach in
graduate preparation programs are not preparing new practitioners with
effective communication and intervention strategies for the diverse student
body on today's college campuses. This lack of diversity training is
antithetical to the guiding philosophy statements put forth by the field
which state that student affairs practioners should do no harm to the
students they serve (ACPA, 1993). When personal identity is ignored by
using only the traditional theories and attempting to apply them to all
cultural groups, educators are doing harm to the students with whom
they work by not acknowledging or embracing their unique characteristics.

Once a multicultural training model has been developed, programs
must also consider the various topical areas to be included in not only a
multicultural course, but in all areas of student affairs preparation. Some
programs may be presenting culture-specific information in a manner
that prohibits inclusion of people with multiple identities. Consequently,
"students may learn to stereotype clients if only normative information
is presented without adequate consideration of within-group differences"
(Ridley, Espelage, & Rubinstein, 1997, p. 136). Addressing issues of
identity development, for example, would require student affairs
administrators and faculty to acknowledge the fact that racial identity
may differ due to the individual's gender and sexual orientation; gender
identity may differ due to race/ethnicity and sexual orientation; and sexual
orientation identity may differ due to gender and race/ethnicity. Training
programs must emphasize the importance of examining identity theories
concurrently and acknowledge the complexity of integrating multiple

social identities and multiple forms of oppression. As students gain an understanding of this complex process, they may begin to move beyond "knowledge and sensitivity;" they can begin to learn practical applications of multicultural approaches and move toward developing multicultural skills (Ridley et al., 1997, p. 136).

Lesbian and bisexual women of color need to find allies and supportive networks to insure their success on campus. This goal can be accomplished if training programs prepare practioners to become sensitive to racial/ gendered individuals as well as to understand diversity issues and factors both between and within racial, gender, and sexual orientation group members.

Many student affairs practitioners know it is important to "walk the walk and talk the talk," but do they really know how to be assertive in uncomfortable situations? Increasing comfort in such situations is one reason why the infusion of a multicultural curriculum and specific course work is so important in our field. Curricula that incorporate a multicultural perspective in theory courses, research, consultation, career, supervision, and counseling courses would assist graduate students in their preparation to work with issues of diversity. Assisting students to recognize and understand oppression based on "isms," their biases and misperceptions about their own and others' culture, and the relevance of sociopolitical and sociocultural contexts would provide them with an awareness that "all people have been shaped by membership in one or more cultures and that these cultural roots or origins influence people's values, behavior, and perception of events" (Pope, Reynolds, & Cheatham, 1997, p. 62). Courses that emphasize the idea of diversity as including multiple identities would help to sensitize students to becoming aware that people do not exist under one identity, but may also be attempting to integrate identities that may be mutually stigmatizing.

Curricula that utilize an integrative approach in which training involves a didactic component (cognitive) and an experiential (affective) component would assist students in recognizing the ways in which their own cultural realities and internalizations interact and affect their work with others (Brown, 1993; Comas-Diaz, 1994). This approach would assist students in becoming more flexible and pluralistic in their teaching and research practices, and program development. Moreover, it would allow student affairs practitioners to gain an understanding of their own cultural development.

McEwen and Roper (1994) suggested that "incorporating multi-culturalism into preparation programs should heighten multicultural awareness and knowledge of graduate students and faculty; embracing multiculturalism represents honest scholarship, rather than scholarship void of consideration of multicultural issues" (p. 49). In addition to coursework and personal exploration, student affairs practitioners should become familiar with the lesbian and bisexual community around them. Talbot (1996) stressed that students in graduate preparation programs should have direct contact and exposure to diverse students, faculty, and staff. For example, personal interaction and participation in dialogues to find out what issues and concerns plague African American lesbian and bisexual women will increase cohesion among these students and administrators. In addition, becoming familiar with community groups off campus can help student affairs administrators and practitioners guide students to referral sources if needed.

Building Bridges of Support
Through Student Affairs Practice

Based upon the reviewed literature, several suggestions for providing a supportive environment for comfort and inclusion among African American lesbians are offered. Administrators can make a strong supportive pronouncement for lesbian, bisexual, and gay rights by supporting the inclusion of a sexual orientation statement in the university nondiscrimination policy. Faculty can assist in this process by becoming members of committees that are developed to address the issue of homophobia and heterosexism on campus. Additionally, strategies to address sensitivity to heterosexism in the classroom, similar to the sexual harassment policies already developed, should be designed by faculty and administrators in a collaborative effort. Demonstrating faculty and administrative support shows students that there is solidarity and advocacy towards this issue.

A support group for lesbian and bisexual women of color should be accessible to students in addition to larger organizations that are inclusive of LGBT students regardless of race or gender. This is one way that lesbians and bisexuals have gained integration of their multiple identities (Garnets & Kimmel, 1993). Garnets and Kimmel stated that such a network provides a sense of community by: (a) creating new extended families that are more sensitive to their needs (p. 336); (b) increasing visibility by acknowledging their presence among the larger racial/ethnic and gay and lesbian populations; and (c) helping them to consolidate efforts toward ameliorating oppression in the respective communities they interact with on a continual basis. It is imperative that some type of network for women of color be established due, in part, to the fact that this cohort is less likely to seek assistance from counselors, thus intensifying their isolation, tension, and loneliness on campus (Greene, 1994).

Inclusion of bisexual women of color should be a focal point for the group because "the gay and especially the lesbian community is embracing bisexuality as never before" (Nichols, 1994, p. 157). If necessary, a group for bisexual women should be established for psychological, social, and emotional support. The bisexual orientation paradigm is relatively new to researchers, practitioners, and counselors. Very little has been written regarding the needs of this population. However, individuals embracing a bisexual identification have unique needs that are separate from those of lesbians and this "paradigm recognizes that sexual orientation is multidimensional; this conception not only includes attraction, behavior, and identity, but also allows for fluid identity over the life cycle" (Nichols, 1994, p. 167).

Establishing "safe places" in classrooms, residential housing, workshops, and student organizations for students to discuss a variety of issues and concerns can help support individuals with multiple identities. Continuing the trend of limiting discussions to "Black" issues, "women's" issues, or "gay, lesbian, bisexual" issues without regard to integrating these issues perpetuates the monolithic, unidimensional paradigm that currently exists. Becoming aware that "Black" issues also include women's and gay, lesbian, and bisexual concerns is an important step in raising the conscience of the campus community.

Conclusion

Traditional student affairs and psychological research historically has excluded or minimized the importance of the individual's social identities (i.e., ethnicity, gender, sexual orientation) and their relationship within individuals' psychological, interpersonal, leadership, and social development. The effects of racism, sexism, and homophobia may differentially affect lesbian and bisexual women of color, and oftentimes in erratic and contradictory ways. As they seek to develop friendships and social activities, the existing separate campus organizations and activities (for example, Black organizations, women's organizations, Greek organizations) may prevent lesbian and bisexual women of color from experiencing themselves as "whole" persons.

Racism, sexism, and heterosexism are forms of oppression perpetrated by respective majority/dominant groups. Moreover, sexism and heterosexism are also forms of oppression in both the communities of color and in the gay/lesbian communities, respectively. Lesbian and bisexual women of color are often in the position of juggling multiple identities and multiple oppressions (Ferguson, 1995). Each social identity carries its own type of oppression, which may be conflicting with another social identity. Being a member of one oppressed group may evoke feelings of fear, denial, or anger that may cause the individual to disavow any membership in another oppressed group (Tajfel, 1981). These factors play a part in how the individual may perceive the salience and importance of a particular social identity relative to the stressors, environment, and people in her life (Ferguson, 1995), and may inhibit her academic and personal/interpersonal growth.

The gay, bisexual, and lesbian population has many within-group differences that should be recognized and addressed in all aspects of student development and student activities on campus. Just as many racial/ ethnic groups are lumped into one monolithic categorization of behaviors or beliefs, so are lesbians, gays, and bisexuals. Continued research and further data are imperative to provide information on the supportive services needed for lesbians and bisexuals of color on college campuses in order to expand our understanding of ways to enrich, transform, and develop multicultural efforts in the field.

References

American College Personnel Association (1993). American College Personnel Association: Statement of ethical principles and standards. *Journal of College Student Development, 34,* 89-92.

Atkinson, D.R., Morten, G., & Sue, D.W. (Eds.). (1998). *Counseling American minorities: A cross-cultural perspective* (5th ed.). Boston: McGraw Hill.

Bell, A., & Weinberg, M. (1978). *Homosexuality: A study of diversity among men and women.* New York: Simon & Schuster.

Brown, L. S. (1993). Anti-domination training as a central component of diversity in clinical psychology education. *Clinical Psychologist, 46,* 83-87.

Carter, R. T. (1995). *The influence of race and racial identity in psychotherapy.* New York: Wiley.

Cass, V.C. (1979). Homosexual identity formation: A theoretical model. *Journal of Homosexuality, 15,* 13-23.

Chickering, A.W., & Reisser, L. (1993). *Education and identity* (2nd ed.). San Francisco: Jossey-Bass.

Coleman, E. (1982). Developmental stages of the coming out process. In J. Gonsiorek (Ed.), *Homosexuality and psychotherapy: A practitioner's handbook of affirmative models* (pp. 31-44). New York: Haworth.

Comas-Diaz, L. (1994). An integrative approach. In L. Comas-Diaz & B. Greene (Eds.), *Women of color: Integrating ethnic and gender identities in psychotherapy* (pp. 287-318). New York: Guilford Press.

Cross, W.E., Jr. (1991). *Shades of Black: Diversity in African-American identity.* Philadelphia, PA: Temple University Press.

Eldridge, N. S., & Barnett, D. C. (1991). Counseling gay and lesbian students. In N. J. Evans & V. A. Wall (Eds.), *Beyond tolerance: Gays, lesbians and bisexuals on campus* (pp. 147-178). Alexandria, VA: American College Personnel Association.

Espin, O. M. (1984). Cultural and historical influences on sexuality in Hispanic/Latina women: Implications for psychotherapy. In C. Vance (Ed.), *Pleasure and danger: Exploring female sexuality* (pp. 149-163). London: Routledge & Kegan Paul.

Evans, N. J., & D'Augelli, A. R. (1996). Lesbians, gay men, and bisexual people in college. In R. C. Savin-Williams & K. M. Cohen (Eds.). *The lives of lesbians, gays, and bisexuals: Children to adults* (pp. 201-226). Fort Worth, TX: Harcourt Brace.

Evans, N. J., Forney, D. S., & Guido-DiBrito, F. (1998*). Student development in college: Theory, research, and practice.* San Francisco: Jossey-Bass.

Fassinger, R. E., & Richie, B. S. (1997). Sex matters: Gender and sexual orientation in training for multicultural counseling competency. In D. B. Pope-Davis & H. L. K. Coleman (Eds.), *Multicultural counseling competencies* (pp. 83-110). Thousand Oaks, CA: Sage.

Ferguson, A. D. (1995). *The relationship between African American lesbians' race, gender, and sexual orientation and self-esteem.* Unpublished doctoral dissertation, University of Maryland, College Park.

Gates, H. L. (1996). The ethics of identity. *Pathways, 20* (3), 3-4.

Garnets, L., & Kimmel, D. (Eds.). (1993). *Psychological perspectives on lesbian and gay male experiences.* New York: Columbia University Press.

Greene, B. (1994). Lesbian women of color: Triple jeopardy. In L. Comas-Diaz & B. Greene (Eds.), *Women of color: Integrating ethnic and gender identities in psychotherapy* (pp. 389-427). New York: Guilford.

Greene, B. (Ed.). (1997). *Psychological perspectives on lesbian and gay issues: Vol. 3. Ethnic and cultural diversity among lesbians and gay men* (pp. 297-300). Thousand Oaks, CA: Sage.

Helms, J. E. (1993). *Black and White racial identity: Theory, research, and practice.* Westport, CT: Praeger.

Helms, J. E., & Richardson, T. Q. (1997). How "multiculturalism" obscures race and culture as differential aspects of counseling competency. In D. B. Pope-Davis & H. L. K. Coleman (Eds.), *Multicultural counseling competencies* (pp. 60-82). Thousand Oaks, CA: Sage.

Hutnik, N. (1991). *Ethnic minority identity.* New York: Oxford University Press.

Kanuha, V. (1990). Compounding the triple jeopardy: Battering in lesbian of color relationships. *Women and Therapy, 9,* 169-183.

Loiacano, D. K. (1989). Gay identity issues among Black Americans: Racism, homophobia, and the need for validation. *Journal of Counseling and Development, 68,* 21-25.

Louise, V. (1989). Coming out. In J. Penelope & S. Wolfe (Eds.), *The original coming out stories.* Freedom, CA: The Crossing Press.

Mays, V., & Cochran, S. (1988). The Black woman's relationship project: A national survey of Black lesbians. In M. Shernoff & W. Scott (Eds.), *The sourcebook on lesbian/gay health care* (2nd ed., pp. 54-62). Washington, DC: National Lesbian and Gay Health Foundation.

McCarn, S. R., & Fassinger, R. E. (1996). Revisioning sexual minority identity development formation: A new model of lesbian identity and its implications for counseling and research. *The Counseling Psychologist, 24,* 508-534.

McEwen, M. L., & Roper, L. D. (1994). Incorporating multiculturalism into student affairs preparation programs: Suggestions from the literature. *Journal of College Student Development, 35,* 46-53.

Morales, E. S. (1989). Ethnic minority families and minority gays and lesbians. *Journal of Homosexuality, 17,* 217-239.

National Association of Student Personnel Administrators (1987). *A perspective on student affairs.* Washington, DC: Author.

Nichols, M. (1994). Therapy with bisexual women: Working on the edge of emerging cultural and personal identities. In M. P. Mirkin (Ed.), *Women in context: Toward a feminist reconstruction of psychotherapy* (pp. 149-169). New York: Guilford.

Pope, M. (1995). The "salad bowl" is big enough for us all: An argument for the inclusion of lesbians and gay men in any definition of multiculturalism. *Journal of Counseling and Development, 73,* 301-304.

Pope, R. L., Reynolds, A. L., & Cheatham, H. E. (1997). American College Personnel Association strategic initiative on multiculturalism: A report and proposal. *Journal of College Student Development, 38,* 62-66.

Ridley, C. R., Espelage, D. L., & Rubinstein, K. J. (1997). Course development in multicultural counseling. In D. B. Pope-Davis & H. L. K. Coleman (Eds.), *Multicultural counseling competencies* (pp. 131-158). Thousand Oaks, CA: Sage.

Smith, A. (1997). Cultural diversity and the coming-out process. In B. Greene (Ed.), *Psychological perspectives on lesbian and gay issues: Vol. 3. Ethnic and cultural diversity among lesbians and gay men* (pp. 297-300). Thousand Oaks, CA: Sage.

Talbot, D. M. (1996). Master's student's perspective on their graduate education regarding issues of diversity. *NASPA Journal, 33,* 163-178.

Tajfel, H. (1981). *Human groups and social categories: Studies is social psychology.* Cambridge: Cambridge University Press.

Tremble, B., Schneider, M., & Appathurai, C. (1989). Growing up gay or lesbian in a multicultural context. *Gay and Lesbian Youth, 17,* 253-267.

Troiden, R. R. (1989). The formation of homosexual identities. *Journal of Homosexuality, 17,* 43-73.

Vazquez, L. A. (1997). A systemic multicultural curriculum model: The pedagogical process. In D. B. Pope-Davis & H. L. K. Coleman (Eds.), *Multicultural counseling competencies* (pp. 159-183). Thousand Oaks, CA: Sage.

Chapter 13

✠

Ethnicity, Race, and Culture: The Case of Latino Gay/Bisexual Men

ROSA CINTRÓN

The basic premise of this chapter is that while homosexuality appears to occur in all cultures, the identification of individuals involved in homosexual behaviors using formal labels such as gay, lesbian, and bisexual is socially constructed and generally unique to a particular culture. The concept of social construction refers to the fact that how we define sexual acts is dependent upon our world view or sociocultural perspective. If the reader accepts the assumption of the social construction of the label "homosexual" s/he will readily accept the notion that homosexuality in the United States has been defined through the only possible prism: the dominant White Anglo-Saxon Protestant (WASP) culture. In this chapter I will discuss homosexuality and the conceptual trilogy of ethnicity, race, and culture using a Latino(a) prism.

Latina lesbians are not the focus of this chapter since it appears that their issues may be different from those of Latino gay/bisexual men. Indeed, referring to the general literature on gays and lesbians, Monteflores and Schultz (1978), indicated that there are differences in the areas of sex-role factors, sex-role violations, and in the political and legal arenas. Moreover, the literature on Latina lesbians is very scarce (Espin, 1987).

First, I will argue that our traditional understandings of homosexuality become problematic, even erroneous, when we generalize socially constructed knowledge from one sociocultural context to another. Second, I will discuss the sociocultural context of Latino gays, emphasizing some of the cultural and socialization forces that, while clarifying the notion of social construction, will help explain particular elements in the Latino culture that shape the social reality of Latino gays.

Ethnicity and Race

To say that homosexual behavior occurs in all cultures tells us very little about how people in various places come to identify themselves or to be considered by others as homosexuals. Murray (1995) argued that there is no single type or unique set of characteristics that typify homosexual behavior. Murray's preference is to talk about homosexualities, a term that emphasizes the multifarious nature of sexuality, including homosexual behaviors. This conceptualization challenges our tendency to reduce complex behavioral dynamics to behaviors reified by one definite and unique variable. For example, let us take the word gay. According to Kutsche (1995), gay is a common English term that defines men who make love to men as homosexuals. In this sense the word "gay" becomes a conceptualization that denies the possibility of a man who prefers to make love to men and who does not define himself as gay. This is a clear example of cultural differences. While in the United States, this man has no option but to call himself gay, in Latin America he is never thought of as gay unless his social demeanor imitates quite obviously that of women (i.e., effeminate). In fact, the term gay is hardly ever heard in Latin America (Kutsche, 1995). As will be discussed later, the Latin American construction of gay underscores the diversity of sexual behavior.

Parallel to Murray's concept of homosexualities is the argument developed by Carrier (1995) that stresses the phrase "bisexually behaving" men. Carrier has studied homosexual and bisexual behaving Mexican men over the past 25 years. In his most recent study (1995), he concluded that men who have sex with men should be conceptualized in terms of their bisexual behaviors and not be labeled simply as bisexuals. Using "bisexual" as a noun to describe this segment of the subpopulation of men obscures the diversity of their lifestyles, motivations, and sexual behaviors. For example, the largest portion of the bisexually behaving subset of Mexican men who have sex with men were single men at the peak of their sexual needs (aged between puberty and late twenties) who identified themselves as being heterosexual. Another significant portion of this bisexually behaving subset was made up of young men who primarily had sex with men as their major source of income. A third group of bisexually behaving men was composed of men who early in their sex lives realized that their interest in homosexual encounters was more intense than that of their similarly involved male friends and yet, defined themselves as being as masculine as their heterosexual male friends.

Another major cultural difference between the United States and Latin America is in the area of jurisprudence. Under the Napoleonic Code, the legal doctrine guiding most of Latin America, all sexual possibilities between consenting adults are equally lawful. By contrast, in the United States, certain sexual acts and most homosexual behaviors are still criminalized (Lambda Legal Defense and Education Fund, 1999). This legal difference has been identified by some authors as "the Latin tradition of tolerance" (Whitam & Mathy, 1986, p. 137). It needs to be clarified that there have been two exceptions to this generally tolerant attitude: Argentina in the 1970s and 1980s and Castro's Cuba. Both of these cases underscore the difference between homosexuality as a political rather than a sexual act. In other words, in most of Latin America, "sexual deviation is not as serious as political deviation, and homosexuality is not a political issue unless it becomes politicized" (Whitam & Mathy, 1986, p. 143). Presently, there seems to be a climate of more tolerance in Cuba (Lumsden, 1996) while it has been reported that in Mexico, Colombia, and Argentina "sexual minorities have been faced with arbitrary arrest, torture and assassination" (Inter-Church Committee on Human Rights in Latin America, 1996).

The scholarship on gays in the United States has traditionally been the monopoly of a white middle-class on two counts: the scholars and their subjects. As a result, the impact of the intersection of race and ethnicity among gays has received little attention in the literature. Perhaps this situation in which the subject under scrutiny cannot give voice to his/her experience of homosexualities, helps to explain how race and ethnicity have been—and continue to be—interchanged carelessly and inconsistently in the literature (Tremble, Schneider, & Appathurai, 1989).

In other words, the sparse scholarship on homosexuals and bisexuals of color has either grouped different racial and ethnic groups under the nomenclature of "minorities" or it has emphasized the African American experience.

Use of the term "minorities" conceals more than it reveals the increasingly heterogeneity and cultural diversity of the students on our campuses (Jones, 1990). In particular, generalizing the African American experience to all other minority groups is incorrect. To say that someone is African American denotes a meaningful social category. It means a distinctive history of slavery, racial subordination, and political activism against inequality, racism, segregation, etc. It denotes the common experiences of this group in the U.S., a society where historically and legally one is either white or black (Myers, Cintrón, & Scarborough, 1994).

In opposition to the previous conceptualization is the racial and national heterogeneity of Latinos. Latinos/Hispanics represent diverse national origin groups. They are diverse not only in when and why they immigrated to the U.S., but also in social class, education, level of acculturation, and as I am arguing, in their racial identity. Latinos are a racially mixed group. For many Latinos, race is not a dichotomy, it is a matter of degrees, of shades of color and diverse physical appearance (the Spanish language contains many words to describe the different racial mixtures among indigenous people, Spaniards, Africans, and other groups). While racial prejudice does exist among Latinos, it does not follow the strict color lines used in the United States. Therefore, while race has been a conceptualization that has served to unite all African-Americans for social action and change, race among the Latino population in this country is secondary to national origin and identity (Myers, et al., 1994).

Although at one time in the scientific literature race was an Herculean construct, some contemporary authors (Cruickshank & Beevers, 1991; Cooper & David, 1986; Rathweld & Philipps, 1986) have questioned its usefulness and have instead supported the use of ethnicity as a more appropriate concept. To this regard, Cruickshank and Beevers (1991) said:

> "Race" and "racial" not only have inflammatory connotations, but are sloppy terms implying a precision of classification between peoples that has no biological basis. . . . the concept "race" has been based on appearances and degree of melanization (skin pigmentation) rather than on repeatable biological or genetic measures. . . .   The term

"ethnic" also has a more appropriate wider context. It includes
individual factors shared by groups (which may be genetic) as well as
the social, economic, dietary and personal habits that characterize
whole societies. By means of experience and education, effort or
invitation, people can alter their social class. However, their ethnic
origin remains relatively unchanged. . . . (p. vii)

Most articles on Latino gay men completely ignore race and treat
ethnic identity and gay identity in a similarly flawed fashion. This problem
is mainly due to the insistence of traditional positivistic frameworks that
require clearly identifiable groupings and effects attributable to a single
variable. In other words, to the extent that researchers try to determine
whether ethnicity or homosexuality plays a greater role in determining
the behaviors of the individuals, we miss the complicated and confusing
reality that frequently describes human behavior. This conceptual
inconsistency might simply be explained by the ubiquitousness of issues
of race and cultural differences in the United States.

The U.S. is the most ethnically diverse nation in history, but this fact
has not increased the ability of its citizens to tolerate differences. This
fact is complicated by the increasing evidence suggesting that ethnic
values and identification are retained for many generations after
immigration (Greeley, 1981) and "play a significant role in family life
and personal development throughout the life cycle. . . . Second-, third-
, and even fourth-generation Americans, as well as new immigrants,
differ from the dominant culture in values, life-styles, and behavior."
(McGoldrick, Pearce, & Giordiano, 1982, p. 4)

An ethnic group has been defined as "those who conceived of
themselves as alike by virtue of their common ancestry, real or fictitious,
and who are so regarded by others" (Shibutani & Kwan, 1965, p. 23).
Ethnicity describes a sense of commonality transmitted over generations
by the family and reinforced by the surrounding community. According
to McGoldrick et al. (1982),

It [ethnicity] is more than race, religion, or national and geographic
origin (which is not to minimize the significance of race or the special
problems of racism). . . . Ethnicity patterns our thinking, feeling,
and behavior in both obvious and subtle ways. It plays a major role in
determining what we eat, how we work, how we relax, how we
celebrate holidays and rituals, and how we feel about life, death and
illness. (p. 4)

Ethnicity is a powerful influence in determining identity. Erikson, in his classic work on identity in 1950, developed a framework for understanding how the individual is linked to the ethnic group and society. He defined identity as a process located in the core of the individual, and yet also in the core of his or her communal culture. In his description, the final stage of human development concerns coming to terms with one's cultural identity: "For only an identity safely anchored in the 'patrimony' of a cultural identity can produce a workable psychosocial equilibrium" (1950, p. 412).

Thus, ethnic identity rather than sexual identity is a particularly salient factor in the identification of minority status individuals (Chin, 1983). However, as we know, Latinos represent a wide variety of ethnicities and races of people and are characterized as multicultural and multiracial (Morales, 1992). American Hispanics trace their origin to Spain or to Mexico, Puerto Rico, Cuba, and many other Spanish-speaking countries of Latin America. The Census Bureau's 1992 projections suggest rapid growth continuing beyond the 20th century. The Hispanic population could rise from 24 million in 1992 to 31 million by the year 2000, 59 million by 2030, and 81 million by 2050 (U.S. Department of Commerce, 1993).

A Latino gay who has made a conscious decision to call himself Latino instead of Hispanic, Chicano, Boricua, Cuban, etc., has gone through an intense and long process of asserting a political and national position. That which one decides to call him/herself is a vital issue that is not to be taken lightly as it is as critical in defining the psychological and social persona as the process that an individual goes through in order to call himself or herself homosexual, lesbian, or bisexual. Writing about the challenge imposed by various identities, Espin (1987) indicated that for Latina lesbians, and I will argue that for Latino gay/bisexual men, too, the dilemma is how to integrate who they are culturally, racially, and ethnically with their identity as homosexuals and men. The identity of each Latino gay/bisexual develops through conscious and unconscious choices that allot relative importance to the different components of the self, and thus of his identity as man, as gay, as Latino (p. 35).

According to Erikson (1975), an integrated identity consists of:

A state of being and becoming that can have a highly conscious quality and yet remain, in its motivational aspects, quite conscious and beset with the dynamics of conflict. Conflict ensues when . . . part of identity must be accounted for in that communality within which an individual finds himself . . . fragments that the individual had to submerge in himself as undesirable or irreconcilable or which his group has taught him to perceive as the mark of fatal 'difference' in sex role or race in class or religion. (pp. 19-21)

According to Espin (1987), for both homosexuals and ethnic minority persons of both sexes "the process of identity development is full of vicissitudes, and it frequently demands the submerging of different fragments of the self" (p. 36).

The racial and ethnic heterogeneity among Latinos becomes more complex when it is remembered that in the same way that there are subcultural, intracultural, and intercultural differences among Latinos there is an "enormous—and frequently conflicting—range of homosexual behaviors, typifications, self-identifications, and meanings . . ." (Murray, 1995, pp. 3-4). Murray cautioned that when making observations about others in different cultures there is a tendency to define sexual roles in a continuum ranging from flexible to rigid. The problem with these interpretations is that the determination of this continuum is done within the frame of reference of the observer. The critical observation to be made is to try to gauge the extent to which the behavior observed is outside the usual rules of sexual behavior for that particular culture.

For example, let us analyze the question "Is Latino culture more tolerant of gay behavior than other cultures?" The first challenge posed by this question is in the use of the descriptor "Latino." To the outside observer Latino or Hispanic as well as twenty-some other national patrimonies based on a particular Latin American country of origin or parental background is as good as any other descriptor. More than likely if confronted on the choice selected, the outside observer would be willing to change from "Latino gays" to "Hispanic gays" in order to be politically correct or just out of simple politeness. What is very often misunderstood, or set aside as a cyclical nomenclature difficulty where some labels are in vogue or passe depending on the political winds of the times, is that how one decides to call him/herself is an issue of intense personal turmoil. The conscious rejection or benign ignorance of this knowledge is the most general way in which racism has affected the scholarship on gays who are members of protected classes. The racism resides in the wholesale application of theories void of a perspective involving race and ethnicity. Latino gays live three different lives among three different communities:

the gay community, the Latino community, and the predominantly heterosexual white mainstream community (Morales, 1990). Clarifying this point, Takagi (1996), writing eloquently about Asian American sexualities, stated:

> Two broad distinctions are worth noting. The first . . . is the relative invisibility of sexual identity compared with racial identity. While both can be said to be socially constructed, the former are performed, acted out, and produced, often in individual routines, whereas the latter tends to be more obviously "written" on the body and negotiated by political groups. Put another way, there is a quality of voluntarism in being gay/lesbian that is usually not possible as an Asian American. One has the option to present oneself as "gay" or "lesbian," or alternatively, to attempt to "pass," or, to stay in "the closet," that is, to hide one's sexual preference. However, these same options are not available to most racial minorities in face-to-face interactions with others. . . .   In other words, many of us experience the worlds of Asian American and gay American as separate places emotionally, physically, intellectually. . . .   Moreover, it is not just that these communities know so little of one another, but, we frequently take great care to keep those worlds distant from one another. (p. 24)

The same author cautioned about the myth of minority homogeneity and the naive conceptualization of some sort of "ethnic model" (p. 24). This model or framework assumes that because of a common minority status we understand the experience of injustice and exploitation of all those who are oppressed. This statement, if not completely erroneous, is decidedly naive and simplistic. Takagi (1996) insisted on our need to understand "the complicated interplay and collision of different identities . . . [and the] perpetual uncertainty and flux governing the construction and expression of identities" (p. 33).

Referring to this uncertainty, Kutsche (1995) discussed a model that describes various layers of sexual structure. On the basis of his preliminary observations of Costa Rican homosexuals, he first concluded that in this country sex between men is two-layered. These consist of a public layer that is homophobic and a private layer that is permissive. However, later on the author's perceptions changed. He reflected that: "Perhaps two layers are not enough to construct an accurate model of the Costa Rican valences toward homosexuality . . ." (p. 112) and proceeded to develop a five-layered sexual structure:

The second layer is contempt for the *maricón* (queer), the butt of ribald jokes. The third layer is police harassment of gays and lesbians. . . The fourth layer consists of ecclesiastical thunder and brimstone against "unnatural behavior. . ." On top of all this is the Napoleonic Code on which Costa Rica laws are based. It treats all sexual possibilities between adult human beings as equally lawful. (p. 112)

Adding to the uncertainty, flux, and layers in the conceptualization of sexual identities are the observations of Taylor (1995). According to him there appear to be three traditions about homosexuality in Mexico: tolerant indifference, fanatic homophobia, and homosexual acceptance (pp. 91-97). Tolerant indifference is based on the Napoleonic doctrine explained earlier in which private consensual sex between adults is legal. Counter to this quasi-personal sexual freedom, there is fanatic homophobia characterized by cruelty, bashings, and even murder of homosexuals. Finally, there seem to be positive attitudes, including an oral tradition that talks about homosexuality at the time of the Aztecs. Certainly, this triad of social traditions clarifies as well as confounds our limited understanding of this topic.

The Case of Latino Gay/Bisexual Men

It could be argued that the scholarship on homosexuality suffers from a lack of a cross-cultural perspective. Again, the literature in this area is circumscribed mainly to the United States and the work is primarily a product of English-speaking writers. Those few scholars who provide an international perspective to this area of inquiry tend to agree that (1) there is considerable cultural variability that has given rise to the notion that some societies have more homosexuals than others, (2) the incidence of homosexual acts on the part of men who are heterosexuals or bisexual varies considerably with culture or circumstances, and (3) homosexuals appear in every society, with equal frequency, regardless of whether or not the society tolerates or represses homosexuality (Whitam & Mathy, 1986).

My first argument was that homosexual behavior appears to occur everywhere. However, as Murray (1995) clarified, not every society has created sociological categories or defined people according to their sexual behavior or preference. In other words, "gay" or "homosexual" are not universal designations with similar meanings everywhere. I have selected this constructionist view of homosexuality to discuss various major cultural differences between Latino and North American gays.

Although some cultural elements and attitudes may not seem different from those of the dominant culture, some authors have insisted that some important differences experienced by Latino gay/bisexual men are indeed directly related to Hispanic cultural patterns (Espin, 1987, p. 40). In a similar vein, Uba (1994) has advanced the notion that the cultural, racial and ethnic backgrounds of individuals affect their personalities and needs. This conceptual trilogy helps to explain why people behave the way they do and that it does not make sense to ignore issues of race and cultural background any more than it makes sense to ignore their gender, age, religion, etc. Even though it would be possible to argue that in some situations these elements might be irrelevant, it would be impossible to discount their effect altogether. In other words, culture, race, and ethnicity cannot always explain the totality of Latino behavior. But the recognition of irrelevancy is in direct proportion to the level of knowledge that one has about a particular situation: it is imperative to have an understanding of the cultural, ethnic, and racial backgrounds of Latinos in order to recognize to what degree these variables are influencing their personality, experiences, and problems.

Several caveats are appropriate at this point. First, Latino cultural values are discussed in order to provide some understanding of the difference between Latinos and the majority cultural values. Second, there are differences among Latinos just as there are among members of other groups. Third, there are innumerable degrees of adherence to the cultural values to be presented herein. Explaining the dynamic and complex nature of these caveats for Asian Americans, Uba (1994) said:

> Individuals do not simply combine traditional Asian values and dominant American values as one would collect rocks: add a few here, throw out a few there. Rather, the very combining and balancing of values within different personal and social contexts is a dynamic, integrated process. Asian American individuals will vary in their syntheses of personal experiences, Asian culture, and American culture as a function of their intelligence, education, gender, exposure to Asian culture (which would depend on place of birth—whether abroad or in the United States—and on age at the time of immigration, if foreign born), and so on. Nevertheless, a benefit can be derived from reviewing traditional Asian values inasmuch as these values constitute some type of context for Asian American values. (p. 14)

As Evans and Levine (1990) reported, there is no definite data concerning the number of gay and bisexual men in the nation, or for that matter, attending colleges and universities. In spite of this lack of empirical data, our students "could benefit from the support of student affairs professionals who are well-informed about the issues faced by this population" (p. 49). Therefore, the discussion that follows on selected cultural elements is intended as a starting point or a frame of reference for the uninitiated, in the hope that this discussion may provide a basis for understanding the behaviors of some Latino gay/bisexual men. The cultural elements to be discussed are: familismo, respeto, buen hijo, macho and buenos sentimientos.

Cultural Elements

A critical difference in the cultural values of North Americans and Latin Americans is the centrality of the family. This notion of *familismo,* includes the nuclear as well as the extended family. It involves a sense of emotional and financial responsibility toward parents, aunts, uncles, other relatives (no matter how distant in terms of blood line), and the godparents of a child. *Familismo* facilitates the functioning of the kinship network through an emphasis on affiliation and cooperation and discouragement of confrontation and competition. Patterns of interaction are characterized by generational interdependence and loyalty to the family of origin, high levels of affective resonance, interpersonal involvement, and controls; a tendency for individuals to live in families—of origin, of procreation, or extended—at every developmental stage; and the fact that all life cycle events and rituals are family celebrations and affirmations of their unity. It is important to emphasize that in spite of this high degree of emotional proximity and interdependency, hierarchies are clearly defined. Rules are organized around age and sex, as they are the most important determinants of authority, with older males being attributed the greatest centrality. The values of family proximity, cohesiveness, and respect for parental authority are present throughout an individual's lifetime. Autonomy and individual achievement are not particularly emphasized (Bernal, 1982; Falicov, 1982; Garcia-Preto, 1982).

Familismo also denotes *respeto* (respect) which is a demeanor of reverence and deference to older people. According to Diaz-Guerrero (1975):

while the word respeto is the same as the English respect, studies
indicate that the internalized meaning of the word varies. For Anglo-
Americans, it reflects a fairly detached, self-assured egalitarianism.
For Latinos, it implies a relationship involving a highly emotionalized
dependence and dutifulness, within a fairly authoritarian framework.
In general, the status of parents is high and that of children low. Thus,
complementary transactions between parents and children are stressed
while symmetrical transactions are discouraged or tolerated only in
jest. . . . Hierarchies are clearly defined, and most parents would not
expect or want to be friends with their children. But most would agree
that parents and children should care about and enjoy each other. (p.
140)

More succinctly, Mann and Mann (1991), defined *familismo* as "a
cultural value that involves individuals' strong feelings of loyalty,
reciprocity, and solidarity among members of the same family" (p. 13).
The power of *familismo* is based on a psychosocial dynamic that involves
the control and sanction of the behavior of family members, especially
public behavior.

Within the traditional value of *familismo,* it is expected that all
unmarried members of a family remain living with their family of origin
until they marry. If an unmarried woman or man leaves their home,
regardless of their age and financial means, the neighbors or *el público*
will understand such a move as indicating that the family does not get
along. To have neighbors talk about one's family affairs is one of the
most damaging offenses against the honor and dignity of one's family
and must be avoided at any cost. In other words, staying with one's
parents does not have the Western classical psychoanalytical interpretation
of dependency, fixation, or undifferentiated ego development that is
common when young North American women and men do not leave
their homes after completion of high school or college. The assumption
is that an unmarried young Latino(a) living on his/her own must have
committed such a grave transgression or *falta de respeto* to offend the
parents and the whole family that it merited expulsion from home. Because
frequent contact and a strong interdependence among family members,
even in adult life, are essential features of Hispanic family life, leading a
double life may become more of a strain. Because of the importance
placed on family and community by most Hispanics, the threat of possible
rejection and stigmatization by the Latin community becomes more of a
psychological burden. Rejection from mainstream society does not carry

the same weight. Espin (1987) clarified this point by stating that "This does not imply that Anglo culture does not stigmatize Latino gay/bisexual men—only that its stigmatization appears not to hold the personal power which Latino culture does" (p. 41).

To avoid stigmatization by the Latin community, Hispanic gay/ bisexual men might seek other groups or networks in which their homosexual orientation will be more accepted than it is in their family and community. However, according to Amaro (1978):

> Reliance on alternative support groups outside the Hispanic community would not occur without a cost. Loss of contact with the ethnic community and culture will mean lack of support for their identity as a Hispanic. On the other hand, staying within the Hispanic community and not "coming out" will represent a denial of the identity associated with sexuality and intimate love relationships. (p. 7)

This cultural element of *familismo* has been an obstacle to gay self-identification and gay community building among Latino gays (Murray, 1995). Murray stated:

> Continued residence with their natal family limits the flamboyance of those inclined to gender variance as well as nearly precluding same-sex couples living together. It also eliminates the possibility of the kind of residential concentration that in the United States and Canada preceded (and enabled) the development of gay institutions and a sense of gay community. . . [In Latin America] finding a place to have sex is very difficult; living together is generally unimaginable. (p. xi-xii)

Open, or more precisely, public, homosexuality is a cause for expulsion from the family home. While this might seem contradictory given the previous discussion of the "Latin tradition of tolerance," judicial tolerance means that homosexuality is not a crime punishable by the law of the land. However, homosexuality is censured by strict social mores that rigidly define the public behavior of men and women. In public, Latino men are expected to behave in a manly or masculine manner, which for the specific purpose of this chapter means that they are expected to make love to women, only. *Un buen hijo* (a good son) would never embarrass his family by behaving in public in a way that casts doubts about his *machismo*. Moreover, as long as he is unmarried he will be frequently asked questions about girlfriends and his sexual prowess. To these questions the *buen hijo* will provide the answers of a *macho*. Therefore, within this cultural frame, the *buen hijo* has a very specific script and deviations from it, as explained before, might result in severing family relations. Someone who holds his family in high esteem, with endearment, and who behaves with a sense of honor and duty toward the family is a person of *buenos sentimientos* (good feelings, affection). This notion of *buen hijo* is a fundamental psychological factor in family dynamics. It not only controls behavior but also defines the essence of a person. In observing the Cuban revolutionary process and the place of homosexuals within it, Lumsden (1996), quoting de la Torre, provided this explanation:

> For Cubans, someone who does not "have *sentimiento* [affection] toward his own *familiares* is not to be trusted by anyone. . . . It is in the expression *of sentimiento* toward his *familiares* that a person reflects the essence of his humanity." Accordingly, it is very rare to encounter anyone who is critical of his family, including those whose decision to emigrate has been partly motivated by the belief that their families were insuperable obstacles to the full realization of their homosexuality within Cuba. (p. 56)

When could a *buen hijo* talk about homosexual behavior—making love to another man exclusively? Never. Some Latino men might boast their sexual prowess by telling stories and jokes of penetration to other men. However, ". . . homosexual experimentation is more acceptable among the unmarried young, but is increasingly threatening to masculine reputation with age and for those whose status is above the working class . . . boasting about fucking men is risky to all but the most solidly established *macho* reputations" (Murray, 1995, pp. 51, 54). In order for a *macho* and/or *buen hijo* to be able to talk about any type of homosexual behavior, then, it must be very clear in the conversation that penetration is not to the exclusion of women and is less pleasurable than vaginal or anal feminine penetration. He must also be the insertor.

The role of insertor does not turn Latinos into homosexuals or give them a gay identity. That is, the social construction of male heterosexuality posits that men "are supposed to experience intense feelings, urges, and sensations that cannot or should not be controlled . . . [and] require immediate release" (Diaz, 1997, pp. 14-15). Women as well as male insertees are seen as appropriate outlets for the immediate release of these strong biologically based sexual impulses. This point, the ostensible distinction between insertors and insertees, is important to understand; however, one must keep in mind that the importance of this differentiation is constantly debated in the literature. Some authors have argued that the duality, insertee-insertor, is clear and that it distinguishes real *machos* from gays (Lancaster, 1992) while others have observed:

> Since the cultural assumption is that gender and sexuality will be consonant, [the Latino culture does] not make the (alien) analytical distinction between gender and sexuality. . . . There are certainly masculine-appearing males who are insertees and effeminate-appearing males who are mostly or exclusively insertors, but the clear, simple masculine/feminine division is paramount in Latino views of gender and sex. (Murray, 1995, p. 63)

As mentioned previously, someone who is a *buen hijo* will never talk about his homosexuality with *familiares*. The only possible exception to this sociocultural reality is described by Diaz (1997): ". . . family acceptance of homosexuality can be achieved only through silence ('They know but we can't talk about it') . . ."(p. 12). In other words, a major coping strategy for both sides is to act as though the behavior is not taking place. Carrier (1995) referred to this situation as the "conspiracy of silence" or "counterfeit secrecy" (pp. 190-191). Another aspect of male coping is activity carried out to divert attention from homosexual involvement that includes social contacts with girlfriends and heterosexual intercourse with prostitutes. In addition, any masculine-type activity may be participated in on a routine basis to promote a heterosexual image. For example, the Hispanic custom of paying a great deal of attention to a passing girl by whistling or making remarks, for instances, may be as avidly carried out by a homosexually involved male as by a heterosexually involved one. Carrier (1995) concluded that "The level of activity required for family coping appears to depend for the most part on the individual's degree of involvement in homosexual encounters and on his relative effeminacy or masculinity" (pp. 190-191).

In Summary

I would like to argue that the cultural elements of *familismo, respeto, buen hijo, macho* and *buenos sentimientos* are major obstacles to the awareness and acceptance of Latino homosexuality. These cultural elements provide a general framework that is useful to college student affairs professionals in dealing with this group of students. Hopefully, the understanding of these elements may serve as the common foundation from which to start multicultural and diverse interactions (Morales, 1992). As services for Latino gay/bisexual men are developed in colleges and universities, it is imperative to understand the cultural nuances that have shaped their lives.

A Note on Limitations

Some important matters have been omitted or treated briefly in my discussion. One variable that might influence the cultural elements presented herein is level of acculturation. It is my contention that Latino gays who have been mostly educated in the United States might define homosexuality in terms similar to non-ethnic gays. I would also predict that their homosexuality, if public, was framed closer to majority values and distant from Latino cultural expectations. These statements are all tentative and in need of empirical verification. To date this is a difficult task because there are few scales of acculturation developed for Latinos (Mann, 1987).

A second major concern is how to study the heterogeneity among Latinos. For example, it is not only that there are few scales for acculturation, but that conceptually those that do exist have been standardized for specific national groups. As we know, the ability to generalize any results from one group to another is a conceptual and statistical challenge.

A third and vital discussion omitted from this chapter and urgently needing lengthy study, is the impact of the AIDS epidemic. As overlapping members of two "high risk" groups—Latinos and men who have sex with men—Latino gay/bisexual men in the United States have been highly and disproportionately affected by the AIDS epidemic (Diaz, 1996a; Diaz, 1996b). During 1990, the death rate (per 100,000) from HIV-related causes was 22.2 for Latinos compared to 8.7 for Whites (National Commission on AIDS, 1992). Also, according to a report by the Centers for Disease Control (CDC), in June 1994, a total of 29, 432 AIDS cases had been diagnosed among Hispanic/Latino men who have sex with men (MSM); Latino MSM thus constituted 52% percent of all reported Latino male AIDS cases in the nation (CDC, 1994). It should be noted that the percentage of Latino AIDS cases accounted for by MSM vary substantially across the major ethnic subgroups. For example, in 1992, 70% of Cubans, 59% of Mexican, and 18% of Puerto Rican AIDS cases were among MSM (CSC, 1993). The CDC has explained the relatively low percentage of MSM among Puerto Rican AIDS cases as reflecting the higher incidence of HIV transmission through injection drug use.

Recommendations

As indicated by Evans and Levine (1990), college student affairs professionals need to understand the impact of multiple identity development processes, how gender and racial identity development intersect with homosexual identity and how these multiple processes relate to student development (p. 56). Similarly, Jones (1990) has indicated that most traditional theories of individual development do not emphasize cultural identity either. Certainly, the serious treatment and inclusion of race, ethnicity, and culture in our preparation programs seems to be a sine qua non if professionals in this area are to remain relevant and current to the needs of all students.

As I have been arguing all along, it is essential to understand the impact of these specific cultural variables on individual students. However, to what degree are racial, cultural, gender, ethnic, and other group differences emphasized in student affairs preparation programs? One danger is that well-intentioned emphasis on being sensitive to diverse groups will lead faculty to reinforce stereotypes. Groups and cultures are not static; just as individuals constantly change, so do their environments. Ethnic behavior and beliefs shift, among generations and across individual life spans. Because those who aspire to help others cannot hope to know the significant cultural elements of all the groups that they will encounter nor everything important about even one group, the indispensable thing to teach is an attitude, a stance, an open-minded way of approaching the helping process with humility and a willingness to learn (Willie, Rieker, Kramer, & Brown, 1995).

Finally, it must be remembered that each man's choices express something about who he is as an individual as well as what his cultural values are. Homosexual and/or bisexual choices, as any set of behaviors that violate strict cultural norms, can present a high personal cost to any man. In the case of Latinos, this high personal cost may additionally involve a loss of support from their ethnic group. Any encouragement of their "coming out" as gay or bisexual should be done with sensitivity to the other components of their identity. There is as much danger in explaining individual differences away as culturally determined as there is in ignoring or rejecting the impact of cultural influences on each man's choices. To understand the multiplicity of tasks involving the development of cultural, ethnic, sexual, and racial identities is the first step in providing services to Latino gay/bisexual men who attend colleges and universities (Willie, et al., 1995).

References

Amaro, H. (1978). *Coming out: Hispanic lesbians, their families and communities*. Paper presented at the National Coalition of Hispanic Mental Health and Human Services Organizations, Austin, TX.

Bernal, G. (1982). Cuban families. In M. McGoldrick, J. Pearce, & J. Giordano (Eds.), *Ethnicity and family therapy* (pp. 187-207). New York: Guilford.

Carrier, J. (1995). *De los otros: Intimacy and homosexuality among Mexican men*. New York: Columbia University Press.

Centers for Disease Control. (1993). *HIV/AIDS surveillance report, 5* (1), 1-27. Atlanta, GA: Centers for Disease Control and Prevention.

Centers for Disease Control. (1994). *HIV/AIDS surveillance report, 6* (1), 1-27. Atlanta, GA: Centers for Disease Control and Prevention.

Chin, J. L. (1983). Diagnostic considerations in working with Asian-Americans. *American Journal of Orthopsychiatry, 53*, 100-109.

Cooper, R., & David, R. (1986). The biological concept of race and its application to public health and epidemiology. *Journal of Health Politics Policy Law, 11*, 97-116.

Cruickshank, J., & Beevers, D. (1991). *Ethnic factors in health and disease*. London: Butterworth-Heinemann.

Diaz, R. (1996a, April). *Cultural-regulation, self-regulation and sexuality: A psychocultural model for HIV risk in Latino gay men*. Paper presented at the International Symposium on "Re-Conceiving Sexuality." Rio de Janeiro.

Diaz, R. (1996b). *Latino gay men and the psycho-cultural barriers to AIDS prevention*. San Francisco: Center for AIDS Prevention Studies/University of California at San Francisco.

Diaz, R. (1997). Latino gay men and the psycho-cultural barriers to AIDS prevention. In M. Levine, J. Gagnon, & P. Nardi (Eds.), *In changing times: Gay men and lesbians encounter HIV/AIDS* (pp. 221-244). Chicago: The University of Chicago Press.

Diaz-Guerrero, R. (1975). *Psychology of the Mexican: Culture and personality*. Austin, TX: University of Texas Press.

Erikson, E. H. (1950). *Childhood and society*. New York: Norton.

Erikson, E. (1975). *Life history and the historical moment*. New York: Norton.

Espin, O. (1987). Issues of identity in the psychology of Latina lesbians. In Boston Lesbian Psychologies Collectives (Ed.), *Lesbian psychologies: Explorations and challenges* (pp. 35-51). Urbana, IL: University of Illinois Press.

Evans, N., & Levine, H. (1990). Perspectives on sexual orientation. In L. Moore (Ed.), *Evolving theoretical perspectives on students* (New Directions for Student Services, no. 51, pp. 49-58). San Francisco: Jossey-Bass.

Falicov, C. (1982). Mexican families. In M. McGoldrick, J. Pearce, & J. Giordano (Eds.), *Ethnicity and family therapy* (pp. 134-163). New York: Guilford.

Garcia-Preto, N. (1982). Puerto Rican families. In M. McGoldrick, J. Pearce, & J. Giordano (Eds.), *Ethnicity and family therapy* (pp. 164-186). New York: Guilford.

Greeley, A. (1981). *The Irish Americans*. New York: Harper & Row.

Inter-Church Committee on Human Rights in Latin America. (1996). *Violence unveiled: Repression against lesbians and gay men in Latin America*. Toronto, Canada: Inter-Church Committee on Human Rights in Latin America.

Jones, W. T. (1990). Perspectives on ethnicity. In L. Moore (Ed.), *Evolving theoretical perspectives on students* (New Directions for Student Services, no. 51, pp. 59-72). San Francisco: Jossey-Bass.

Kutsche, P. (1995). Two truths about Costa Rica. In S. Murray (Ed.), *Latin American male homosexualities* (pp. 111-137). Albuquerque, NM: University of New Mexico Press.

Lambda Legal Defense and Education Fund (1999, February 19). *State-by-state sodomy law update* [online]. Available: http://www.lambdalegal.org/cgi-bin/pages/documents/record?record=275

Lancaster R. (1992). *Life is hard: Machismo, danger, and the intimacy of power in Nicaragua*. Berkeley: University of California Press.

Lumsden, I. (1996). *Machos, maricones, and gays: Cuba and homosexuality*. Philadelphia, PA: Temple University Press.

Mann, B. (1987). Development of a short acculturation scale for Hispanics. *Hispanic Journal of Behavioral Sciences, 9* (2), 183-205.

Main, G., & Main, B. (1991). *Applied Social Research Methods Series: Vol. 23. Research with Hispanic populations*. Newsbury Park, CA: Sage.

McGoldrick, M., Pearce, J., & Giordano, J. (1982). *Ethnicity and family therapy*. New York: Guilford.

Monteflores, C., & Schultz, S. (1978). Coming out: Similarities and differences for lesbians and gay men. *Journal of Social Issues, 34* (3), 59-72.

Morales, E. (1990). Ethnic minority families and minority gays and lesbians. *Marriage and Family Review, 14*, 217-239.

Morales, E. (1992). Counseling latino gays and latina lesbians. In S. Sworkin & F. Gutierrez (Eds.). *Counseling gay men and lesbians* (pp. 125-140). Alexandria, VA: American Association for Counseling and Development.

Murray, S. (1995). *Latin American male homosexualities*. Albuquerque, NM: University of New Mexico Press.

Myers, L., Cintr6n, M., & Scarborough, K. (1994). Latinos: The conceptualization of race. In J. E. Hendricks & B. Byers (Eds.). *Multicultural perspectives in criminal justice and criminology* (pp. 155-184). Springfield, IL: Charles C. Thomas.

National Commission on AIDS. (1992). *The challenge of HIV/AIDS in communities of color*. Washington, DC: National Commission on AIDS.

Rathweld, T., & Philipps, D. (1984). *Health, race and ethnicity*. London: Croom Helm.

Shibutani, T., & Kwan, K. (1965). *Ethnic stratification*. New York: Macmillan.

Takagi, D. (1996). Maiden voyage: Excursion into sexuality and identity politics in Asian America. In R. Leong (Ed.), *Asian American sexualities: Dimensions of the gay and lesbian experience* (pp. 21-36). New York: Routledge.

Taylor, C. (1995). Legends, syncretism, and continuing echoes of homosexuality from pre-Columbian and colonial Mexico. In S. Murray (Ed.), *Latin American male homosexualities* (pp. 80-99). Albuquerque, NM: University of New Mexico Press.

Tremble, B., Schneider, M., & Appathurai, C. (1989). Growing up gay or lesbian in a multicultural context. *Journal of Homosexuality, 17* (3/4), 253-267.

U.S. Department of the Commerce, Bureau of the Census, Ethnic and Hispanic Branch. (1993, November). *We the American Hispanics*. Washington, DC: Government Printing Office.

Uba, L. (1994). *Asian Americans: Personality patterns, identity, and mental health*. New York: Guilford.

Whitam, F., & Mathy, R. (1986). *Male homosexuality in four societies*. Westport, CT: Praeger.

Willie, C., Rieker, P., Kramer, B., & Brown, B. (1995). *Mental health, racism, and sexism*. Pittsburgh, PA: University of Pittsburgh Press.

Chapter 14

℘)☯

Faith, the Bible, and Lesbians, Gay Men, and Bisexuals

VALSIN L. DUMONTIER II

Lesbian, gay, and bisexual college students face many challenges as they begin to understand their identity. Their development is hindered by the many institutions that contribute to the prejudice against these students including family, schools, and religion (Evans & D'Augelli, 1996; Russell & Ellis, 1993; Savin-Williams & Cohen, 1996). As the field of student affairs is committed to the development of the whole student, which includes physical, social, emotional, and spiritual dimensions, as well as intellectual dimensions (American Council on Education, 1994), developmental models become lenses through which practitioners view the educational opportunities they face when dealing with students (Brown, 1980; Widick, Knefelkamp, & Parker, 1980). One area that is often neglected is faith development (Hoffman, 1994). Furthermore, the role of faith development in the formation of lesbian, gay, and bisexual identity development is misunderstood and understudied.

While recognizing the broad range of religious traditions from which lesbian, gay, and bisexual students come, this chapter will focus specifically on those within the Judeo-Christian tradition. The chapter begins with a discussion of the parallel processes of faith development and lesbian, gay, and bisexual identity development. Next, the *Bible's* role in the faith development of lesbians, gay men, and bisexuals, its inappropriate use, and recent scholarly findings that support and nurture sexual minorities are presented. Finally, recommendations for student affairs professionals are suggested.

Faith Development

In a search of the literature, one finds scant discussion of faith development. There is one qualitative study detailing respondents' discussion of the impact that religion has had on their development as sexual minorities (Sears, 1991). There is evidence that suggests that research neglects faith development, particularly among lesbians (Engelken, 1996). One can find some discussion about religion and lesbians (Beck, 1982; Zanotti, 1986), the intersection of religion, ethnicity, and sexual orientation (Chan, 1995; Wall & Washington, 1991), and non-Christian religions and gay male sexual orientation (Bouldrey, 1995). However, there is no attempt to explain the processes of faith development and lesbian, gay, and bisexual identity development. Fowler's (1981) faith development model and Cass's (1979) homosexual identity development model will inform this exploration.

According to Fowler (1981), faith is a:

> person's or group's way of moving into the force field of life. It is our way of finding coherence in and giving meaning to the multiple forces and relations that make up our lives. Faith is a person's way of seeing him or herself in relation to others against a background of shared meaning and purpose. . . . We require meaning. We need purpose and priorities; we must have some grasp on the big picture. (p. 4)

Thus, faith is a trust in another and loyalty to a transcendent center of value and power. Faith is also understood as a dynamic process and commitment to a collective understanding of how people act with one another irrelevant of a commitment to God or a higher power (Heyward, 1984; Williams, 1993). But, as a result of a lesbian, gay man, or bisexual's religious upbringing, there is also a fear of faith (Wilson, 1996). Most organized religious systems are not supportive of, and are even hostile to non-heterosexuals. A sense of loss and grief is all too often associated with one's affirmation of being a lesbian, gay man, or bisexual person (Fortunato, 1982; Heyward, 1984). So, how does someone make any sense of this journey? What could it possibly mean? How does being lesbian, gay, or bisexual fit into the larger picture of life?

Faith is a means by which some people come to this understanding. It has been posited as the fundamental prerequisite for understanding humanity. "Faith . . . is generic, a universal feature of human living, recognizably similar everywhere despite the remarkable variety of forms and contacts of religious practice and belief" (Fowler, 1981, p. 14).

Building upon the theories of Piaget (1954), Perry (1968), Selman (1976), and Kohlberg (1981), Fowler's (1981) faith development model attempts to bring together the knowing and the feeling aspects of cognitive and structural theories of development. Faith is a focus on how beliefs and values come to be important, and not on what those beliefs and values necessarily are. Each stage of the model is a structural whole, sequential to another stage, hierarchical in nature, and universal. As a search for meaning, faith becomes a universal aspect of living, is an active process, and is a journey of ordering life in relation to images of the larger world view. Faith is how people become aware of self, others, and the transcendent. It is how people make meaning out of, and commitment based upon what they have become, learned, or discovered.

Although according to Fowler there are six stages through which an individual's understanding of faith progresses, people use different methods of meaning-making. These can be categorized as: a) forms of logic, b) social perspective taking, c) forms of moral judgment, d) bounds of social awareness, e) locus of authority, f) forms of world coherence, and g) symbolic function (Fowler, 1981). Fowler's six stages are defined as follows:

Undifferentiated Faith

In what is considered a pre-stage, children from birth to the age of 3 experience the needs of trust, courage, hope, and love, and these needs are brought together in undifferentiated ways. Infants contend with the sense of threat of abandonment, as well as the inconsistencies and deprivations of their surroundings. How these factors are established and developed underlies or threatens to undermine all that comes later in faith development. A transition to Stage 1 is initiated with the convergence of thought and language, opening up the use of symbols in speech and ritual play.

Intuitive-Projective Faith (Stage 1)

Ranging from ages 3 to 7, children in this stage begin using imagination and fantasy which are powerfully and permanently influenced by the moods, examples, actions, and stories of the faith of the primary adults in their life who may or may not be the immediate family. This is the stage of first awareness as related to egocentrism. It is at this stage when the adults close to the child convey their perspectives on death, sex, taboos, and religion. Therefore, the understanding and interpretation of the *Bible*, used by adults as a pedagogical tool, is a primary influence on the understanding of these perspectives. In transition to the next stage of faith, children begin to have a growing concern for understanding how things are and clarifying for themselves the bases of distinctions between what is real and what only seems real.

Mythic-Literal Faith (Stage 2)

Children, adolescents or adults take on the stories, beliefs, and observances that symbolize belonging to their community. Beliefs, rules, and attitudes are learned and become internalized in a literal sense. Symbols are one-dimensional and, along with stories, become the primary way of giving unity, meaning, and value to experiences. Life and the concept of fairness are seen as reciprocal. There is no attempt to be reflective or to develop a conceptual meaning of events or encounters. The primary tool one gains in this stage is the ability to use narrative to find and give meaning to experiences. Stories, drama, and myths are a few examples of narratives.

A transition to stage 3 is marked by the clash in stories and their meaning (for example, creation and the theory of evolution). Also at this time, authority is challenged and a personal understanding of what has previously been learned and discovered is required. However, the focus of authority changes from primary adults to other circles of influence.

Synthetic-Conventional Faith (Stage 3)

Visible in adolescents and adults, this period is categorized by conformity and agreement beyond the familiar (that subscribed to by immediate family or other primary adults). Individuals are influenced by friends, school, work, the media, and to some extent, the religion in which they were reared. It becomes crucial at this stage for faith to assist in helping to reconcile the diversity of viewpoints and experiences related by others. The unity that forms the understanding of meaning and power is experienced in personal relationships. It is a conformist stage, since individuals do not have a good understanding of their own identity or autonomous judgment to maintain or construct an independent perspective. The faith that is closely held is one that is held in the context of the group with which the person most identifies, generally his or her family. The person's faith is built on the doctrines, stories, traditions, and creeds that are part of the religious beliefs of this group. There is no sense of reflective understanding.

Transition out of the Synthetic-Conventional Faith stage is marked by a sense of leaving the familiar. Any encounter that leads to an inward reflectiveness and allows an individual to understand how beliefs and values are beginning to change results in a shift to Fowler's Stage 4. This understanding is also extended to how a person sees him or herself in relationship to others.

Individual-Reflective Faith (Stage 4)

As a movement to stage 4 occurs, a person begins to take on the burden of responsibilities for his or her own commitments, beliefs, and attitudes. Certain unavoidable conflicts arise with respect to (a) individuality versus group identity, (b) subjectivity to understanding one's strong unexamined feelings versus objectivity to a critical reflectiveness, and (c) relativity versus dualism or an absolute. The critical component of this stage is the development of the self moving away from a definition held by others and moving towards one in which the individual begins to define and take responsibility for a world view that is internally driven. At this stage, the individual is faced with a constant struggle; what was held sacred now becomes internalized and driven by the individual. A person begins to search for a community, religious or secular, that will support and nurture this internalized view. This differentiated perspective assists the person in understanding the reactions, interpretations, and judgments of others and their differences. Awareness may occur prior to Stage 5 of Fowler's faith development, but, depending on the security of the individual, may result in moving back to Stage 3, or even Stage 2, if old faith systems are held tightly. Stage 4 is full of dissonance and characterized by hard questions about what was learned early in life or what is part of popular belief. Support from others and the search for those who can affirm the new sense of self is important for progression to Stage 5.

Conjunctive Faith (Stage 5)

Building upon the previous faith journey of Stages 1 – 4, a person uses this foundation to establish and acknowledge a very individualistic faith that eventually becomes uniquely owned. This stage, rarely seen prior to age 30, is a full integration of a person's family of origin, life experience, religious affiliation, education, and social awareness. Aspects of this faith may be very similar to what was adhered to in earlier stages, but this personalized faith is not influenced or supported by family, a religious tradition, or an influential social sphere. It is clearly owned and affirmed by the self. Unique to this stage is the ability to see other perspectives, identify with others who are different, and find meaning and understanding from cross-cultural experiences.

Universalizing Faith (Stage 6)

Fowler's (1981) last stage is marked by an ultimate environment that is inclusive of all human beings. He acknowledged that very few people reach this stage of faith development. Those who do are actualizers of the spirit of an inclusive and fulfilled human community. Seen as radical in their vision of a just community in the political, social, economic, and ideological realm, individuals who reach this stage challenge the perceived norms of justice and elevate these "norms" to higher standards for all human beings. Examples of individuals who have attained this stage are Martin Luther King Jr. and Mahatma Ghandi. These people are seen as more fully human than other people. The human community is seen in a universal context. Fowler suggested that individuals at this stage are easily able to interact with others at various stages of faith development and other faith traditions.

Gay Identity Development

Cass's (1979) sexual identity development model is frequently used to explain the psychological and social aspects of adjusting to being gay, lesbian, or bisexual (Chan, 1995). There are points in which the evolution of gay identity development may be connected and integral to faith development as outlined in Fowler's (1981) model. There are six stages in Cass' model: Identity Confusion, Identity Comparison, Identity Tolerance, Identity Acceptance, Identity Pride, and Identity Synthesis. A progression through these stages may parallel the progression of the stages of faith development proposed by Fowler (1981). (See Table 1.)

Since Cass's (1979) perspective on gay identity development focuses on an awareness of thoughts, feelings, or behaviors that may be homosexual, the pre-stage and stage 1 of Fowler's (1981) model find no parallel in Cass's model. Fowler's initial stages focus on ordering the environment in undifferentiated ways. Because language is crucial to the expression of feelings, thoughts and behaviors, Fowler's early stages appear irrelevant here to sexual identity development as outlined by Cass precisely due to an inability to express one's experience.

Cass's Stage 1, Identity Confusion, finds its genesis in the self-awareness of an individual. Fowler's Stage 2 may present challenges in understanding a developing lesbian, gay, or bisexual identity. Feelings, thoughts and behaviors are seen and internalized in a literal sense at this stage of Fowler's theory. For the most part, institutions and society support the notion that all people are heterosexual. Most religions that are foundations for a developing faith are sources of this misconception. These misconceptions may conflict with the developmental aspects of the emerging homosexual self. How a person perceives and internalizes what he or she regards as an authority on beliefs, rules, and attitudes may greatly influence how she or he resolves the incongruencies of the emerging gay, lesbian, or bisexual identity. Cass's Stage 1, Identity Confusion, is marked by an incongruence between the self and what is held as the "heterosexual" norm for sexuality. Fowler's Stage 2 presents faith as the capacity to make meaning out of myths, stories, and narratives. For the most part, these myths, stories, and narratives support heterosexual identity as the norm and appropriate form of sexual identity. When these narratives conflict with the emergence of a homosexual identity, Cass's Stage 1 may present challenges that could result in moving to Stage 2, Identity Comparison. Likewise, the contradictions in various stories in faith development may lead into Fowler's Stage 3.

In Stage 2 of Cass's model, Identity Comparison, information is gathered and attempts are made to reach out to the lesbian, gay, and bisexual community. This information seeking may take many forms ranging from personal contact to reading literature and investigating other resources. This pattern may parallel the movement to Fowler's Stage 3 in which individuals begin to move away from the beliefs and values held by the adults closest to the individual. The sphere of influence becomes larger. Individuals in Fowler's Stage 3 of Faith Development, who seek support and begin to incorporate the shared beliefs of the larger community to which they belong, may or may not be moving into Cass's Stage 2, Identity Comparison. It is only when the person begins to seek others who are gay, lesbian, or bisexual that this stage of Cass's model becomes a focal point.

Increased conflict with others (depending on its resolution), and resulting dissonance may lead the individual into either Fowler's Stage 4 or Cass's Stage 3, Identity Tolerance, or into both stages. Both stages are seen as leaving the familiar and allowing the individual to incorporate a personal identity as either a gay, lesbian, or bisexual person, a faith development that is personally owned, or both. A more reflective self emerges in both stages.

Identity Tolerance, Cass's Stage 3, may be part of the continuous struggle that Fowler describes in his Stage 4. As an individual begins to increase his or her contact with the lesbian, gay, and bisexual community, he or she may be affirmed in the emerging identity. However, fear of societal, peer, mainstream community, and adult authority may be strong enough to overwhelm the emerging identity and, therefore, result in a continued presentation of the individual as heterosexual.

With the progression to Cass's Stage 4, Identity Acceptance, dissonance increases between the self and others' perceptions and is potentially very stressful and intense. Behaviors such as continuing to pass as "straight," limited contact with non-homosexuals or beginning to disclose to those who are perceived as supportive and affirming, assist the person in resolving the internal conflict. If the coping mechanisms are sufficient to sustain a person, he or she may stay at this stage. Otherwise, the individual moves into Cass's Stage 5, Identity Pride.

In Identity Pride, a person begins to fully integrate his or her sexual orientation. As the person moves into this stage, Fowler's Stage 5 may also become a part of his or her development. This identity and faith development becomes uniquely owned in the lesbian/gay/bisexual community. This community may become the place in which the person gains a better sense of affirmation and self-worth that is apart from the heterosexual community. The person's faith and identity is clearly one's own and is not influenced by family, a religious tradition, or the larger mainstream society. A firmer commitment to the lesbian, gay, or bisexual identity may be made at this stage of Cass's model. As a result, anger may be directed towards the straight community. Furthermore, an individual may become immersed in the lesbian/gay/bisexual community thus isolating herself or himself from the heterosexual community. This pattern can also be seen in Fowler's Stage 5 as the person begins to integrate a personal faith that is unique. For lesbians, gay men, and bisexuals, isolation and immersion in the non-heterosexual community may assist with the development of the conjunctive faith of this stage in Fowler's schema. Hence, Cass's Stage 5 may overlap in the area of Fowler's Stages 4 and 5.

Stage 6, the last stage of Cass's model, Identity Synthesis, may be associated with Fowler's Stage 5, Conjunctive Faith. As an understanding of others' points of view is integral to both stages, an individual's receptiveness to both the lesbian/gay/bisexual and heterosexual communities is a fundamental aspect of these stages. Both stages celebrate differences. Sexual orientation, in particular, is seen as a part of a larger whole of the human experience. As conflicts are always present due to the continuous need to "come out" to others, this final stage of Cass's model is one of integration, appreciation of self and others, celebration, and nurturance.

Models are used to understand and order complex ideas. They are not linear but cyclical in nature. However, progress from one stage to another is dependent upon the success in a previous stage. Being heavily influenced by environmental factors, individuals progress in these stages in a fluid manner. In reviewing these models, it appears that a lesbian, gay, or bisexual person may be influenced by a particular stage of faith and that a person's stage of faith may be influenced by his or her identity development. However, even though there are similarities in faith and identity development, how a person reaches a lesbian, gay, or bisexual identity stage may not be related to faith at all and vice versa. This discussion is an attempt to show the similarities of these processes and how one may impact the other.

In using both of these models, the student affairs professional may be able to understand the parallel and possibly interconnected journeys of lesbians, gay men, and bisexuals as they attempt to make meaning of their unique experiences. Fowler's model allows practitioners to view the development of lesbian, gay, and bisexual students from a perspective

Figure 1. **Suggested Parallel Process of Fowler and Cass**

Cass's Identity Development   Fowler's Faith Development

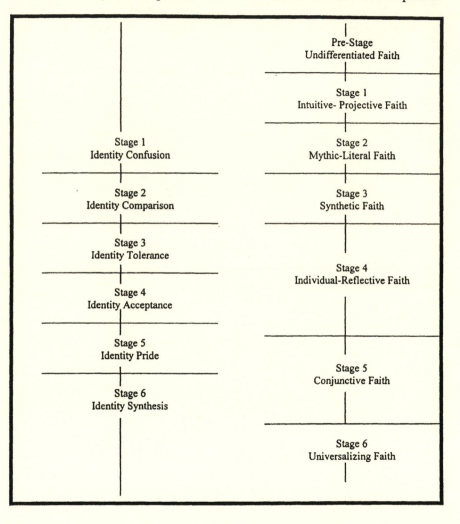

of how students make meaning, understand their own faith, and incorporate an emerging non-heterosexual identity. With the assistance of Fowler's and Cass's developmental models, practitioners may be able to listen more attentively and assist lesbian, gay, and bisexual students as these students progress in their sexual identity development and evolving faith development. This increased understanding may facilitate the growth and development of lesbian, gay, and bisexual college students as they face the integration of information, experiences, thoughts, feelings, and beliefs about the lesbian/gay/bisexual community and the heterosexual community.

The Bible—*Its Inappropriate Use*

As an instrument in the development of Christian faith, the *Bible*, particularly its literal interpretation, has often been used as a means of justifying prejudice and discrimination. "It is not unusual for lesbians and gay men, in their efforts at dealing with these issues, to cite the Bible frequently as validation for their very painful conviction that they are bad or evil" (McDonald & Steinhorn, 1990, p. 55). In addition to supporting the lower-class treatment of women, people of color, and Jews, as well as harassment and violence directed at these populations, Gomes (1996) argued that the *Bible* has been used to justify attacks on lesbians, gay men, and bisexuals. For example, the Baptist pastor Fred Phelps is known for picketing funeral services of individuals who have died of complications from AIDS and marching in front of businesses owned by or employing lesbians, gays, or bisexuals (Bull, 1993). The pastor's signs include the phrases, "Thank God for AIDS," and "No tears for queers," as well as several inaccurate quotes from the Bible, such as "God hates fags, Romans 9:13." Additionally, some right-wing Christian organizations have made attempts to legislate anti-gay initiatives across the country (Gallagher, 1993). The concept of sinfulness and the stigma associated with being lesbian, gay, or bisexual obviously contribute to the difficult journey of homosexual identity, especially within a faith perspective.

The Bible—*The Good News for Professionals*

As suggested, religion can be seen as a dynamic of faith. This dynamic contributes to a person's understanding of the larger schema of his or her life's purpose and journey. The *Bible* is an influential aspect of this faith development for both Christians and Jews. As a historical document, the *Bible* is a canon sacred to a group of people, which documents their faith journey towards an understanding of God.

"Too often the valid witness of faith of gay [men]/lesbian[s] . . . has been rejected due to a misconstrued or distorted interpretation of scripture" (Alexander & Preston, 1996, p. xvi). Despite pockets of strength within their own faith communities, many believers are at a loss in their response to those who use the *Bible* as a means to express and justify their position against lesbians, gay men, and bisexuals. Cultural contexts, the translations from one language to another, and the evolution of word meanings are all important factors in understanding scripture (Boswell, 1981).

One of the most prominent stories from the Old Testament is the fall of the cities of Sodom and Gomorrah in the Book of Genesis. Some scholars suggest that the story's theme is inhospitality and its results (Boswell, 1981; Gomes, 1996; McNeill, 1988). Here we understand that Lot's activities result from his apprehension regarding harm to his male guests. In order to protect these guests, Lot offers his daughters for sexual relations to the citizens of Sodom. Hospitable concern motivates the compromise offer.

The offering of Lot's daughters is understood to be the most tempting means of focusing the crowd away from the visitors. In understanding the event, twentieth century society would think it unethical to offer daughters as an exchange. But in cultural context, Lot's daughters are seen and valued as his property. As Lot himself was a visitor to Sodom, it is understood in recent scholarly studies that the custom of visitors being introduced to the city was part of the culture. The men of Sodom were suspicious of Lot's visitors for they understood them to be messengers bringing news of destruction to the city. Lot was fearful of these messengers' physical safety at the hands of the town's people. The mission of the messengers (or angels of God) is discussed prior to this story in the eighteenth chapter of Genesis. So, it can be clearly assumed that the sin of Sodom is one of abuse and the neglect of strangers; that is, inhospitality to outsiders and people who are unknown.

Further references to Sodom make no mention of homosexuality. On the contrary, these references refer to the assistance of travelers and strangers in need (for example, Ezekiel 16:48-49 and Wisdom 19:13). In the New Testament, Jesus refers to the sin of Sodom as hostility to God's messengers (Matthew 10:5-15). One should additionally consult Isaiah 1:10-17 and 3:9, Jeremiah 23:14, and Zephaniah 2:8-11, sources that detail oppression and injustice as Sodom's sin (Helminiak, 1995).

As a result of these findings,

> we are dealing with one of the supremely ironic paradoxes of history. For thousands of years in the Christian West homosexuals have been the victim[s] of inhospitable treatment. Condemned by the Church, they have been the victim[s] of persecution, torture, and even death. In the name of a mistaken understanding of the crime of Sodom and Gomorrah, the true crime of Sodom and Gomorrah has been and continues to be repeated every day. (McNeill, 1988, p. 50)

There is a joke within the gay, lesbian, and bisexual community in which a card contains an inscription on the outside: "What Jesus said about homosexuality. . ." and the inside is blank; there are no words. Nothing is mentioned. Gomes (1996) indicated that the gospels of Matthew, Mark, Luke, and John make no reference to Jesus' teaching on the topic. The New Testament references in Paul's writing are often used to support condemnation of lesbians, gays, and bisexuals. But it was not until the early twentieth century translations of the Bible that the word homosexual was used (Boswell, 1981). One must view any scriptural reference within a larger context. Thus, Romans 1:18-27 must be seen in light of the entire letter. The specific text about homosexuality refers to homosexual acts. However, the debate is focused on what the definitions of "natural" and "unnatural" are. Paul did not understand "natural" to mean an abstract construct of nature or something derived from the laws of nature. His understanding was more concrete (Boswell, 1981; Gomes, 1996; Helminiak, 1995).

> What is patently unknown to Paul is the concept of a homosexual nature, that is, using Paul's sense of the word "nature," something that is beyond choice, that is not necessarily characterized by lust, avarice, idolatry, or exploitation, and that aspires to a life under the jurisdiction of the Holy Spirit. All Paul knew of homosexuality was the debauched pagan expression of it. He cannot be condemned for

that ignorance, but neither should his ignorance be an excuse for our own. To base the church's principled objections to homosexuality and homosexuals on the basis of Paul's imperfect knowledge is itself unprincipled, and indeed quite beside all the heroic points that Paul intends to make in Romans 1. (Gomes, 1996, p. 158)

There are other points in the *Bible*, both in the Old and New Testaments, which have been used as arguments against homosexuality. For example, the creation story as well as sections from the book of Leviticus and the first letters to the Corinthians and of Timothy are often cited. Boswell (1981), Helminiak (1995), and McNeill (1988) offered evidence and insight into the misrepresentation of these passages. They went further and suggested that the relationship between Jesus and the chosen disciple, John, is one of same-sex love, and that the celebration of same-sex relationships is evidenced in the companionships of Ruth and Naomi, Jonathan and David, and Saul and David (Boswell, 1981; Helminiak, 1995).

Suggestions, Recommendations and Further Reading

As student affairs professionals confront their own ignorance of the *Bible* and work to support gay, lesbian, and bisexual students on campus, the models of Fowler and Cass help to frame our understanding in working with these challenging issues. The following suggestions provide a structure for dealing with gay, lesbian, and bisexual students and the campus climate.

1. *Self reflection.*
As professionals, we should be aware of our own biases and actively work to confront the internalized homophobia that is reflective of our campus cultures and society. Engelken (1996) suggested that gay, lesbian, and bisexual professionals should be out and visible. This recommendation could be extended to straight allies who may play a key function in the support of gay, lesbian, and bisexual students, as well as provide leadership to non-gay students (Washington & Evans, 1991). Sharing an understanding of faith and its impact on sexual orientation may provide an opportunity for everyone to learn, grow, and develop. Small discussion groups on the topic of sexual orientation and faith for both gay and non-

gay participants provide a structure for dialogue. Furthermore, information about various religious organizations that are inclusive of gay, lesbian, and bisexual people can be valuable opportunities for students who are familiar with a particular religious foundation and are attempting to integrate their identity development. Provided at the end of this chapter is a list of some of these organizations.

2. *University and community resources.*

The university community has a large impact on the spiritual and sexual identity development of students. Campus ministries are particularly influential. Obear (1991) advocated the involvement of campus ministers as resources, since they can strongly impact the spiritual development of students. Knowledge about various ministers and their particular ability to deal with the concerns of lesbian, gay, and bisexual people may be helpful for students who are struggling with their sexual orientation. As this chapter suggests, knowledge and insight into the *Bible* and its misuse by some is helpful to student affairs professionals and gay, lesbian, and bisexual students.

3. *Key administrators and their support*

The president and other high level administrators provide obvious leadership on college campuses. Their voices in support of lesbian, gay, and bisexual students can contribute to the tone and climate of a university community. Religious-based institutions, in particular, could use the mission statement of the university or college in supporting and advocating justice in a Christian tradition (Gutierrez, 1987). Levine and Love (Chapter 4, this volume) discuss this topic further.

4. *Utilize the university's language and values.*

Incorporating the language and values of the academic community in facilitating a climate that is welcoming of gay, lesbian, and bisexual students is important. This strategy may be of particular assistance to staff in residence halls, student activities, career planning and placement, and admissions offices. The mission of the institution and its language is a fundamental start. Furthermore, the purpose of the organizations that support the academic mission within the institution may have reference to seeking the truth, and, though it may be contradictory to present understanding and knowledge, furthering the cause of justice and celebrating diversity and various cultures in all their forms. These values help shape the support services and give credence to the work of the individual parts for the common good. Lesbians, gay men, and bisexuals are part of the common good and placing their identity development and education in the context of the institution's mission conveys a message to all in the campus community. For religious-affiliated campuses in particular, the interpretation of Scripture to combat ignorance and support the equal treatment of gay, lesbian, and bisexual students on campus could be useful. Levine and Love discuss these ideas further in Chapter 4.

5. *Knowledge and leadership*

Counseling centers may provide workshops for therapists to become more knowledgeable about the spiritual needs of gay, lesbian, and bisexual students (Johnson, 1988). Residence life organizations could provide training regarding sexual orientation and faith development to professional and paraprofessional staff. University unions and student activities offices may investigate lectures and speakers on the topic. Furthermore, the opportunity for a cross-section of the college community to collaborate on workshops, retreats, or research that will allow non-heterosexual students an opportunity for exploring faith in the context of their emerging identity exists abundantly. Role modeling, experiential opportunities, and attention to both the emotional and cognitive sides of faith will assist young lesbians, gay men, and bisexuals in their developing faith.

Discussing the topic of one's own faith and religion is never easy. Compounded with understanding the lives and experiences of lesbians, gay men, and bisexuals, the situation becomes even more complex. Aarons (1995), Blumenfeld and Raymond (1988), Laushway (1994), Marcus (1993), Morrison (1995), and Scanzoni and Mollenkott (1978) provide more information on this topic and are valuable resources. Educators have a responsibility to students to challenge themselves and, in turn, challenge one another as they support lesbian, gay, and bisexual students. It is a leap of faith for everyone that lands us in the direction of learning and discovering more about the community in which we are all members— the human family.

Resources

Baptist: Association of Welcoming and Affirming Baptists, P. O. Box 2596, Attleboro Falls, MA 02763-0894, Rev. Brenda J. Moulton, Coordinator, 508.226.1945, <http://members.aol.com/wabaptists/index.html>.

Catholic: Dignity/USA (National Office), 1500 Massachusetts Avenue NW, #11W, Washington DC 20005, 202.861.0017, <http://www.dignityusa.org/>.

Christian Scientists: Emergence International, P. O. Box 6061-423, Sherman Oaks, CA 91413, 818.994.6653, <http://www.geocities.com/WestHollywood/1892/>.

Episcopal: Integrity, P. O. Box 5255, New York, NY 10185-5255, 908.220.1914, <http://members.aol.com/natlinteg/index.html>.

Jewish: World Congress of Gay and Lesbian Jewish Organizations, P. O. Box 23379, Washington DC 20026-3379, <http://www.wcgljo.org/wcgljo/>.

Lutheran: Lutherans Concerned—North America, Bob Gibeling, Program Executive, 2466 Sharondale Drive, Atlanta, GA 30305, 404.266.9615, <http://www.lcna.org/>.

Mennonite: Brethren/Mennonite Council for Lesbian and Gay Concerns, P. O. Box 6300, Minneapolis, MN 35406-0300, 615.305.0315, <http://www.webcom.com/bmc/welcome.html>.

Methodist: Broadway United Methodist Church: Reconciling Congregation, 3344 N. Broadway, Chicago, IL 60657, 773.348.2679, <http://hwmin.gbgm-umc.org/churches/broadwayumc/>.

Mormons: Affirmation, Gay and Lesbian Mormons—Chapter at Large, <http://members.aol.com/affirmchlg/index.html>.

Non-Denominational: Universal Fellowship of Metropolitan Community Churches, 8704 Santa Monica Blvd. 2nd Floor, Los Angles, CA 90069, 310.360.8640, <http://ufmcc.com/mccla.html>. Index of Metropolitan Community Churches, <http://www.geocities.com/WestHollywood/2326/worldwide.html>.

Presbyterian: Presbyterian for Lesbian and Gay Concerns, James D. Anderson, SCILS Building, Dean's Office, 4 Huntington Street, New Brunswick, NJ 08903, 908.932.7501, <http://www.epp.cmu.edu/~riley/PLGC.html>.

Seventh Day Adventist: P. O. Box 7320, Laguna Niguel, CA 92607, 714.248.1299, <http://www.qrd.org/qrd/www/orgs/sda-kinship/>.

Unitarian Universalist: Interweave—Unitarian Universalist for Lesbian, Gay, Bisexual and Transgender Concerns, 167 Milk Street # 406, Boston, MA 02215, <http://www.qrd.org/qrd/www/orgs/uua/uu-IW.html>.

References

American Council on Education. (1994). The student personnel point of view. In. A. L. Rentz (Ed.), *Student affairs: A profession's heritage* (2nd ed., pp. 108-123). Washington, DC: American College Personnel Association. (Original work published in 1949)

Alexander, M. B., & Preston, J. (1996). *We were baptized too: Claiming God's grace for lesbians and gays*. Louisville, KY: Westminster John Knox Press.

Aarons, L. (1995). *Prayers for Bobby: A mother's coming to terms with the suicide of her gay son* (1st ed.). New York: HarperCollins.

Beck, E. T. (1982). *Nice Jewish girls*. Trumansburg, NY: Crossing Press.

Blumenfeld, W. J., & Raymond, D. (1988). *Looking at gay and lesbian life*. New York: Philosophical Library.

Boswell, J. (1981). *Christianity, social tolerance, and homosexuality*. Chicago: The University of Chicago Press.

Bouldrey, B. (1995). *Wrestling with the angel: Faith and religion in the lives of gay men*. New York: Riverhead Books.

Brown, R. D. (1980). The student development educator role. In U. Delworth, G. R. Hanson, & Associates, *Student services: A handbook for the profession* (pp. 191-208). San Francisco: Jossey-Bass.

Bull, C. (1993, November 2). Us vs. them: Fred Phelps. *The Advocate*, pp. 42-45.

Cass, V. C. (1979). Homosexual identity formation: A theoretical model. *Journal of Homosexuality, 4*, 219-235.

Chan, C. S. (1995). Issues of sexual identity in an ethnic minority: The case of Chinese American lesbians, gay men, and bisexual people. In A. R. D'Augelli & C. J. Patterson (Eds.), *Lesbian, gay, and bisexual identities over the lifespan: Psychological perspectives* (pp. 87-101). New York: Oxford Press.

Engelken, L. C. (1996). *Integrating sexual and spiritual identity: Educating student affairs professional to facilitate gay, lesbian, and bisexual students' journey toward wholeness*. Unpublished master's thesis, The University of Vermont, Burlington.

Evans, N. J., & D'Augelli, A. R. (1996). Lesbians, gay men, and bisexual people in college. In R. C. Savin-Williams & K. M. Cohen (Eds.), *The lives of lesbians, gays, and bisexuals* (pp. 201-226). Orlando, FL: Harcourt Brace.

Fortunato, J. E. (1982). *Embracing the exile: Healing journeys of gay Christians*. New York: Seabury Press.

Fowler, J. W. (1981). *Stages of faith*. San Francisco: Harper and Row.

Kohlberg, L. (1981). *The philosophy of moral development*. New York: Harper and Row.

Gallagher, J. (1993, November 2). Us vs. them: State of the Union. *The Advocate,* pp. 46-51.

Gomes, P. J. (1996). *The good book: Reading the Bible with mind and heart.* New York: William Morrow.

Gutierrez, F. J. (1987, March). *Managing the campus ecology of gay/lesbian students on Catholic college campuses.* Paper presented at the Annual Meeting of the American College Personnel Association, Chicago.

Helminiak, D. A. (1995). *What the Bible really says about homosexuality.* San Francisco: Alamo Square Press.

Heyward, C. (1984). *Our passion for justice: Images of power, sexuality, and liberation.* New York: Pilgrim Press.

Hoffman, D. (1995, March). *New perspectives on spirituality: Creating developmental communities and assessment measures.* Paper presented at the American College Personnel Association, Boston, MA.

Johnson, T. (1988). Spiritual questions in gay counseling. In M. Shernoff & W. A. Scott (Eds.), *The sourcebook on lesbian/gay health care* (2nd. ed., pp. 136-141). Washington, DC: National Lesbian/Gay Health Foundation.

Laushway, F. A. (1994). The Christian response to AIDS: A reflection. *Listening: Journal of Religion and Culture, 29,* 137-152.

Marcus, E. (1993). *Is it a choice?: Answers to 300 of the most frequently asked questions about gays and lesbians.* New York: HarperCollins.

McDonald, H. B., & Steinhorn, A. I. (1990). *Homosexuality: A practical guide to counseling lesbians, gay men, and their families.* New York: Continuum Publishing.

McNeill, J. J. (1988). *The church and the homosexual* (3rd. ed.). Boston, MA: Beacon Press.

Morrison, M. (1995). *The grace of coming home: Spirituality, sexuality, and the struggle for justice.* Cleveland, OH: Pilgrim Press.

Obear, K. (1991). Homophobia. In N. J. Evans & V. A. Wall (Eds.), *Beyond tolerance: Gays, lesbians and bisexuals on campus* (pp. 36-66). Alexandria, VA: American College Personnel Association.

Perry, W. (1968). *Forms of intellectual and ethical development in the college years.* New York: Holt, Rinehart and Winston.

Piaget, J. (1954). *The construction of reality in the child.* New York: Basic Books.

Russell, C. D., & Ellis, J. B. (1993, March). *Religiosity, gender, sex anxiety, and AIDS attitudes as they affect attitudes towards homosexuals.* Paper presented at the Annual Meeting of the Southeastern Psychological Association, Atlanta.

Savin-Williams, R. C., & Cohen, K. M (1996). Psychosocial outcomes of verbal and physical abuse among lesbian, gay and bisexual youths. In R. C. Savin-Williams & K. M. Cohen (Eds.), *The lives of lesbians, gays, and bisexuals* (pp. 181-200). Orlando, FL: Harcourt Brace.

Scanzoni, L., & Mollenkott, V. R. (1978). *Is the homosexual my neighbor? Another Christian view.* New York: Harper and Row.

Sears, J. T. (1991). *Growing up gay in the south: Race, gender, and journeys of the spirit.* New York: Harrington Park Press.

Selman, R. (1976). Social-cognitive understanding: A guide to educational and clinical practice. In T. Lickona (Ed.), *Moral development and behavior: Theory, research, and social issues* (pp. 299-316). New York: Holt, Rinehart and Winston.

Wall, V. A., & Washington, J. (1991). Understanding gay and lesbian students of color. In N. J. Evans & V. A. Wall (Eds.), *Beyond tolerance: Gays, lesbians and bisexuals on campus* (pp. 67-78). Alexandria, VA: American College Personnel Association.

Washington, J., & Evans, N. J. (1991). Becoming an ally. In N. J. Evans & V. A. Wall (Eds.), *Beyond tolerance: Gays, lesbians and bisexuals on campus* (pp. 195-204). Alexandria, VA: American College Personnel Association.

Widick, C., Knefelkamp, L., & Parker, C. A. (1980). Student development. In U. Delworth, G. R. Hanson, & Associates, *Student services: A handbook for the profession* (pp. 75-116). San Francisco: Jossey Bass.

Williams, R. (1993). *Just as I am: A practical guide to being out, proud and Christian* (1st ed.). New York: HarperPerennial.

Wilson, N. L. (1996). Fear of faith. *The Harvard Gay & Lesbian Review, 3* (4), 18-19.

Zanotti, B. (1986). *A faith of one's own: Explorations by Catholic lesbians.* Trumansburg, NY: Crossing Press.

PART V

ADDRESSING CAMPUS ISSUES

Chapter 15

඲ශ

Ways of Being an Ally to Lesbian, Gay, and Bisexual Students

ELLEN M. BROIDO

The term "ally" can be defined in many different ways. Within the context of social justice work, however, the word has a very specific connotation. I will retain the usage of the term "ally" as developed by Washington and Evans (1991). They define the word as "a person who is a member of the 'dominant' or 'majority' group who works to end oppression in his or her personal and professional life through support of, and as an advocate with and for, the oppressed population" (p. 195). In the context of this paper, then, an ally for lesbian/gay/bisexual issues is by definition someone who identifies as heterosexual, and who works to end homophobia and heterosexism.

Ally work can be conducted both within dominant and within targeted populations. Although the most obvious beneficiaries of ally work are members of the targeted social group, many authors (for example, Katz, 1978; McIntosh, 1988) have noted that the elimination of oppression has positive ramifications for members of the dominant social group as well. Such benefits include a greater ability to relate to and work with all members of society, broader personal relationships, congruence between one's values and one's actions, a stronger sense of self-efficacy, and increased self-esteem (Katz, 1978; McIntosh, 1988; Washington & Evans, 1991).

This chapter will review models and theories of how people come to be allies, before proceeding to a discussion of ways in which people can act as allies. Because the literature in this area is so sparse, models of dominant identity development will be considered as well as models specific to allies to lesbians, gay men, and bisexual people. Additionally, two non-developmental models that examine attitudes toward lesbian, gay, and bisexual people will be described. Following these descriptions of how people come to be allies, ways of being an ally will be discussed. Because of the paucity of literature specific to allies in the area of lesbian/gay/bisexual oppression, literature from other types of ally work will be considered as well.

The Development of Heterosexual Allies

As yet there is only one model or theory (Chojnacki & Gelberg, 1995) that traces the development of allies in the area of lesbian/gay/bisexual issues. This development has been proposed as paralleling the gay identity formation process described by Cass (1979, 1984). The Chojnacki/Gelberg model is no more than a basic outline, and as yet has no empirical support. In general, few models exist that identify the development of ally attitudes regarding any social justice issues. Those that do exist and are well articulated primarily deal with the development of White identity. One model of White identity development (Hardiman 1979, 1982) has been expanded to create a "generic" model of dominant identity development (Jackson & Hardiman, 1982), which can be applied to heterosexuals as well as any other dominant group. Like the Chojnacki/Gelberg model, neither the Hardiman nor the Jackson/Hardiman model has empirical support. Both Chojnacki and Gelberg's and Jackson and Hardiman's models will be discussed here.

Choinacki/Gelberg Model

Chojnacki and Gelberg (1995) have proposed a model of how heterosexual counselors might develop as allies. Their model is based upon their experiences as facilitators of a support group for lesbian, gay, and bisexual students on a university campus, and mirrors Cass's (1979, 1984) model of sexual identity formation. Although only roughly conceptualized, and lacking empirical validation, it stands unique as the only published attempt at explaining how heterosexuals might become allies to people who are lesbian, gay, or bisexual.

Stages of the Model

In Chojnacki and Gelberg's (1995) model, counselors in the first stage, *confusion,* question the need for services for lesbian and gay clients and are unaware of the oppression of gays and lesbians. Contact with people who are lesbian and gay moves counselors toward the second and third stages, *comparison* and *tolerance.* Here counselors begin to experience doubt and confusion as they try to be more gay-affirming. Lack of professional role models and concerns about experiencing both homophobia from the larger society and rejection by people who are lesbian, gay, or bisexual can heighten a counselor's fear and confusion.

The fourth stage, *acceptance,* is marked by greater risk-taking as an ally. There is more "coming out" as an ally, and therefore greater contact with professional colleagues who affirm this position. Greater activism, such as starting a lesbian/gay/bisexual support group, may happen while counselors are in this stage. In the fifth stage, *pride,* most feelings of confusion, fear, and anxiety dissipate. Chojnacki and Gelberg (1995*)* reported that those feelings were replaced by feelings of "increased self-esteem and efficacy in our activities, and at the same time we experienced greater alienation from homophobic colleagues and organizations" (p. 354). In the final stage of the model, *integration,* the values counselors espouse in their professional lives are continued in their personal lives. The development of one's identity as an ally is seen as life-long and cyclical.

Implications of the Model

Within the Chojnacki and Gelberg (1995) model, development is assumed to occur though a combination of two forms of contact. The first includes contact with clients, family members, or friends who are lesbian, gay, or bisexual. The second is through contact with and support from colleagues. This model was developed within the context of a profession in which there are individuals who are affirmative of lesbian, gay, and bisexual identities. In that way, this model seems particularly suitable for translation to a student affairs context, where there is increasing recognition of the challenges faced by students and colleagues who are lesbian, bisexual, or gay, and an increasing number of heterosexual allies who can provide support and act as role models to those seeking to become allies.

Hardiman and Jackson/Hardiman Models

Hardiman's model of White identity development was developed from her examination of models of ethnic/racial identity development and women's identity development. From these models she first developed a generic model of dominant identity development and then used autobiographies of anti-racist Whites to tailor the model to the development of an anti-racist White identity. Working with Bailey Jackson, she has developed a general model of social identity development that describes the development of people in "dominant" social groups and those in "target" social groups. The Jackson/Hardiman model will be examined here for its relevance to heterosexual ally development.

The Jackson/Hardiman model of social identity development is based upon an examination of models of learning and unlearning oppression (specifically Paulo Freire's [1994/1970] model), as well as models of racial and gender identity development, and draws from the perspectives of sociology, psychology, and anthropology (Hardiman, 1982). From these models Hardiman was able to identify common themes, and from those themes she developed a "generic" model of social identity development that could be applied both to those with dominant social identities and to those with targeted social identities. This broad model was made more specific by applying it separately to dominant and target groups (Jackson & Hardiman, 1982), and even more particularly to White identity development (Hardiman, 1982). The Social Identity Development Model, although far more thoroughly articulated than the Chojnacki and Gelberg model, is similarly lacking in empirical validation.

The Social Identity Development Model is based on the premise that oppression is a learned phenomenon, and as such it can be unlearned (see also Ponterotto & Pederson, 1993). As Jackson and Hardiman (1982) specify, "The transition from one stage to another is typically motivated by a recognition that the world view of the current stage is either illogical, detrimental to a healthy self-concept, impractical or in general no longer serving some important self-interest" (p. 2).

There are five stages to the model of dominant identity development: naive, acceptance, resistance, redefinition and internalization, two of which, acceptance and resistance, can take two forms: active and passive. It is the intermediate level of specificity, the model of dominant identity development (Jackson & Hardiman, 1982), which is most useful in trying to understand the development of heterosexual allies, and which will be discussed here. Each stage of the model will be described both in its generic form, and as it might be applied to heterosexual ally development.

Stages of the Model

1. Naive. The first stage of dominant identity development, Naive, describes the stage everyone enters into at birth, whether she or he has a dominant or a target identity. This stage is a period prior to any social consciousness, a stage of early childhood that usually lasts until about 4 years of age. In this stage, differences between people usually are noticed by children, but are not evaluated in a good/bad sense. Movement to the next stage begins as children are socialized to accept the dominant views that some groups are better, or more normal, than others, and that there are negative consequences if one does not abide by the dominant worldview.

Heterosexual Naive. People are born with no understanding that love and physical affection for those of the other gender are to be valued over love and physical affection for the same gender. No assumptions are made that some behaviors are appropriate for only one gender.

2. Acceptance. The stage of Acceptance describes the time during which a person accepts, consciously or unconsciously, the dominant worldview regarding the nature and worthiness of particular social groups. Acceptance can take two forms, passive or active. In Passive Acceptance the person "unconsciously identifies with the social system and the social group that gives the person privilege. The person denies the existence of social oppression and blames the oppressed for their condition" (Hardiman & Jackson, 1992, p. 7). She or he agrees to help the oppressed to the extent that they are willing to conform to the dominant way of being.

Active Acceptance refers to the process of "conscious identification with the social system that gives the person privilege as a member of an oppressor group" (Hardiman & Jackson, 1982, p. 7). People in this stage believe, act on and promulgate stereotypes about members of targeted groups, and sanction members of both the oppressed and the dominant group who challenge the system.

Many people spend their entire lives in Acceptance. Movement to the stage of Resistance begins if and when the person begins to see that some of the challenges to the dominant way of thinking may have some validity, or that there may actually be some injustice or discrimination against targeted group members in society. According to Hardiman and Jackson (1992),

> The transition generally evolves over time and usually results from a number of events that have a cumulative effect. People in acceptance consciousness begin to be aware of experiences that contradict the acceptance world views, experiences they had earlier ignored or passed off as isolated, exceptional events. Gradually, as a person begins to encounter more dissonant issues, the isolated incidents form a discernible pattern. (p. 27)

Thus, when the person's worldview can no longer assimilate dissonant information, the person moves into a new way of understanding the world.

Heterosexual Acceptance. Through parental and family influence, teachers and religious doctrine, as well as through images in the media, books, and teasing from adults and peers, people learn that the only "right" or "normal" emotional and physical intimacy is to be with people of the other gender. Negative stereotypes about people who are lesbian, bisexual, and gay are learned and believed. Attitudes toward lesbian, gay, and bisexual people range between revulsion and pity. Except in the most progressive environments, most people are probably in Active (rather than Passive) Acceptance. This is evidenced by the consequences for not joining in behaviors indicative of Active Acceptance: Not laughing at anti-gay jokes, or not joining in the expression of anti-gay comments often causes one to be labeled as gay oneself.

3. Resistance. As people enter Resistance they begin to become aware of, and increase their knowledge of the ways in which this particular form of oppression operates in their and other's lives. They begin to recognize the multiple ways in which oppression operates. There is a shift in worldview such that the "problem" no longer is thought to lie in members of targeted groups, but rather in the dominant group. One's identity as a member of the dominant group becomes explicit, and oppression is seen everywhere. Feelings of guilt, shame, and anger are common in people in Resistance.

People in Passive Resistance feel overwhelmed by the problem, and may feel incapable of changing anything. They will challenge expressions of oppression only in safe situations. They therefore try to "drop out" of the dominant culture, believing that they will then at least not be perpetuating the oppression. However, they rarely try to challenge or change the system itself

People in Active Resistance, however, deliberately confront and question social norms and individual behaviors that perpetuate particular forms of oppression. They actively dissociate themselves from other members of the dominant group, and often try to become part of the target group, or at least try to reject the privilege they accrue as members of the dominant group. Their inability to accomplish this leads to a need to redefine their identity, and spurs movement into the next stage.

Heterosexual Resistance. As people become aware that not all lesbian, gay, or bisexual people match the stereotypes they have been taught, as they come to know lesbians, bisexual people, or gay men, or because they enter an environment more affirming of lesbian, gay, and bisexual people, some people enter into the stage of Resistance. People in this stage begin to recognize the ways in which lesbian, gay, and bisexual people are hurt by homophobia, and how they as straight people benefit from heterosexism. As people become increasingly aware of the ways in which lesbian, gay, and bisexual people are discriminated against, they try to dissociate themselves from their homophobic peers, and may experience feelings of anger or guilt. Depending on the environment, they may challenge homophobic comments and jokes. During this stage there is also an attempt to learn about gay culture, usually through less risky avenues such as watching mainstream films that deal with lesbian/gay/bisexual issues.

4. Redefinition. In Redefinition one returns to an examination of one's own identity. Until now, the only way to be a member of the dominant group was as an oppressor. People in this stage seek ways to recreate, or rename their identity in order to find new ways of being heterosexual, white, male, etc., without being oppressive. The question being asked and answered in this period is "Who am I?" There is a search for like-minded others who are struggling with the same issues, looking for new ways to define being a member of the dominant group. As non-oppressive ways and histories are found, there is a new pride and comfort in being heterosexual, White, etc. As people move though this stage they begin to gain an understanding of the inter-relatedness of all types of oppression, which leads them into the next stage, Internalization.

Heterosexual Redefinition. In the Redefinition period, heterosexual allies focus on using their own privilege within their spheres of influence to bring about social change. They band together with other heterosexual people who are working to find non-oppressive ways of being straight. As they continue to advocate for the elimination of heterosexism, they come to understand how heterosexism relates to sexism, racism, classism, and other forms of oppression.

5. Internalization. During Internalization the identity acquired in Redefinition becomes more stable, requiring less of a conscious effort, and becomes integrated with the person's way of seeing her or himself The understanding of how one's dominant identity(ies) are related to all aspects of one's life becomes clearer, and people begin working to end all types of oppression. Very few people reach this position, and Hardiman has said that it may actually be more of a hypothetical construct than a real stage (personal communication, September 30, 1992).

Heterosexual Internalization. During Internalization, heterosexual allies integrate their work against homophobia and heterosexism into their work on other areas of oppression. Once a very salient identity, their identities as heterosexual allies now are one of many identities that coexist with minimal tension.

Attitude Change

What causes people to move from homophobic attitudes toward more positive attitudes, and eventually to ally attitudes and behaviors? While a fairly substantive body of research exists that explores various correlates of prejudice, be it racial prejudice, homophobia, sexism, or other "-isms," there is essentially no research that explores how people experience the transition to becoming an ally, or even on correlates of this transition.

The research that does exist on correlates of homophobia indicates that female gender, the perception that sexual orientation is innate rather than a choice, contact with lesbians and gays, and liberal views all correlate with more positive attitudes toward lesbian, gay, and bisexual people (Herek & Capitanio, 1995; Herek & Glunt, 1993). Positive attitudes toward lesbians were found, in one study of college students, to be correlated with positive contact with lesbians, lesbian friends, contemporary attitudes toward women (that is, more egalitarian views on the roles of women in society), and more permissive sexual attitudes (Simon, 1995). However, this research is focused more on demographic correlates of relatively positive attitudes than on the development of positive attitudes, and none of the research examines correlates of ally behavior.

Models of attitude change can be found in the more general literature on oppression and social justice. Roberta Harro (1996) has developed a schematic diagram of how oppression is perpetuated (the "Cycle of Socialization") and how it is challenged (the "Cycle of Liberation"). In her model, as people reflect on the realities of a society organized to enhance the power and privilege of only certain groups, they may become aware of the contradictions inherent in the current system and experience dissonance. This dissonance motivates people to begin a process of consciousness raising, which must happen in collaboration with others who are experiencing the same dissonance. Unlearning the assumptions and stereotypes we have all been taught leads to feelings of anger and guilt, but also to feelings of pride, love, and empowerment as people begin to take action to challenge the system of oppression. As a result of this challenge, people begin to redefine what it means to be a member of the dominant group, and to see that it does not inherently make one a "bad" or a "good" person. Because there are negative social consequences for taking action against the system of oppression, people begin to be treated differently, which leads to further consciousness raising, and continued progress through the cycle of liberation.

In the particular case of heterosexual allies, increasing contact with people known to be lesbian, gay, or bisexual may lead to greater knowledge of the legal, social, and structural inequities experienced by people who are lesbian, gay, and bisexual. This knowledge may in turn lead people to become more open advocates for equitable treatment, and thus have their own sexual orientation called into question, continuing the process of greater awareness of the environments experienced by lesbian, gay, and bisexual people.

Non-developmental Models of Attitudes toward Lesbians, Gay Men, and Bisexual People

The Chojnacki and Gelberg (1995) model and the Jackson/Hardiman (1982) model are both developmental models. They assume there is a linear progression from one set of attitudes and behaviors to another, that people pass through each stage, and that change is in the direction of increasingly positive attitudes and behaviors. In contrast to these models, the two models considered below are not developmental. Although Riddle's (1996) model may in fact be developmental, she has not conceptualized it as such. Neither Herek's (1986) nor Riddle's models assumes attitudes to be static, but theoretically people's attitudes toward lesbian, bisexual, and gay people could change without passing through contiguous positions, and change would not have to be in a positive direction.

Herek's Model

Gregory Herek has studied attitudes toward lesbians and gay men from the perspectives of social psychology, and that discipline's theories of how attitudes are formed and how they change. Herek (1986) takes a functionalist approach to the study of attitudes, arguing that attitudes "are strategies for satisfying psychological needs" (p. 99). Some attitudes and their consequent behaviors are thought to result from self-interest while other actions seem to come more from one's long held values and beliefs about society. These two types of motivations are referred to as "instrumental" and "symbolic." Herek has developed a model that indicates under what circumstances each of these motivations takes precedence, and has applied the model to attitudes toward people who are lesbian, gay, and bisexual.

Herek (1986) has found that heterosexual students' attitudes toward lesbians and gay men often serve an expressive function. "Lesbians and gay men (the attitude object) seemed to serve primarily as a symbol or vehicle, and the attitude's function lay primarily in the social and psychological benefits derived from its expression (e. g., acceptance by others, enhancement of self-esteem, reduction of anxiety)" (p. 106). Expressive attitudes, then, serve a symbolic function, and benefit their holder not through their relation to the attitude object (lesbians and gay men), but rather by the consequences of articulating the attitude. Expressive attitudes are best predicted by "the individual's group identifications, self-concept, and intrapsychic dynamics" (p. 106).

Herek (1986) indicated that efforts at attitude change should be different for attitudes serving different functions, and that "messages are most likely to change attitudes when they are resonant with the person's dominant function" (p. 111). For expressive attitudes "changes in the consequences for asserting the attitude will be of primary importance" (p. 111). Positive attitudes toward people who are lesbian or gay would be most likely to be elicited when the situation makes salient a person's underlying values of equality, justice, or compassion, when significant others support attitudes affirming of people who are lesbian, gay, or bisexual, or when situations help people resolve intrapsychic conflicts they may have about people who are lesbian, gay, or bisexual.

The Riddle Scale

The Riddle scale, developed by psychologist Dorothy Riddle (1996), outlines an eight-point scale of attitudes toward lesbian and gay people and issues. The scale has made its way into the workshop and training circuit, and is used in many heterosexism/homophobia training sessions within the student affairs profession, perhaps because of its strong "face validity." The scale was developed in the 1970s, based on the author's awareness that there were different attitudes toward gay and lesbian people evident in the participants attending her workshops on gay and lesbian issues. From her observations she developed an initial schematic, which was shared with other experts on attitudes toward lesbians and gay men. From this schematic she developed a questionnaire that was distributed throughout the state of Arizona. The eight attitudes that made up the final scale were developed from a factor analysis of the results of the questionnaire (Riddle, personal communication, October 18, 1996).

Dorothy Riddle's scale identifies eight possible attitudes toward lesbians and gays, which she presents in order of increasingly positive attitudes. However, her model does not specify whether these attitudes are stable or are capable of changing. It would seem likely that in some circumstances or environments development through the levels might be possible. Riddle has stated that she believes that attitude change is possible, but is very unlikely unless there is personal contact with someone who has suffered severe discrimination because of her or his sexual orientation. She stated as well that she believes that attitude change is more likely among those who are most hostile, and much rarer among those in the middle stages of the scale (Riddle, personal communication, October 18, 1996).

Levels of the Scale

The eight levels in the scale are divided into four homophobic levels of attitude and four positive levels of attitude. The levels are as follows:

1. *Repulsion*: Homosexuality is pathological and immoral, and as such, any method is appropriate to eradicate it.
2. *Pity*: Heterosexuality is the only right or normal sexual orientation, and those who are unable to be or become heterosexual should be pitied.
3. *Tolerance*: Lesbian and gay identities are merely an adolescent phase, which individuals will or should grow out of. Lesbians and gays are therefore to be treated as children.
4. *Acceptance*: It's OK if I don't have to see it or know about it. Homosexuality is something distasteful which must be accepted, but it is not to be embraced.
5. *Support*: Homophobia is wrong. People in this stage have a basic awareness of homophobia's existence, although they may not yet be comfortable with lesbians and gays.
6. *Admiration*: It is difficult to be lesbian or gay. People in this stage are willing to examine their own homophobia.
7. *Appreciation*: People in this stage recognize the contributions of lesbians and gay men, and see them as an important part of the human community. These people are willing to address their own homophobia and that of others.
8. *Nurturance*: People in this stage genuinely and fully embrace lesbians and gay men. They are willing to be advocates for lesbian/gay issues.

Implications of the Riddle Scale

The importance of the Riddle scale is its implication (although it does not say so explicitly) that homophobic/homo-hating attitudes are not indelible, that the development of positive attitudes toward lesbian, gay and bisexual people is a process. These changes are not limited to those with initially homophobic attitudes. Riddle's model indicates also that those with "neutral" attitudes have room to grow in their understanding of gay and lesbian issues, and in their appreciation of lesbian, gay, and bisexual people. The scale also indicates that attitudes such as "tolerance" and "acceptance," seemingly positive attitudes, still carry beliefs that are detrimental to lesbians and gay men.

Strategies for Being an Ally

The literature on ways in which heterosexuals can be allies to lesbian, gay, and bisexual people is scant. Two notable exceptions are Gary Rapp's article "From the Heart: Being an Ally to the Lesbian, Gay and Bisexual Community" (1995) and Jamie Washington and Nancy Evans's chapter "Becoming an Ally" (1991). Useful parallels, however, can be drawn from some works that speak to how Whites can be allies to people of color. In one such article "Something about the Subject Makes it Hard to Name" Gloria Yamato (1996) advised:

> *Whites who want to be allies to people of color*: You can educate yourselves via research and observation rather than rigidity [sic], arrogantly relying solely on interrogating people of color. Do not expect that people of color should teach you how to behave non-oppressively. Do not give in to the pull to be lazy. Think, hard. Do not blame people of color for your frustration about racism, but do appreciate that fact that people of color will often help you get in touch with that frustration. Assume that your effort to be a good friend is appreciated, but don't expect or accept gratitude from people of color. Work on racism for your sake, not "their" sake. Assume that you are needed and capable of being a good ally. Know that you'll make mistakes and commit yourself to correcting them and continuing on as an ally, no matter what. Don't give up. (p. 11)

Yamato's recommendations can be adapted, and apply equally well to heterosexual allies. For example, allies should teach themselves about lesbian/gay/bisexual cultures and issues rather than relying on lesbian, gay, and bisexual people to teach them. There are books in most larger libraries and bookstores that provide accurate perspectives both on the diversity and on the commonalties in lesbian, gay, and bisexual cultures (see, for example, *Looking at Gay and Lesbian Life*, Blumenfield & Raymond, 1988; *Sisters, Sexperts and Queers: Beyond the Lesbian Nation*, Stein, 1993). Similarly, subscribing to or purchasing magazines directed toward the lesbian/gay/bisexual communities (for example, *The Advocate, Curve*) provides information on current issues in the lesbian/gay/bisexual communities. These two magazines, in particular, are available in large or progressive bookstores and libraries. Additionally, displaying copies of these magazines in the workspace signals that one is receptive to lesbian/gay/bisexual issues.

Be allies without expecting praise from lesbian, gay, and bisexual people. Know that it will take time to overcome the conditioning that has taught the presumed superiority of heterosexual lifestyles and that has kept most people, regardless of sexual orientation, ignorant of lesbian, gay, and bisexual lives. Allies will make mistakes, feel awkward and at times out of place, but this is to be expected (Rapp, 1995) and should not be taken as a valid reason to cease ally work.

Roles for heterosexual allies can be divided, very roughly, into three primary categories: support, education, and advocacy. These roles are not without overlap, although for conceptual clarity they will be discussed in this chapter as separate functions. Their overlap is evident in the conclusions of an informal survey of over 100 members of the National Association for Women Deans, Administrators, and Counselors (Hollingdale & Kennedy, 1991). Forty-eight of those who participated in the study identified themselves as lesbian or bisexual university faculty or staff. They indicated the following types of responses to the question "In what ways can your non-gay colleagues be supportive of you?"

- Don't assume everyone is straight
- Don't treat me differently [from heterosexual colleagues]: ask about my partner, the rest of my life
- Confront homophobic behavior and statements
- Don't out me
- Advocate for gay issues/against heterosexist policies
- Educate yourself about lesbian/gay/bisexual issues
- Include lesbian/gay/bisexual issues in the rubric of diversity
- Include lesbian/gay/bisexual issues in staff training
- Ask questions

Although these responses were given by university faculty and staff, the same behaviors would be perceived as supportive by lesbian, gay, and bisexual students.

Providing Support to Lesbian. Gay, and Bisexual Students and Staff

As long as the campus environment remains hostile to lesbian, gay, and bisexual students, faculty, and staff, there will be a need for faculty, administrators, and staff members to provide safe spaces, to develop mentor programs and support systems, and to coordinate programming on lesbian, gay, and bisexual issues. As long as there remain negative consequences to students, faculty, and staff for being out, as long as those not explicitly identified as heterosexual risk being "tainted" as lesbian or gay for providing lesbian, gay, and bisexual affirmative programs, there will be a role for allies in providing direct services in support of students and colleagues who are lesbian, gay, and bisexual. In short, there is still a need to "help" people who are lesbian, gay, and bisexual to counteract the effects of the hostile climate in which they must work and study. One of the simplest ways of being an ally is to recognize and affirm the legitimate existence of lesbian, gay, and bisexual people. This affirmation is a necessary part of ally strategies, and in itself is a significant step in countering the climate on most campuses.

Educating Oneself

The first step in becoming an ally is to know oneself. This can be a frustrating place to begin because it is not active, not overtly helpful to the group to be "helped." However, it is critical that one first become aware of one's own feelings about lesbian, gay, and bisexual people so one can deal with any negative or uncomfortable feelings before offering oneself as an ally. Only once such feelings are resolved can one be effective as an ally (Rapp, 1995; Washington & Evans, 1991).

Similarly, to be an effective support person it is important to learn more about lesbian/gay/bisexual culture and issues (Hollingdale & Kennedy, 1991; Washington & Evans, 1991). Attending lesbian/gay/ bisexual events (for example, National Coming Out Day events, pride rallies, dances, films, etc.) allows one to learn about lesbian/gay/bisexual issues. It also increases the political impact of such events (because of greater attendance), and makes visible one's identity as an ally—to the heterosexual community and to lesbians, gay men, and bisexual people (Croteau & Lark, 1995).

Letting People Know One is an Ally

In order to provide support, one must first be visible as a person who is willing and able to provide such support. Allies frequently ask "How can I let lesbian and gay people know I am an ally?" There are many ways. As Clark (1987) makes clear, actions speak louder than words. Many people perceive a pressure to be "politically correct" that may result in pro-gay statements being heard as reactions to that pressure, rather than as true sentiments. Some of the simplest ways of demonstrating one is an ally are through one's use of language and through items in one's office such as a poster of a same-sex couple, display of a button stating "I Support Gay Rights" or "Straight but Not Narrow," or having gay-titled books on one's bookshelves (Bertolino, 1992; Obear, 1991).

Language

The use of non-heterosexist language provides support and affirmation to lesbian, gay, and bisexual people. Use gender-neutral questions when asking about relationships, or when responding to people's references to relationships. Making references to a person's "significant other" or "partner" implies that one does not assume an other-gender relationship.

Use of the words "lesbian," "gay," or "bisexual" rather than "homosexual" indicates a recognition that sexual orientation is not a clinical issue, or just about sex, but rather is an identity. Use of "sexual orientation" rather than "sexual preference" or "alternative lifestyle" implies knowledge of current identifiers used by the lesbian/bisexual/ gay communities. It also implies recognition that sexual orientation is not a choice or preference (at least for most people), and recognition that the term "lifestyle" trivializes an identity by equating it with, for example, the decision to live in the country rather than the city.

Join or Start a Support Network/Safe Space Program

Probably the most common ally programs on college campuses are "safe space" or support network type programs. In these programs people who are willing to provide support to lesbian, gay, and bisexual people display a button, poster, or sticker that identifies them as someone "safe" to talk to about lesbian/gay/bisexual issues. These programs generally are open both to lesbian, gay, and bisexual people and to heterosexual allies. Some universities have a screening process for potential members, although more commonly anyone who wishes to designate her or himself as "safe" can do so. Occasionally training sessions or resources materials are provided to members of the program.

Advise Lesbian/Bisexual/Gay Student Groups

While having an "out" lesbian, gay, or bisexual advisor to lesbian/gay/bisexual student groups is certainly desirable, heterosexual allies can and do make excellent advisors, both in the absence of a gay advisor, and as co-advisors. Especially on smaller or more conservative campuses, there may be no lesbian, gay, or bisexual faculty or staff who are willing to advise such groups, and unless a straight ally is willing to do so, a lesbian/gay/bisexual student group may not be able to exist (Bourassa & Broido, 1993; Croteau & Lark, 1995).

Education

While there is a need to provide support to lesbians, gay men, and bisexual people, there is also a great, if not greater, amount of work to be done with the heterosexual community that can best be accomplished by fellow heterosexuals. While providing support to students is necessary, it does not change the social structure that sustains heterosexism and homophobia. Only by educating heterosexuals and advocating for social change will the climate in which lesbian, bisexual, and gay people live and work change (Hogan & Rentz, 1996).

Educational actions can include: (a) challenging homophobic comments, (b) correcting misinformation and stereotypes, (c) including lesbian, gay, and bisexual histories, cultures, and issues in curricula, and (d) including sexual orientation issues in diversity training. Training about lesbian/gay/bisexual issues can be done with faculty, staff, teaching assistants, and academic advisors, among many others (Obear, 1991). Campus media outlets can be taught the importance of giving coverage to lesbian/gay/bisexual events and issues. Other ways of educating include bringing up lesbian/gay/bisexual issues with colleagues, and pointing out and acting upon incidents of discrimination or harassment.

Challenging Homophobic Words and Actions

In one study of university faculty and staff attitudes only 40.6% of the almost 600 respondents indicated they were likely or very likely to challenge an anti-gay comment or joke, while 38.4% indicated they were unlikely or very unlikely to challenge such comments (Rankin, 1994). Consistently and firmly addressing such statements has two positive outcomes: it tends to reduce the expression of such sentiments, and it sends a message about what is valued or important that will become known beyond the individual who was confronted (Obear, 1991). Challenging homophobic comments also challenges the myth that all good or moral people condemn homosexuality.

Develop a Lesbian/Gay/Bisexual Speakers Program

Students and administrators at many institutions have developed lesbian/gay/ bisexual speakers programs as one way of addressing homophobia and heterosexism on their campuses (Geasler, Croteau, Heineman, & Edlund, 1995; Green, Dixon, & Gold-Neil, 1993). These programs often are initiated or advised by student affairs staff members (Geasler, et al., 1995), although faculty members can and do play this role as well. These advisors' responsibilities can include articulating the need for such programs, locating and training participants, and publicizing the program. None of these responsibilities need be restricted to lesbian, gay, or bisexual staff or faculty. In fact, having heterosexual allies involved as advisors in such programs can lend a stamp of credibility to the program. In addition, students who are heterosexual allies can participate in panels and discuss their "coming out" experience as allies.

Advocacy: The Importance of Visibility

Working to change heterosexist policies and advocating for lesbian/ gay/bisexual issues can be done both by straight allies and by lesbian, gay, and bisexual people. Often the advocacy of allies is more effective than that of lesbian, gay, or bisexual people because allies are not seen as advocating for their own benefit, but rather because they truly believe in the merits of their arguments. Depending on the campus, advocacy may be necessary for some or all of the following issues: including sexual orientation in the institution's non-discrimination policy; developing majors in lesbian/gay/bisexual studies; funding research on lesbian/gay/bisexual issues; addressing police, faculty, staff, and/or student harassment of people who are lesbian, gay, or bisexual; hiring and compensation policies; service provision to lesbian, gay, and bisexual students; developing a lesbian/gay/bisexual student center; ensuring access to family housing; and obtaining athletic facility and ticket privileges for domestic partners of students, staff, and faculty. This is only a partial list of issues that commonly arise on college and university campuses with regard to people who are lesbian, gay, or bisexual. While this list is restricted to issues immediately within the purview of the institution, often there is as great a need to address lesbian/gay/bisexual issues in the surrounding community, most often safety and housing access.

Heterosexual allies can utilize many tactics in their advocacy for these issues. They can join existing committees or groups working to address the climate for people who are lesbian, gay, or bisexual; they can write letters of support to institutional decision makers (for example, members of the board of trustees, the institution's president, senior administrators); they can speak up about these issues with their colleagues, supervisors, and supervisees; they can initiate or participate in protests and boycotts. It is not enough to personally support the adoption of policies affirmative of lesbian, bisexual, and gay people. In whatever fashion, it is crucial for heterosexual allies to make their support for lesbian/gay/bisexual issues and people visible.

Consequences of Being an Ally

If there is minimal literature available suggesting ways in which heterosexual allies develop, and ways in which people can be allies to people who are lesbian, bisexual, or gay; there is virtually no literature that describes in any substantive way the consequences of being an ally in this area. This lack of literature may have a number of causes, but the most probable seems to be the recency of academic interest in lesbian/gay/ bisexual issues. The literature published to date is focused on the experiences of lesbian, gay, and bisexual students, faculty, and staff, and the extent of negative attitudes on the part of heterosexuals. Exploration of the experiences and development of allies are second order questions that largely appear to be unasked, and as yet are unanswered.

In contrast to the logical parallels that can be drawn between the development of White allies and heterosexual allies, the literature exploring the experiences of allies in the area of racism seems to be less relevant in forecasting the experiences of allies against homophobia and heterosexism. This is because allies in the area of racism, as well as sexism, never need to worry that because of their advocacy they will be mistaken for members of the group whom they are supporting. While Whites participating in the Civil Rights movement were sometimes killed or beaten (McAdam, 1988), they were never thought to be Black. However, it is often assumed that anyone advocating for gay rights, or who is supportive of gay people, must her or himself be gay, lesbian, or bisexual (Rhoads, 1995a; Schreier, 1995). Thus, ally behavior in support of lesbian/gay/bisexual issues may have some consequences quite different than ally behaviors regarding sexism or racism, at least in contemporary times.

Personal consequences for being an ally thus may echo the consequences for being "out" for lesbian, gay, and bisexual people. Such consequences may include verbal abuse, scorn, avoidance, or ostracism by family and friends. In some professional settings advocacy for lesbian/ gay/bisexual issues may be seen as too liberal or radical (Schreier, 1995). Senior level administrators whose institutions have conservative boards of trustees or state legislatures may find their employment or authority jeopardized if they advocate or implement policies supportive of lesbian, gay, and bisexual people. The drive for domestic-partner benefits and the establishment of lesbian/gay/bisexual student centers has been divisive in many state legislatures, and in at least one instance (Pearlman, 1994; Wimmer, 1994) has led to the threat to eliminate $500,000 of state funding for the institution.

Implications for Student Affairs

While most research has indicated that more positive attitudes toward lesbian/ bisexual/gay issues are correlated with contact with people who are lesbian, bisexual, or gay (Herek & Capitanio, 1995; Herek & Glunt, 1993; Obear, 1991; Rankin, 1994; Simon, 1995), the developmental models reviewed in this paper, Herek's (1986) model of attitude function, and Harro's (1996) "Cycle of Liberation" each indicate that the development of ally attitudes and behaviors is facilitated by contact with other heterosexual allies. This argument has not been made before, at least not in any explicit way. This conclusion highlights the importance of allies making themselves visible, not only to people who are lesbian, gay, or bisexual, but also to their heterosexual colleagues. It also affirms Croteau and Lark's (1995) call for increased training about lesbian/gay/bisexual issues within graduate preparation programs, so that allies will begin to develop early in their career as student affairs professionals.

Certainly there are risks to doing ally work. However, like gay people who find most (although certainly not all) of their fear of negative consequences for coming out to be unfounded (Rhoads, 1995b), in most situations the reactions to ally behaviors will be more positive than negative. As Yamato (1996) has advised, it is important that allies not give up. More than 20 years ago, Williamson and Biggs (cited in Arminio & McEwen, 1996) called upon student affairs professionals to be agents of social change. The call for student affairs educators to affirm people of diverse identities has been well articulated in recent years. It is time to move beyond affirmation to advocacy (Hogan & Rentz, 1996).

Conclusion

This chapter has reviewed models of how people become allies to lesbians, gay men, and bisexual people, other models that may be extrapolated to this process, and strategies for being an ally. Common to the models, and to the strategies is the theme of the importance of being visible as an ally, both to support people who are lesbian, gay, or bisexual, and to aid the development of new allies.

Society seems to have successfully promulgated a pervasive myth that all good, moral, and responsible heterosexuals will condemn homosexuality and anyone who identifies as lesbian, gay, or bisexual. What else would explain the near universal fear people have during their coming-out process that they will be ostracized, abused, or otherwise assaulted (Obear, 1991)? The myth far too often represents reality, but it is not always accurate. Simply by making public their existence, allies challenge this hegemonic ideology and affirm that lesbian, gay, and bisexual existence is to be nurtured, not condemned.

References

Arminio, J. W., & McEwen, M. K. (1996). White connections of family, place, race, and ethnicity: Implications for student affairs. *Journal of College Student Development, 37,* 315-323.

Bertolino, J. A. (1992). *Being an ally: Assisting gay, lesbian and bisexual students.* Paper presented at the MACUHO Resident Advisor Conference, Shippensburg University, PA.

Blumenfield, W. J., & Raymond, D. (1988). *Looking at gay and lesbian life.* Boston: Beacon Press.

Bourassa, D. M., & Broido, E. M. (1993, March). *Educational interventions which address the developmental needs of lesbian, gay and bisexual students.* Paper presented at the annual meeting of the National Association for Women in Education, Seattle, WA.

Cass, V. C. (1979). Homosexual identity formation: A theoretical model. *Journal of Homosexuality, 4,* 219-235.

Cass, V. C. (1984). Homosexual identity formation: Testing a theoretical model. *Journal of Sex Research, 20,* 143-167.

Chojnacki, J. T., & Gelberg, S. (1995). The facilitation of a gay/lesbian/bisexual supporttherapy group by heterosexual counselors. *Journal of Counseling and Development, 73,* 352-354.

Clark, D. (1987). *The new loving someone gay.* Berkeley, CA: Celestial Arts.

Croteau, J. M., & Lark, J. 5. (1995). A qualitative investigation of biased and exemplary student affairs practice concerning lesbian, gay and bisexual issues. *Journal of College Student Development, 36,* 472-482.

Freire, P. (1994). *Pedagogy of the oppressed* (Rev. ed.). New York: Continuum. (Original work published 1970)

Geasler, M. J., Croteau, J. M., Heineman, C. J., & Edlund, C. J. (1995). A qualitative study of students' expression of change after attending panel presentations by lesbian, gay and bisexual speakers. *Journal of College Student Development, 36,* 483-491.

Green, S., Dixon, P., & Gold-Neil, V. (1993). The effects of a gay/lesbian panel discussion on college student attitudes toward gay men, lesbians, and person with AIDS (PWAs). *Journal of Sex Education & Therapy, 19,* 47-63.

Hardiman, R. (1979). *White identity development theory.* Unpublished manuscript, University of Massachusetts, Amherst.

Hardiman, R. (1982). *White identity development: A process-oriented model for describing the racial consciousness of White Americans.* Unpublished doctoral dissertation, University of Massachusetts, Amherst.

Hardiman, R., & Jackson, B. W. (1992). Racial identity development: Understanding racial dynamics in college classrooms and on campus. In M. Adams (Ed.), *Promoting diversity in college classrooms: Innovative responses for the curriculum, faculty and institutions.* (New Directions in Teaching and Learning, no. 52, pp. 21-37). San Francisco: Jossey-Bass.

Harro, R. (1996). Cycle of socialization. In M. Adams, P. Brigham, P. Dalpes, & L. Marchesani (Eds.), *Diversity and oppression: Conceptual frameworks* (p. 50). Dubuque, IA: Kendall/Hunt Publishing.

Herek, G. M. (1986). The instrumentality of attitudes: Toward a neofunctional theory. *Journal of Social Issues, 42,* 99-114.

Herek, G. M., & Capitanio, J. P. (1995). Black heterosexuals' attitudes toward lesbians and gay men in the United States. *Journal of Sex Research, 32* (2), 95-105.

Herek, G. M., & Glunt, E. K. (1993). Interpersonal contact and heterosexuals' attitudes toward gay men: Results from a national survey. *Journal of Sex Research, 30,* 239-244.

Hogan, T. L., & Rentz, A. L. (1996). Homophobia in the academy. *Journal of College Student Development, 37,* 309-314.

Hollingdale, L. A., & Kennedy, J. A. (1991, March). *Breaking the silence: How to support our lesbian/gay colleagues.* Paper presented at the meeting of the National Association of Women Deans, Administrators and Counselors, Boston, MA.

Jackson, B., & Hardiman, R. (1982). *Social identity development model.* Unpublished manuscript.

Katz, J. H. (1978). *White awareness: Handbook for anti-racism training.* Norman, OK: University of Oklahoma Press.

McAdam, D. (1988). *Freedom summer.* New York: Oxford University Press.

McIntosh, P. (1988). *White privilege and male privilege: A personal account of coming to see correspondences through work in women's studies.* Wellesley, MA: Wellesley College Center for Research on Women.

Obear, K. (1991). Homophobia. In N. J. Evans & V. A. Wall (Eds.), *Beyond tolerance: Gays, lesbians and bisexuals on campus* (pp. 39-66). Washington, DC: American College Personnel Association.

Pearlman, R. (1994, October 20). Brand defends GLB office decision. *Indiana Daily Student,* p.1, back page.

Ponterotto, J. G, & Pederson, P. B. (1993). *Multicultural aspects of counseling: Vol. 2. Preventing prejudice: A guide for counselors and educators.* Newbury Park, CA: Sage Publications.

Rankin, S. (1994). *The perspectives of heterosexual faculty and administrators toward gay men and lesbians.* Unpublished dissertation, The Pennsylvania State University.

Rapp, G. (1995, May). From the heart: Being an ally to the gay, lesbian, and bisexual community. *Campus Activities Programming,* 33-37.

Rhoads, R. A. (1995a, January 27). The campus climate for gay students who leave "the closet." *The Chronicle of Higher Education,* p. A56.

Rhoads, R. A. (1 995b). Learning from the coming-out experiences of college males. *Journal of College Student Development, 36,* 67-74.

Riddle, D. (1996). Riddle homophobia scale. In M. Adams, P. Brigham, P. Dalpes, & L. Marchesani (Eds.), *Social diversity and social justice: Gay, lesbian and bisexual oppression* (p. 31). Dubuque, IA: Kendall/Hunt Publishing.

Schreier, B. A. (1995). Moving beyond tolerance: A new paradigm for programming about homophobia/biphobia and heterosexism. *Journal of College Student Development, 36,* 19-26.

Simon, A. (1995). Some correlates of individuals' attitudes toward lesbians. *Journal of Homosexuality, 29,* 89-103.

Stein, A. (Ed.). (1993). *Sisters, sexperts, queers: Beyond the lesbian nation.* New York: Plume.

Washington, J., & Evans, N. J. (1991). Becoming an ally. In N. J. Evans & V. A. Wall (Eds.), *Beyond tolerance: Gays, lesbians and bisexuals on campus* (pp. 195-204). Washington, DC: American College Personnel Association.

Wimmer, A. (1994, October 4). Burton to meet with GLB leaders. *Indiana Daily Student.* pp. 1, back page.

Yamato, G. (1996). Something about the subject makes it hard to name. In M. Adams, P. Brigham, P. Dalpes, & L. Marchesani (Eds.), *Social diversity and social justice: Racism* (pp. 9-11). Dubuque, IA: Kendall/Hunt Publishing.

Chapter 16

ഇറ്റ

Navigating the Minefield: Sexual Orientation Issues and Campus Politics

MARK VON DESTINON, NANCY EVANS,
AND VERNON A. WALL

There is a growing need on college and university campuses to increase attention paid to lesbian, gay, bisexual, and transgender (LGBT) students and employees by providing personal and institutional support and by educating heterosexual students and staff about homosexuality (Evans & Levine, 1990). Doing so, however, can be controversial. Because of the heterosexist nature of U. S. society, the conservative religious and political values held by many campus constituencies, and personal discomfort with dealing publicly with issues related to sexual orientation, openly addressing the concerns of LGBT students and staff can be a difficult proposition. As LGBT groups become more visible and vocal on campus, staff and administrators may feel ill prepared to respond to their demands. Equally, members of student organizations who wish to bring about change in relation to sexual orientation issues may feel helpless.

The purpose of this chapter is to provide a framework that campus leaders can use to understand and respond to requests for support and action relating to sexual orientation issues and that students, faculty, and staff can use to manage change in this area. A combination of identity development and organizational decision-making theories are used to foster this understanding. The Probability of the Adoption of Change (PAC) model, developed by Creamer and Creamer (1990) is introduced as a means for assessing the likelihood of change on college campuses and as a guide for developing intervention strategies to facilitate change. Finally, recommendations are provided for LBGT individuals and groups, allies and advocates, and administrators who wish to more effectively navigate the political minefields associated with addressing sexual orientation issues on campus.

The Politics of Identity

A number of theorists and researchers have explored issues related to lesbian, gay, and bisexual identity development (Cass, 1979; Coleman, 1981-1982; D'Augelli, 1991, 1994; Elkins, 1986; Herdt, 1992, Miranda & Storms, 1989; Rhoads, 1994; Troiden, 1989). Development is presented in most models as linear; however, that is not necessarily the case. It is possible that a person may be politically at one level, socially at another, and personally at a third (Cain, 1991; McCarn & Fassinger, 1996). Additionally, identity appears to be fluid—with the environment, significant others, and life experiences affecting how persons identify at various points during their life (D'Augelli, 1994).

"Coming out" is a term used to described the process of and extent to which one identifies oneself as lesbian, gay, or bisexual (Crooks & Baur, 1987). As such, it is a major aspect of the identity development process. Coming out is not a one-time occurrence. It is an on-going process where disclosure of one's sexual orientation is made again and again, and which some people find more difficult than others (Evans & Broido, 1998). Although persons may consider themselves out and open about their sexual orientation, the heterosexual assumption that dominates society causes many people to overlook behaviors and expressions through which LGBT individuals communicate their identity. The more positive responses the disclosing person receives, the easier the coming out process can be. Yet, there are some people who never come out of the closet. They consider the risk just too great.

The coming out process is influenced by relationships with parents, environment, friends, role models, mental state, developmental stage, and patience (Troiden, 1989). Students affairs is grounded in conceptions of how students socially and intellectually interact within the context of the college environment. For many LGBT students, the coming-out process is a significant part of their college experience (Evans & Broido, 1998).

The developmental models of the coming-out process provide an understanding of the identity formation of individuals with same-sex feelings. The models do not describe a political process, yet developmental stages that are representative of personal crisis and growth are fraught with political overtones. As they move through the various stages of coming out, individuals' behaviors and statements are often highly political in nature.

We view the coming-out process as a political act in a number of ways. First, the process of disclosure is political by virtue of the fact that LGBT people make their presence known. This revelation makes others aware that not all people are heterosexual and often causes cognitive dissonance within the campus community. The reflections of two women interviewed as part of a study of the experiences of LGB students in residence halls (Evans & Broido, 1997) illustrate the varying impact disclosure can have. The first woman noted, "Most of the people that live on my floor that I've personally come out to, they've all been really supportive. There are some people on my floor that have suspicions and they've said things to friends of mine . . . People talk but they won't say anything right to your face. It's that kind of situation." The second woman viewed being out as leading to more negative reactions from others: "The more out you seem to be and active and proclaiming this, the more hostility you tend to meet from people."

Second, the process of coming out is political because persons who choose to come out begin to gain a greater level of political consciousness as a result of their self-awareness and the responses of others to their disclosure. Another student in the residence hall study noted that the harassment he experienced for being bisexual affirmed his commitment to activism. He stated, "I was more pissed off and committed to changing the entire university as a result of it."

Third, persons who decide to come out are also choosing to affiliate with a community based on their sexual orientation and they begin to construct an empathic world that is tolerant and nurturing of other differences. A fourth student interviewed as part of the residence hall study stated, "Being exposed to other LGBs really helped in making it possible for me to relay the good that I felt about being LGB in general."

Finally, the process of coming out may contribute to the discovery or further development of a political consciousness when the individual is faced with the legal constraints that society has placed on same-sex unions. Attempts to gain equal treatment under the law are political by nature. For example, a new professional seeking her first professional position as a residence hall director quickly discovered that very few institutions allow same-sex partners to live together in residence halls. As a political act, she limited her search to those that did.

LGBT students, faculty, and staff who push for change in the area of sexual orientation policy and issues are doing so from their individual level of identity development. For example, a student in a later stage of identity development might be comfortable and vocal to administrators while a student in an earlier stage may have concerns relating to being quoted (and therefore "outed") in the student newspaper. Student affairs professionals working to eliminate various forms of oppression on the college and university campus must keep in mind the role of identity development, as well as other aspects of cognitive and psychosocial development, on individuals with and for whom they are working.

Examples from the study of the experiences of LGB students living in residence halls noted earlier (Evans & Broido, 1997) illustrate the interaction of identity development and political activism. In this study, 20 LGB students at a large eastern university participated in in-depth interviews concerning the impact of their living environment on their identity development, perceptions of college, and involvement in college life. Students who were in the early stages of coming out were very reluctant to join the very political LGBT student organization or to attend rallies and marches. Even the seemingly simple political act of displaying a pin was difficult for one student. She reflected, "The hardest thing was to put a pin on my bag . . . If somebody's walking behind me on campus . . . I think that they are going to see it. I'm not really comfortable with it completely."

Another woman in the study reported having been very involved in LGB organizations as a sophomore. She noted that her grades fell and that she felt the two events were related. Speaking of her current involvement, she reported, "I've actually started taking some stuff off my door, because if you would have looked at my door, it looked like I was a lesbian feminist and that's it. And there's much more to my world than that." Now as a senior, this woman seemed to be entering the identity integration stage of Cass's (1979) model where she viewed other aspects of her life as being as important as sexual orientation. The same woman also disclosed that conflicts about newly discovered attractions to men had led her to pull back from being a part of the LGBT Speaker's Bureau. She stated, "Right now I don't feel like I can [be part of the Speaker's Bureau]. I don't feel like I'm in the right mind-set because I'm dealing with all these issues with men right now, which I haven't dealt with for like three or four years, so now everything's evolving again." This statement supports D'Augelli's (1994) argument that identity is constantly evolving. Educators and administrators must keep this fluidity and its concurrent psychological impact in mind when interpreting the changing level of involvement of students (and staff) in LGBT advocacy.

Another student related the negative effects of his activism: "I knew that everyone on the floor knew about me . . . It was a nerve-racking time because I was constantly living in fear . . . I was at a high point in terms of my visible outness and activism, so I decided I didn't want to go through that anymore and I moved off campus." However, at the time of the interview this student was a candidate for a Resident Assistant position because he wanted to make a difference in the lives of others. He reflected that "knowing what I know now gives me strength in terms of how to handle a situation." This student's experiences suggest that events that may be stressful at one point in development can provide opportunities for learning that encourage the development of a more confident sense of self. This more secure identity will, at a later time, enable the student to work more effectively for change within the institution.

Political Decision Making

The decision-making model developed by Baldridge (1971) describes decision-making in academic institutions as a political process. As we discuss the issue of sexual identity within the academic structure in this chapter, it seems appropriate to use the political model to define the struggles for acceptance and a place at the table for LGBT students, faculty, staff, and alumni.

Decisions surrounding the issues of LBGT people are political in nature due to the legislation pertaining to, and social acceptance of, same-sex relationships. Policy decisions, which are also seen as political in nature, provide a foundation to influence the acceptance and inclusion of sexual orientation on our campuses. Baldridge's model is based on assumptions about policy making within a political decision-making process in six areas: Prevalent Inactivity, Interest Group Pressures, Fluid Participation, Conflict, Limitations on Formal Authority, and External Interest Groups. A review of Baldridge's assumptions provides evidence of the opportunity to influence the political decision-making processes.

Prevalent Inactivity is the assumption that not everyone is included in or even interested in the decision-making process. This level of apathy results in less participation, thereby allowing decisions to be made by small interest groups. There are several ways in which the concept of prevalent inactivity affects decision-making about LGBT issues on college campuses. Societal pressures are such that students and staff are often afraid to reveal their sexual identity. Their inactivity, sometimes due to fear of identification, may mislead administrators into believing that, "it's not an issue here." Awareness of prevalent inactivity on the part of groups and individuals needs to be considered in decision-making for campus governance. What may not appear to be an issue this year may be a crisis next year.

Interest Group Pressures refer to the actions of stakeholders within the political process. There are often strong feelings by committed groups either for or against the acceptance and inclusion of LGBT interests. One example of these conflicting pressures is the LGBT student group that seeks and receives funding from the student government only to face public opposition after the fact from right-wing student groups. The effects of interest group pressures may be mitigated through environmental scanning, a technique by which institutions survey "the campus and community for groups that may have an impact" on the organization (Woodard & von Destinon, 1994, p. 73). Knowing the interest groups on the horizon helps decision-makers to be proactive when issues arise.

Fluid Participation suggests the way in which participants move in and out of the decision-making process. This movement, the result of changing populations and priorities, affects the focus, pressure, and continuity of political scrutiny. This pattern is especially important in the collegiate model where one group of students graduates each year and another enters. Continuity of social activism for LGBT issues at the collegiate level is dependent upon the foundation that LGBT students are able to establish and maintain. Such a foundation provides a focal point for continuity and permits incoming students ease in connecting to others like themselves. The importance of institutionally sanctioned LGBT student organizations and support services can not be stressed enough.

Conflict is seen as natural to the process of decisionmaking and may be an asset in promoting healthy change if all parties have the opportunity to voice their concerns. The caution here is not to let the conflict undermine the process. This dynamic often occurs on campuses when disagreement over policy decisions turn into attacks on character, threats, and occasionally violent acts. These tendencies are particularly problematic with regard to sexual orientation concerns given the emotionally volatile nature of the issues. However, it must be remembered that some degree of conflict contributes to the growth of understanding through the resolution process.

The assumption of *Limitations on Formal Authority* recognizes that decisions are the result of compromises and represent those interests or conditions affecting the issue. One example of this principle is those institutions that create a gray area of acceptance by adding sexual orientation to their non-discrimination statements even though the community, state, and national legislation does not extend the same recognition. Thus, the ability of the campus to affect change on LGBT issues in the face of political scrutiny is often compromised.

External Interest Groups are those external agencies attempting to influence the policy-making process. Examples of such groups are state legislators who threaten funding cuts based upon institutional actions recognizing sexual orientation or religious groups outside the institution who agitate for or against a specific issue.

Awareness of these assumptions can help administrators begin to understand the complexity of sexual orientation issues and work to "trouble shoot" potential reactions. Students, faculty, and staff attempting to initiate change can also use knowledge of these assumptions to maneuver in campus politics with better understanding and savvy, regardless of the institutional size or type.

Each of the six assumptions in the political decision-making model both influence and are influenced by the level of development of the individuals involved. The level of individuals' personal awareness, their willingness to disclose, their ability to lead, their fear of retaliation, and many other factors each weave themselves into the political decision-making paradigm. College administrators must be aware not only of the level of awareness that students, faculty, and staff possess in relation to sexual orientation issues but also the impact their level of awareness has on their behaviors and feelings during the political process of change.

The Probability of the Adoption of Change Model

Individuals interested in addressing sexual orientation issues on campus face many barriers. Before investing significant amounts of time and energy attempting to create change, it is helpful to have a framework to assess the likelihood of success and to provide guidance in structuring interventions. The Probability of the Adoption of Change (PAC) model (Creamer & Creamer, 1990) is a useful tool for analyzing the potential of change occurring and for developing strategies to increase the odds for a positive outcome.

The PAC model is based on qualitative and quantitative analyses of planned change in higher education (Creamer & Creamer, 1990). In this model, Creamer and Creamer identify nine key variables within an organization that influence the potential for change: leadership, championship, top-level support, circumstances, value compatibility, idea comprehensibility, practicality, advantage probability, and strategies. Three of these variables—leadership, championship, and top-level support (collectively referred to as superintendence variables)—were found to play a major role in determining the outcomes of change-oriented interventions (Creamer, D. & Creamer, E., 1986; Creamer, E. & Creamer, D., 1986; 1988; 1989). These three variables, in turn, influenced the other six variables in the PAC model.

Leadership refers to the activities of the director of the project and the roles this person plays in initiating change. The involvement of successful leaders includes: (a) developing a clear vision, (b) securing support from top-level administrators, (c) recruiting key people, including a project coordinator, to be involved in the initiative, (d) assuring that necessary financial and human resources are available to carry out the project, (e) empowering the project coordinator with the responsibility to carry out the initiative, (f) obtaining support for the project across the system, and (g) assuring that support for the project is maintained throughout the life of the project (Creamer, E. & Creamer, D., 1986). Creamer and Creamer (1990) noted that "successful projects in student affairs were found to have a clearly recognizable leader with strong personal identification to the project" (p. 184).

Leadership for projects focusing on LGBT issues offers some unique challenges. On most college campuses, no administrator is specifically responsible for addressing the needs of LGBT students. And on the small minority of campuses that do have an LGBT support office, many are staffed by entry-level professionals with little credibility on campus. Leadership may be provided by student affairs staff who view their role as serving the needs of all students, including those who are LGBT. In other instances, LGBT students provide leadership themselves, sometimes with the support and encouragement of LGBT faculty and staff. Too often, however, no one is willing to take on a major leadership role and issues remain unaddressed. Creamer and Creamer's (1990) model would certainly suggest that identifying an individual who is knowledgeable about LGBT issues and willing to invest time and energy in making change happen for the LGBT population is a crucial first step in any organized effort.

Championship is an advocacy role played by an individual or group who favors the project during its initial stages of development and has responsibility for seeing that the goals of the project are implemented. Champions are particularly important in obtaining support for the project throughout the institution. Most often, advocacy comes from the LGBT community and its allies. Unfortunately, fear of discrimination or harassment can stop many LGBT individuals from taking an active role in championing LGBT-related initiatives (D'Augelli, 1989). Senior-level staff and tenured faculty often are in the best position to take on the role of advocate (Rankin, 1998). LGBT student organizations can also play a part in raising awareness and pushing for needed change on campus (D'Augelli, 1989). A "top-down, bottom-up" strategy involving both senior-level faculty and staff and students can be particularly effective in championing new initiatives (Rankin, 1998).

Campus-wide commissions, committees, or task forces created to advise the president or other senior-level administrators on diversity issues, especially groups focusing specifically on LGBT issues, can be major forces for initiating change on campus. Such committees are generally charged with examining the campus climate and recommending necessary steps to improve the environment for LGBT students and staff. As such, their role is to serve as advocates for change. While few institutions currently have this type of oversight group, advocating for the creation of an advisory committee can be an important first step in creating conditions for advocacy and change regarding LGBT issues.

Top-level support refers to the role played by the chief executive officer or institutional governing body. Institutional leaders can make or break a project by actively supporting or opposing it. Gaining the support of the chief executive officer usually takes a coordinated and sustained effort on the part of LGBT staff and faculty, LGBT students, and allies. Relating the needs and concerns of LGBT students and staff to the mission and goals of the institution can be an effective strategy. For instance, support for a "Safe Zone" program at Iowa State University was obtained by stressing the importance of a safe environment for recruiting and retaining students, important goals frequently stated by the ISU president. National educational reports calling for creation of inclusive and welcoming learning communities (for example, Association of American Colleges and Universities, 1995; Boyer, 1990) can also be used as leverage to gain the attention of senior administrators. Many campuses are facing increased pressure to respond to multicultural concerns on campus. Demonstrating that the issues facing LGBT students and staff are similar to those of other nondominant groups can be effective when seeking equitable treatment. For example, D'Augelli (1989) reported that an effort to get sexual orientation included in the nondiscrimination policy at Penn State was successful in part because it built on the gains of other minority groups on campus.

Once the three superintendence variables are in place, individuals playing these key leadership roles need to attend to the other six variables that the PAC model includes. *Circumstances*, such as felt need and timing, must favor implementation of change. For instance, a series of "gay bashings" in one college town provided leverage for the creation of a joint campus-community task force on anti-gay violence, a project that had been under consideration for some time. On the other hand, pushing for domestic partner benefits at a time when a university is being scrutinized by a very conservative legislature is an initiative likely to fail.

Value compatibility refers to the extent to which values underlying a project reflect the values of the institution as a whole. One Catholic women's college justified support of a lesbian and bisexual student organization by referring to its commitment to social justice expounded in its statement of Catholic identity. The intention of the Safe Zone project at Iowa State to create a safe and welcoming community was promoted as being compatible with the institution's overall goals of providing a learning community inclusive of all students.

Idea comprehensibility "refers to the degree of clarity, simplicity, and timing of the idea" (Creamer & Creamer, 1990, p. 183). Ideas must be clearly stated to all constituents. Short proposals that address specific issues in a straightforward and politically neutral way are more likely to gain approval than lengthy treatises heavy on ideology and jargon.

The *practicality* of projects must be demonstrated. Leaders must show that the resources are available to carry out a project. Proposals should include a detailed budget, an indication of where financial resources will be obtained, and a discussion of who will be involved in carrying out the project. Having commitments for staffing and financial support prior to submitting proposals for new projects can eliminate an argument typically used to block change—a lack of resources.

Advantage probability "refers to the perception of demonstrable gains, the likelihood of achievement of stated goals, and the probability of solving vexing problems many people feel" (Creamer & Creamer, 1990, p. 183). Showing that a project will benefit the institution and truly address felt needs is very helpful in gaining support. For instance, after a series of incidents on one college campus in which attacks of various types were made against Jewish students, African American students, and LGBT students, representatives from various multicultural student organizations came together to propose a public forum to demonstrate their unity in the face of oppression. Because their project addressed a deeply felt need for a strong statement in support of multiculturalism and anti-oppression on campus, administrators quickly approved it.

Strategies include the steps necessary to implement a project once it is approved. Specifying goals, action steps, and evaluation plans ahead of time creates a sense of confidence that the leaders of a project have thought through what will be required to implement it and are competent to carry it out. Collaborative efforts in which the support and assistance of individuals from various offices are secured are particularly effective in assuring that a project will come to fruition. A proposal submitted under the signatures of many different campus officials is much harder to turn down than a proposal submitted by one person alone. The Safe Zone Project at Iowa State is again a good example. In 1996, a proposal for funding such a project was submitted by the LGBT Student Services director and was rejected. In 1997, the proposal was resubmitted by a campus-wide advisory group and bore the names of 17 different individuals representing every major unit in student affairs. It was approved with no questions asked.

Recommendations

Issues surrounding sexual orientation and the acceptance of sexual differences can be complex and frustrating for students, faculty, and staff as well as for campus leaders. In this section we provide some guidelines for negotiating the difficult and stressful arena of LGBT change agentry and advocacy.

Individuals and Groups

The following guidelines are suggested for students, both individuals and groups, who are committed to creating change on campus:

1. *Choose battles strategically.* There are many issues of concern to LGBT people on college campuses. Each year groups have to choose specific issues on which to focus their energies. This choice has to be strategic. As previously mentioned, there are institutions that add sexual orientation to their affirmative action disclaimer, in spite of the fact that federal, state, and local laws do not recognize it. Strategically, a campus group may choose to focus on a less comprehensive issue upon which they would have greater control and impact in order to actually contribute to change for the human condition rather than joust with the federal and state giants.

2. *Know the decision-making process of the campus and use it to benefit the group.* To accomplish this goal, students must learn the five P's of their institution: policies, procedures, politics, people, and power structure. These are the factors that both enter into and affect the decision making process. Which would be more effective, student petitions presented to the Governing Board, a rally on the mall, or a sit-in at the library? Each requires an expenditure of energy to accomplish and which action will have the greater impact on campus decision-making will vary by campus structure and culture.

3. *Plan and be organized.* Planning is addressed in the first two guidelines. The admonition here is to think through the possible actions and possible consequences. Individuals and student groups often forget that organization is the key to planning and successful completion of any project.

4. *Identify internal and external allies*. The stereotypical LBGT underground has always consciously or unconsciously made these connections. This guideline suggests that identification be made a conscious process. It is important to know who one's friends and opponents are and remember that the old adage, "politics makes strange bedfellows" (Bartlett & Beck, 1980, p. 603), applies especially in activism.

5. *Know the law*. This includes the rules and regulations for the institution as well as the federal, state, and local laws and the legislative process. LGBT activists need to be cognizant of the rules and the possible consequences of their actions. Part of dissent and protest is the expectation that dissenters not only know the consequences of their actions but are willing to face the sanctions resulting from their actions in order to make their point.

6. *Be aware of the personal consequences of activism*. Personal consequences may differ greatly from the legal or administrative consequences. This guideline looks not at a legal charge of unlawful assembly and resultant penalties, but the personal consequences of legal fees and public recognition and acknowledgment of an association with LGBT issues. Many times students are unpleasantly surprised when their families, either local or at a distance, learn of their sexual orientation following a public review of a campus action.

Allies and Advocates

As an activist, it is important to develop "allies" who understand the issues surrounding sexual orientation and the acceptance of sexual differences. Campus communities benefit from the contributions of students and employees who are at peace with themselves, who are comfortable and confident in their identities and who can participate in the campus community without fear. Because the roots of discrimination are grounded in fear and divisiveness, allies can help. In Chapter 15, Broido discussed the steps that individuals can take to become allies to the LGBT community.

Administrators

As mentioned earlier, campus administrators are a very important component in the change process relating to sexual orientation issues.

Broido's recommendations for allies combined with the guidelines for individuals and groups produces the following guidelines for heterosexual administrators who must develop, deliver, and support the institutional response:

1. *Look before leaping.* The concept presented here is one that is intended to transcend the traditional management philosophy of planning before acting. Looking before leaping requests that administrators take some extra time to examine exactly what is going on in a given situation before making a decision. This strategy draws from symbolic interaction theory and asks that the question of "What's going on here?" be considered (Freeman, 1980). What may appear to the administration to be a simple question over appropriate use of a facility may be a freedom of assembly issue or one of equitable treatment of campus groups. Looking deeper into the problem at hand may reveal an LBGT student group or interest of which the administration had not previously been aware. The civil rights of the people involved, the developmental stages of those individuals, and the political ramifications of the decision all need to be carefully weighed.

2. *Apologize when necessary.* Although common courtesy dictates that people politely express their regrets for misdeeds, administrators often do not think about doing that. The myriad of issues surrounding LGBT students and staff are interwoven with the civil rights and political correctness movements. Ignorance of an item of cultural taboo or tradition is not uncommon. A lot of damage can be repaired or crises averted by a simple statement of regret followed by a request for cooperation and understanding.

3. *Personalize.* Meet with groups. The dynamics of any exchange becomes more manageable when it is between two people rather than two organizations. Be willing to meet with LGBT student groups and affirm their self-worth. A dismissal of their issues based on an assumption of a lack of interest by the student population may not be the best course of action. Meeting with a student group and showing a willingness to learn their names and work with them gives evidence that, whether or not their request can be honored, they are viewed as significant.

4. *Seek education*. This suggestion encourages administrators to think about things that, as heterosexuals, they may never have thought about before, but rather accepted as fact. Is sexual orientation included in the institution's affirmative action disclaimer? Are domestic partnerships recognized by the institution? If the institution's insurance carrier does not recognize them, are they recognized in the residence halls? What are the issues that LGBT students and staff might be interested in and why are those issues important to that community? Administrators do not have to become conversant about the details of every issue. At the same time, they should not ignore the existence of these issues and hope that LGBT activism never arises on campus. There are numerous court cases where rules of law have been established by precedence. Administrators must not assume that their institution is the first one ever to be faced with a particular LGBT issue.

5. *Know the law*. This recommendation is the same as that for individuals and groups, albeit with a different twist. The admonition to activists is to be aware of the consequences of their actions and to accept the penalties as part of their protest. For administrators, knowing the law means not allowing circumstances to escalate through omission or ignorance that could precipitate a lengthy court action and/or unnecessary negative publicity for the institution.

6. *Explain one's thought process and decisions to groups*. "Because I said so" is not an adequate explanation. Grant individuals and groups the courtesy of an opportunity to understand the decision by providing a rationale for one's decision. They may not agree with it, but agreement is not the goal. Understanding the factors influencing the decision is the goal.

Conclusion

It is the responsibility of institutions and student affairs personnel to support, encourage, and protect students, regardless of sexual orientation. While sexual orientation issues can be a minefield, we hope that these guidelines can help LGBT students, faculty, and staff as well as student affairs professionals to provide environments of inclusion, appreciation, and empowerment for all students. Decision-making is never an easy process and the political realities of the decisions on college campuses are not without dissent. Compassion and understanding, as well as the acceptance of the relevance of LGBT issues, will help to insure that the politics of institutional decision-making are conducted in an atmosphere of mutual respect.

References

Association of American Colleges and Universities. (1995). *The drama of diversity and democracy: Higher education and American commitments.* Washington, DC: Author.

Baldridge, J. (1971). *Academic governance: Research on institutional politics and decision making.* Berkeley, CA: McCuthan.

Bartlett, J., & Beck, E. M. (Eds.). (1980). *Bartlett's quotations.* Boston: Little, Brown, & Co.

Boyer, E. (1990). *Campus life: In search of community.* Princeton, NJ: The Carnegie Foundation for the Advancement of Teaching.

Cain, R. (1991). Sigma management and gay identity development. *Social Work, 36,* 67-73.

Cass, V. C. (1979). Homosexual identity formation: A theoretical model. *Journal of Homosexuality, 4,* 219-235.

Coleman, E. (1981-1982). Developmental stages of the coming out process. *Journal of Homosexuality, 7,* 31-43.

Creamer, D. G., & Creamer, E. G. (1986). Applying a model of planned change to program innovation in student affairs. *Journal of College Student Personnel, 27,* 19-26.

Creamer, D. G., & Creamer, E. G. (1990). Use of a planned change model to modify student affairs programs. In D. G. Creamer & Associates, *College student development: Theory and practice for the 1990s.* Alexandria, VA: American College Personnel Association.

Creamer, E. G., & Creamer, D. G. (1986). The role of leaders and champions in planned change in student affairs. *Journal of College Student Personnel, 27,* 431-437.

Creamer, E. G., & Creamer, D. G. (1988). Predicting successful organizational change: Case studies. *Journal of College Student Development, 29,* 4-11.

Creamer, E. G., & Creamer, D. G. (1989). Testing a model of planned change across student affairs and curriculum reform projects. *Journal of College Student Development, 30,* 27-34.

Crooks, R., & Baur, L. (1987). *Our sexuality* (3rd ed.) Menlo Park, CA: Benjamin/Cummings.

D'Augelli, A. R. (1989). Lesbians and gay men on campus: Visibility, empowerment, and educational leadership. *Peabody Journal of Education, 66,* 124-142.

D'Augelli, A. R. (1991). Gay men in college: Identity processes and adaptations. *Journal of College Student Development, 32,* 140-146.

D'Augelli, A. R. (1994). Identity development and sexual orientation: Toward a model of lesbian, gay, and bisexual identity development. In E. J. Trickett, R. Watts, & D. Birman (Eds.), *Human diversity: Perspectives on people in context* (pp. 312-333). San Francisco: Jossey-Bass.

Elkins, J. (1986, April). *Coming out: The five stages of death.* Paper presented at the conference of the American College Personnel Association, New Orleans.

Evans, N. J., & Broido, E. (1997). [The experiences of lesbian, gay, and bisexual students in college residence halls]. Unpublished raw data.

Evans, N. J., & Broido, E. (1998, March). *Coming out on campus: Negotiation, meaning-making, challenges, supports.* Paper presented at the conference of the American College Personnel Association, St. Louis, MO.

Evans, N. J., & Levine, H. (1990). Perspectives on sexual orientation. In L. V. Moore (Ed.), *Evolving theoretical perspectives on students* (New Directions for Student Services, no. 51, pp. 49-58). San Francisco: Jossey-Bass.

Freeman, C. R. (1980). Phenomenological sociology and ethnomethodology. In J. D. Douglas (Ed.), *Introduction to the sociologies of everyday life* (pp. 158-175). Boston: Allyn & Bacon.

Herdt, G. (1992). *Gay culture in America: Essays from the field.* Boston: Beacon Press.

McCarn, S. R., & Fassinger, R. E. (1996). Revisioning sexual minority identity formation: A new model of lesbian identity and its implications for counseling and research. *Counseling Psychologist, 24,* 508-534.

Miranda, J., & Storms, M. (1989). Psychological adjustments of lesbians and gay men. *Journal of Counseling and Development, 68,* 41-45.

Rankin, S. (1998). Campus climate for lesbian, gay, bisexual, and transgendered students, faculty, and staff: Assessment and strategies for change. In R. Sanlo (Ed.), *Working with lesbian, gay, and bisexual students: A guide for administrators and faculty* (pp. 277-284). Westport, CT: Greenwood.

Rhoads, R. (1994). *Coming out in college: The struggle for a queer identity.* Westport, CT: Bergin & Garvey.

Troiden, R. (1989). The formation of homosexual identities. *Journal of Homosexuality, 17,* 43-73.

Woodard, D. B., & von Destinon, M. (1994). Identifying and working with campus constituencies. In Barr, M. (Ed.), *Handbook for student affairs administration* (pp. 69-82). San Francisco: Jossey-Bass.

Chapter 17

୧୬ୠ

Parting Thoughts: An Agenda for Addressing Sexual Orientation Issues on Campus

NANCY J. EVANS AND VERNON A. WALL

The preceding chapters in this book suggest that progress has been made during the last decade with regard to addressing lesbian, gay, bisexual, and transgender (LGBT) concerns on college campuses. Institutions are more aware of the issues and have begun to publicly address them. Student services staff more regularly provide support, education, and advocacy to address the needs of LGBT students, and the complexity of issues facing a diverse LGBT population is being acknowledged. But LGBT advocates should not be lulled by current successes into believing that LGBT people are now accepted and that their issues are a standard part of the diversity agenda of colleges and universities. Much more work must be done if LGBT people are to be

We wish to thank Houston Dougharty, Associate Dean for Student Services, University of Puget Sound, and Mark von Destinon, Dean of Student Services, Cochise College, for their contributions to this chapter.

fully included and equitably treated on college campuses and in society. In this concluding chapter, we reflect on the progress made to date and offer our thoughts concerning issues that must still be addressed, strategies that appear promising for furthering LGBT advocacy, and cautions to consider when engaging in this work

Institutional Issues

Three words seem to capture the institution-wide concerns of LGBT persons on campus: visibility, normalcy, and equity. LGBT issues are receiving greater visibility as more faculty, staff, and students take the risk of openly identifying as lesbian, gay, bisexual, or transgender and actively work to increase the awareness of institutions about the needs and concerns of LGBT people. More heterosexual allies are openly joining their LGBT colleagues in this effort. Issues are being raised in administrative board rooms, at meetings of Boards of Trustees, and in faculty governance meetings. A student affairs administrator recently commented that when she arrived at her institution five years ago, she never heard the words "lesbian, gay, or bisexual" in an upper level administrative meeting. Recently, however, because of the activism of LGBT students and the positive advocacy of LGBT staff and allies on her campus, questions are now being raised and administrators, including her president, are asking for more information about LGBT issues.

Visibility can be created using a number of avenues. A university-wide advisory committee on LGBT concerns can be a powerful vehicle for keeping issues before individuals in positions of power. Such a committee might authorize or conduct an LGBT climate study to highlight the experiences of LGBT people on campus and provide leverage for needed interventions. It might also promote educational symposiums or invite speakers to campus to raise visibility. Review of existing policies and procedures could also be undertaken with recommendations forwarded to appropriate administrators. Annual reports to the president or Board of Trustees would certainly help to educate these individuals and keep issues in their awareness.

Curricular integration is key factor for increasing LGBT visibility. In the last decade we have seen diversity enter the curriculum. Non-Western ideas are being presented and studied along with those of Western societies. The culture and concerns of the diverse racial and ethnic populations found in the United States are being examined. The history, literature, art, culture, psychology, and sociology of LGBT people must be considered along with those of other nondominant populations. Lack of information is the primary cause of fear, hatred, and inability to accept people who are different. Education will help to dispel the misinformation individuals have acquired and will contribute to the intergenerational transfer of learning that helps to remove threat and fear. The college student of today is the PTA parent of tomorrow—and also the local school board member or college administrator. The power of individual knowledge and experience is greater than the rantings of vitriolic fanatics.

With visibility comes the threat of backlash. The more attention a particular population receives, the more threatened are those who fear that population. Certainly this dynamic has been consistently apparent in the movement for racial and ethnic equality. It is no less present as LGBT people become more active and forceful in advocating for their rights. Conservative legislators will threaten the withholding of funds for universities that have an active LGBT presence, fundamentalist groups will picket LGBT events, letters to the editor will decry the teaching of "pornographic" material, and so on. Universities must be prepared to respond to these attacks in a rational and educational manner. It is important to recognize that such attacks, while distressing, do garner attention and provide the opportunity for "teachable" moments. In addition, extremists often "hang themselves" with their incoherent and violent rhetoric.

Not only must LGBT issues become more visible on campus, but they must also come to be viewed as legitimate. The existence of an LGBT resource center with appropriate staff to serve the needs of the LGBT population on campus is one sign of the acceptance of LGBT people as an important constituency on campus. In addition, promotional materials discussing the services provided by the college or university should include services targeted toward LGBT individuals along with those designed for honors students, women, fraternity and sorority members, and so forth.

That LGBT people are "normal" is certainly underscored when students are taught and advised by LGBT individuals who are open about their identities. It is also reinforced when students live with an open LGBT roommate, work with an LGBT peer, or collaborate on a group assignment with someone who is LGBT. Research consistently supports the finding that individuals who know someone who is LGBT are much more likely to be supportive of the rights of LGBT people and to become allies (see D'Augelli & Rose, 1990; Herek & Glunt, 1993; Malaney, Williams, & Geller, 1997; Simoni, 1996; Wells & Franken, 1987).

We must continue to work to create environments in which students, faculty, and staff feel safe and comfortable being who they are. One vehicle for indicating the safety of a campus for LGBT people is a safe zone project. Such a project provides the opportunity for individuals and offices on campus to display a sticker conveying the message that they are supportive of LGBT issues and people; in effect that they are "safe zones" in an otherwise homophobic environment. A formal evaluation of the safe zone project at Iowa State University (Dougharty, Evans, Nelson, & Lund, 1998) suggested that such an effort was significant in providing the support needed for many faculty, staff, and students to identify themselves to others as LGBT.

If others are to assume that the concerns of LGBT people are worthy of attention and that LGBT people play an important role in the life of the campus, then LGBT individuals and their allies must resist any temptation to be apologetic about their expectation to be included "at the table." Self-confidence and a refusal to back down in the face of criticism or foot dragging will slowly win over those who are uncertain and lack knowledge of the issues. Appearing calm, rational, and persistent, while at the same time presenting well documented arguments, does eventually convince those who are less invested in the position they hold (Barr & Keating, 1979).

Equity is the third goal we must achieve. On an overwhelming majority of campuses, LGBT people still do not have the rights or protections accorded to every other individual. As Boden, Leppo, and Stenta clearly noted in their chapter, domestic partner benefits, particularly insurance benefits, are offered by only a few institutions. In effect, the lack of such benefits means that LGBT faculty and staff are compensated significantly less that their heterosexual counterparts. In addition, on many campuses no policies are in place to protect LGBT students, faculty, or staff from harassment or discrimination. Employment policies fail to consider LGBT people a protected population. Little is done to prevent violence or to prosecute perpetrators or crimes against LGBT people.

On a positive note, we must acknowledge that in recent years the courts have often favored equal treatment for LGBT people. While legal battles are long, expensive, and hard-fought, LGBT issues are gaining visibility and the rights of LGBT individuals are supported more often than they are dismissed. If they do not voluntarily promote equal rights and policies for LGBT students and staff, institutions of higher education may be forced to do so by the courts. The issue could eventually come down to money. Either colleges and universities will comply with legal mandates or they will not receive federal financial support.

In the meantime, constant pressure must be placed on institutions to put into place policies and practices that insure equal treatment for LGBT people. In addition to providing a consistent message that such efforts are "the right thing to do," information about the effects of such policies at other institutions and presentation of research findings related to costs, outcomes, and the impact of inequitable practices on individual lives must be regularly shared with those in positions of power. Often, individual stories can convey the importance of such policies when the numbers presented in quantitative studies are ignored. Testimony before university policy-making committees can be persuasive.

On a cautionary note, LGBT people and their allies must not be lulled into complacency by small victories. It should never be assumed that university administrators "get it." It will take several generations of enlightened and committed faculty, staff, and students to "hard-wire" the inclusion of LGBT issues in the academy.

Student Affairs Issues

As the chapters in the Student Affairs section indicate, the issues facing the student affairs profession as it attempts to address the needs of LGBT students are numerous. As students become more active in advocating for their rights and as staff educate themselves in this area, the task can often appear overwhelming. In addition, in too many cases, student affairs initiatives are built around the interests and commitment of one or a few student affairs staff. As a result, there is a lack of consistency in offerings from year to year as staff come and go or those who are working on the issues lose energy or become disillusioned when their efforts are only moderately successful.

To become an integral and ongoing part of the student affairs program, LGBT issues must be seen in the larger context of the student affairs mission and goals. Fostering human growth and development needs to be the foundation upon which all student affairs programs and services are built. To accomplish this goal, individual differences must be respected, valued, and addressed. Sexual orientation must always be included among the differences to which we are sensitive.

Effectively addressing LGBT concerns within student affairs must occur at several levels. These include policy, provision of resources, programming, individual support, and staff selection and development. A comprehensive program that will truly make a difference in creating an inclusive environment for LGBT individuals must attend to all of these areas simultaneously and with the total commitment of the student affairs division.

Student affairs policies are usually the ones with which students are most familiar. Even if university policy is noninclusive of LGBT people, policies related to housing, student organizations, campus safety, and other areas under the purview of student life can send an important message to students about the rights and responsibilities of all students. Policies should clearly indicate that all students have equal rights. LGBT students should be assured of their right to form advocacy groups, support groups, and social organizations and to have these groups recognized, funded, and publicized in the same manner as other student organizations.

Policies should also indicate that the safety and comfort of students are of paramount concern. For example, room change policies should be written to allow students to move immediately if they are living in an environment in which they are being harassed or feel unsafe. Policies concerning the establishment or funding of student organizations should be sensitive to the need of LGBT groups to keep their membership lists private to insure the safety and comfort of their members. Policies that protect the victims of hate crimes by omitting their names from published crime reports should be instituted. Policies should also inform students that acts of victimization, harassment, and discrimination will be addressed quickly and publicly.

All student affairs policies must be widely disseminated to all students. Student handbooks, pre-enrollment information, orientation presentations, and other public vehicles for reaching students must clearly and succinctly inform students that the environment of the college or university is a humane one in which all people will be treated with respect and that violations of these policies will not be tolerated. Then student affairs staff must see that these policies are strictly enforced. Too often, policies are on the books but are not clearly presented to students or backed up with action when violated. As a result, a message is sent that the student affairs division may pay lip service to equality but really doesn't mean it when enforcement becomes necessary.

Provision of resources is particularly important to show support for LGBT students. LGBT resource centers with well-stocked libraries in convenient but non-public places provide information for questioning students, students interested in researching LGBT topics for classes or personal interest, and students just looking for reading material featuring LGBT characters and topics. Resource centers can also be useful in providing background material when preparing proposals or advocating for services for LGBT students. Centers might also provide meeting space for LGBT groups or informal lounges in which students could congregate to relax and socialize. Ideally, centers should be staffed by an LGBT coordinator who can provide support, short-term counseling, referral services, and outreach to the LGBT community and the entire campus. Resource centers obviously require a major commitment on the part of student services in the form of financial support, facilities, and staffing. Establishment of such centers needs to be a high priority to insure comprehensive attention to the needs of LGBT students and staff.

Electronic listservs and websites that address LGBT issues and provide information about services, programs, off-campus events, and national news of interest to LGBT individuals are becoming a major vehicle for reaching out to LGBT individuals who may be reluctant to openly seek advice and information. They also help to connect the LGBT community and provide a forum for discussion of current issues and concerns on and off-campus. Providing computer support and space is a fairly easy way to make a significant impact on the quality of life for LGBT students. Making sure that students have access to the internet is important on all campuses; it has some particular benefits for LGBT students who often fear accessing information in any other way.

Student affairs programming must target both LGBT students and heterosexual students. LGBT students need to know that their concerns and interests warrant attention when programming decisions are made. LGBT speakers, entertainers, and artists should be considered as part of the regular speakers series, performing arts programming, or popular entertainment series. Much too often, programming such acts is left to the LGBT student organization and occurs only as part of Coming Out Week or Pride Week events. In addition to providing affirmation to LGBT students, including LGBT-oriented performers in the mainstream programming of the college or university also sends a message to heterosexual students that such programming is legitimate and normal.

Student affairs staff can also provide assistance with the establishment of LGBT support groups and student organizations. Unlike other student organizations there is a very real risk in attempting to start an LGBT-oriented group. Students must be secure in their own identity if they are to publicly advocate for such activities. Advocacy and promotion from a trusted student affairs staff member can be of great assistance. Finding a facilitator or an advisor for such groups is another hurdle not easily overcome. Volunteering for these roles is an excellent way to provide support for students.

Many LGBT students feel isolated and alone on campus (Evans, in press). They need opportunities to find each other and to develop a social network on campus. Events such as LGBT dances, coffee houses, or receptions can provide comfortable alcohol-free environments in which to meet people and to socialize with friends. These types of activities should be built into the regular social programming provided by residence life and the student union.

Programs about coming out, LGBT identity development, and other topics of interest to LGBT students should be presented regularly. Such programs should not be promoted as strictly for LGBT students since many students will avoid coming for fear of being labeled. In addition, heterosexual students should also be encouraged to attend in order to learn about the experiences and issues facing LGBT individuals. Such programs provide an educational vehicle to explore material often not presented in the classroom and to assist LGBT students in learning that their experiences are normal and natural.

Much more programming must be done to educate non-LGBT students. Unfortunately, most heterosexual individuals have little awareness of the existence of LGBT people and no appreciation for their contributions to the campus. Education should focus on what LGBT students add to the fabric of the university community, both as a group and as individuals. Learning that active student leaders, members of athletic teams, honors scholars, resident assistants, and perhaps one's best friend could be LGBT contributes to the development of individuals' realization that all students contribute to the university environment, including LGBT students, and that all students, again including those who are LGBT, are entitled to a welcoming, supportive, and inclusive college experience.

Unfortunately, the students who most need accurate information are the ones least likely to attend programs on LGBT issues. Passive programming, such as bulletin boards and posters about LGBT topics, is one way of addressing this concern. It can do much to raise awareness of students who must walk past such displays on their way to classes, the dining hall, or the student lounge (Evans, in press). In addition, seeing visible evidence of their existence gives LGBT students a feeling that the university cares about them.

LGBT students are especially appreciative of personal support they receive from student affairs staff (Evans, in press). Because they do not expect to be treated fairly or to be valued for who they are, even small acts of kindness can be meaningful. Checking to make sure a student's roommate situation is working out, asking about a student's partner, or attending a program sponsored by the LGBT student organization can let LGBT students know that they are accepted for who they are. Even having LGBT-themed posters on the wall or books on one's bookshelf sends an important message of inclusion. Participating in a campus safe zone program is a more formal way that allies can let students know that they are accepting and appreciative of LGBT persons.

Careful attention to the selection and training of staff is crucial if student affairs divisions are to provide active support for LGBT students. Individuals who are homophobic, ambivalent, or even just uninformed will be ineffective in carrying out even the most enlightened LGBT agenda. LGBT staff who are open about their orientation should be actively encouraged to apply for student affairs positions. Such individuals serve as important role models for all students. Allies are equally important in demonstrating that values of inclusion and equity are a high priority in student affairs.

All promotional materials for student affairs positions should include statements about the values of the organization as well as the characteristics sought in potential employees. Knowledge of diversity issues and a demonstrated commitment to inclusiveness should be stressed. Addressing LGBT issues should be specifically mentioned in job descriptions as an expectation of the division. Resumes and reference checks should be reviewed with these requirements in mind. Interviews should contain opportunities to specifically address the candidate's knowledge of and commitment to LGBT issues.

Staff training and on-going staff development should include comprehensive exposure to LGBT concerns and the developmental issues of LGBT students. Most student affairs staff, like other educated people, have had little formal introduction to these topics. Their work will be enhanced through in-depth study of these topics. Staff development for resident assistants, orientation leaders, and other student staff is especially crucial since undergraduate staff often have the most contact with LGBT students and can have a major impact on their experience in college (Evans, Broido, Dragon, Eberz, & Richards, 1997). These staff are also less likely to be sensitive to the needs of LGBT students. Since personally knowing LGBT people is an important factor in breaking down stereotypes, including opportunities for staff to meet and interact with LGBT students, faculty, and staff should be built into training programs (Evans, et al., 1997).

Diversity within the LGBT Community

As the fourth section of this book suggested, the LGBT community is very diverse and the issues this diversity creates must be considered in any attempt to provide services and support for the LGBT population. Too often diversity becomes divisive and is seen as a problem rather than a factor that contributes in a positive way to the richness of the LGBT community. Different ideas, perspectives, experiences, and viewpoints that arise in a group because people come from varied backgrounds create a wealth of knowledge, sensitivities, and skills that make a community stronger and more effective in achieving its goals. The positive aspects of diversity should constantly be underscored in all interactions and programming efforts.

Unfortunately, attention often centers around the ways individuals hurt each other by being insensitive to the issues and concerns of those from whom they differ. Historically, the movement for equal rights and recognition has focused on the concerns of white gay men. These issues continue to plague the LGBT community. For example, during the summer of 1998, the listserv of the LGBTA Alliance at Iowa State had a dialog about the perceived dominance of white gay men in the organization and what could be done to make the group more inclusive.

In recent years, lesbians have played a larger role in the LGBT movement, holding major leadership positions in national LGBT organizations and becoming important and visible advocates for LGBT causes. However, on many college campuses sexism is significant in keeping men and women separated. Lesbians congregate in certain locations while gay men frequent others. Separate groups exist for men and women, often lessening the impact of the entire LGBT community. Most importantly, fights break out between gay men and lesbians, creating a hostile atmosphere in which those from whom they should be receiving support hurt individuals and nothing is accomplished with regard to furthering the LGBT agenda on campus.

Similar issues face bisexual men and women whose sexual orientation is often questioned by both homosexual and heterosexual individuals. As Robin and Hamner clearly point out in their chapter, bisexual men and women feel pressured from both sides to "make a decision." They are often teased and excluded from lesbian and gay groups (even when such groups use the initials "LGBT") because they are not "gay enough." Finding partners who accept their bisexual orientation may also be an issue.

Transgender students are often not understood or welcomed by the LGB community. Since their gender identification, rather than their sexual orientation, is the cause of their oppression, many LGB individuals question if their issues are similar enough to warrant their inclusion in political efforts to gain equality. Other LGBT people fear that their efforts to be seen as "normal" will be undermined by transgender individuals who garner sensationalistic headlines and make "extreme" statements.

LGBT individuals who are also members of racial and ethnic minority groups fight for true acceptance and understanding from both of the nondominant groups of which they are a part. White students usually are the majority of any LGBT student organization and they bring to these groups the same prejudices and stereotypes about racial and ethic populations as any other white student. Their lack of sensitivity and concern about the issues faced by racial and ethnic minority students frequently drive these students away, often deeper into the closet to maintain acceptance from their racial or ethnic peer group.

Other types of diversity can also disrupt the LGBT community. Many LGBT students struggle with issues related to religion. As DuMontier noted in his chapter, some maintain their faith in the face hostility and misunderstanding, others move to a more accepting church organization, and others adopt a personal spirituality that sustains them. Many LGBT individuals, however, end up totally rejecting religion and spirituality. Unfortunately, they often deride the beliefs of other LGBT individuals and create a hostile environment when issues of spirituality are raised.

Differences among students with regard to identity development level can also create divisiveness. Students who are just beginning to come out have very different concerns than those students who have been extensively out for several years. Students who are questioning their sexual orientation have different needs than those students who have known they were LGBT since they were very young. Often students fail to put themselves in the position of their peers and make little attempt to understand alternative viewpoints. Challenges from the outside are especially likely to bring developmental differences out into the open. For example, the announced visit of a notorious anti-LGBT fanatic threw the LGBT community at Iowa State into disarray. Attempts to develop a strategy for addressing the visit resulted in much argument and criticism of the ideas of others. Advocated plans ranged from totally ignoring the visit, to initiating an educational effort using the local media, to staging a "clean-up" after the visit, to holding a counter-protest. Individuals at different levels of development who held different philosophies were unable or unwilling to hear each other.

How, then, do we acknowledge and work to incorporate diversity as part of a united and mutually supportive community? First, support must be provided for individuals who are members of diverse groups. This goal can be a challenge when numbers are small. If a campus has only one identified Asian-American lesbian, it's hard to provide a support group for that person. But perhaps a group could be held to discuss the issues facing individuals who are members of two or more nondominant populations. It must be recognized that having a place to share with others who have had similar experiences (e.g., lesbians, people of color, bisexuals) provides an opportunity for personal growth and nurturing that enables people to come back to the larger community stronger, more creative, and more energized to address the common issues.

Second, programs must be developed to educate the LGBT community about the diversity that exists within the community. A workshop on transgender issues was very helpful to the Penn State Commission on LGB Equity in providing information and confronting fears and stereotypes about transgendered individuals. Likewise, anti-racism and anti-sexism workshops, programs on spirituality, and seminars about LGBT identity development could increase sensitivity to the issues related to difference in the LGBT community.

Finally, focusing on commonalities helps to build and nurture a strong community. As members of nondominant populations, all LGBT people struggle with certain issues related to inclusion, acceptance, and equity. In addition, as individuals pursuing an education, LGBT students face common challenges related to learning, succeeding, and forging future plans and goals. Finally, as human beings in today's society, LGBT people face the common demands of living in an increasingly complex and sophisticated world. Efforts to engage LGBT students in an exploration of their commonalities and ways to develop strong internal support systems within the community are crucial to the community's well-being.

Tensions will always be present as we attempt to both recognize and honor our differences and to identify those things we have in common. The potential for discord within the LGBT community is great, particularly in the face of attacks from the outside by individuals who work to divide and conquer. Building unity and nurturing the whole LGBT community is of primary importance if attempts to educate the non-LGBT population are to be successful. A strong and consistent message must be presented in order to secure the rights that will benefit everyone.

References

Barr, M. J., & Keating, L. A. (1979). No program is an island. In M. J. Barr & L. A. Keating (Eds.), *Establishing effective programs* (New Directions for Student Services, No. 7, pp. 13-28). San Francisco: Jossey-Bass.

D'Augelli, A. R., & Rose, M. L. (1990). Homophobia in a university community: Attitudes and experiences of heterosexual freshmen. *Journal of College Student Development, 31,* 484-491.

Dougharty, W. H., Evans, N. J., Nelson, J., & Lund, C. (1998, October). *Creating and evaluating a Safe Zone project.* Presented at the Iowa Student Personnel Association conference, Des Moines, IA.

Evans, N. J. (in press). The experiences of lesbian, gay, and bisexual youths in university communities. In A. R. D'Augelli & C. Patterson (Eds.), *The experiences of gay, lesbian, and bisexual youth.* New York: Oxford.

Evans, N. J., Broido, E., Dragon, M., Eberz, A., & Richards, K. (1997, March). *Gay, lesbian, and bisexual students' development in residence halls.* Paper presented at the joint conference of the American College Personnel Association and the National Association of Student Personnel Administrators, Chicago, IL.

Herek, G. M., & Glunt, E. K. (1993). Interpersonal contact and heterosexual attitudes toward gay men: Results from a national survey. *Journal of Sex Research, 30,* 239-244.

Malaney, G. D., Williams, E. A., & Geller, W. W. (1997). Assessing campus climate for gays, lesbians, and bisexuals at two institutions. *Journal of College Student Development, 38,* 365-375.

Simoni, J. M. (1996). Pathways to prejudice: Predicting students' heterosexist attitudes with demographics, self-esteem, and contact with lesbians and gay men. *Journal of College Student Development, 37,* 68-78.

Wells, J. W., & Franken, M. L. (1987). University students' knowledge about and attitudes toward homosexuality. *Journal of Humanistic Education and Development, 26,* 81-95.

Resources

ॐ

JOHN LEPPO

Resources are provided below that will assist in addressing sexual orientation and transgender issues on campus. The lists are not exhaustive, but represent those that have been particularly helpful to others working on these issues.

The first section presents books and articles from periodicals organized by related topical areas. It opens with a list of books of general interest on Lesbian, Gay, Bisexual, and Transgender topics. The next topical areas addressed are: AIDS and Health Issues; Coming Out, Youth, and Educational Issues; Counseling LGBT People; Diversity; Domestic Violence, Sexual Assault, and Violence topics; Family, Marriage, and Relationships; Religion and Spirituality; Resources for the Curriculum; and Workplace Issues.

Following sections present various publications available for LGBT people, allies, and those who work with LGBT people; resource organizations and associations; resources available on the World Wide Web; national hotlines; and mail order bookstores.

The author offers many thanks to all who responded to a request for resources to be included in this chapter.

Books of General Interest on Lesbian, Gay, Bisexual, and Transgender Topics

The Alyson Almanac: 1996 edition, the fact book of the lesbian and gay community. (1996). Boston: Alyson.

Baldwin, G. (1993). *Ties that bind: The SM—leather fetish erotic style.* San Francisco: Daedalus.

Bannon, R. (1993). *Learning the ropes: A basic guide to safe and fun SM lovemaking.* San Francisco: Daedelus.

Bawer, B. (Ed.). (1996). *Beyond queer: Challenging gay left orthodoxy.* New York: Simon & Schuster/Free Press.

Bawer, B. (1993). *A place at the table.* New York: Simon & Schuster/Poseidon.

Blumenfeld, W. (Ed.). (1992). *Homophobia: How we all pay the price.* Boston: Beacon.

Brelin, C. (Ed.). (1996). *Strength in numbers: A lesbian, gay and bisexual resource.* Detroit: Visible Ink.

Caster, W. (1993). *The lesbian sex book: A guide for women who love women.* Boston: Alyson.

Coles, M. A. (1996). *Try this at home: A do-it yourself guide to instituting lesbian and gay civil rights policy.* New York: New Press.

Davidoff, R., & Nava, M. (1994). *Created equal: Why gay rights matter to America.* New York: St. Martin's.

Fahey, U. (1995). *How to make the world a better place for gays and lesbians.* New York: Warner.

Feinberg, L. (1996). *Transgender warriors: Making history from Joan of Arc to RuPaul.* Boston: Beacon.

Galindo, R., & Marcus, E. (1996). *Icebreaker: The autobiography of Rudy Galindo.* New York: Pocket Books.

Garber, M. (1996). *Vice versa: Bisexuality and the eroticism of everyday life.* New York: Simon & Schuster.

Geller, T. (Ed.). (1990). *Bisexuality: A reader and sourcebook.* Novato, CA: Times Change.

George, S. (1993). *Women and bisexuality.* Milford, CT: LPC/InBook.

Grahn, J. (1990). *Another mother tongue: Gay words, gay worlds.* Boston: Beacon.

Harvard Law Review. (1990). *Sexual orientation and the law.* Cambridge, MA: Harvard University Press.

Hausman, B. L. (1995). *Changing sex: Transsexualism, technology, and the idea of gender*. Durham, NC: Duke University Press.

Hay, H. (1996). *Radically gay: Gay liberation in the words of its founder*. Boston: Beacon.

Hutchins, L., & Kaahumanu, L. (Eds.). (1991). *Bi any other name: Bisexual people speak out*. Boston: Alyson.

Jay, K. (Ed.). (1996). *Dyke life: From growing up to growing old, a celebration of the lesbian experience*. New York: Basic Books.

Kirk, M., & Madson, H. (1989). *How America will conquer its fear and hatred of gays in the 90's*. New York: Plume.

Klein, F. (1993). *The bisexual option* (2nd ed.). New York: Harrington Park.

Klein, F., & Wolf, T. J. (1985). *Two lives to lead: Bisexuality in men and women*. New York: Harrington Park.

LeVay, S., & Nonas, E. (1995). *City of friends: A portrait of the gay and lesbian community in America*. Cambridge, MA: MIT Press.

Louganis, G., & Marcus, E. (1995). *Breaking the surface*. New York: Random House.

Loulan, J. (1984). *Lesbian sex*. San Francisco: Spinsters.

Marcus, E. (1993). *Is it a choice? Answers to 300 of the most frequently asked questions about gays and lesbians*. San Francisco: HarperSanFranscisco.

Marcus, E. (1993). *Making history: The struggle for gay and lesbian equal rights*. New York: HarperCollins.

McNab, C., & Gedan, S. (1997). *The loving lesbian*. Tallahassee, FL: Naiad.

Miller, N. (1989). *In search of gay America: Women and men in a time of change*. New York: Atlantic Monthly Press.

Mohr, R. D. (1994). *A more perfect union: Why straight America must stand up for gay rights*. Boston: Beacon.

Perry, T., & Swicegood, T. (1991). *Profiles in gay and lesbian courage*. New York: St. Martin's.

Ramsey, G. (1996). *Transsexuals: Candid answers to private questions*. Freedom, CA: Crossing.

Roberts, J. (1993). *Who's who and resource guide to the international transgender community 1995*. King of Prussia, PA: Creative Design.

Rosario, V. A. (Ed.). (1996). *Science and homosexualities*. New York: Routledge.

Rust, P. C. (1995). *Bisexuality and the challenge to lesbian politics: Sex, loyalty, and revolution*. New York: New York University Press.

Rutledge, L. (Ed.). (1989). *The gay fireside companion*. Boston: Alyson.

Sadownick, D. (1996). *Sex between men: An intimate history of the sex lives of gay men, postwar to present*. San Francisco: Harper.

Silverstein, C., & Picano, F. (1993). *The new joy of gay sex* (Rev. ed.). New York: HarperCollins.

Singlar, B. L., & Deschamps, D. (1994). *Gay and lesbian stats: A pocket guide of facts and figures*. New York: New Press.

Stewart, W., & Hamer, E. (Eds.). (1995). *Cassell's queer companion: A dictionary of lesbian and gay culture*. New York: Cassell.

Taylor, J. (1990). *A dyke's bike repair handbook*. LaMesa, CA: Clothespin Fever Press.

Thompson, M. (Ed.). (1994). *Long road to freedom*. New York: St. Martin's.

Thompson, M. (Ed.). (1992). *Leather-folk: Radical sex, people, politics, and practice*. Boston: Alyson.

Townsend, L. (1996). *The leatherman's handbook: The original* (4th ed.). Portland, OR: LT Publications.

Tucker, N. (1995). *Bisexual politics: Theories, queries, and visions*. New York: Harrington Park.

Vaid, U. (1996). *Virtual equality: The mainstreaming of gay and lesbian liberation*. Garden City, NY: Doubleday.

VanGelder, L., & Brandt, P. R. (1996). *The girls next door: Into the heart of lesbian America*. New York: Simon & Schuster.

Vida, G. (Ed.). (1996). *New our right to love: A lesbian resource book*. New York: Simon & Schuster/Touchstone.

Walker, M. (1994). *Men loving men: A gay guide and consciousness book* (2nd ed.). San Francisco: Gay Sunshine.

Weinberg, M., Williams, C., & Pryor, D. (1993). *Dual attraction: Understanding bisexuality*. New York: Oxford University Press.

Witt, L., Thomas, S., & Marcus, E. (1995). *Out in all directions: The almanac of gay and lesbian America*. New York: Warner.

Wright, L. (1997). *The bear book: Readings in the history and evolution of a gay male subculture*. New York: Harrington Park.

AIDS & Health Issues

American Medical Association. (1990). *Early care for HIV infection.* Washington: Author.

Barouh, G. (1992). *Support groups: The human face of the HIV/AIDS epidemic.* Huntingdon Station, NY: Long Island Association for AIDS Care.

Bartlett, J. G., & Finkbeiner, A. K. (1996). *Guide to living with HIV infection: Developed at the Johns Hopkins AIDS clinic* (3rd ed.). Baltimore: Johns Hopkins University Press.

Berer, M. (Ed.). (1993). *Women and HIV/AIDS: An international resource book.* San Francisco: HarperSanFrancisco.

Boston Women's Health Book Collective. (1996). *New our bodies, ourselves: 25th anniversary edition.* New York: Simon & Schuster/ Touchstone.

Burris, S., Dalton, H., Miller, J., & Yale AIDS Law Project. (1993). *AIDS law today: A new guide for the public* (2nd ed.). New Haven, CT: Yale University Press.

Capossela, C., & Warnock, S. (1995). *Share the care: How to organize a group to care for someone who is seriously ill.* New York: Simon & Schuster/Fireside.

Dilley, J., Pies, C., & Helquist, M. (1989). *Face to face: A guide to AIDS counseling.* Berkeley, CA: Celestial Arts.

Doress-Worters, P. B., & Siegal, D. L. (1994). *The new ourselves, growing older: Women aging with knowledge and power.* New York: Simon & Schuster/Touchstone.

Eidson, T. (1988). *AIDS caregiver's handbook.* New York: St. Martin's.

Greif, J., & Golden, B. A. (1994). *AIDS care at home: A guide for caregivers, loved ones, and people with AIDS.* New York: Wiley.

Haigh, R., & Harris, D. (Eds.). (1995). *AIDS: A guide to the law* (2nd ed.). New York: Routledge.

Hedgepeth, E., & Helmich, J. (1996). *Teaching about sexuality and HIV: Principles and methods for effective education.* New York: New York University Press.

King, E. (1996). *Rubber up!* Milford, CT: LPC InBook.

King, E. (1993). *Safety in numbers: Safer sex and gay men.* New York: Cassell.

Kloser, P., Kloser, C., & MacLean, J. (1994). *Woman's HIV sourcebook: A guide to better health & well-being.* Rochester, MI: Taylor.

McCormack, T. P. (1990). *The AIDS benefits handbook.* New Haven, CT: Yale University Press.

Moffat, B. C. (1986). *When someone you love has AIDS: A book of hope for family and friends.* Santa Monica, CA: IBS Press/Love Heals.

Moffat, B. C., Spiegel, J., Parrish, S., & Helquist, M. (Eds.). (1989). *AIDS: A self care manual* (3rd ed.). Santa Monica, CA: IBS Press.

Morales, J., & Bok, M. (1993). *Multicultural human services for AIDS treatment and prevention.* New York: Harrington Park.

Morin, J. (1986). *Anal pleasure and health: A guide for men and women* (2nd ed.). San Francisco: Down There Press.

O'Sullivan, S., & Parmar, P. (1992). *Lesbians talk (safer) sex.* Milford, CT: LPC InBook.

Patton, C., & Kelly, J. (1988). *Making it: A woman's guide to sex in the age of AIDS.* Ithaca, NY: Firebrand.

Pinsky, L., Douglas, P. H., & Metroka, C. (1992). *The essential HIV treatment fact book.* New York: Pocket Books.

Rimer, R., & Connolly, M. (1993). *HIV+: Working the system.* Boston: Alyson.

Rofes, E. (1995). *Reviving the tribe: Regenerating gay men's sexuality and culture in the ongoing epidemic.* New York: Haworth.

Rubenstein, W. B., Eisenberg, R., & Gostin, L.O. (1996). *The rights of people who are HIV positive: An ACLU handbook.* Carbondale, IL: Southern Illinois University Press.

Sankar, A. (1991). *Dying at home: A family guide for caregiving.* Baltimore: Johns Hopkins University Press.

Schwartzberg, S. (1996). *Crisis of meaning: How gay men are making sense of AIDS.* New York: Oxford University Press.

Siano, N., & Lipsett, S. (1993). *No time to wait: A complete guide to treating, managing, and living with HIV infection.* New York: Bantam.

Sutherland, R., & Shelp, E. (1990). *Handle with care: A handbook for care teams serving people with AIDS.* Nashville, TN: Abingdon.

Tatchell, P. (1994). *Safer sexy: The guide to gay sex safely.* New Milford, CT: LPC InBook.

Watney, S. (1997). *Policing desire: Pornography, AIDS, and the media* (3rd ed.). Minneapolis, MN: University of Minnesota Press.

Wilton, T. (1996). *Finger licking good: The ins and outs of lesbian sex.* New York: Cassell.

Coming Out, Youth, and Education

Aarons, L. (1995). *Prayers for Bobby: A mother's coming to terms with the suicide of her gay son.* San Francisco: HarperSanFrancisco.

American Friends Service Committee. (1988). *Bridges of respect: Creating support for lesbian and gay youth.* Philadelphia: Author.

Bernstein, R. (1994). *Straight parents, gay children: Keeping families together.* New York: Thunder's Mouth.

Berzon, B. (1995). *Positively gay: New approaches to gay and lesbian life* (2nd ed.). Berkeley, CA: Celestial Arts.

Borhek, M. V. (1983). *Coming out to parents.* New York: Pilgrim.

Buxton, A. P. (1992). *The other side of the closet: The coming out crisis for straight spouses.* New York: Amity.

Central Toronto Youth Services. (1988). *Often invisible: Counseling gay and lesbian youth.* Toronto: Author.

Clark, D. (1987). *New loving someone gay* (Rev. ed.). Berkeley, CA: Celestial Arts.

Cook, A. (1991). *The role of sexual identity in youth suicide.* (Respect All Youth Issue Paper). Washington, DC: Parents & Friends of Lesbians and Gays.

Corley, R. (1990). *The final closet: The gay parent guide for coming out to their children.* Miami: Editech press.

Crew, L. (Ed.). (1978). *The gay academic.* Palm Springs, CA: ETS Publications.

Crist, S. (1990). *Out on campus: A how-to manual of gay and lesbian campus activism.* Bloomington, IN: Association of College Unions— International.

DeCrescenzo, T. (Ed.). (1994). *Helping gay and lesbian youth: New policies, new programs, new practices.* New York: Haworth.

Due, L. (1995). *Joining the Tribe – Growing up gay & lesbian in the 90's.* Boston: Anchor Books.

Eichberg, R. (1991). *Coming out: An act of love.* New York: NAL/ Dutton.

Evans, N. J., & Wall, V. A. (1991). *Beyond tolerance: Gays, lesbians and bisexuals on campus.* Washington, DC: American College Personnel Association.

Fairchild, B. (1989). *Now that you know: What every parent should know about homosexuality* (2nd ed.). New York: Harvest Books.

Garber, L. (Ed.). (1994). *Tilting the tower.* New York: Routledge.

Harbeck, K. M. (Ed.). (1992). *Coming out of the classroom closet: Gay and lesbian students, teachers, and curricula.* New York: Harrington Park.

Herdt, G. (Ed.). (1989). *Gay and lesbian youth.* New York: Harrington Park.

Herdt, G., & Boxer, A. (1996). *Children of Horizons: How lesbian and gay teens are leading a new way out of the closet.* Boston: Beacon.

Heron, A. (Ed.). (1995). *Two teenagers in twenty: Writings by gay and lesbian youth.* Boston: Alyson.

McNaught, B. (1989). *On being gay: Thoughts on family, faith, and love.* New York: St. Martin's.

Malinowitz, H. (1995). *Textual orientations: Lesbian and gay students and the making of discourse communities.* Portsmouth, NH: Boynton/Cook.

O'Neill, C., & Ritter, K. (1992). *Coming out within: Stages of spiritual awakening for lesbians and gay men.* San Francisco: HarperSanFrancisco.

Pollack, R., & Schwartz, C. (1995). *The journey out: A guide for and about lesbian, gay, and bisexual teens.* New York: Puffin.

Powers, B., & Ellis, A. (1996). *A family and friend's guide to sexual orientation.* New York: Routledge.

Remafedi, G. (Ed.). (1994). *Death by denial: Studies of suicide in gay and lesbian teenagers.* Boston: Alyson.

Rhoads, R. (1994). *Coming out in college: The struggle for a queer identity.* Westport, CT: Bergin & Garvey.

Romesburg, D. (Ed.). (1995). *Young, gay, and proud!* (4th ed.). Boston: Alyson.

Sanlo, R. (Ed.). (1998). *Working with lesbian, gay, and bisexual students: A guide for administrators and faculty.* Westport, CT: Greenwood.

Sears, J. T. (1991). *Growing up gay in the south: Race, gender, and journeys of the spirit.* New York: Harrington Park.

Sherrill, J. M., & Hardesty, C. A. (1994). *The gay, lesbian, and bisexual students' guide to colleges, universities, and graduate schools.* New York: New York University Press.

Signorile, M. (1996). *Outing yourself: How to come out to your family, your friends, and your coworkers.* New York: Simon & Schuster/Fireside.

Tierney, W. (1993). *Building communities of difference: Higher education in the twenty-first century.* Westport, CT: Bergin & Garvey.

Unks, G. (1995). *The gay teen: Educational theory and practice.* New York: Routledge.

Woog, D. (1995). *School's out: The impact of gay and lesbian issues on America's schools.* Boston: Alyson.

Counseling Lesbian, Gay, Bisexual, and Transgender People

Alexander, C. J. (Ed.). (1996). *Gay and lesbian mental health: A sourcebook for practitioners.* New York: Harrington Park.

American Psychological Association, Committee on Lesbian and Gay Concerns. (1990). *Final report of the task force on bias in psychotherapy with lesbian women and gay men.* Washington, DC: Author.

Boston Lesbian Psychologies Collective. (1987). *Lesbian psychologies: Explorations and challenges.* Champaign, IL: University of Illinois Press.

Cabaj, R., & Stein, T. (Eds.). (1996). *Textbook of homosexuality and mental health.* Washington, DC: American Psychiatric Press.

Carl, D. (1990). *Counseling same-sex couples.* New York: Norton.

D'Augelli, A. R. (1994). Identity development and sexual orientation: Toward a model of lesbian, gay, and bisexual development. In E. J. Trickett, R. J. Watts, & D. Birman (Eds.), *Human diversity: Perspectives on people in context* (pp. 312-333). San Francisco: Jossey Bass.

D'Augelli, A. R., & Patterson, C. J. (Eds.). (1995). *Lesbian, gay, and bisexual identities over the lifespan.* New York: Oxford University Press.

Davis, N. D., Cole, E., & Rothblum, E. D. (Eds.). (1996). *Lesbian therapists and their therapy: From both sides of the couch.* New York: Harrington Park.

DeCecco, J., & Coleman, E. (Ed.). (1987). *Integrated identity for gay men and lesbians: Psychotherapeutic approaches for emotional well being.* New York: Harrington Park.

Duberman, M. (1992). *Cures: A gay man's odyssey.* New York: NAL/ Dutton.

Dworkin, S., & Guiterrez, F. (1992). *Counseling gay men and lesbians: Journey to the end of the rainbow.* Washington, DC: American Association for Counseling and Development.

Falco, K. L. (1991). *Psychotherapy with lesbian clients: Theory into practice.* New York: Brunner/Mazel.

Garnets, L., & Kimmel, D. (Eds.)(1993). *Psychological perspectives on lesbian and gay male experiences.* New York: Columbia University Press.

Glassgold, J., & Lasenza, S. (Eds.). (1995). *Lesbians and psychoanalysis*. New York: Simon & Schuster/Free Press.

Isay, R. (1989). *Being homosexual*. New York: Farrar Straus Giroux.

Isensee, R. (1991). *Growing up gay in a dysfunctional family: A guide for gay men reclaiming their lives*. New York: Prentice Hall.

Kain, C. D. (1996). *Positive: HIV affirmative counseling*. Washington, DC: American Counseling Association.

Kaufman, G., & Raphael, L. (1996). *Coming out of shame*. New York: Doubleday.

Kus, R. J. (Ed.). (1995). *Addiction and recovery in gay and lesbian persons*. New York: Haworth.

Kus, R. J. (1990). *Keys to caring: Assisting your gay and lesbian clients*. Boston: Alyson.

Laird, J., & Green, R. (Eds.)(1996). *Lesbians and gays in couples and families: A handbook for therapists*. San Francisco: Jossey Bass.

Milton, A. (1995). *Lavender light: Daily meditations for gay men in recovery*. Berkeley, CA: Berkeley.

Moore, S., & Rosenthal, D. (1993). *Adolescent sexuality in social context*. New York: Routledge.

Nealy, E. (1995). *Amazon spirit: Daily meditations for lesbians in recovery*. Berkeley, CA: Berkeley.

Odets, W., & Shernoff, M. (Eds.). (1995). *The second decade of AIDS: A mental health handbook*. New York: Hatherliegh.

Ryan, C., & Futterman, D. (1998). *Lesbian and gay youth: Care & counseling*. New York: Columbia University Press.

Shernoff, M. (Ed.). (1996). *Human services for gay people: Clinical & community practice*. Binghamton, NY: Haworth.

Siegel, S., & Lowe, E., Jr. (1995). *Uncharted lives: Understanding the life passages of gay men*. New York: NAL/Dutton.

Silverstein, C. (1991). *Gays, lesbians, and their therapists: Studies in psychotherapy*. New York: Norton.

Steinhorn, A. I. (1990). *Homosexuality: A practical guide for those who help others*. New York: Crossroads.

Weinstein, D. L. (1992). *Lesbians and gay men: Chemical dependency treatment issues*. New York: Harrington Park.

Woodman, N. J. (1992). *Lesbian and gay lifestyles: A guide for counseling and education*. New York: Irvington.

Woodman, N. J., & Lenna, H. P. (1980). *Counseling with gay men and women: A guide for facilitating positive life styles.* San Francisco: Jossey-Bass.

Young, V. (1996). *The equality complex: A guide to anti-oppressive practice for lesbians in therapy.* New York: Cassell.

Ziebold, T. O., & Mongeon, J. E. (Eds.). (1985). *Gay and sober: Directions for counseling and therapy.* New York: Harrington Park.

Diversity in the Gay, Lesbian, Bisexual, and Transgender Community

Adelman, M. (1996). *Lesbian passages in true stories as told by women over 40* (Rev. ed.). (Original title: *Long time passing: Lives of older lesbians*). Boston: Alyson.

Anzaldua, G. (1987). *Borderlands/La frontera*. San Francisco: Spinsters/ Aunt Lute.

Asian Women United of California (Eds.). (1989). *Making waves: An anthology of writings by and about Asian American women*. Boston: Beacon.

Beam, J. (1986). *In the life: A Black gay anthology*. Boston: Alyson.

Berger, R. (1995). *Gay and gray: The older homosexual man* (2nd ed.). New York: Harrington Park.

Brown, L. B. (Ed.). (1996). *Two-spirit people: American Indian lesbian women and gay men*. New York: Haworth.

Boykin, K. (1996). *One more river to cross: Black and gay in America*. New York: Anchor.

Jalal al-Din Rumi, M. (1997). *The essential Rumi*. (C. Barks, Trans.). Edison, NJ: Castle.

Lee, J. (Ed.). (1991). *Gay mid-life and maturity*. New York: Haworth.

Leong, R. (Ed.). (1995). *Asian American sexualities: Dimensions of the gay and lesbian experience*. New York: Routledge.

Longres, J. F. (Ed.). (1996). *Men of color: A context for service to homosexually active men*. New York: Harrington Park.

Lorde, A. (1984). *Sister outsider*. Freedom, CA: Crossing.

Lorde, A. (1983). *Zami: A new spelling of my name*. Freedom, CA: Crossing.

Luczak, R. (1993). *Eyes of desire: A deaf gay & lesbian reader*. Boston: Alyson.

Moraga, C., & Anzaldua, G. (Eds.). (1980). *This bridge called my back: Writings by radical women of color*. Boston: Persephone.

Ramos, J. (1994). *Copanaras: Latina lesbians*. New York: Routledge.

Roscoe, W. (1989). *Living the spirit: A gay American Indian anthology*. New York: St. Martin's.

Roscoe, W. (1991). *The Zuni man-woman*. Albuquerque, NM: University of New Mexico Press.

Schmitt, A. (Ed.). (1991). *Sexuality and eroticism among males in Moslem societies*. New York: Haworth.

Thompson, K., & Andrzejewski, J. (1988). *Why can't Sharon Kowalski come home?* San Francisco: Spinsters.

Williams, W. L. (1992). *Spirit and the flesh: Sexual diversity in American Indian culture.* Boston: Beacon.

Domestic Violence, Sexual Assault, Violence

Bart, P., & O'Brien, P. (1985). *Stopping rape: Successful survivor strategies*. New York: Pergamon.

Bass, E., & Davis, L. (1992). *Courage to heal: A guide for women survivors of child sexual abuse*. New York: HarperCollins.

Benedict, H. (1994). *Recovery: How to survive sexual assault for women, men, teenagers, their family and friends* (Rev. ed.). New York: Columbia University Press.

Comstock, G. (1991). *Violence against lesbians and gay men*. New York: Columbia University Press.

Elliott, P. (1996). Shattering illusions: Same-sex domestic violence. *Journal of Gay and Lesbian Social Services, 4* (1), 1-8.

Funk, R. E. (1993). *Stopping rape: A challenge for men*. Philadelphia: New Society.

Hunter, M. (1990). *Abused boys: The neglected victims of sexual abuse*. New York: Fawcett Columbine.

Herek, G., & Berrill, K. (Eds.). (1991). *Hate crimes: Confronting violence against lesbians and gay men*. Newbury Park, CA: Sage.

Hickson, F. C. I., Davies, P. M., Hunt, A. J., Weatherburn, P., McManus, T. J., & Coxon, A.P.M. (1994). Gay men as victims of nonconsensual sex. *Archives of Sexual Behavior, 23,* 281-294.

Island, D., & Letellier, P. (1991). *Men who beat the men who love them*. New York: Harrington Park.

Langelan, M. J. (1993). *Back off! How to confront and stop sexual harassment and harassers*. New York: Simon & Schuster.

Lew, M. (1990). *Victims no longer: Men recovering from incest and other childhood sexual abuse*. New York: HarperCollins.

Lobel, K. (Ed.). (1986). *Naming the violence: Speaking out about lesbian battering*. Seattle, WA: Seal.

McMullen, R. (1990). *Male rape: Breaking the silence on the last taboo*. Boston: Alyson.

Merrill, G. S. (1996). Ruling the exceptions: Same-sex battering and domestic violence theory. *Journal of Gay and Lesbian Social Services, 4* (1), 9-21.

Pennacchia, Y. M. (1995). *Healing the whole: The diary of an incest survivor*. New York: LPC InBook.

Rafkin, L. (1995). *Street smarts: A personal safety guide for women*. San Francisco: HarperSanFrancisco.

Renzetti, C. (1992). *Violent betrayal: Partner abuse in lesbian relationships*. Newbury Park, CA: Sage.

Renzetti, C. M., & Miley, C. H. (Eds.). (1996). *Violence in gay and lesbian domestic partnerships*. New York: Harrington Park.

Sanday, P. R. (1990). *Fraternity gang rape: Sex, brotherhood and privilege on campus*. New York: New York University Press.

Slater, B. (1993). Violence against lesbian and gay male college students. *Journal of College Student Psychotherapy, 8,* 177-202.

Taylor, J., & Chandler, T. (1985). *Lesbians talk violent relationships*. Milford, CT: LPC InBook.

Waldron, C. M. (1996). Lesbians of color and the domestic violence movement. *Journal of Gay and Lesbian Social Services, 4* (1), 43-51.

Waterman, C. K., Dawson, L. J., & Bologna, M. J. (1989). Sexual coercion in gay male and lesbian relationships: Predictors and implications for support services. *The Journal of Sex Research, 26* (1), 118-124.

Family, Marriage, and Relationships

Arnup, K. (Ed.). (1995). *Lesbian parenting: Living with pride and prejudice*. New York: LPC InBooks.

Ayers, T., & Brown, P. (1994). *The essential guide to lesbian and gay weddings*. San Francisco: HarperSanFrancisco.

Barret, R. L., & Robinson, B. E. (1990). *Gay fathers*. Lexington, MA: Lexington Books.

Berzon, B. (1988). *Permanent partners*. New York: Plume Books.

Bozett, F. W. (Ed.). (1987). *Gay and lesbian parents*. New York: Praeger.

Bozett, F. W. (Ed.). (1989). *Homosexuality and the family*. New York: Harrington Park.

Clunis, D. M., & Green, G. D. (1988). *Lesbian couples: Creating healthy relationships for the 90's*. Seattle, WA: Seal.

Clunis, D. M., & Green, G. D. (1995). *Lesbian parenting book: A guide to creating families and raising children*. Seattle, WA: Seal.

Duff, J., & Truitt, G. (1991). *The spousal equivalent handbook: A legal and financial guide to living together*. Houston, TX: Sunny Beach.

Isensee, R. (1990). *Love between men: Enhancing intimacy and keeping your relationship alive*. Englewood Cliffs, NJ: Prentice Hall.

Johnson, S. E. (1990). *Staying power: Long term lesbian couples*. Tallahassee, FL: Naiad.

Johnson, S. E. (1995). *For love and for life: Intimate portraits of lesbian couples*. Tallahassee, FL: Naiad.

Leslie, M. (1994). *The single mother's companion: Essays & stories by women*. Seattle, WA: Seal Press.

Lewin, E. (1993). *Lesbian mothers: Accounts of gender in American culture*. Ithaca, NY: Cornell University Press.

Marcus, E. (1988). *The male couple's guide*. New York: Harper & Row.

Martin, A. (1993). *The lesbian and gay parenting handbook*. New York: HarperCollins.

McDaniel, J. (1995). *The lesbian couples' guide: Finding the right woman and creating a life together*. New York: HarperCollins.

McWhirter, D. P., & Mattison, A. M. (1984). *The male couple: How relationships develop*. Englewood Cliffs, NJ: Prentice Hall.

Morgen, K. (1995). *Getting Simon: Two gay doctors' journey to fatherhood*. Las Vegas, NV: Bramble Company.

Pies, C. (1988). *Considering parenthood* (2nd ed.). San Francisco: Spinsters/Aunt Lute.

Ricketts, W. (1991). *Lesbians and gay men as foster parents*. Portland, ME: University of Southern Maine.

Silverstein, C. (1982). *Man to man: Gay couples in America*. New York: Morrow.

Strasser, M. (1997). *Legally wed: Same-sex marriage and the Constitution*. Ithaca, NY: Cornell University Press.

Sullivan, A. (Ed.). (1997). *Same-sex marriage: Pro and con, a reader*. New York: Vintage Books.

Tessina, T. (1989). *Gay relationships for men and women: How to find them, how to improve them, how to make them last*. Los Angeles: Tarcher.

Uhrig, L. (1984). *The two of us: Affirming, celebrating, and symbolizing gay and lesbian relationships*. Boston: Alyson.

Wells, J. (1997). *Lesbians raising sons*. Boston: Alyson.

Weston, K. (1991). *Families we choose: Lesbians, gays, and kinship*. New York: Columbia University Press.

Religion and Spirituality

Balka, C., & Rose, A. (Eds.). (1989). *Twice blessed: On being lesbian and gay and Jewish.* Boston: Beacon.

Boswell, J. (1981). *Christianity, social tolerance, and homosexuality.* Chicago: University of Chicago Press.

Bouldrey, B. (Ed.). (1995). *Wrestling with the angel: Faith and religion in the lives of gay men.* New York: Putnam.

Brooten, B. J. (1996). *Love between women: Early Christian responses to female homoeroticism.* Chicago: The University of Chicago Press.

Evans, A. (1977). *Witchcraft and the gay counterculture.* Boston: Fag Rag Books.

Glaser, C. (1994). *Word is out: The Bible reclaimed for lesbians and gay men.* San Francisco: HarperSanFrancisco.

Helminiak, D. (1994). *What the Bible really says: Top scholars put homosexuality into perspective.* San Francisco: Alamo Square.

Hill, J., & Cheadle, R. (1996). *The Bible tells me so: Uses and abuses of holy scripture.* New York: Anchor.

Isom, K. (1996). *Congregations in conflict: The battle over homosexuality.* Princeton, NJ: Rutgers University Press.

Klein, A. C. (1994). *Meeting the great bliss queen: Buddhists, feminists, and the art of the self.* Boston: Beacon.

McNeill, J. J. (1994). *The church and the homosexual* (4th ed.). Boston: Beacon.

O'Neill, C., & Ritter, K. (1992). *Coming out within: Stages of spiritual awakening for lesbians and gay men.* San Francisco: HarperSanFrancisco.

Piazza, M. (1994). *Holy homosexuals: The truth about being gay or lesbian and Christian.* Dallas, TX: Sources of Hope.

Roscoe, W. (1995). *Queer spirits: A gay men's myth book.* Boston: Beacon.

Scanzini, L., & Mollenkott, V. (1994). *Is the homosexual my neighbor?: A positive Christian response.* San Francisco: HarperSanFrancisco.

Shokeid, M. (1995). *A gay synagogue in New York.* New York: Columbia University Press.

Stone, M. (1978). *When god was a woman.* New York: Harcourt Brace Jovanovich.

Thompson, M. (Ed.). (1994). *Gay soul: Finding the heart of gay spirit and nature.* San Francisco: HarperSanFrancisco.

Waldherr, K. (1996). *The book of goddesses.* Hillsboro, OR: Beyond Words.

Resources for the Curriculum

Abelove, H., Barale, M. A., & Halperin, D. (Eds.). (1993). *The lesbian and gay studies reader*. New York: Routledge.

Abramson, A. (1986). *TAHs guide for overcoming homophobia in the classroom*. Berkeley, CA: University of California.

Adams, M. (1992). Cultural inclusion in the American college classroom. In L. L. B. Border & N. V. N. Chism (Eds.), *Teaching for diversity*. (New Directions for Teaching and Learning, no. 49, pp. 5-17). San Francisco: Jossey-Bass.

Baker, R. (1995). *Drag: A history of female impersonation in performing arts*. New York: New York University Press.

Beam, J. (Ed.). (1986). *In the life: A black gay anthology*. Boston: Alyson.

Bell, A., & Weinberg, M. (Eds.). (1978). *Homosexualities: A study of diversity among men and women*. New York: Simon and Schuster.

Bergman, D. (1993). *Camp grounds: Style and homosexuality*. Boston: University of Massachusetts.

Berube, A. (1991). *Coming out under fire: Gay men and women during World War II*. New York: Plume/NAL.

Blumenfeld, W., & Raymond, D. (1988). *Looking at gay and lesbian life*. Boston: Beacon.

Boswell, J. (1994). *Same-sex unions in pre-modern Europe*. New York: Villard.

Bullough, V., & Bullough, B. (1993). *Cross dressing, sex, and gender*. Philadelphia: University of Pennsylvania.

Cantarella, E. (1992). *Bisexuality in the ancient world*. Hartford, CT: Yale University Press.

Collis, R. (1994). *Portraits to the wall: Historic lesbians lives unveiled*. New York: Cassell.

Cowan, T. (1996). *Gay men and women who enriched the world*. Boston: Alyson.

D'Augelli, A. R. (1991). Teaching gay and lesbian development: A pedagogy of the oppressed. In W. G. Tierney (Ed.), *Culture and ideology in higher education* (pp. 213-233). New York: Praeger.

Davis, W. (Ed.). (1994). *Gay and lesbian studies in art history*. New York: Haworth.

Duberman, M. (1991). *About time: Exploring the gay past*. New York: Plume.

Duberman, M. (1993). *Stonewall*. New York: Dutton.

Duberman, M., Vicinus, M., & Chauncey, G., Jr. (Eds.). (1989). *Hidden from history: Reclaiming the gay and lesbian past*. New York: New American Library/Penguin.

Dyer, K. (Ed.). (1990). *Gays in uniform: The Pentagon's secret reports*. Boston: Alyson.

Faderman, L. (1991). *Odd girls and twilight lovers: A history of lesbian life in twentieth century America*. Hamilton, NY: Colgate University Press.

Garber, M. (1991). *Vested interests: Cross-dressing and cultural anxiety*. New York: HarperCollins.

Gilbert, L., & Kile, C. (1996). *SurferGrrrls: Look, Ethel! An Internet guide for us!* Seattle, WA: Seal.

Gough, C., & Greenblatt, E. (1990). *Gay and lesbian library service*. Jefferson, NC: McFarland & Company.

Grau, G., & Schoppmann, C. (1994). *Hidden holocaust: Lesbian and gay persecution in Germany 1933-45*. New York: LPC InBooks.

Haggerty, G. E., & Zimmerman, B. (Eds.). (1995). *Professions of desire: Lesbian and gay studies in literature*. New York: Modern Language Association.

Herdt, G. (Ed.). (1996). *Third sex, third gender: Beyond sexual dimorphism in culture and history*. New York: Zone Books.

Holmlund, C., & Fuchs, C. (Eds.). (1997). *Between the sheets, in the streets: Queer, lesbian, and gay documentary*. Minneapolis, MN: University of Minnesota Press.

Jennings, K. (Ed.). (1994). *Becoming visible: A reader in gay and lesbian history for high school and college students*. Boston: Alyson Publications.

Katz, J. N. (1992). *Gay American history: Lesbians and gay men in the USA* (Rev. ed.). New York: Meridian/NAL.

Kimmel, M. (1995). *Manhood in America: A cultural history*. New York: Simon & Schuster/Free Press.

LeVay, S. (1996). *Queer science: The use and abuse of research into homosexuality*. Boston: MIT Press.

Lewins, F. (1995). *Transsexualism in society: A sociology of male-to-female transsexuals*. Concord, MA: Paul.

Malinowski, S., Brelin, C., & Boyd, M. (1995). *Gay & lesbian literary companion*. Detroit, MI: Visible Ink.

McDowell, D. (1995). *The changing same: Black women's literature, criticism, and theory*. Bloomington, IN: Indiana University Press.

Miller, N. (1992). *Out in the world: Gay and lesbian life from Buenos Aires to Bangkok*. New York: Vintage Books.

Miller, N. (1995). *Out of the past: Gay and lesbian history from 1869 to the present*. New York: Vintage Books.

National Museum & Archive of Lesbian and Gay History (1996). *The gay almanac*. New York: Berkley Publishing Group.

National Museum & Archive of Lesbian and Gay History (1996). *The lesbian almanac*. New York: Berkley Publishing Group.

Peterson, K. J. (Ed.). (1996). *Health care for lesbians and gay men: Confronting homophobia and heterosexism*. New York: Harrington Park.

Plant, R. (1986). *The pink triangle: The Nazi war against homosexuals*. New York: Holt.

Russo, V. (1995). *The celluloid closet* (Rev. ed.). New York: Quality Paperback Book Club.

Summers, C. J. (Ed.). (1995). *Gay and lesbian literary heritage: A reader's companion to the writers and their works, from antiquity to the present*. New York: Holt.

Teal, D. (1995). *The gay militants: How gay liberation began in America, 1969-1971*. New York: St. Martin's.

Thadani, G. (1996). *Salkhiyani: Lesbian desire in ancient and modern India*. New York: Cassell.

Tully, C. T. (Ed.). (1995). *Lesbian social services: Research issues*. New York: Haworth.

Wardlow, D. L. (Ed.). (1996). *Gays, lesbians, and consumer behavior: Theory, practice, and research issues*. New York: Harrington Park.

Wilton, T. (1995). *Lesbian studies: Setting an agenda*. New York: Routledge.

Winkler, B. S. (1996). *Straight teacher/queer classroom: Teaching as an ally*. In K. J. Mayberry (Ed.), *Teaching what you're not: Identity politics in higher education* (pp. 47-69). New York: New York University Press.

Zeeland, S. (1993). *Barracks buddies and soldier lovers: Dialogues with gay young men in the U.S. military*. New York: Harrington Park.

Zeeland, S. (1995). *Sailors and sexual identity*. New York: Harrington Park.

Zeeland, S. (1996). *The masculine marine: Homoeroticism in the U.S. Marine Corps*. New York: Harrington Park.

Workplace Issues

Baker, D, Strub, S., & Henning, B. (1995). *Cracking the corporate closet*. New York: HarperBusiness.

Banta, W. (1993). *AIDS in the workplace: Legal questions and practical solutions*. New York: Lexington.

Ellis, A. L., & Riggle, E. D. B. (1996). *Sexual identity on the job: Issues and services*. New York: Harrington Park.

Friskopp, A., & Silverstein, S. (1996). *Straight jobs, gay lives: Professionals, the Harvard business school, and the American workplace*. New York: Simon & Schuster/Scribner.

Kirk, S., & Rothblatt, M. (1995). *Medical, legal & workplace issues for the transsexual*. Waltham, MA: Together Lifeworks.

Loden, M., & Rosener, J. (1991). *Workforce America: Managing employee diversity as a vital resource*. Homewood, IL: Business One Irwin.

McNaught, B. (1993). *Gay issues in the workplace*. New York: St. Martin's.

Mickens, E. (1994). *100 best companies for gay men and lesbians*. New York: Pocket Books.

Powers, B., & Ellis, A. (1995). *Manager's guide to sexual orientation in the workplace*. New York: Routledge.

Rasi, R., & Rodriguez-Nogues, L. (Eds.). (1995). *Out in the workplace: The pleasures and perils of coming out on the job*. Boston: Alyson.

Winfeld, L., & Spielman, S. (1995). *Straight talk about gays in the workplace*. New York: AMACOM (American Management Association).

Woods, J. D. (1993). *The corporate closet: The professional lives of gay men in America*. New York: Simon & Schuster/Free Press.

Zuckerman, A.J., & Simons, G. F. (1996). *Sexual orientation in the workplace: Gay men, lesbians, bisexuals and heterosexuals working together*. Thousand Oaks, CA: Sage.

Publications

Able-Together Magazine

AT Magazine, PO Box 460053, San Francisco CA 94146-0053. Tel: (415) 522-9091. http://www.well.com/user/blaine/abletog.html. Organization and quarterly magazine for men with or without disabilities.

The Advocate

PO Box 4371, Los Angeles CA 90078-4371. Tel: (213) 871-1225. http://www.advocate.com
Biweekly newsmagazine for gay men and lesbians. Online edition available.

Alternative Family Magazine

AFM Publishing, PO Box 7179, Van Nuys CA 91409. Tel: (818) 909-0314. http://www.altfammag.com.
International parenting magazine for gay, lesbian, bisexual, and transgender parents and their children.

Anything That Moves: Beyond the Myth of Bisexuality

2261 Market St. #496, San Francisco CA 94114-1600. Tel: (415) 626-5069. http://www.anythingthatmoves.com.
Monthly magazine with news, events, fiction and non-fiction.

Bisexual Resource Guide

Available from: Bisexual Resource Center, PO Box 639, Cambridge MA 02140. Tel: (617) 424-9595. http://www.biresource.org.
Listings of bisexual groups in 20 countries, annotated bibliography, conferences, merchandise sources.

BLK

PO Box 83912, Los Angeles CA 90083-0912. http://www.blk.com
Magazine for black lesbians and gays.

Common Lives, Lesbian Lives

PO Box 1553, Iowa City IA 52244. Tel: (319) 335-1486.
Covers all aspects of lesbian culture.

CTN Magazine

PO Box 14431, San Francisco CA 94114. Fax: (415) 626-9033.
National magazine for deaf, hard-of-hearing, and hearing-signing
lesbians, gays, bisexuals.

Curve

One Haight St., Suite B, San Francisco CA 94102. Tel: (415) 863-
6538. http://www.curvemag.com
Formerly known as *Deneuve*. News, politics, sports, arts,
entertainment, and trends. Fiction, poetry, and profiles.

Electronic Gay Community Magazine

Land of Awes, PO Box 16782, Wichita KS 67216-0782. Tel: (316)
269-0913. http://www.awes.com/egcm.
Collects, distributes, and archives news of or about gays and lesbians.

Harvard Gay & Lesbian Review

Box 180722, Boston MA 02118. Tel: (617) 499-9570. http://hglc.org/
hglc/review
Quarterly scholarly and literary journal.

Hikane: The Capable Woman

PO Box 841, Great Barrington MA 01230.
Magazine for networking and empowerment of lesbians with
disabilities and non-lesbian wimmin allies.

Journal of Gay, Lesbian, and Bisexual Identity

Human Sciences Press Inc., 233 Spring St., New York NY 10013-
1578. Tel: (800) 221-9369.

Journal of Gay & Lesbian Psychotherapy

Haworth Press, 10 Alice St., Binghamton NY 13904-1580. Tel: (800)
342-9678.

Journal of Gay & Lesbian Social Services

Haworth Press, 10 Alice St., Binghamton NY 13904-1580. Tel: (800)
342-9678.

Journal of Homosexuality
  Haworth Press, 10 Alice St., Binghamton NY 13904-1580. Tel: (800) 342-9678.

Journal of Lesbian Studies
  Haworth Press, 10 Alice St., Binghamton NY 13904-1580. Tel: (800) 342-9678.

off our backs
  2337-B 18th St. NW, Washington DC 20009. Tel: (202) 234-8072. Feminist newsjournal.

POZ Magazine
  PO Box 1279, New York NY 10113-1279. Tel: (212) 242-2163. http://www.poz.com.
  National lifestyle magazine for those affected by AIDS/HIV.

Qv Magazine
  PO Box 9700, Long Beach CA 90810. Tel: (818) 766-0023. http://www.qvmagazine.com
  National gay Latino men's journal.

Second Stone
  PO Box 8340, New Orleans LA 70182-8340. Tel: (504) 899-4014. National gay and lesbian Christian newspaper.

Trikone Magazine
  PO Box 21354, San Jose CA 95151-1354. Tel: (408) 270-8776. http://www.trikone.org
  For LGB South Asians.

The Washington Blade
  1408 U. St. NW, 2nd flr., Washington DC 20009. Tel: (202) 797-7000. Online edition at http://www.washblade.com.
  Gay weekly of the nation's capital. National news and local news focus.

XY Magazine
  4104 24th St. #900, San Francisco CA 94114. Tel: (415) 552-6668. http://www.xymag.com.
  National glossy fashion-and-style magazine for young gay men.

Organizations

Affirmation (gay & lesbian Mormons)

PO Box 46022, Los Angeles CA 90046. Tel: (213) 255-7251. http://www.affirmation.org.

Educational, social, and support group for lesbian and gay Latter Day Saints, their families, and friends. Local chapters.

Affirmation: United Methodists for Lesbian, Gay, and Bisexual Concerns

PO Box 1021, Evanston IL 60204. Tel: (847) 733-9590.

American Baptists Concerned

PO Box 16128, Oakland CA 94610. Tel: (510) 6562.

American Civil Liberties Union, Lesbian and Gay Rights Project

132 West 43rd St., New York NY 10036-6599. Tel: (212) 944-9800 x 545. http://www.aclu.org.

The ACLU Lesbian and Gay Rights Project is involved with legal cases which advance the civil liberties of lesbians and gay men. Their webpage features information about cases and current issues such as same sex marriage, student groups, employment discrimination, the military ban, and ACLU publications on these topics.

American Foundation for AIDS Research

733 3rd Ave. 12th flr., New York NY 10017-3204. Tel: (212) 682-7440.

Publishes AIDS/HIV Treatment Directory and AIDS/HIV Clinical Trial Handbook.

American Library Association, Gay, Lesbian, and Bisexual Task Force

c/o O.L.O.S., 50 E. Huron St., Chicago IL 60611.

Publications include: list of bookstores with LGBT titles, directory of publishers of LGBT books, directory of professional groups of gays and lesbians.

American Psychological Association, Committee on Lesbian, Gay, and Bisexual Concerns

750 1st St. NE, Washington DC 20002-4242. Tel: (202) 336-6037.

Association for Gay, Lesbian, and Bisexual Issues in Counseling
Box 216, Jenkintown PA 19046.
Seeks to eliminate discrimination and educate counselors. Publishes newsletter.

Association for Gay, Lesbian, and Bisexual Issues in Counseling
59999 Stevenson Ave., Alexandria VA 22304-3300. Tel: (703) 823-0252.

Association of Gay and Lesbian Psychiatrists
24 Olmstead St., Jamaica Plain MA 02401. Tel: (617) 522-1267.

Association of Gay and Lesbian Psychotherapists
209 N. 4th St. #D-5, Philadelphia PA 19106. Tel: 215-925-5008.

ASTRAEA—National Lesbian Action Foundation
116E 16th St., 7th flr., New York NY 10003-2112. Tel: (212) 982-3321.
Grants, scholarships, training, and technical assistance to lesbian organizations, writers, film and video makers.

Bisexual Resource Center
PO Box 639, Cambridge MA 02140. Tel: (617) 424-9595. http://www.biresource.org.
Non-profit educational organization that provides resources on bisexuality. Telephone information and referral serves for support groups. Bisexual Archive online. Speakers Bureau. Publishes Bisexual Resource Guide and newsletter; sources for pamphlets, buttons. Books available to order online.

Bridges Project, American Friends Service Committee
1501 Cherry St., Philadelphia PA 19102. Tel: (215) 241-7133.
Quaker project on LGBT youth issues.

Center for Lesbian and Gay Studies, CUNY
CUNY Graduate Ctr., 33 W 42nd St. #404N, New York NY 10036-8099. Tel: (212) 642-2924.
Publishes CLAG News and Directory of Lesbian and Gay Scholarship.

Children of Lesbians and Gays Everywhere (COLAGE)
3543 18th St. #17, San Francisco CA 94110. Tel: (415) 861-5437.
http://www.colage.org.
Affiliated with Gay and Lesbian Parents Coalition International,
COLAGE provides a newsletter, pen pal service, conferences, and
other information to support children of gays and lesbians.

Community United Against Violence
973 Market St. #500, San Francisco CA 94103. Tel: (413) 777-
5500. 24 hr crisis line: (415) 333-HELP. http://www.xq.com/cuav/
index.html.
Considered nation's oldest community project focused on anti-queer
hate violence. Information on hate crimes prevention and advocacy;
same-sex domestic violence; transgender issues; lesbian and gay
speakers bureau; youth empowerment; recent statistics and incidents;
action alerts.

Deaf Queer Resource Center
PO Box 14431, San Francisco CA 94114. Tel: (415) 626-9033 TTY.
http://www.deafqueer.org.
Resources include a bulletin board for deaf queers, organizations,
HIV/AIDS resources, library, e-zine.

Delta Lambda Phi Fraternity National Office
1008 10th St. #374, Sacramento CA 95814 Tel: (800) 587-FRAT.

Dignity USA (LGBT Catholics)
1500 Massachusetts Ave. NW #11, Washington DC 20005 Tel: (202)
861-0017. http://www.dignityusa.org.
Provides resources, information about local chapters, for LGBT
Catholics.

Disabled Womyn's Educational Project
PO Box 8773, Madison WI 53708-8773. Tel: (608) 256-8883.
Lesbians with disabilities. Speakers bureau, newsletter (available in
Braille, large print, and audiocassette).

Family Pride Coalition (formerly Gay and Lesbian Parents Coalition International)

PO Box 34337, San Diego CA 92163. Tel: (612) 296-0699. http://www.familypride.org.

Resources and information on adoption rights, legal resources for custody, parenting, newsletter, conferences.

Friends for Lesbian and Gay Concerns (Quakers)

143 Campbell Ave., Ithaca NY 14850. Tel: (607) 277-1024.

Fund for Lesbian and Gay Scholarships, Whitman Brooks Foundation

PO Box 48320, Los Angeles CA 90048. Tel: (213) 650-5752.

Gay Men's Health Crisis

129 W. 20th St., New York NY 10011. Tel: (212) 807-6655.

Publishes *Treatment Issues*.

Gay, Lesbian, Straight Education Network

122 West 26th St. Suite 1100, New York NY 10001. Tel: (212) 727-0135. Fax: (212) 727-0254. http://www.glsen.org/respect.

GLSEN has 40 chapters nationwide composed of teachers, parents, and concerned citizens who work to insure that schools are places where all people are respected and valued regardless of their sexual orientation. Homepage has information about the annual Back to School Campaign, chapters list, fact sheets about the impact of homophobia, violence prevention, true life stories, etc.

Gay and Lesbian Alliance Against Defamation

150 W. 26th St. Suite 503, New York, NY 10001. Tel: (800) GAY-MEDIA. http://www.glaad.org.

Works for fair, accurate, and inclusive portrays of lesbians and gay men in the media. Homepage has media contact information, GLAAD publications, Gay Newswire service, GLAAD Alerts with "instant" replies, links to statements by religious radicals, positive gay news stories, etc.

Gay and Lesbian Association of Retiring Persons (GLARP)
10940 Wilshire Blvd. Suite 1600, Los Angeles CA 90024. Tel: (310) 966-1500. http://www.gaylesbianretiring.org.
Organization designed to provide information and advocate for the needs of gays and lesbians who are retiring, such as retirement homes, benefits, medical discounts, etc.

Gay and Lesbian Medical Association
211 Church St., Suite. C, San Francisco CA 94114. Tel: (415) 255-4547.
Physicians and medical students, local chapters nationwide.

Hetrick Martin Institute
2 Astor Place, New York NY 10003. Tel: (212) 674-2600.
Recognized as a leader in work with LGBT youth, HMI offers a speakers bureau and consultation to those working with lesbian, gay, bisexual, or transgender youth.

Human Rights Campaign
1101 14th St. NW #200, Washington DC 20005. Tel: (202) 628-4160. Fax: (202) 347-5323. http://www.hrc.org.
HRC is active in legislative lobbying on the national and state level. Their homepage makes email activism easy with Action Email feature—the program determines your Senator and Representative. Links to information on other issues—such as Employment Non-Discrimination Act, AIDS legislation, anti-gay legislation, and lesbian health issues and policy. Partnered with regional LGB student conferences.

Institute for Lesbian Studies
PO Box 25568, Chicago IL 60625.
Publishes on lesbian theory for use in classrooms.

Integrity, Inc.
PO Box 5255, New York NY 10185-5255. Tel: (201) 868-2485.
Lesbian and gay justice ministry of the Episcopal church.

International Association of Lesbian/Gay Pride Coordinators, Inc.
1390 Market St. Suite 1225, San Francisco CA 94102. http://www.interpride.org.
Worldwide coordination organization for pride events coordinators in local cities. Website provides information about pride events around the world, contact information for local groups.

International Foundation for Gender Education
PO Box 229, Waltham MA 02154. Tel: (617) 899-2212.
Publishes *Transgender Tapestry Journal*. Network of support organizations and services, information, referrals, speakers bureau.

International Gay and Lesbian Human Rights Commission
1360 Mission St., Suite 200, San Francisco CA 94103. Tel: (415) 255-8680.
Mobilizes activists worldwide and operates in many languages.

Interweave: Unitarian Universalists for Gay, Lesbian, Bisexual, and Transgender Concerns
25 Beacon St., Boston MA 02108-2800. Tel: (617) 742-2100 x 470.

Lambda Legal Defense and Education Fund
120 Wall Street, New York NY 10005-3904. Tel: (212) 809-8585. http://www.lambdalegal.org.
Takes judicial action to support gay and lesbian rights. Offers specialized assistance to other attorneys.

Lesbian, Gay and Bisexual People in Medicine
c/o American Medical Student Association, 1902 Association Dr., Reston VA 22091. Tel: (703) 620-6600.
AMSA standing committee.

Lesbian Health Project—Whitman Walker Clinic
1407 S. St. NW, Washington DC 20009.
Active in breast cancer awareness, education, research.

Lesbian Herstory Archives

Lesbian Herstory Educational Foundation Inc., PO Box 1258, New York NY 10116. Tel: (718) 768-3953.

Founded 1974. Publishes newsletter. Open to the public by appointment.

Lutherans Concerned/North America

2466 Sharondale Dr., Atlanta GA 30305-0461.

Mautner Project for Lesbians with Cancer

PO Box 90437, Washington DC 20090.

More Light Presbyterians (formerly Presbyterians for Lesbian and Gay Concerns)

PO Box 38, New Brunswick NJ 08903-0038. Tel: (732) 249-1016. http://www.mlp.org

NAMES Project

310 Townsend St., Suite 310, San Francisco CA 94107. Tel: (415) 882-5500. Fax: (415) 882-6200. http://www.aidsquilt.org.

Website has information about the quilt; order form for memorabilia and information; how to make a panel; how to arrange for a display; local chapters list; display locations; newsletter; AIDS information.

National Association of Black and White Men Together

1747 Connecticut Ave. NW, Washington DC 20009. Tel: (202) 462-3599. http://www.nabwmt.com.

Local chapters are sometimes called Men of All Colors Together.

National Association of Lesbian and Gay Alcoholism Professionals

1147 S. Alvarado St., Los Angeles CA 90006.

National Association of People With AIDS

1413 K St. NW 7th flr, Washington DC 20005. Tel: (202) 789-2222.

National Black Lesbian and Gay Leadership Forum
1612 K Street NW, Suite 500, Washington DC 20006. Tel: (202) 483-6786. http://www.nblglf.org.

National Center for Lesbian Rights
870 Market St., Suite #570, San Francisco CA 94102. Tel: (415) 392-6257. Fax: (415) 392-8442.
Legal resource for lesbians and gay men, provides telephone consultation. Has lesbians of color and gay youth projects. Custody and parenting issues, employment benefits, and newsletter.

National Gay and Lesbian Domestic Violence Victims' Network
3506 S. Ouray Cir., Aurora CO 80013.
Support group for people abused by their partners, promotes victims advocacy, speakers bureau, resources.

National Gay and Lesbian Task Force
2320 17th St. NW, Washington DC 20009-2702. Tel: (202) 332-6483. Fax: (202) 332-0207. TTY: (202) 332-6219. http://www.ngltf.org.
Engages in lobbying, advocacy. Sponsors annual Creating Change Conference, Workplace Issues Conference, and youth leadership training institute to train local activists. Website has general information, press releases, publications, conference information, reports on gay related legislation, etc.

National Latino/a Lesbian and Gay Organization
1612 K St. NW #500, Washington DC 20009. Tel: (202) 466-8240. Develops leadership and advances progressive political agenda. Newsletter and conferences.

National Native American AIDS Prevention Center
2100 Lakeshore Ave. #A, Oakland CA 94606-1123. Tel: (510) 444-2051.

National Organization for Women, Lesbian Rights Program
PO Box 96824, Washington DC 20090-6824. Tel: (202) 331-0066. TTY: (202) 331-9002. http://www.now.org.
Support, education, advocacy, and lobbying on women's and lesbian issues.

National Women's History Project
7738 Bell Road, Windsor CA 95492. Tel: (707) 838-6000. Fax: (707) 838-0478. http://www.nwhp.org.
Women's History information, includes lesbian material and merchandise.

Network of Gay and Lesbian Alumni/ae Associations (NetGALA)
PO Box 53188, Washington DC 20009.
Publishes a newsletter.

ONE Institute—International Gay and Lesbian Archives
PO Box 69679, West Hollywood CA 90069. Tel: (310) 854-0271.
Publishes a newsletter.

!OutProud! The National Coalition for Gay, Lesbian, Bisexual, and Transgender Youth
454 LaGallinas Ave. #261, San Rafael CA 94903-3618. Tel: (415) 269-6125. http://www.outproud.org.
Support, education, and advocacy. Offers peer counseling, webpage has list of links and resources for youth, links to e-zines for youth.

Partners Task Force for Gay and Lesbian Couples
Box 9685, Seattle WA 98109-0685. Tel: (206) 935-1206. http://www.buddybuddy.com.
Resources and information on legal marriage, ceremonial marriage, domestic partnerships, resources and links to other sites.

PFLAG: Parents and Friends of Lesbians and Gays
1101 14th St. NW, Suite 1030, Washington DC 20005. Tel: (202) 638-4200. http://www.pflag.org.
Support, education, and advocacy. Supplies educational materials at low cost. Safe Spaces for Youth Project, Project Open Mind counters anti-gay propaganda. Website has list of chapters; press releases; membership information; youth suicide statistics; hate crimes statistics.

Project Inform
1965 Market St., Suite 220, San Francisco CA 94103. Tel: (800) 822-7422 (hotline).
Informs HIV infected of life saving strategies and gives means to make informed decisions about the most promising treatments.

Quatrefoil Library
1619 Dayton Ave., Suite 105, St. Paul MN 55104-6206. Tel: (612) 641-0969.
Devoted to gay, lesbian, and other sexual minority materials. Open to the public, publishes a newsletter.

Renaissance Transgender Association
987 Old Eagle School Rd #719, Wayne PA 19087. Tel: (610) 975-9119. http://www.ren.org.
Peer support and counseling on transgender issues. Newsletter, list of local chapters. How to start a local support group or speakers bureau. Gender education materials for helping professionals and the general public. Publishes monthly *Transgender Community News* magazine.

Senior Action in a Gay Environment (SAGE)
305 7th Ave., 16th flr., New York NY 10001. Tel: (212) 741-2247.
Bulletin, North American conference. Centered in New York City. Inservice training for human services professionals. Social activities, peer counseling, resources.

Servicemembers Legal Defense Network
PO Box 53013, Washington DC 20009. Tel: (202) 328-3244. http://www.sldn.org.
A national legal aid and watchdog group that assists men and women targeted by the "Don't Ask—Don't Tell" anti-gay military policy. Website includes advice for a person under investigation.

StopAIDS Project—San Francisco
201 Sanchez St., San Francisco CA 94114. Tel: (415) 575-1545. http://www.stopaids.org.
Information on website about safer sex, effective AIDS education, research into behavior change, etc.

Straight Spouse Support Network
C/o Family Pride Coalition, PO Box 34337, San Diego CA 92163. Tel: (612) 296-0699. http://www.familypride.org.
Maintains a support mailing list and connections to other resources on the web page.

Trikone
Box 21354, San Jose CA 95151. Tel: (408) 270-8776. http://www.trikone.org.
Gay and lesbian South Asians. Website has list of community organizations, events, merchandise, newsletter.

Uncommon Legacy Foundation, Inc.
150 W. 26th St. #503, New York NY 10011. Tel: (212) 366-6507. Small grants to lesbian projects and organizations, and scholarships to lesbian students.

Universal Fellowship of Metropolitan Community Churches (MCC)
8704 Santa Monica Blvd., 2nd flr., West Hollywood CA 90069-4548. Tel: (310) 360-8640. http://www.ufmcc.com.
Church founded to minister to lesbians and gay men. Churches across the nation.

Web Resources

FTM International: http://www.ftm-intl.org/
Support group for FtM transvestites and transsexuals. Newsletter, resource guide, contacts, and bibliography.

Gay Workplace Issues Home Page: http://www.nyu.edu/pages/sls/gaywork/
Lists and resources about many workplace issues, including non-discrimination statements, corporate employee groups, gay and professional business organizations, employers offering domestic partners benefits, gay population statistics, etc.

International Gay and Lesbian Review: http://www.usc.edu/Library/oneigla/onepress
USC Doheny Reference Center. Interactive electronic journal focused on reviews of books relating to gay, bisexual, lesbian, transgender, queer, and sexual variance topics.

LGBT Campus Resource Center Directors: http://www.uic.edu/orgs/lgbt/index.html
Links to campus LGBT center homepages.

Queer Resources Directory: http://www.qrd.org/qrd/www/index.html
Central reference area for LGBT topics: family issues, youth, religion, health, on-line resources, media, events, culture, history, business, legal, politics, organizations, publications, etc.

Safer Sex Home Page: http://www.safersex.org
Information about various sexual activities and how to use condoms properly.

Scholarships of Interest to Lesbian, Gay, and Bisexual Students: http://www.finaid.org/otheraid/gay.phtml
Website created by the Task Force on Lesbian, Gay, and Bisexual Issues of the California Association of Student Financial Aid Administrators.

Social Support Youth—Gay, Lesbian, Bi: http://www.youth.org/ssyglb

Website contains information about the newsgroup which provides peer-based support, understanding, and friendship to young people coming to terms with their sexual orientation. FAQ and other resources.

Transgender Forum Resource Center: http://www.tgforum.com

Provides a support group, calendar of events.

Youth Action Online: http://www.youth.org

Web based support system for lesbian, gay, and questioning youth. Their homepage features several LGBT e-zines, "I might be gay/lesbian, what do I do?", coming out resources, peer support mailing lists, and links to other resources to assist youth.

Hotlines

AIDS Hotline, Center for Disease Control

National AIDS Hotline, CDC Prevention Information Network, PO Box 6003, Rockville MD 20849-6003. Tel: (800) 342-AIDS. TTY: (800) 243-7889. Spanish: (800) 344-7432.. http://www.cdcpin.org. Internet order form for HIV/AIDS related publications; CDC services (National AIDS Hotline, CDC Automatic Telephone Services); AIDS Clinical Trials Information; HIV/AIDS Treatment Information. Netlinks to other sites. Daily news posting.

Gay and Lesbian National Hotline

332 B Bleecker St. Suite F-18, New York, NY 10014. Hotline: (888) THE-GLNH. http://www.glnh.org.

Available any weekday evening, 6 pm – 10 pm, Saturday Noon – 5 pm EDT. Offers peer counseling, information, referrals without charge, anonymously. Crisis suicide intervention, listing of shelters and runaway services, recovery centers, local organizations. Webpage has links to other organizations.

Gay and Lesbian Victims Assistance Hotline

Lambda Services AVP, PO Box 31321, El Paso TX 799931-0321. Hotline: (800) 259-1538. Office: (915) 533-6024.

Helps document violence against gays and lesbians; has referral information and resources.

Gay and Lesbian Youth Hotline

PO Box 20716, Indianapolis IN 46220. Tel: (317) 541-8726. Hotline: (800) 347-TEEN. Email: iygteen@aol.com.

Operates Sunday through Thursday, 7 pm – 10 pm; Friday and Saturday, 7 pm – midnight. Operated by Indianapolis Youth Group with trained peer (youth) counselors. Confidential and anonymous. Operates youth penpal program.

U.S. Department of Justice Hate Crimes Hotline

Tel: 800-347-HATE.

For reporting bias-related crimes; statistics are compiled by the FBI.

Bookstores (Mail Order)

A Different Light
>   151 W 19th St., New York NY 10011. Tel: (212) 989-4850.
>   489 Castro St., San Francisco CA 94114. Tel: (415) 431-0891.
>   8853 Santa Monica Blvd., West Hollywood CA 90069. Tel: (310) 854-6601.
>   http://www.adlbooks.com/~adl.

Lambda Rising
>   1625 Connecticut Ave. NW, Washington DC 20009. Tel: (202) 462-6969.
>   241 W. Chase St., Baltimore MD 21201. Tel: (410) 234-0069.
>   39 Baltimore Ave., Rehoboth Beach DE 19971. Tel: (302) 227-6969.
>   9229 Granby St., Norfolk VA 23503. Tel: (757) 480-6969.
>   lrstaff@aol.com.

Paths Untrodden
>   PO Box 430, Seattle WA 98111-0430.
>   Catalog of hard to find/out of print/small press/imported books. Catalog $3.

People Like Us Books
>   3321 N. Clark St., Chicago IL 60657.

About the Authors

Kathleen J. Bieschke is an associate professor of Counseling Psychology at The Pennsylania State University. She obtained a B.S. in Psychology and her M.S. in Clinical Psychology from Illinois State University in 1982 and 1985, respectively, and was awarded her Ph.D. in Counseling Psychology from Michigan State University in 1991. Dr. Bieschke has written extensively on gay, lesbian, and bisexual issues. Most recently, she co-edited the *Handbook of Counseling and Psychotherapy with Gay, Lesbian, and Bisexual Clients* with Ruperto Perez and Kurt DeBord.

Scott R. Boden is currently an Assistant Director of Residence Life at The Ohio State University. Over the course of several years, he has worked on research and education about domestic partnership and gay, lesbian, and bisexual issues on campus. He received his Master's degree in College Student Personnel from Western Illinois University in 1989, and a Bachelor of Science degree in Speech Communication from Ithaca College in 1987.

Kathleen Brock is a doctoral student in Counseling Psychology at the University of Missouri—Columbia. She is currently completing her internship at the University of California—Irvine Counseling Center and recently accepted a postdoctoral fellowship at the Traumatic Stress Institute in South Windsor, Connecticut. Areas of research, clinical, and political interest include sexual trauma, eating disturbances, white racial identity development, and anti-racism.

Ellen M. Broido is currently an assistant professor of University Studies and Coordinator of University Studies/Student Affairs Partnerships at Portland State University. She received her doctorate in Counselor Education from the Pennsylvania State University and her masters in College Student Personnel and Counseling and Guidance from Indiana University. Her current research interests focus on how college students come to understand issues of diversity and social justice, with particular attention to the development of social justice allies in college.

James M. Croteau received his Ph.D. in Counseling Psychology from Southern Illinois University in 1986. He is an associate professor in the Counselor Education and Counseling Psychology Department at Western Michigan University. He was one of the group of professionals who founded the ACPA Standing Committee on Lesbian, Gay, Bisexual, and Transgendered Awareness and served as its second chairperson. Lesbian, gay, and bisexual concerns have been a focus of his research and scholarship especially with regard to career development, professional training, and the field of student affairs. More recently, he has also begun scholarly work concerning White professionals and their racial awareness.

Kelly A. Carter is the Assistant Director for Programming and New Student Orientation Coordinator at Northwestern University, Evanston, Illinois. She received her bachelors degree from Virginia Polytechnic Institute and State University (Virginia Tech) and her masters of education from The Pennsylvania State University. She has served on the directorate for the Standing Committee for Lesbian, Gay, Bisexual, and Transgender Awareness for the American College Personnel Association as a Member at Large for Transgender Education.

Rosa Cintrón is an assistant professor in the Department of Educational Leadership and Educational Policy Studies at the University of Oklahoma. She holds a Ph.D. degree from Florida State University and the M.A. and B.A. degrees from the University of Puerto Rico. Before becoming a faculty member, Dr. Cintrón held professional positions in student affairs at the State University of New York/Old Westbury and at Northern Illinois University. She is an active member in ACPA, NASPA and ASHE. She is co-editor of *Building a Working Policy for Distance Education* with Connie Dillon (1997) and co-author with Jerome C. Weber of *Issues in Higher Education: Enduring Enigmas in American Higher Education* (1999).

Sandy L. Colbs is currently the Associate Director of the Counseling Center at Georgia State University. She received her Ph.D. in Counseling Psychology from Southern Illinois University, and worked for many years at University Counseling Services, Virginia Commonwealth University. In the mid-1980s, she helped to establish what is now the ACPA Standing Committee for LGBT Awareness. More recently, she worked to develop the Section for GLB Awareness in Division 17 of APA, and was a founding member of the Association for Coordination of Counseling Center Clinical Services(ACCCCS). Her professional interests focus on women's mental health, group therapy, and counseling center administration.

Mark Connolly is currently an Associate Researcher for the LEAD Center at the University of Wisconsin—Madison and completing a Ph.D. in Higher Education at Indiana University Bloomington. He earned a B.A. in English from Western Illinois University and an M.Ed. in Student Personnel in Higher Education from the University of Georgia. He has worked in residence life, student activities, health education, and counseling outreach at the Universities of Georgia, San Francisco and Vermont. His professional efforts to improve student learning are shaped by his scholarly work on college teaching, assessment and evaluation, postsecondary faculty, and redefining theory/practice connections.

Kurt A. DeBord earned his Ph.D. in counseling psychology from the University of Missouri—Columbia after receiving a B.S. in psychology from Ball State University. He is currently an assistant professor of psychology at Lincoln University in Jefferson City, Missouri. He has published research in the areas of rape prevention, gender roles, drug and alcohol involvement, and lesbian, gay, and bisexual concerns. He is currently involved in research on the relationship between racism and biphobia as well as research on teaching interventions.

Valsin L. DuMontier II is a doctoral student in the Cultural Studies in Education department at the Ohio State University. He received his B.S. from Louisiana State University and his M.A. from the Ohio State University. He previously held positions in student affairs at Cornell University and the University of Virginia. His research interests include the interconnection of spirituality and lesbian, gay, and bisexual identity development and the role of spirituality in the lives of lesbian, gay, and bisexual people.

Amy Bowers Eberz is a doctoral candidate in the counseling psychology program at the Pennsylvania State University. She is currently completing her predoctoral internship at the Center for Counseling and Student Development at the University of Delaware. Her professional interests include lesbian, gay, and bisexual issues (particularly providing affirmative counseling and educational training) and women's issues. She plans to work as a psychologist in a college counseling center upon completing her degree.

Wallace Eddy is currently a doctoral student in College Student Personnel Administration at the University of Maryland. He earned the Bachelor's degree from Castleton State College (Vermont) in Communication and holds a Master's degree from Western Illinois University in College Student Personnel. His areas of research interest are the scholar-practitioner identity in student affairs and the use of phenomenological inquiry as a way to tell the stories of marginalized students.

Angela DeSharn Ferguson is a Clinical Assistant Professor at the University of Florida's Counseling Center. She received her doctorate from the University of Maryland, College Park in Counseling Psychology and has worked in a variety of clinical, educational, and organizational settings during the past 15 years prior to her arrival at the University of Florida. She has presented and published in the areas of women's leadership styles, the effects of multiple identities on self-esteem, diversity, and multicultural counseling issues. Her clinical interests include racial, gender, and sexual orientation identity development, women's issues, and the integration of psychodynamic psychotherapy with multicultural issues.

Deanna S. Forney is a professor in the College Student Personnel program at Western Illinois University. Previously, she served as a student affairs practitioner at several institutions. She holds a Ph.D. in Counseling and Personnel Services from the University of Maryland—College Park and is a past Chair of ACPA's Commission XII—Professional Preparation, as well as a current member of the Editorial Board of the Journal of College Student Development. She is a co-author of *Student Development in College: Theory, Research, and Practice*, and she has received ACPA's Annuit Coeptis Award and WIU's Faculty Excellence Award.

Mary F. Howard-Hamilton received her B. A. and M. A. degrees from the University of Iowa in the areas of Speech and Dramatic Arts as well as College Student Personnel Administration and Counseling. She received an Ed.D. in Counselor Education and Psychology from North Carolina State University. Dr. Howard-Hamilton has 13 years of full time experience as a student affairs administrator at four institutions. She is currently an Associate Professor and Coordinator of the Student Personnel in Higher Education Program in the Department of Educational Leadership and Policy Studies at the University of Florida. Dr. Howard-Hamilton has published numerous articles and book chapters on issues related to multiculturalism and gender role socialization.

Karl M. Hamner is an independent evaluation consultant with experience working with federal, state, county and community-based agencies to assess the impact of health-related programs. He is also a social activist in the areas of health problem prevention, preventing violence against lesbians, gay men, bisexuals, and transgendered people, and general bisexual issues. Previously he was Director of Evaluation Research at Sociometrics Corporation and a Research Associate at the Vanderbilt Institute for Public Policy Studies, Vanderbilt University. Dr. Hamner received his Ph.D. in Sociology from the University of California, Los Angeles (UCLA) in 1993.

Claire N. Kaplan has served as Sexual Assault Education Coordinator at the University of Virginia since Fall, 1991. She received her B. S. degree from the University of California, Davis and her Masters in Professional Writing degree from the University of Southern California. Kaplan co-authored "Womens Centers Respond to Sexual Violence," with Myra Hindus, Elizabeth Mejia, Lee LaDue, and Jane Olsen, in *Handbook for College and University Womens Centers* and is writing a book, *Shared Trauma: The Longterm Impact of Sexual Assault on Couples*, with Linda BloomBecker. She is also currently a doctoral student in Social Foundations of Education at the Curry School of Education at the University of Virginia.

John Leppo is the Associate Director for Building Services of the University Student Commons at Virginia Commonwealth University. He holds a M.Ed. from the University of South Carolina and a B.S. from Duquesne University. He serves as the Resource Clearinghouse Coordinator for the Standing Committee for Lesbian, Gay, Bisexual, and Transgender Awareness of the American College Personnel Association.

Heidi Levine is the Associate Director of the Center for Counseling and Student Development at Radford University, where she also teaches in the counseling psychology program. Dr. Levine received her Ph.D. in counseling psychology from Temple University and has a Master's in Student Personnel Services from the Pennsylvania State University. Her areas of professional and research interest include gay/lesbian identity development, campus climate, and counseling issues with LGB students.

Patrick G. Love is an Associate Professor and Coordinator of the Higher Education Administration and Student Personnel Program at Kent State University. He earned his Ph.D. in Higher Education and Student Affairs from Indiana University and his M.S./C.A.S. in Counseling Psychology and Student Development from the University at Albany. His areas of research and scholarship include cognitive development and learning; organizational culture; lesbian, gay, and bisexual issues; and spiritual development.

Ross A. Papish is currently the Director of Student Life at Occidential College. He will be receiving his Ph.D. in the Student Affairs Administration program from the University of Georgia during the fall of 1999. Current research emphases are on student learning and student development. Ross received his B.A. in Psychology from Purchase College in 1987 and an M.Ed. in College Student Personnel from Colorado State University in 1989. Ross has been actively involved in the American College Personnel Association, the Association of College and University Housing Officers—International, and the National Affiliate of College and University Residence Halls.

Ruperto M. Perez is a counseling psychologist and Counseling Services Coordinator in the Counseling and Testing Center at the University of Georgia in Athens, Georgia. He received his doctorate in counseling psychology from the University of Missouri—Columbia in 1993. He is actively involved in the American College Personnel Association (ACPA) and is currently Chair-elect for ACPA's Commission VII (Counseling & Psychological Services). Dr. Perez is also active in Division 17 (Counseling Psychology) of the American Psychological Association (APA) and in the Division's Section for Lesbian, Gay, and Bisexual Awareness and the Section on Ethnic and Racial Diversity. He is co-editor of the *Handbook of Counseling and Therapy with Lesbian, Gay, and Bisexual Clients* soon to be published by APA Press.

Leah Robin evaluates HIV and STD prevention interventions for youth in high risk situations, including gay and bisexual youth, in Atlanta. She received a Ph.D. and M. A. in sociology from the University of California, Los Angeles. She has worked on evaluation studies including gay, lesbian, and bisexual youth, runaway and homeless youth, HIV-positive youth, youth whose parents are HIV-positive, and youth in alternative schools. She is also involved in dissemination projects that implement research-based programs in a variety of applied settings.

Donald A. Stenta is currently the Coordinator of Student Involvement in the Office of Student Activities at the Ohio State University. He is also a doctoral student in the Higher Education and Student Affairs program at Ohio State. Don received his Master's degree from the University of Vermont's Higher Education and Student Affairs program in 1991, and a Bachelor of Arts degree from Binghamton University in 1988. Don is currently involved in dissertation work and a research team exploring leadership, service-learning, and student learning.

Donna M. Talbot received her Ph.D. in College Student Personnel Administration in 1992 from the University of Maryland—College Park. She is an Associate Professor and Coordinator of the Student Affairs Graduate Programs in the Department of Counselor Education and Counseling Psychology at Western Michigan University. Donna began her involvement with ACPA through the Standing Committee on Multicultural Affairs; currently, she is the Chair of Commission XII: Graduate Preparation. As an Asian American, a person of color, Donna has always had a strong professional and research interest in multicultural and diversity issues. Her research has focused especially on how multiculturalism is addressed through graduate and professional training.

Mark von Destinon is the Dean of Student Services at Cochise Community College in Southern Arizona. He holds a B.A. (1978) in political science, an M.Ed. (1985) in higher education, and a Ph.D. (1989) in higher education, all from the University of Arizona. He has been very active in both ACPA and NASPA in the following roles: NASPA Journal editorial board; former chair of the NASPA Gay, Lesbian and Bisexual Concerns Network; former member of the NASPA Research and Program Development Division, NASPA National Executive Board, ACPA Standing Committee on Lesbian, Gay and Bisexual Awareness Directorate, ACPA Commission XI (Student Development in Two Year Colleges) Directorate, and ACPA Campus Violence Project. Dr. von Destinon co-authored three chapters in the second edition of *The Handbook of Student Affairs Administration*.

Jamie Washington serves as Assistant Vice President of Student Affairs and an affiliate faculty member in the departments of Sociology and American Studies at the University of Maryland—Baltimore County. He is also founder of New Visions, a multicultural organizational development firm, and serves as a Senior Consultant with Equity Institute and Elsie Y. Cross Associates. He earned his B. S. from Slippery Rock State College in Therapeutic Recreation and Music and his M. S. from Indiana University—Bloomington in Higher Education Administration and Counseling. He holds a Ph. D. in College Student Development from the University of Maryland—College Park. Dr. Washington is a nationally known speaker and consultant on multicultural and leadership issues.

M. D'Andre Wilson is currently a pre-doctoral intern at The Pennsylvania State University Center for Counseling and Psychological Services. He obtained a B.S. in Computer Science from Ball State University and an M.A. in Counseling and Social Psychology also from Ball State University in 1989 and 1995 respectively. He is in his fourth year of work toward a Ph.D. in Counseling Psychology at The Pennsylvania State University. His research interests include cross cultural supervision and counseling, racial identity, domestic violence, and GLB issues.

About the Editors

Vernon A. Wall is Assistant Dean of Students and Director of the Student Activities Center at Iowa State University. He received his B.S. in Political Science from North Carolina State University and his M.S. in College Student Personnel Administration from Indiana University. Vernon has experience in new student orientation, Greek life, student activities, leadership development, and university housing and has receive several awards for his contributions to the quality of student life on campus. Co-editor of *Beyond Tolerance: Gays, Lesbians and Bisexuals on Campus*, he has written several articles on the topics of social justice, multi-culturalism, and leadership and is a nationally-known speaker, presenter, and trainer. Vernon is active in several regional, state and national organizations and has served on the Executive Council of the American College Personnel Association.

Nancy J. Evans is Associate Professor and Higher Education Program Coordinator in the Department of Educational Leadership and Policy Studies at Iowa State University. Dr. Evans holds a B.S. in Social Science from SUNY—Potsdam, an M.S.Ed. in Higher Education from Southern Illinois University—Carbondale, a Ph.D. in Counseling Psychology from the University of Missouri—Columbia, and an M.F.A. in Theatre from Western Illinois University. She is the co-editor, with Vernon Wall, of *Beyond Tolerance: Gays, Lesbians and Bisexuals on Campus;* co-author with Deanna S. Forney and Florence Guido-DiBrito, of *Student Development on Campus: Theory, Research and Practice;* co-editor with Christine E. Phelps Tobin, of *The State of the Art of Preparation and Practice in Student Affairs: Another Look*, and editor of *Facilitating the Development of Women*. She is a recipient of the Contribution to Knowledge Award from the American College Personnel Association and is currently an ACPA Senior Scholar. Her research interests focus on the impact of the college environment on student development, particularly the experiences of gay, lesbian, bisexual, and transgendered students on campus.